SAFe® 4.0 Distilled

SAFe® 4.0

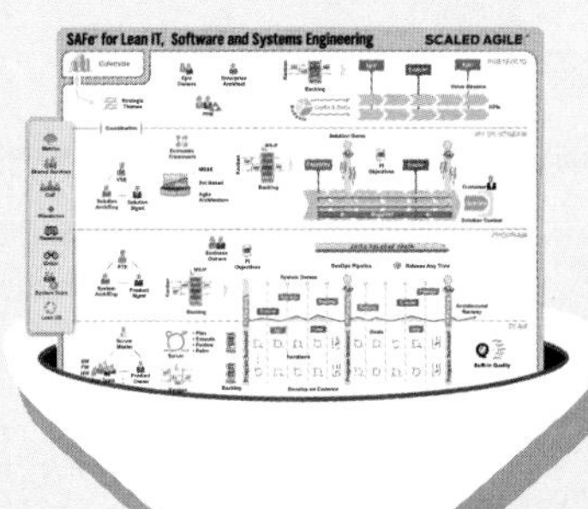

SAFe® DISTILLED

APPLYING THE SCALED AGILE FRAMEWORK® FOR LEAN SOFTWARE AND SYSTEMS ENGINEERING

Richard Knaster
Dean Leffingwell

Addison-Wesley

Boston • Columbus • Indianapolis • New York • San Francisco • Amsterdam • Cape Town
Dubai • London • Madrid • Milan • Munich • Paris • Montreal • Toronto • Delhi • Mexico City
São Paulo • Sydney • Hong Kong • Seoul • Singapore • Taipei • Tokyo

For information about buying this title in bulk quantities, or for special sales opportunities (which may include electronic versions; custom cover designs; and content particular to your business, training goals, marketing focus, or branding interests), please contact our corporate sales department at corpsales@pearsoned.com or (800) 382-3419.

For government sales inquiries, please contact governmentsales@pearsoned.com.

For questions about sales outside the U.S., please contact intlcs@pearson.com.

Visit us on the Web: informit.com/aw

Library of Congress Control Number: 2016961165

ISBN-13: 978-0-13-420942-5
ISBN-10: 0-13-420942-7

1 17

From Richard

To my wife, Ilise, and our sons, Jason and Cole, for their love and support on this journey. Without their patience and sacrifices this book would not have been possible.

From Dean

Dedicated to my father H.D "Rusty" Leffingwell, 1924–2016. Rest in peace, Dad.

Contents

Preface xiii
Acknowledgments xvii
About the Authors xix

PART I: Overview 1

1 Business Need for SAFe 3
Why Do Businesses Need SAFe? 3
The Challenge of System Development 4
Applying New Bodies of Knowledge 5
Improving System Development Outcomes 9
The Business Benefits of SAFe 10
Summary 13

2 SAFe Overview 15
The Big Picture 15
The Levels 17
The Foundation 22
The Spanning Palette 24
Summary 25

PART II: The Foundation of SAFe 27

3 Lean-Agile Mindset 29
Overview 29
Thinking Lean 30
Embracing Agility 33
Applying the Agile Manifesto at Scale 37
Summary 40

4 Lean-Agile Leaders 41
Exhibit the Lean-Agile Mindset 42
Lead the Change 42
Know the Way and Emphasize Lifelong Learning 47
Develop People 48
Inspire and Align with Mission. Minimize Constraints 52
Decentralize Decision-Making 53
Unlock the Intrinsic Motivation of Knowledge Workers 54
Evolve the Development Manager Role 55
Summary 58

5 SAFe Principles 61
Why Focus on Principles? 61
Principle #1: Take an Economic View 62
Principle #2: Apply Systems Thinking 70
Principle #3: Assume Variability; Preserve Options 74
Principle #4: Build Incrementally with Fast, Integrated Learning Cycles 76
Principle #5: Base Milestones on Objective Evaluation of Working Systems 79
Principle #6: Visualize and Limit WIP, Reduce Batch Sizes, and Manage Queue Lengths 80
Principle #7: Apply Cadence; Synchronize with Cross-Domain Planning 83
Principle #8: Unlock the Intrinsic Motivation of Knowledge Workers 87
Principle #9: Decentralize Decision-Making 89
Summary 91

PART III: Program and Team Level 93

6 The Agile Release Train 95
Overview 95
ART Organization 97
Develop on Cadence. Release Any Time 100
Vision 102
Features 103
Program Backlog 104
Roadmap 104
Agile Teams Power the Train 105
User Stories and the Team Backlog 107
Summary 111

7 Planning a Program Increment 113
Overview 113
Preparation for the PI Planning Event 115
Day 1—Create and Review Draft Plans 118
Day 2—Finalize Plans and Commit 125
Summary 133

8 Executing a Program Increment 135
Overview 135
The Iteration Cycle 136
Building Quality In 140
Improving Team Flow with Kanban 143
Managing ART Flow 146
System Demo 154
Innovation and Planning 154
Inspect and Adapt 156
Summary 156

9 Inspect and Adapt 159
Overview 159
PI System Demo 160
Quantitative Measurement 160
Retrospective and Problem-Solving Workshop 162
Inspect and Adapt at the Value Stream Level 166
Summary 167

PART IV: Value Stream Level 169

10 Value Stream Overview 171
Overview 171
Economic Framework 173
Capabilities and the Value Stream Backlog 176
Value Stream Epics 177
Defining and Building the Solution 178
Value Stream Flow 179
Summary 180

11 Defining Large and Complex Solutions 183
Overview 183
The Solution 184
Solution Intent 186
Fixed and Variable Solution Intent 187
Developing Solution Intent 188
Documenting Solution Intent 191
Solution Context 192
Summary 196

12 Coordinating ARTs and Suppliers 197
Overview 197
Value Stream PI Planning 198
ART PI Planning 200
Value Stream Post-PI Planning 201
Frequent Solution Integration 204
Value Stream Sync 206
Solution Demo 206
Value Stream Inspect and Adapt 207
Summary 207

PART V: Portfolio 209

13 Portfolio Level Overview 211
Overview 211
Connecting the Portfolio to the Business 213
Defining Strategic Themes for a Portfolio 213
Influence of Strategic Themes 214
Measuring Progress against Strategic Themes 215
Portfolio Roles 215
Lean-Agile Program Portfolio Management 218
Advancing Solution Behavior with Portfolio Epics 221
Establishing Enterprise Value Flow 223
Coordinating Value Streams 225
Summary 228

14 Lean-Agile Budgeting, Forecasting, and Contracting 231
Introduction 231
Lean-Agile Budgeting 231
Lean-Agile Planning and Forecasting 235

Lean-Agile Contracting....237
Agile Capitalization Strategies....243
Summary....247

PART VI: Implementing SAFe....249

15 The Guiding Coalition....251
Introduction....251
The Implementation Roadmap....252
Reaching the Tipping Point....253
The Need for a Powerful Coalition....255
Train Lean-Agile Change Agents....255
Train Executives, Managers, and Leaders....256
Charter a Lean-Agile Center of Excellence....257
Summary....258

16 Design the Implementation....259
Introduction....259
Create the Implementation Plan....265
Summary....268

17 Implementing Agile Release Trains....269
Introduction....269
Prepare for the ART Launch....270
Train Teams and Launch the ART....277
The Quick-Start Approach to ART Launch....280
Coach ART Execution....281
Launch More ARTs in the Value Stream....282
Launch More Value Streams in the Portfolio....284
Summary....285

18 Sustain and Improve....287
Introduction....287
Advance Organizational Maturity....288
Implement Agile HR Practices....292
Measure and Take Action....293
Improve Agile Architecture and Technical Practices....295
Focus on DevOps and Continuous Delivery....297
Reduce Time to Market with Value Stream Mapping....298
Summary....299

19 Essential SAFe 301
Overview 301
Lean-Agile Principles 303
Agile Teams and Release Trains 306
Cadence and Synchronization 308
Essential Team and Program Roles 310
PI Planning 312
System Demo 313
Inspect and Adapt 314
IP Iteration 315
DevOps Pipeline 316
Lean-Agile Leadership 317
Summary 319

Abbreviations 321

Glossary 323

Index 335

Preface

On behalf of the entire Scaled Agile, Inc., team and the SAFe contributors, it is our personal pleasure to introduce you to *SAFe® 4.0 Distilled: Applying the Scaled Agile Framework for Lean Software and Systems Engineering.*

It seems like only yesterday, but it was back in 2011 that we launched V1.0 of the Scaled Agile Framework. We did so without much fanfare, as we were a brand-new company, and we certainly had no marketing department. The earliest release had a simple Big Picture and only abstracts, which we scrambled madly to fulfill info full-fledged articles in the few months after launch. But the website was free, and it was useful.

Fast forward to today. Now SAFe Version 4.0 (soon to be 4.5; yes, you heard that here first!)—now renamed "SAFe for Lean Software and Systems Engineering"—has emerged as the world's leading framework for adopting Lean-Agile development practices at enterprise scale.

The reason is simply that it works. As documented by dozens of case studies (see ScaledAgileFramework.com/case-studies), software and systems builders worldwide are achieving substantial business benefits, which routinely include:

- 20% – 50% increases in productivity
- 50%+ increases in quality
- 30% – 75% faster time to market
- Measurable increases in employee engagement and job satisfaction

As you can imagine, with results like those, SAFe is spreading rapidly across the world. A significant majority of Fortune 100 U.S. companies have certified SAFe practitioners and consultants already on site, as do an increasing percentage of the Global 1000 enterprises.

Scaled Agile, Inc. (ScaledAgile.com), the company that owns SAFe, has grown as well. In addition to continued development of the framework, we have established a comprehensive role-based training curriculum, and a worldwide network of over one hundred tooling, training, consulting and service delivery partners, to help assure your success.

Why SAFe?

As we noted in the companion *SAFe® 4.0 Reference Guide* (http://www.scaledagile.com/reference-guide/):

> The world's economy, and the health and welfare of society as a whole, is increasingly dependent on software and systems. In support of this need, systems builders are creating increasingly complex software and cyber-physical systems of unprecedented scope and complexity with requirements for utility and robustness exceeding those that have come before them. The methods that systems builders use to create these systems must keep pace with this larger mandate.
>
> However, the assumptive, one-pass, stage-gated, waterfall methods of the past are not scaling to the new challenge. New development methods are needed. Agile shows the greatest promise, but it was developed for small teams and, by itself, does not scale to the needs of larger enterprises and the systems they create. What's needed is a new way of working, one that applies the power of Agile but leverages the more extensive knowledge pools of systems thinking and Lean product development.

About This Book

Several months ago, we published the *SAFe® 4.0 Reference Guide*, which is a handy reference to largely the same content that is on the website. But admittedly, SAFe is a big framework. What more could we expect if one is to effectively address the needs of faster time-to-market and higher quality for people building some of the world's biggest, and most important, systems?

While bigger is better in this case, it doesn't make the framework necessarily more understandable. After all, the framework is a website, logically divided into 50–60 individual primary articles, a glossary, guidance articles, case studies, and more. The SAFe website is designed for as-needed, random access, for those who need just-in-time information to do their job. As such, it doesn't really "tell a story." That is the purpose of this book.

The book is divided into six parts, each with a specific purpose.

Part I makes the business case for SAFe and provides an overview of the major elements of the framework. While we didn't write it to stand alone, it does make a pretty good introduction for those just needing to get a basic understanding of SAFe.

Part II provides the foundational principles that make SAFe effective, including the role of Lean-Agile leaders, the Lean-Agile mindset, and the all-important SAFe principles and values.

Part III describes the program and team level, which is the "heart" of SAFe, the people and their practices. You'll learn the primary value delivery mechanisms of SAFe, and how people are organized into Agile teams and Agile Release Trains. You will also learn how to plan and execute a program increment, and how to achieve relentless improvement with inspect and adapt.

Part IV is the value stream level, intended to help those building the world's largest, most complex, and most critical, systems. Here you will find an overview of the value stream level, how to define large and complex systems, and how to execute value stream program increments.

Part V describes the portfolio level. Here you will learn the basic roles, responsibilities, activities, and artifacts of the portfolio level. In addition, you'll learn how to implement advanced, Lean portfolio concepts including Lean-Agile budgeting, forecasting, and contracting. You'll also gain insights into potential Agile development capitalization strategies.

Part VI, Implementing SAFe, is all-new content that describes how to implement SAFe. Here you will learn a step-by-step approach to implementation, including: how to form a sufficiently powerful guiding coalition, how to design the implementation, how to launch Agile Release Trains, and how to sustain and continuously improve the benefits of your SAFe Lean-Agile implementation. Finally, we'll introduce "Essential SAFe," a summary view of the ten most critical factors in achieving a successful Lean-Agile implementation.

We hope that you will enjoy reading this book as much as we liked writing it (well, more, actually). But most importantly, our sincerest hope is that it will help you—those who build the world's most important systems—build better systems more quickly to the benefit of your enterprise, as well as the individuals and society who use these systems.

And as we wrote this book for you the practitioner, we strongly believe that building such great systems should be fun, too!

—*Richard Knaster and Dean Leffingwell*

Register your copy of *SAFe® 4.0 Distilled* at informit.com for convenient access to downloads, updates, and corrections as they become available. To start the registration process, go to informit.com/register and log in or create an account. Enter the product ISBN (9780134209425) and click Submit. Once the process is complete, you will find any available bonus content under "Registered Products."

Acknowledgments

First and foremost, this is a book about SAFe and therefore the authors are deeply indebted to all those who have contributed to the development of the framework. There are over 100 books and authors who (knowingly or unknowingly) contributed to the bodies of knowledge that underlie SAFe. In addition, there are another 100 or so contributors, reviewers, commenters, editors, graphic designers, etc. that make SAFe what it is. But if we were to take time to thank all those who contributed, we wouldn't be able to call this book "Distilled." Fortunately, the SAFe "Contributors" page (www.scaledagileframework.com/contributors) does an honorable job of acknowledging those contributions, so we needn't repeat that here.

However, it is most appropriate to thank all those who contributed directly to this work. These include SAFe methodologist Alex Yakyma, SAFe Fellow Inbar Oren, SAFe SPCT Joe Vallone, our Addison-Wesley acquisition editor Greg Doench, and Scaled Agile, Inc. graphic and production designers Jeff Long and Regina Cleveland. And last but certainly not least, Alan Sharavsky, SAI copy editor, who helped improve the readability of the book.

About the Authors

Richard Knaster is a SAFe Fellow, Principal Consultant, and a member of the Framework team at Scaled Agile, Inc., which develops new versions of SAFe. He has over 25 years' experience in software development in roles ranging from developer to executive and has been involved in large-scale Agile transformations for well over a decade.

Dean Leffingwell is recognized as one of the world's foremost authorities on Lean-Agile best practices and is an author, entrepreneur, and software development methodologist. He currently serves as CEO and Chief Methodologist to Scaled Agile, Inc., which he co-founded in 2011.

Part I
Overview

If you can't describe what you are doing as a process, you don't know what you're doing.

—W. Edwards Deming

SAFe® for Lean IT, Software and Systems Engineering

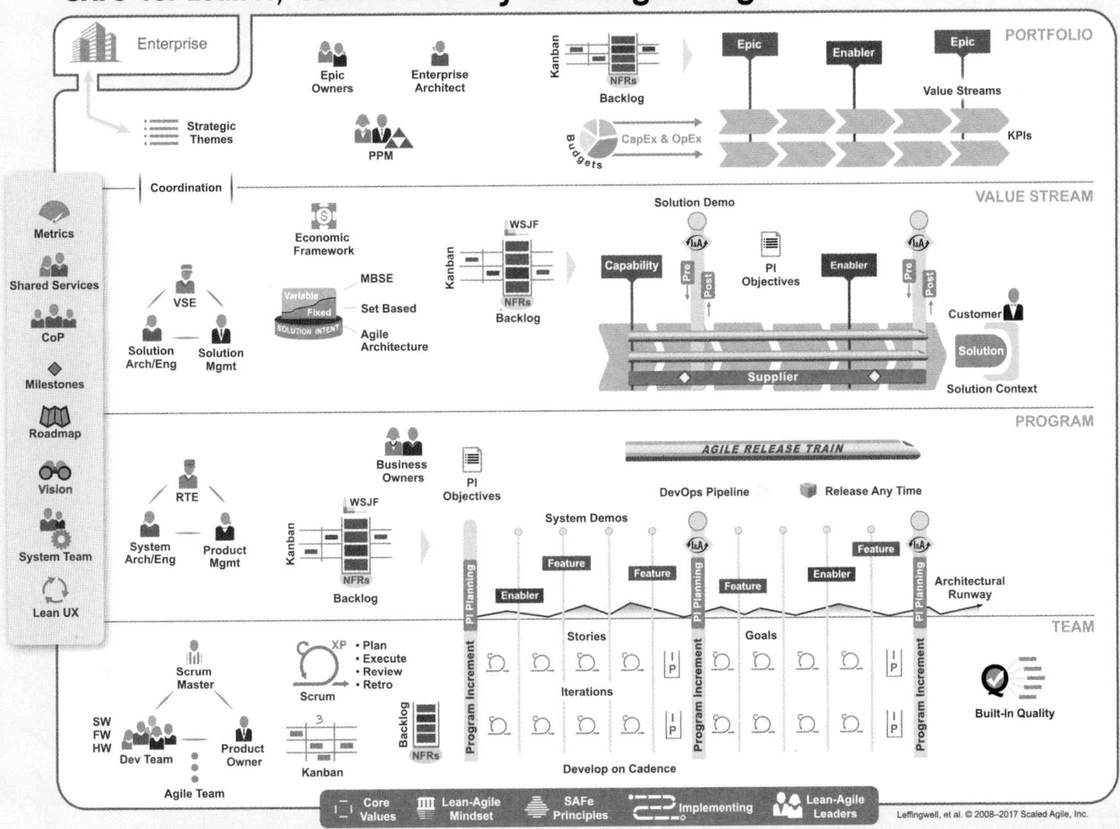

- Chapter 1 – Business Need for SAFe
- Chapter 2 – SAFe Overview

1

Business Need for SAFe

Learning is not compulsory; neither is survival.

—W. Edwards Deming

Why Do Businesses Need SAFe? 3
The Challenge of System Development 4
Applying New Bodies of Knowledge 5
Improving System Development Outcomes 9
The Business Benefits of SAFe 10
Summary 13

Why Do Businesses Need SAFe?

In today's fast-paced digital economy, businesses must respond rapidly to advances in technology to maintain a competitive edge. Software and systems are everywhere, driving business innovation and new ways of working, while replacing aging business models.

However, many enterprises struggle to develop significant software and systems—the modern fabric of nearly every product, in every industry across the planet.

Companies that understand the urgency to move and adapt faster—and change their ways of working—will succeed. Those that don't will struggle, or simply fade away. The business world is littered with examples: Blockbuster, Kodak, Tower Records, Borders, Palm Computing, Nokia, and Compaq were all iconic market leaders that couldn't adapt to new business models and technology innovations ahead of their competitors.

The lesson is simple: Enterprises must learn how to adapt quickly to changing technology and economic conditions or they will become extinct, no matter their size, smarts, or strength. This holds true even for businesses that don't consider themselves Information Technology (IT) or software companies. Professional services, financial services, healthcare institutions, and government entities are all highly dependent on their ability to produce new technology-based products and services.

The Challenge of System Development

Our development methods must keep pace with an increasingly complex and interconnected world. This includes innovations in mobile, big data, social media, and the Internet of Things (IoT). At the same time, organizations must maintain legacy systems while also defending against cyber-attacks and theft of digital information and intellectual property. Systems are larger, they are more integrated, and their impact on the global economy is significant. Failure of a critical system can have unacceptable social and economic consequences.[1] The size of the technology group and the range of technical skills that an enterprise needs are constantly expanding. Although outsourcing has helped meet many of these challenges, it adds risks and complexities, such as delayed communication, dependency on external providers, and loss of internal capabilities. Outsourcing also presents difficulties in maintaining solution quality and regulatory compliance.

Despite these challenges, many companies still use waterfall development methods, which rely on sequential phases and phase-gate approvals. Unfortunately, this way of working was created more than 40 years ago, when the rate of innovation was slower and the development tools and processes were less complex. If the enterprise's processes and systems are still based on traditional, sequential ways of thinking and working, even teams that have adopted Agile methods will be unable to deliver value quickly. And organizations will still struggle to scale their people, processes, and technology to keep up with the digital economy. Figure 1-1 shows some common software and systems development problems that some industries experience.

W. Edwards Deming, renowned author and management consultant, has taught us that the source of these problems is not poor employee performance. *Rather, the problems are with the system in which the employees work.*

1. https://en.wikipedia.org/wiki/2010_Flash_Crash

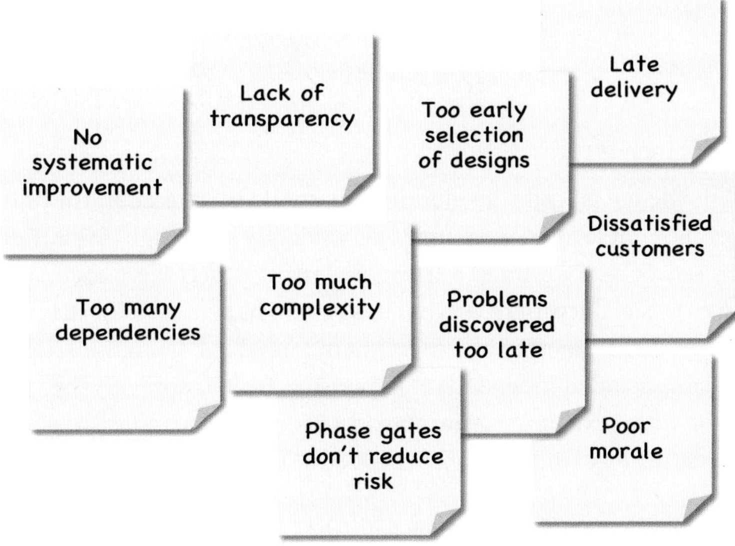

Figure 1-1. Common issues from retrospectives conducted across many industries

To achieve broader change, the entire development value stream—from concept to deployment—must become leaner and more responsive to change. Moreover, the organizational structures, processes, and cultures of most businesses were developed more than a century ago. They were built for control and stability, not for speed and agility. Small, incremental changes to how businesses manage, strategize, and execute are insufficient to remain competitive. True transformation to leaner and more Agile approaches requires sweeping change that has a positive, long-lasting effect on the entire enterprise.

Applying New Bodies of Knowledge

When considering the challenges enterprises face to achieve more effective large-scale solution development and taking into account the systemic nature of problems, it makes sense to apply all the tools and contemporary knowledge available.

Fortunately, the last few decades have provided three such bodies of knowledge: Agile development, systems thinking, and Lean product development. Understanding these newer areas of knowledge is critical to applying the values, principles, and practices of the Scaled Agile Framework (SAFe). Each is described in the following sections.

Agile Development

We are uncovering better ways of developing software by doing it, and helping others do it.

—Agile Manifesto

One body of knowledge is Agile development, initially pioneered in the late nineties by a number of thought leaders working independently. Jim Highsmith, Kent Beck, Martin Fowler, Ken Schwaber, Brian Marick, and many others were each experimenting with alternatives to the document-driven, heavyweight processes of that era. In 2001, seventeen of them came together at a meeting in Snowbird, Utah, looking for common ground. Attendees included independent experts, as well as some of the creators of the lighter-weight software development frameworks, including Extreme Programming (XP), Scrum, and Dynamic System Development Method (DSDM).

What emerged was the *Manifesto for Agile Software Development*, igniting an industry-wide movement that unified various philosophies and practices behind a common belief system:

AGILE MANIFESTO

"Through this work we have come to value:

- Individuals and interactions over processes and tools
- Working software over comprehensive documentation
- Responding to change over following a plan
- Customer collaboration over contract negotiation

That is, while there is value in the items on the right, we value the items on the left more."[2]

Based on accounts by Martin Fowler,[3] "in the latter part of the Snowbird meeting, and in the following couple of months, we worked on identifying the twelve principles." Fowler goes on to say, "The manifesto is a rallying cry: it says what we stand for and also what we are opposed to. Several items were worded to clearly make a distinction between our views and that of many others in the software industry. I hope the manifesto will make clear what is and isn't agile."

2. www.agilemanifesto.org (last updated 2001)
3. http://martinfowler.com/articles/agileStory.html (July 9, 2006)

The manifesto unleashed a dramatic and entirely new way of thinking and working for software developers, one that unlocks the intrinsic motivation of those who do the work.

The importance of this breakthrough cannot be overstated. SAFe is founded on the culture and innovative team-based methods that Agile embraces. If we can't be Agile, we can't be SAFe. Indeed, the manifesto is a critical part of the *SAFe Lean-Agile mindset.*

Systems Thinking

A system must be managed. It will not manage itself. Left to themselves, components become selfish, independent profit centers and thus destroy the system. ... The secret is cooperation between components toward the aim of the organization.

—W. Edwards Deming

The second body of knowledge that underlies SAFe is systems thinking, probably best represented by the formative work of Deming. Systems thinking is a holistic approach to solution development, which views a system as an interrelated set of elements. Key aspects of systems thinking include the following:

- Optimizing a component does not optimize the whole system. Indeed, the opposite may be true.
- A system exhibits emergent behavior, which occurs only as a result of the interaction from all the system elements.
- A system operates in its own environment, the context in which it deliver its value. Moreover, the very operation of a new system changes that environment.
- The value of a system passes through its interconnections. Therefore, special attention should be given to interfaces (such as APIs, physical connections, networks, and so on) and dependencies among system elements since they are critical elements of providing ultimate value.

Systems thinking also acknowledges that two entities must be considered: the system built for the benefit of the customer, and the organization building the system. The path to improvement requires a constant focus on all the basic systems principles, both for the system under development and for the organization building it. After all, the organization building the system is itself a system.

Fundamental to the design and implementation of SAFe is understanding that individuals, teams, programs, and business units are all part of the product development system. And as Deming noted, "a system must be managed" in order to be effective.

Lean Product Development

All we are doing is looking at the timeline from when the customer gives us an order to when we receive the cash, and we are reducing the timeline by eliminating the non-value added wastes.

—Taiichi Ohno, father of the Toyota Production System

The third body of knowledge, Lean product development, is a hybrid of Lean thinking and product development flow largely based on the *Toyota Production System*, a remarkably rich and deep source of guidance. In the earlier quote, Ohno distills Lean to its very essence: the continuous evaluation of existing processes with the goal of eliminating waste and delays. This enables the Lean enterprise to achieve its ultimate and perpetual goal of *delivering value in the shortest sustainable lead time.*

In the last few decades, thought leaders such as Allen Ward, Michael Kennedy, Don Reinertsen, Eric Ries, and many others have brought the science of Lean from manufacturing to product development. They've provided an extensive body of knowledge that we can use to dramatically improve the process. Highlights include the following:

- Focusing on understanding the full value stream. The value stream is the sequence of steps needed to take a concept from idea to market. Avoiding waste and delays in the value stream is a constant focus.
- Developing and managing a sustainable flow of value. Cadence and synchronization, batch size reduction, managing queue lengths, and visualizing and limiting Work in Process (WIP) are key to achieving flow.
- Respecting people and culture. Lean recognizes that people do all the work, and respecting people—while embracing the cultural changes that support newer and leaner habits—is key to Lean.
- Accelerating innovation by releasing a Minimum Viable Product (MVP) to get fast feedback with the least amount of effort.
- Embracing kaizen, which is a culture of continuous improvement, where every person in the organization is dedicated to relentless improvement and better outcomes.

- Empowering the leadership. The responsibility for implementation and continuous improvement of Lean-Agile development lies in large part with management. Only they can change the system by first being trained in and then becoming trainers of these leaner ways of thinking and working.

These practices are at work in SAFe and covered throughout this book.

Improving System Development Outcomes

Based largely on these three bodies of knowledge, SAFe has evolved as a proven approach for developing complex systems and software in a Lean-Agile manner. It helps enterprises answer the following types of questions:

- How do we align the enterprise toward common business and technical goals?
- How do we deliver new value on a predictable schedule so that the rest of the business can plan and execute?
- How do we improve the quality of our solutions and delight our customers?
- How do we organize teams around value so that our programs deliver it effectively and avoid the delays and bureaucracy inherent in a traditional, hierarchical structure?
- How do we scale Agile practices from the team to the larger program and business unit, and across the enterprise, to deliver better results?
- How do we manage and minimize dependencies between teams, programs, and value streams?
- How do we make better decisions to improve our economic outcomes?
- How do we create an environment that fosters collaboration, innovation, and relentless improvement? How do we unlock the intrinsic motivation of the people who do this work?
- How can we change our culture so that it tolerates failure and rewards risk-taking and continuous learning?
- How do we know that the new ways of working are more effective? How do we know what our Agile teams are doing and measure how well they're performing? How can we help our teams improve without getting in the way?

By adopting SAFe—and applying its well-described set of values, principles, and practices—the enterprise can address these questions and realize greater business and individual benefits.

That is the subject and purpose of this book.

The Business Benefits of SAFe

Three years into this effort, our SAFe transformation has taken strong root, leading to high-quality, predictable software delivery and architectural runways.

—Robert F. Crudup, SEI Investments, executive vice president and CIO

Now in its fourth major revision, SAFe 4.0 is improving business outcomes for companies of all sizes across the world. It has produced dramatic increases in time to market, employee engagement, higher quality, higher customer satisfaction, and overall improved economic outcomes. It also helps create cultures that are more productive, rewarding, and fun.

Figure 1-2 highlights these benefits as derived directly from case studies written by SAFe end users (see ScaledAgileFramework.com/case-studies/).

Figure 1-2. Business results from customer-developed case studies

These, and other benefits, are highlighted in the following sections.

Quality

Built-in quality practices increase customer satisfaction and provide faster and more predictable value delivery. They also improve the ability to innovate. Without quality, the Lean goal of maximum value in the shortest sustainable lead time cannot be achieved. Enterprises that apply SAFe typically get rapid and compelling increases in solution quality.

- "95% decrease in defects." —Telstra
- "5x reduction in deployment impact." —CSG International
- "55% defect reduction rate." —Hynix Semiconductor
- "44% decrease in post-release defects." —Mitchell International
- "50% warranty expense decrease." —John Deere
- "20–25% increase in client satisfaction." —SEI Investments

Productivity

When productivity increases, system development economics improves, as does employee engagement. For team members, productivity is a critical, personal need. Everyone feels better when they're contributing more and doing less wasteful work.

- "Productivity has increased by at least 20–25%." —Discount Tire
- "Team productivity is up by 20–50%." —BMC Corporation
- "A single defect gets fixed only once now." —TomTom

Employee Engagement

According to the Society of Human Resource Management (SHRM), employees with the highest level of commitment perform 21 percent better and are 65 percent less likely to leave the organization. Clearly, employee engagement is directly linked to business performance.

- "Employee engagement increased 9.8%." —John Deere
- "Employee happiness rating went from 47–67% in 10 weeks." —Medical systems company
- "Improved productivity and morale." —Valpak
- "Overall happier teams." —Elekta

Faster Time to Market

Lean-Agile frameworks allow businesses to deliver value to the market more quickly. Companies that adopt Agile development practices routinely gain first-mover advantages and enjoy the higher gross margins afforded to market leaders. SAFe enterprises typically see a 30–75 percent (as much as 3x!) improvement in time to market.

- "Delivery down from one year to 126 days." —TomTom
- "Decreased time to market by 27 weeks." —Here.com
- "Time to market and level of quality have increased dramatically." —Discount Tire
- "Delivered higher-value business results in a shorter delivery cycle." —SEI Investments
- "Releases went from 12–18 months to 3–4x per year." —BMC Corporation

In addition to these "big four" benefits, SAFe users report other advantages as well, as highlighted in the following sections.

Program Execution

One of SAFe's core values is program execution. Mastering this means that Research and Development (R&D) or IT can become trusted and respected partners of the business—people who do what they say they're going to do. That allows other team members to plan and execute more effectively.

- "50% improved delivery predictability." —SK Hynix Memory Solutions
- "SAFe principles key to delivering on time." —French National Employment Agency
- "Since adopting SAFe, we routinely meet 95% of our commitments." —CA-Rally
- "A positive and significant increase in net promoter score from the business." —Royal Melbourne Institute of Technology

Alignment

When management and teams are aligned to a common mission, all the energy is directed toward helping the customer. Everyone is on the same team and working toward the same purpose. Alignment communicates the intent of the mission and enables teams to focus on how to accomplish the objectives.

- "Management aligned and supportive of Agile teams." —Nordea Bank
- "Program Increment (PI) planning provides both vertical and horizontal alignment." —Elekta
- "Better alignment to common vision." —Infogain
- "SAFe makes it easier for us to focus on what has the most business value." —Travis Perkins
- "To see a waterfall program manager embrace SAFe only two days after participating in a PI planning session is remarkable." —Nordea Bank

Transparency

You can't manage a secret. Transparency builds trust. Trust, in turn, is essential for performance, innovation, risk-taking, and relentless improvement.

- "There is transparency through showcases. There is much better trust." —Royal Melbourne Institute of Technology
- "Better managed expectations." —Lego
- "Improved transparency through Rally reports and SAFe ceremonies." —Elekta
- "The SAFe recipe helped highlight dependencies and risks far in advance of what we saw before." —Intel

A final quote from Peter Vollmer, distinguished technologist at Hewlett Packard Enterprise, sums up the benefits of SAFe: *"With a proven framework, we can deliver solutions much faster and with less effort. SAFe defines the roles, teams, activities, and artifacts to apply Lean and Agile principles at enterprise scale, and provides outstanding training and coaching materials to increase our chance of success."*

Summary

This chapter discussed the challenges and principles of improving systems development, demonstrating why businesses need and will benefit from implementing SAFe.

The key takeaways are as follows:

- To maintain a competitive edge in today's fast-paced digital economy, businesses must respond rapidly to technological advances. Companies that understand this—and change their ways of working—will succeed. Those that don't will struggle, or simply go out of business.
- Common challenges of software and systems development include late delivery and discovery of problems, dissatisfied customers, phase gates that cause delays but don't reduce risk, too many dependencies, lack of transparency, and no means for systematic improvement.
- If the enterprise's processes and systems are still based on traditional, sequential ways of thinking and working, even Agile teams will be unable to deliver value quickly.
- SAFe combines the power of Agile with systems thinking and Lean product development. As a result, SAFe provides dramatic improvements to business agility, including productivity, time to market, quality, and employee engagement, and more. Case studies written by customers confirm these benefits.

Now that you know what the framework can do for your business and your people, we invite you on an exciting learning journey. You'll discover what SAFe is, how it works, and how to apply it. More important, you'll gain the knowledge and tools you'll need to create an environment where your people and organization can survive, and thrive, well into the future.

2

SAFe Overview

This would all be a lot easier to understand if you would just draw me a picture.

—Global 100 executive

The Big Picture 15
The Levels 17
The Foundation 22
The Spanning Palette 24
Summary 25

The Scaled Agile Framework (SAFe) helps businesses address the significant challenges of developing and delivering enterprise-class software and systems in the shortest sustainable lead time. It is an online, freely revealed knowledge base of proven success patterns for implementing Lean-Agile software and systems at enterprise scale.

Developed in the field, SAFe draws from three primary bodies of knowledge: Agile development, systems thinking, and Lean product development. It synchronizes alignment, collaboration, and delivery for large numbers of Agile teams. Scalable and configurable, SAFe allows each organization to adapt it to its own business needs. It supports smaller-scale solutions employing 50–125 practitioners, as well as complex systems that require thousands of people.

The Big Picture

An extensive body of knowledge, SAFe describes the roles, responsibilities, artifacts, and activities necessary to implement Lean-Agile development. To illustrate SAFe concepts, the website (www.scaledagileframework.com) features an interactive Big Picture graphic, which is a visual overview of the framework and is the primary user interface to the knowledge base. Each icon of the image is clickable, offering access to an article on that topic, as well as links to related information.

There are three different configurations of the framework, which provide a key part of SAFe's scalable and modular approach:

1. *Essential SAFe.* The most basic configuration of the framework is illustrated in Figure 2-1. Essential SAFe provides the minimal elements necessary to be successful with SAFe. (See chapter 19, "Essential SAFe," for an overview of these elements.)

SAFe® for Lean IT, Software and Systems Engineering

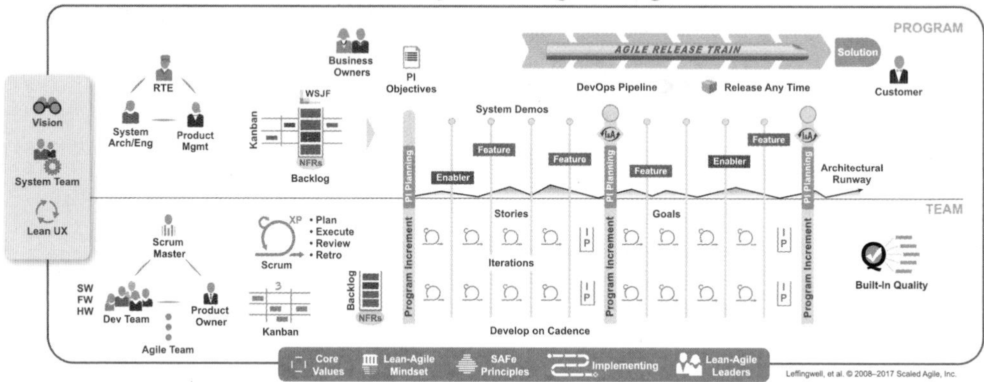

Figure 2-1. Essential SAFe

2. *Three-level SAFe.* This configuration, illustrated in Figure 2-2, is intended for those building solutions that require a modest number (perhaps 5–10) of Agile teams. In larger enterprises, it can also be used effectively to support the development of multiple solutions, so long as they are largely independent of each other.

SAFe® for Lean IT, Software and Systems Engineering

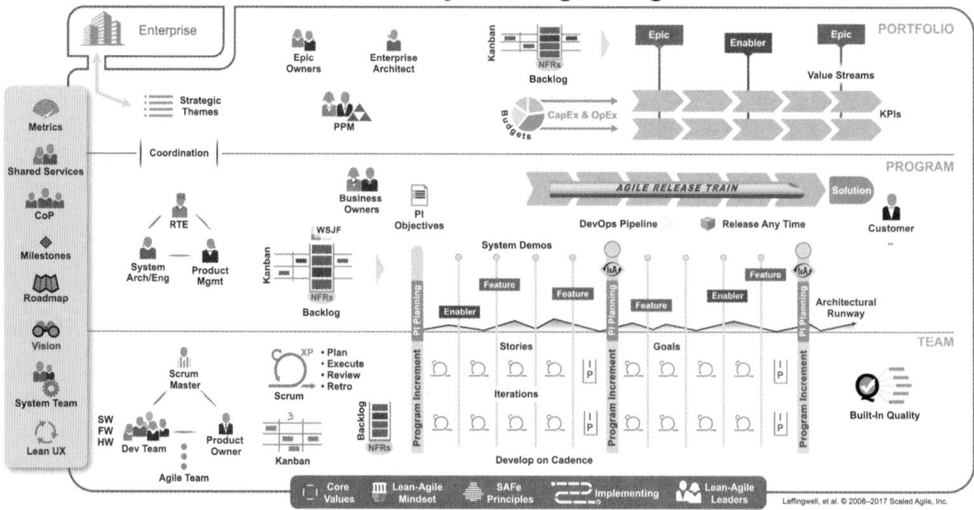

Figure 2-2. Three-level SAFe

3. *Four-level SAFe.* Figure 2-3 illustrates the most comprehensive configuration. It supports those enterprises building large, integrated solutions that typically require hundreds of people or more to develop and maintain.

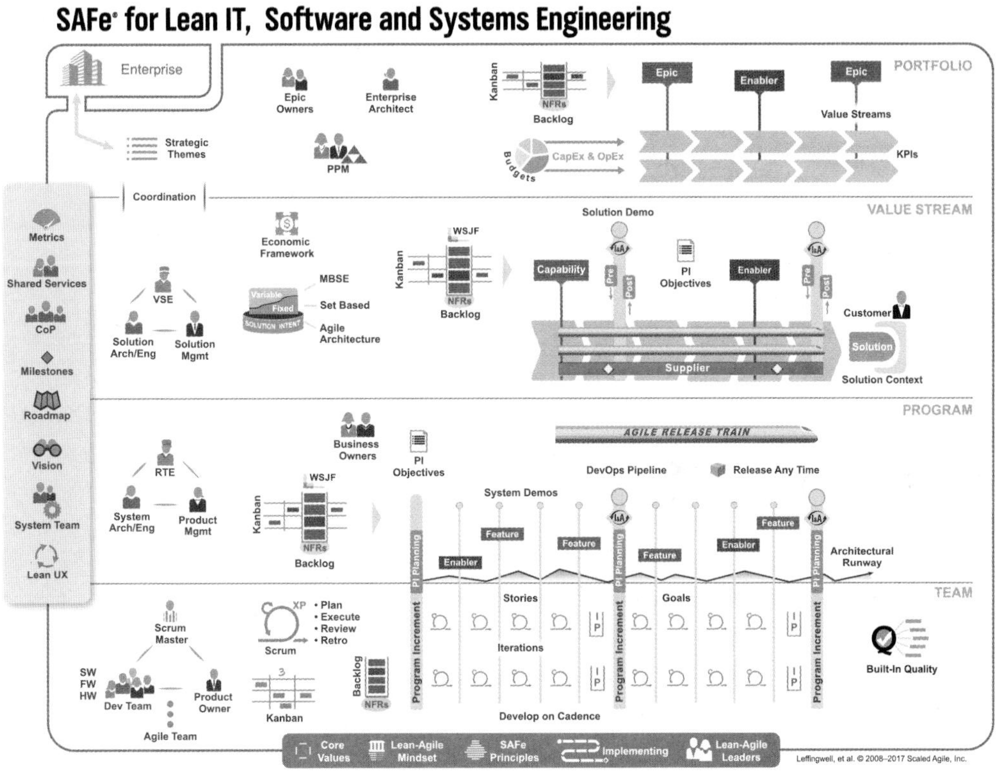

SAFe® for Lean IT, Software and Systems Engineering

Figure 2-3. Four-level SAFe

The Levels

SAFe provides guidance for all the levels of the enterprise that are actively engaged in solution development—*team, program, value stream,* and *portfolio*—along with a supporting foundation element. Each level is described in the following sections.

Team Level

The team level, shown at the bottom of Figure 2-4, describes the structure and activities of the Agile teams that build the solution. Each team has dedicated individual contributors, covering all the roles necessary to build a quality increment of value for an iteration. Teams can deliver software, hardware, and any combination.

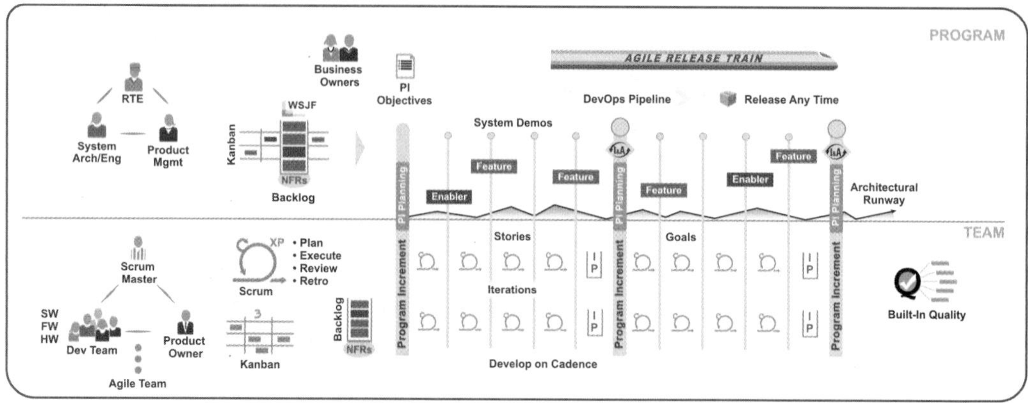

Figure 2-4. The team and program level

Teams apply software quality practices including continuous integration, test-first, refactoring, pair work, collective ownership, and more. Hardware quality is supported by exploratory early iterations, frequent system-level integration, design verification, modeling, and set-based design. Agile architecture supports software and hardware quality.

Highlights of the team level include the following:

- Each team delivers valuable, tested, working systems at least every two weeks.
- Teams implement user stories and enablers, which describe small pieces of functionality needed to develop features.
- Scrum teams have three to nine team members. Their roles include the Scrum Master, Product Owner, dedicated individual contributors, and any specialty resources needed to deliver value.
- Kanban team roles are less rigorously defined, though many kanban teams implement Scrum roles and team size limits.

Program Level

The heart of SAFe is the program level (Figure 2-4), where Agile teams, key stakeholders, and other resources are dedicated to an important, ongoing solution mission using a construct called the Agile Release Train (ART). The ART is a self-managing and organizing team-of-Agile-teams that plans, commits, and executes together. Agile teams are dedicated to one, and only one Agile Release Train (ART). Each is responsible for defining, building, and testing stories from their backlog in a series of timeboxed iterations.

ARTs are virtual organizations (typically five to twelve Agile teams), formed to span functional reporting structures and eliminate unnecessary handoffs and steps across silos. Value in SAFe is delivered by ARTs, each of which realizes a portion of a value stream or, in some cases, the whole thing. They accelerate the delivery of solutions by implementing Lean-Agile practices.

Since ARTs are organized around a value stream, they allow teams to stay together for long periods of time; this is versus projects, where teams are formed and then disbanded after the project is completed. ARTs also differ from a traditional program, which typically has start and end dates and temporary resources. Instead, ARTs have a long-lived structure and mission. Many ARTs span organizational and geographic boundaries; others follow a line of business or product line management reporting structure.

Highlights of the program level include the following:

- The ART aligns management, teams, and stakeholders to a common mission through a single vision, roadmap, and program backlog.
- ARTs deliver the features (user functionality) and the enablers (technical infrastructure) needed to provide value on a sustainable basis.
- Team iterations are synchronized and use the same duration and start and end dates. Each ART delivers valuable and tested system-level increments every two weeks.
- Program Increments (PIs) provide a fixed timebox for planning, execution, and inspecting and adapting. Solutions can be released at any time, during or at the end of a PI, based solely on the needs of the business.
- Key ART roles include the Agile teams plus Product Management, System Architect/Engineering, and the Release Train Engineer (RTE), who is the chief Scrum Master for the train. Business owners are also part of the ART.
- The system demo synchronizes the work of all teams on the train every two weeks and provides an opportunity for ART sponsors, stakeholders, and customers to assess the value and progress of the solution.
- Frequent or continuous integration of the work from all teams is the ultimate measure of progress.
- ARTs use face-to-face PI planning to assure collaboration, alignment, and rapid adaptation.

- ARTs build and maintain a DevOps pipeline, which is used to continuously develop and release small increments of value.
- ARTs provide common and consistent approaches to user experience using Lean UX principles and practices (see chapter 8, "Executing a Program Increment" for more details).

Value Stream Level

The value stream level (Figure 2-5) helps enterprises that face the biggest challenges—building large-scale, multidisciplinary software, hardware and complex IT systems. Building these solutions requires additional roles, artifacts, events, and coordination.

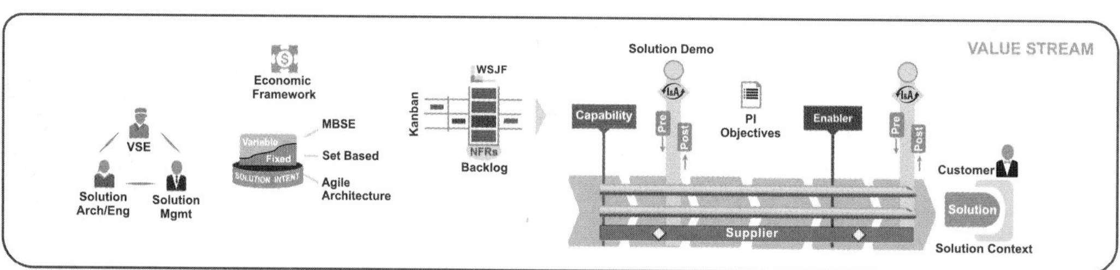

Figure 2-5. SAFe value stream level

Enterprises that build largely independent systems or those that can be built with a few hundred practitioners may not need this level. In those cases, the portfolio operates with the three-level configuration. Even then, elements from the value stream level may be incorporated into the three-level configuration as needed. For example, solution intent, solution context, and economic framework are all described in the value stream level, but may also support a single ART.

Highlights of the value stream level include the following:

- An economic framework that provides financial boundaries for value stream and ART decision-making
- Solution intent, which is a repository for current and future solution behaviors, and can be used to support verification and validation
- Solution context, which describes how the system will interface and be packaged and deployed in its operating environment
- System engineering disciplines, including Agile architecture, set-based design, and model-based systems engineering

- Capabilities and enablers that describe the larger behaviors of the solution
- Additional roles to support the ARTs, including Solution Management, Solution Architect/Engineer, Value Stream Engineer (VSE), supplier, and customer

Like the program level, the value stream level is organized around PIs, which are synchronized across all ARTs. This enables cadence and synchronization of multiple ARTs and suppliers. That includes pre- and post-PI planning meetings and the solution demo.

Portfolio Level

The portfolio level organizes the Lean-Agile enterprise around the flow of value through one or more value streams. Each develops the systems and solutions needed to meet the portfolio's business objectives. The portfolio level contains these elements and provides the budgeting and other oversight necessary to assure that value stream investments meet their financial goals.

As shown in Figure 2-6, each portfolio funds and governs a set of value streams to meet the business strategy.

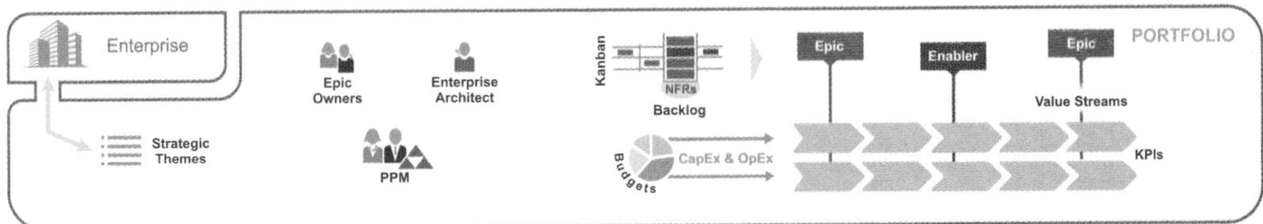

Figure 2-6. SAFe portfolio level

Highlights of the portfolio level include the following:

- Strategic themes, which are the business objectives that connect the portfolio to the evolving strategy of the enterprise
- The enterprise value streams, which are responsible for delivering the solutions, products, and services that help the enterprise achieve its mission
- The Program Portfolio Management (PPM) function, which consists of the executive and management stakeholders who have the highest level of accountability for business results
- Epics, which are significant initiatives that require multiple value streams, help guide development toward the larger aim of the portfolio

- Epic Owners, who are responsible for guiding epics through the portfolio kanban system, developing the business case, and working with key ART stakeholders on implementation
- Enterprise Architects, who work with business stakeholders and Solution/System Architects to guide technology initiatives (enabler epics) and drive enterprise standards across value streams
- A Lean-Agile budgeting mechanism that funds value streams (instead of projects), empowering decision makers and accelerating value delivery
- Objective metrics that support Lean-Agile governance and continuous improvement

The portfolio has bidirectional connections to the larger business. One direction establishes the strategic themes that guide the business to changing objectives. The reverse provides a constant flow of feedback. This includes the current state of the portfolio's solutions, as well as key performance indicators and other business factors affecting the portfolio.

The Foundation

As illustrated in Figure 2-7, SAFe's foundation contains the supporting principles, values, mindset, implementation guidance, and leadership roles needed to successfully deliver value at scale. Each foundation element is briefly described next.

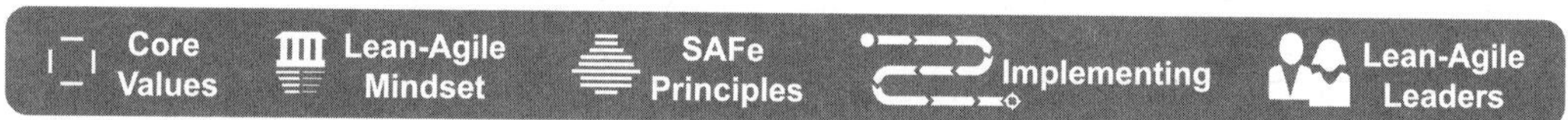

Figure 2-7. The foundation

- *Core values.* Four core values define the belief system for SAFe: alignment, built-in quality, transparency, and program execution. These are described in more detail in the following section.
- *Lean-Agile mindset.* Lean-Agile leaders are lifelong learners and teachers. They understand and embrace Lean and Agile principles and practices. The SAFe House of Lean and the Agile Manifesto provide the basis for these new ways of thinking and are discussed in chapter 3, "Lean-Agile Mindset."
- *SAFe principles.* SAFe practices are grounded in nine principles that synthesize Agile methods, Lean product development, systems thinking, and decades of field experience. These Lean-Agile principles are covered in chapter 5, "SAFe Principles."

- *Implementing.* Implementing the changes necessary to become a Lean-Agile technology enterprise is a substantial change for most companies. SAFe provides an implementation roadmap to help guide organizations on this journey. Part VI, the final five chapters of this book, is dedicated to this purpose.
- *Lean-Agile leaders.* Management has the ultimate responsibility for business outcomes. To achieve that, leaders must be trained in, and become trainers of, these leaner ways of thinking and operating. To this end, SAFe describes a new style of leadership exhibited by the enterprise's leaders. This is covered in chapter 4, "Lean-Agile Leaders."

Core Values

The following core values are key to SAFe's effectiveness:

1. *Alignment.* Alignment ensures that many people act as one unit or team, all pulling in the same direction. Alignment in SAFe is achieved when everyone in the portfolio, and every team member on every ART, understands the strategy and the part they play in achieving it. SAFe delivers alignment by orchestrating strategic themes, vision, roadmap, and PI planning. Economic prioritization and the visible flow of work through the various kanban systems and backlogs provide visibility and transparency.
2. *Built-in quality.* The economic impact of poor quality is much greater in larger systems. Problems accumulate. A small issue with a subsystem can have an enormous impact on the whole system. Built-in quality practices, however, help ensure that each solution element, at every increment, achieves appropriate quality standards throughout development. This results in a fast, continuous flow of value, with reduced delays due to rework. It also boosts productivity, and employee and customer satisfaction.
3. *Transparency.* Large-scale solution development is hard. Things don't always work out as planned. Transparency—sharing progress and facts openly across all levels—is key to building trust and improving performance. It enables fast, decentralized decision-making and higher levels of employee empowerment and engagement. SAFe helps achieve transparency by providing visibility into the work of the portfolio, value streams, programs, and teams. The Inspect & Adapt (I&A) event provides visibility into the business value achieved and the retrospective of the PI. Status reporting is based on objective measures of working systems.

4. *Program execution.* Of course, none of this matters if teams can't execute and continuously deliver value. That is why SAFe places an intense focus on working systems and business outcomes. That's the purpose of the ART. The success of the value stream depends on the combined success of the ARTs. If they struggle—and they will, because complex solution development is hard—they'll have the support of the I&A workshops to rely on. The workshop closes the loop and improves execution every PI.

But program performance can't be only a team-based, bottom-up thing. Successful execution also requires the active support of Lean-Agile leaders, who combine internal leadership with their orientation toward systems thinking, objective measures, and customer outcomes.

The Spanning Palette

The spanning palette (Figure 2-8) contains various roles and artifacts that may be applicable to a specific team, program, value stream, or portfolio context. An element of SAFe's flexibility and configurability, the spanning palette permits organizations to apply only the elements needed for each level.

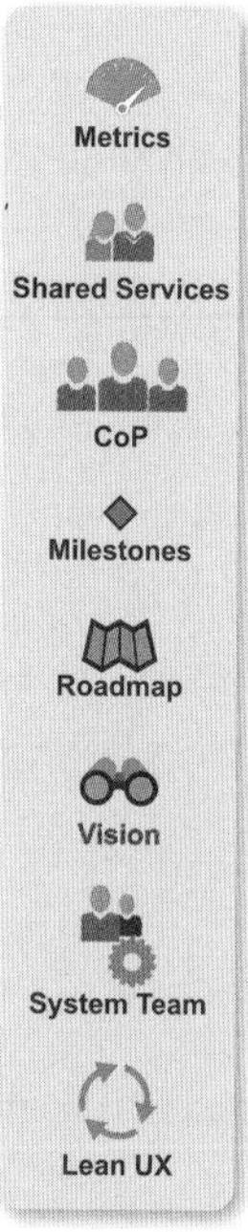

Figure 2-8. The spanning palette

Below is a brief description of each element of the spanning palette:

- *Metrics.* The primary measure in SAFe is the objective measurement of working solutions. Moreover, SAFe defines a number of additional intermediate and long-term measures as well, metrics that teams, programs, and portfolios can use to measure progress.
- *Shared services.* Represents the specialty roles that are necessary for the success of an ART or value stream, but that cannot be dedicated full time to any specific train.
- *CoPs.* Communities of Practice (CoPs) is an informal group of team members and other experts, acting within the context of a program or enterprise, that has a mission of sharing practical knowledge in one or more relevant domains.
- *Milestones.* Milestones are used to track progress toward a specific goal or event. These include fixed-date milestones, PI milestones, and learning milestones.
- *Roadmap.* The roadmap communicates planned ART and value stream deliverables and milestones over a timeline.
- *Vision.* The vision describes a future view of the solution to be developed, reflecting customer and stakeholders needs, as well as features and capabilities, which are proposed to address those needs.
- *System Team.* This a special Agile team that provides assistance in building and using the Agile development environment, including continuous integration and test automation and automating the delivery pipeline.
- *Lean UX.* Lean UX is the application of lean principles to user experience design. It uses an iterative, hypothesis driven approach to product development, through constant measurement and learning loops (build – measure – learn). In SAFe, Lean UX is applied at scale, with the right combination of centralized and decentralized UX design and implementation.

Summary

This chapter gave a brief overview of SAFe, which provides guidance for scaling Lean-Agile development across the entire enterprise.

The key takeaways from this chapter are as follows:

- SAFe helps businesses address the significant challenges of developing and delivering enterprise-class software and systems in the shortest sustainable lead time.
- SAFe is scalable and configurable, allowing each organization to apply it to its own business model.
- There are three configurations of the framework. Essential SAFe is the most basic subset, which describes the minimal elements necessary to be successful with SAFe. The three-level configuration works best for smaller systems and a modest number of Agile teams. The four-level configuration supports building and maintaining large, integrated solutions that typically require hundreds of practitioners.
- SAFe teams use an Agile team framework, combining the best of Scrum project management, built-in quality technical practices, and kanban to manage the flow of work. Each Agile team includes all the roles necessary to build a quality increment of a working system in each iteration.
- The heart of SAFe is the program level, which revolves around an organization called the ART. It includes all the roles necessary to move ideas from concept through deployment. Each ART aligns teams to a common mission and vision using a single program backlog. It produces valuable and tested system-level solutions, which can be evaluated by stakeholders at least every two weeks. Under the guidance of architects and user experience designers, ARTs use a fixed PI planning and an execution timebox.
- The optional value stream level helps enterprises that face the biggest challenges, building large-scale software and systems. Developing such solutions in a Lean-Agile manner requires additional constructs, artifacts, and coordination. Value streams are implemented by creating one or more ARTs, which are organized to work across functional silos to accelerate delivery.
- Each portfolio has the value streams, people, and processes necessary to fund and govern the products, services, and solutions required to fulfill its business strategy.

Part II
The Foundation of SAFe

The foundation for any successful change is the right leadership, values, principles, and mindset.

—The authors

- Chapter 3 – Lean-Agile Mindset
- Chapter 4 – Lean-Agile Leaders
- Chapter 5 – SAFe Principles

3

Lean-Agile Mindset

People are already doing their best. The problem is with the system. Only management can change the system. It is not enough that management commit themselves to quality and productivity, they must know what it is they must do. ... Such a responsibility cannot be delegated.

—W. Edwards Deming

Overview 29
Thinking Lean 30
Embracing Agility 33
Applying the Agile Manifesto at Scale 37
Summary 40

Overview

Deming's quotes remind us of a basic premise of the Scaled Agile Framework (SAFe): The ultimate responsibility for the success of the enterprise, and thereby any significant change to the way of working, lies with management. And there's no question that moving to a Lean-Agile paradigm will be a huge change. Not only are the practices different, but the belief system, core values, culture, and management philosophy are different as well.

To begin this journey of change and instill new habits into the culture, leaders and managers should learn and adopt the Lean-Agile mindset, as shown in Figure 3-1.

House of Lean

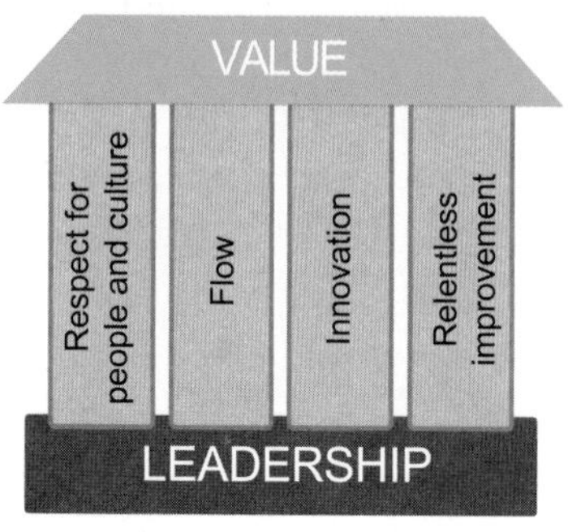

Value in the shortest sustainable lead time

Agile Manifesto

Individuals and interactions over processes and tools

Working software over comprehensive documentation

Customer collaboration over contract negotiation

Responding to change over following a plan

That is, while there is value in the items on the right, we value the items on the left more.

Figure 3-1. The aspects of a Lean-Agile mindset

There are two primary aspects of a Lean-Agile mindset, described here:

- *Thinking Lean.* Organized around six key concepts, much of the thinking is pictured in Figure 3-1. The roof represents the goal of delivering value. The pillars support this goal through the concepts of respect for people and culture, flow, innovation, and relentless improvement. Lean leadership provides the foundation on which everything else stands.
- *Embracing agility.* SAFe is built entirely on the skills, aptitude, and capabilities of Agile teams and their leaders. And while there's no single definition of what an Agile method is, the manifesto provides a value system that introduced Agile methods into mainstream software development.

Together, these help create the Lean-Agile Mindset, which is a large part of a new management approach and an accelerator to cultural improvement. It provides the thinking tools and belief system that leadership needs to guide a successful enterprise transformation. In turn, this helps both individuals and businesses achieve their goals. Each is described further in the following sections.

Thinking Lean

While initially derived from Lean manufacturing,[1] the principles and practices of Lean thinking as applied to software, product, and systems development are now deep and

1. James P. Womack, Daniel T. Jones, and Daniel Roos, *The Machine That Changed the World: The Story of Lean Production—Toyota's Secret Weapon in the Global Car Wars That Is Revolutionizing World Industry* (Free Press, 2007).

extensive. For example, Allen Ward,[2] Don Reinertsen,[3] Mary and Tom Poppendieck,[4] Dean Leffingwell,[5] and others have described aspects of the core principles and practices of Lean thinking using a product development context. In combination with these factors, we developed the SAFe House of Lean, inspired by the Toyota "House of Lean" and others.

Goal: Value

The roof of the house represents value. The goal is to deliver the *maximum value in the shortest sustainable lead time*, while providing the highest possible quality to customers and to society as a whole. High morale, emotional and physical safety, and customer delight are further goals with economic benefits.

Pillar 1: Respect for People and Culture

A Lean-Agile approach doesn't implement itself or perform any real work. People do all the work. Respect for people and culture is a basic human need. People are empowered to evolve their own practices and improvements. Management challenges people to change and may help steer them toward improvement. However, the teams and individuals learn problem-solving and reflection skills and are accountable for making the appropriate improvements.

To evolve into a Lean organization, the culture will need to change substantially. For that to happen, the organization and its leaders must change first. And respect for people and culture should extend to relationships with suppliers, partners, customers, and the broader community. After all, they are key to the success of the enterprise.

When there is true urgency for change, improvements in culture will naturally occur. First, understand and implement SAFe values and principles. Second, deliver winning results. Changes to culture will surely follow.

---

2. Allen Ward and Durward Sobek II, *Lean Product and Process Development* (Lean Enterprise Institute, 2014).
3. Donald G. Reinertsen, *The Principles of Product Development Flow: Second Generation Lean Product Development* (Celeritas, 2009).
4. Mary Poppendieck and Tom Poppendieck, *Implementing Lean Software Development: From Concept to Cash* (Addison-Wesley, 2006).
5. Dean Leffingwell, *Agile Software Requirements: Lean Requirements Practices for Teams, Programs, and the Enterprise* (Addison-Wesley, 2011).

Pillar 2: Flow

The key to successfully implementing SAFe is establishing a continuous flow of incremental value delivery based on continuous fast feedback and adjustment.

Continuous flow enables faster value delivery, effective built-in quality practices, constant improvement, and evidence-based governance.

The principles of flow are an important part of the Lean-Agile mindset. These include understanding the full value stream, visualizing and limiting Work in Process (WIP), and reducing batch sizes and managing queue lengths. Additionally, Lean focuses on reducing delays and eliminating waste, meaning activities that add no value.

Pillar 3: Innovation

Flow builds a solid foundation for the delivery of value. But without innovation, both the product and process will steadily decline. In support of innovation, Lean-Agile leaders must do the following:

- Understand and implement the Japanese concept of "Gemba." It advises management to "get out of the office" and into the workplace. This is where value is actually produced and products are created and used. As Toyota's Taiichi Ohno said, "No useful improvement was ever invented at a desk."
- Provide a regular time and space for people to be creative. Time for innovation must be purposeful and become part of the natural development rhythm. SAFe's Innovation and Planning (IP) iteration provides one such opportunity.
- Avoid the trap of focusing on the "tyranny of the urgent." Innovation rarely occurs with 100 percent people utilization and constant firefighting.
- Apply innovation accounting.[6] Establish nonfinancial, actionable metrics that provide fast feedback on the important elements of the solution's new concepts, business model, and/or features.
- Validate innovations with customers and then pivot without mercy or guilt when the hypothesis needs to change.

---

6. Eric Ries, *The Lean Startup: How Today's Entrepreneurs Use Continuous Innovation to Create Radically Successful Businesses* (Crown Business, 2011).

Pillar 4: Relentless Improvement

The fourth pillar is relentless improvement. It guides the business to become a learning organization through continuous reflection and adaptation. A constant sense of competitive danger drives it to aggressively pursue improvement opportunities. Leaders and teams systematically do the following:

- Optimize the whole organization and the development process, not just parts
- Consider facts carefully and then act quickly
- Apply Lean tools and techniques to determine the root cause of problems, and apply effective countermeasures quickly
- Reflect at key milestones to openly identify and address process shortcomings at all levels

Foundation: Leadership

The foundation of Lean is leadership, the key enabler for team success. The ultimate responsibility for the adoption and success of the Lean-Agile paradigm lies with the enterprise's managers, leaders, and executives. To be successful, leaders must be trained in these new and innovative ways of thinking and exhibit the principles and behaviors of Lean-Agile leadership.

Embracing Agility

The right half of the Lean-Agile Mindset is, of course, Agile. In chapter 1, "Business Need for SAFe," we introduced the Agile Manifesto. It provides the foundation for empowered cross-functional, self-organizing, self-managing teams. The rest of this chapter is devoted to it.

SELF-MANAGING AND SELF-ORGANIZING

The manifesto and the methods that support it all rely on self-managing, self-organizing teams. To traditional management, this can be a disturbing notion, so some explanation is warranted. A self-organizing, self-managing team is a group of people who work together to achieve a goal or objective with minimal direction. They have the authority and autonomy to plan and execute their work, make decisions, and adapt to changing conditions. They determine when and how the work will be done and by whom. Self-managing teams monitor their own progress, solve problems together, and continuously improve their process. All of this occurs with subtle or no management control. The teams, however, align with common goals, architecture, user experience, and enterprise standards.

The Values of the Agile Manifesto

Figure 3-2 illustrates the Agile Manifesto and is followed by a description of its four values.

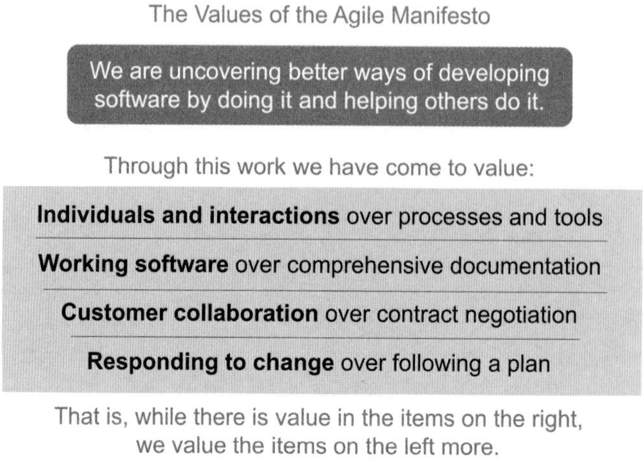

The Values of the Agile Manifesto

We are uncovering better ways of developing software by doing it and helping others do it.

Through this work we have come to value:

Individuals and interactions over processes and tools

Working software over comprehensive documentation

Customer collaboration over contract negotiation

Responding to change over following a plan

That is, while there is value in the items on the right, we value the items on the left more.

Figure 3-2. The Manifesto for Agile Software Development

We Are Uncovering Better Ways

The first phrase of the manifesto deserves emphasis: *"We are uncovering better ways of developing software by doing it and helping others do it."*

We interpret this phrase as an ongoing journey of discovery to increasingly embrace Agile behaviors, a journey that has no ending. SAFe is not a fixed, frozen-in-time framework. As soon as we uncover better ways of working, we adapt the framework, as evidenced by more than four major releases as of this writing.

Where We Find Value

We'll discuss the values shortly, but the final phrase of the manifesto is important and sometimes overlooked: *"That is, while there is value in the items on the right, we value the items on the left more."*

Some people may misinterpret the value statements as a decision between two choices (for example, working software versus comprehensive documentation). But that is not the intent. Both items have value; however, the item on the left has more value (for example, working software). The Agile Manifesto is a mantra for us not to be rigid or dogmatic in our approach but instead to embrace the need to balance the values depending on the context.

Individuals and Interactions over Processes and Tools

People build software and systems, and that requires teams to work together effectively. Processes and tools are important, but they do not replace individuals and interactions.

With respect to process, Deming notes, "If you can't describe what you are doing as a process, then you don't know what you are doing." So, Agile processes in frameworks like Scrum, kanban, and SAFe do matter. However, a process is only a means to an end. When we're captive to a process that isn't working, you may know "what you're doing," but "what you're doing may not be working." So, *favor individuals and interactions* and then modify processes accordingly.

In a distributed environment, tools are critically important to assist with communication and collaboration (for example, video conferencing, instant messaging, ALM[7] tools, wikis), especially at scale. However, tools should not be used as a substitute for regular, face-to-face communication.

Working Software over Comprehensive Documentation

Documentation is important and can provide great value (for example, user help, models, story mapping, regulatory/compliance documentation). However, creating documents for the sake of complying with outdated corporate governance models does not provide value. As part of a change program, governance needs to be updated to reflect the Lean-Agile way of working.

Software requirements specifications are tricky, and one could assume that the authors of the manifesto were particularly concerned about them. Too often, they cause Big Design Up Front (BDUF) and project delays consistent with waterfall thinking. They frequently constrain development to overly detailed written specs that are not always practical (or desirable) to implement. Moreover, people usually do not know what they want until they see it working in action.

Therefore, it's more valuable to show your customer working software and get fast feedback, rather than create comprehensive documentation (especially the wrong kind) too early in the process. The goal of software development, after all, is to create innovative solutions, not a library of documents. Therefore, favor *working software*. Document only what's necessary.

---

7. Application Lifecycle Management

Customer Collaboration over Contract Negotiation

Customers are the ultimate deciders of value. Determining value requires close collaboration on a daily basis. Contracts are often necessary for communicating and agreeing on the rights, responsibilities, and economic concerns of each party. But all too often, contracts over-regulate what is to be done and how to do it. No matter how well they're written, contracts are not a replacement for regular communication, collaboration, and trust. Contracts should be written to be win-win propositions. Win-lose contracts usually result in poor economic outcomes and distrust, creating short-term relationships instead of long-term business partnerships. Favor *customer collaboration*.

> **LEARN MORE**
>
> For a more contemporary view of contracts in Agile development, see chapter 14, "Lean-Agile Budgeting, Forecasting, and Contracting."

Responding to Change over Following a Plan

Change is a natural part of software and systems development, a reality that must be reflected in the process. The strength of Lean-Agile development is in how it embraces change. The process of product development is about converting uncertainty to knowledge. As the system evolves, so does the understanding of the problem and solution domain. Business stakeholder understanding also improves over time, and customer needs evolve as well. Indeed, this variability adds value to our system.

Of course, the phrase "over following a plan" means that there actually is a plan. Planning is an important part of Agile development. Indeed, Agile teams and programs plan more often and more continuously than teams using a waterfall process. However, plans must be adaptable as new learning occurs, new information becomes visible, and the situation changes. Worse, measuring conformance to a plan drives the wrong behaviors (following the plan over empiricism) and should be avoided.

Agile Manifesto Principles

The manifesto has 12 principles that support its values. Listed here, the principles take the values one step further and describe more specifically what it means to be Agile:

1. Our highest priority is to satisfy the customer through early and continuous delivery of valuable software.
2. Welcome changing requirements, even late in development. Agile processes harness change for the customer's competitive advantage.

3. Working software is the primary measure of progress.
4. Deliver working software frequently within a couple of weeks to a couple of months, preferring a shorter timeline.
5. Business people and developers must work together daily throughout the project.
6. Build projects around motivated individuals. Give them the environment and support they need, and trust them to get the job done.
7. The most efficient and effective method of conveying information to and within a development team is face-to-face conversation.
8. Agile processes promote sustainable development. The sponsors, developers, and users should be able to maintain a constant pace indefinitely.
9. Continuous attention to technical excellence and good design enhances agility.
10. Simplicity—the art of maximizing the amount of work not done—is essential.
11. The best architectures, requirements, and designs emerge from self-organizing teams.
12. At regular intervals, the team reflects on how to become more effective, and then fine-tunes and adjusts its behavior accordingly.

Most of these are self-explanatory, so no further elaboration is needed, except for a discussion of applying the Agile Manifesto at scale, covered next.

This combination of values and principles in the manifesto creates a framework for what the Snowbird attendees believed to be the essence of Agile. The industry is the recipient of the extraordinary business and personal benefits of this new way of thinking and working. We are grateful.

Applying the Agile Manifesto at Scale

The brief document that launched this industry movement is more than 15 years old. Since then, not a word has been changed. It's legitimate to ask, given all the advancements in the last 15 years, whether or not the manifesto is still relevant. Or should it be treated like a historical document that has served its purpose?

Moreover, it was defined for small, potentially fast-moving software-only teams, raising another legitimate question: Does the manifesto scale to the needs of enterprises developing the biggest and most complex software and systems? Does it serve those that require hundreds of people to build and have unacceptably high costs of failure? Although the manifesto might not have been designed for them, can it be applied?

Rather than judge these questions on our own, what better way to assess its practicality than by asking those who are actively engaged in building these new systems? Specifically, we ask SAFe students to do the following exercise in class, as described in Figure 3-3.

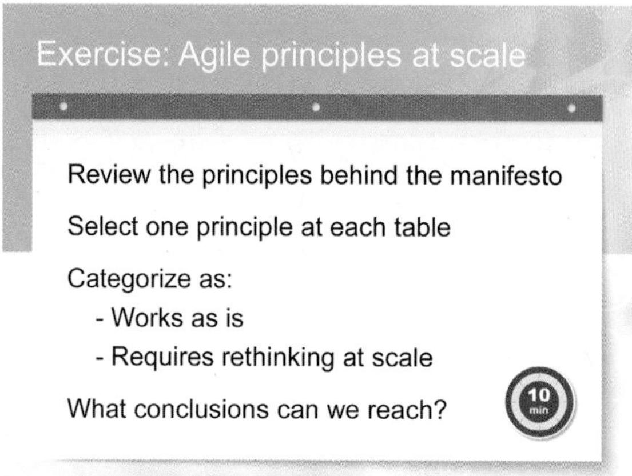

Exercise: Agile principles at scale
Review the principles behind the manifesto
Select one principle at each table
Categorize as:
- Works as is
- Requires rethinking at scale
What conclusions can we reach?
10 min

Figure 3-3. Agile Manifesto class exercise

The typical response is principles 1, 3, 4, 7, 9, and 12 "work as-is." The conclusion is that most Agile principles scale without requiring any rethinking for scale. The other principles typically need some further discussion, as highlighted here:

- *Principle #2*—Welcome changing requirements, even late in development. *Agile processes harness change for the customer's competitive advantage.* The answer here is largely "it just depends." This isn't an attitude problem on the part of the class participants. Rather, it's a practical recognition that the cost of change for some types of late modifications may create a situation that is not feasible. (For example, can we change the optical resolution of a geophysical satellite a few months before launch?) And yet, if it's a software-only change and the program can still meet any compliance and validation criteria and launch on time, then of course we want to make that change.
- *Principle #5*—Business people and developers must work together daily throughout the project. For this concept, the spirit is certainly willing. However, there are limitations regarding the economic practicality and convenience of daily onsite feedback from customers of large programs. But we fully respect the sentiment. SAFe addresses this need through

certain roles, such as the Product Manager and System Architect/Engineer. We also engage the customer directly at system and solution demos and other points throughout the development process.

- *Principle #6*—The most efficient and effective method of conveying information to and within a development team is face-to-face conversation. Attendees always agree with the intent of this principle. And SAFe largely addresses it with periodic face-to-face PI planning events. This probably addresses the majority of needs for efficient communication. However, if you needed a supplier to build a smart power device to fit the physical and thermal constraints of your satellite, you would indeed want to speak to them continuously. In addition, you will certainly want to document the results of those decisions. Fortunately, "working software over comprehensive documentation" does not mean "instead of." So, most serious Agilists proceed with knowledge of the intent, as well as the practical limitations of that principle.
- *Principle #11*—The best architectures, requirements, and designs emerge from self-organizing teams. Nearly everyone agrees with this principle, depending on how you define a team and how you define the subject and scope of the decisions. All agree that local decisions are generally best. After all, that's part of SAFe principle #9—decentralize decision-making. However, that principle also provides the economic rationale for when some decisions are most efficient when they're centralized.

Principle #11 may be the tricky one, and yet it clearly is the essence of Agile. Let's test it with a scenario. For example, let's discuss the User Interface (UI) design for a significant software application, a system where many teams are implementing numerous elements.

- If each team made their own local decisions, they would be unlikely to produce a design that supported the significant cross-cutting usage scenarios that they may not even be able to envision. The functions may work, but the usability of the solution may frustrate the customer. For that we'd need a centralized view, which if not created by the teams, would need to be imposed on them. And yet, the role of a User Experience (UX) lead is clearly articulated as an Agile Release Train (ART) role in SAFe. In that case, the best requirements and designs do emerge from the ART team. But, again, it does depend on how you define the team.
- In the larger view, decisions as to how the UI would work across multiple platforms in a large value stream may go beyond the limits of ART level design. Those judgment calls may need to occur at a higher level.

The conclusion from this exercise is that the Agile Manifesto does indeed scale, even though some principles require a somewhat expanded perspective. It remains as relevant today as it was when it was written. We're fortunate to have it, and it plays a vital role in SAFe.

Summary

This chapter gave an overview of the Lean-Agile mindset, which is critical for supporting Lean-Agile development at scale across the entire enterprise.

The key takeaways from this chapter are as follows:

- The ultimate responsibility for the success of the enterprise, and thereby any significant change to the way of working, lies with management.
- To begin the Lean-Agile journey of change and instill new habits into the culture, leaders and managers should adopt the mindset, principles, and values provided in SAFe's House of Lean and Agile Manifesto.
- The SAFe House of Lean consists of the following elements:
    1. Goal (the roof): Value
    2. Pillar 1: Respect for People and Culture
    3. Pillar 2: Flow
    4. Pillar 3: Innovation
    5. Pillar 4: Relentless Improvement
    6. Foundation: Leadership
- The *Manifesto for Agile Software Development* has four simple values and twelve principles that define what it means to be Agile, and it is often referred to as the Agile Manifesto.
- The Agile Manifesto does indeed scale, even though some principles require a somewhat expanded perspective.

4

Lean-Agile Leaders

Ultimately, leadership is about keeping your team focused on a goal and motivated to do their best to achieve it. ... It is about laying the groundwork for others' success, and then standing back and letting them shine.

—Chad Hadfield, Astronaut and ISS Commander

Exhibit the Lean-Agile Mindset 42
Lead the Change 42
Know the Way and Emphasize Lifelong Learning 47
Develop People 48
Inspire and Align with Mission. Minimize Constraints 52
Decentralize Decision-Making 53
Unlock the Intrinsic Motivation of Knowledge Workers 54
Evolve the Development Manager Role 55
Summary 58

The enterprise's executives, leaders, and managers are ultimately responsible for the success of Lean-Agile adoption and the results it delivers. Only they can change and continuously improve the system in which people work.

To accomplish this change, managers must first become "Lean-thinking manager-teachers," by receiving training in lean ways of thinking and operating. As they evolve into Lean-Agile leaders, management goes from task-based direction to mission-led direction.

Based on empirical evidence from hundreds of SAFe implementations, there are eight key behaviors leaders can focus on to fulfill their roles in the successful adoption and evolution of SAFe, as follows:

1. Exhibit the Lean-Agile mindset.
2. Lead the change.

3. Know the way and emphasize lifelong learning.
4. Develop people.
5. Inspire and align with mission. Minimize constraints.
6. Decentralize decision-making.
7. Unlock the intrinsic motivation of knowledge workers.
8. Evolve the role of the development manager.

Exhibit the Lean-Agile Mindset

To effectively implement SAFe, the enterprise's leaders must embrace the Lean-Agile mindset, which was described as part of the House of Lean and the Agile Manifesto in chapter 3, "Lean-Agile Mindset." However, continuous learning of these in-depth principles is required. Becoming a Lean-Agile leader is a journey, not a destination.

But if leaders support the Lean-Agile mindset only through their words and not their actions, people will quickly recognize this as a half-hearted attempt at change. And then the journey will end before it begins, without leading to the personal or economic benefits of SAFe. So, let's proceed to understand the deeper thinking behind these concepts in the hope that once you've started the journey, the knowledge and rewards will reinforce the need to exhibit a Lean-Agile mindset.

Lead the Change

Successful change management for implementing SAFe requires a significant commitment from executives and senior managers. After all, leadership is the foundation of the House of Lean. What else would we expect? As for the *how*, we'll take our cues from the book *Leading Change*, where Dr. John Kotter offers these eight keys to successful change:

1. Establish a sense of urgency.
2. Create a powerful guiding coalition.
3. Develop the vision and strategy.
4. Communicate the vision.
5. Empower employees for broad-based action.

6. Generate short-term wins.
7. Consolidate gains and produce more wins.
8. Anchor new approaches in the culture.

The following sections describe each of these steps.

Establish a Sense of Urgency

Never underestimate the magnitude of the forces that reinforce complacency and that help maintain status quo.

—John Kotter

According to Kotter, the biggest mistake an organization can make when promoting change is the "failure to establish a sense of urgency."

By communicating the current shortfall of technical development capabilities and its business impact, leaders can create a strong bias for action. They should also call out issues in the marketplace and the dangers imposed by competitive threats and potential digital disruptions. For many, the survival of the business depends on enhanced software and systems development capabilities. And it's needed now!

Leaders should also communicate the goals of the change, identify critical development programs, and set Lean-Agile metrics and success criteria to assess progress.

Create a Powerful Guiding Coalition

Change is extremely hard. And the larger the enterprise, the harder it is. Accomplishing it requires a broad and powerful coalition of change agents, Agile coaches, managers, and senior leadership dedicated to making the transformation happen.

This typically involves forming a change transformation team, which is an example of a Community of Practice (CoP), and establishes a base of operations. This guiding coalition is sometimes called a Lean-Agile Center of Excellence (LACE). As part of this effort, the enterprise will typically train and certify some number of SAFe Program Consultants (SPCs) as change agents, who are often active in the team and also have a material role in program execution. But the responsibility for change cannot be delegated. Even with a strong group, senior leadership must actively drive the need and support the mechanisms for change, overcoming the impediments that will inevitably occur.

Develop the Vision and Strategy

Lean-Agile leaders must create a vision for change. In their book *Switch*, Dan and Chip Heath describe this as "a postcard from the future."[1] This vision must paint a picture of a future motivating enough to encourage others to come along on the journey. However, to change behavior, people need to know what to do differently. Therefore, leaders should do the following:

- Describe the rollout strategy, including training, coaching, and timeline.
- Discuss how roles and responsibility will change.
- Provide the reasoning for organizing teams around value streams and Agile Release Trains (ARTs).
- Ensure that the transformation teams are sufficiently empowered.

Then, everyone will know what's expected of them and the parts they'll play in that desirable future state. After all, if people can't envision a new identity for themselves in the new organization, they won't support the change. And, why should they?

Communicate the Vision

Kotter identifies that "under-communication of the vision for change by a factor of 10 (or 100 or even 1000) is a key reason for failure."[2] He also goes on to say that "without credible communication, and a lot of it, employees' hearts and minds are never captured." Lean-Agile leaders must communicate the need and vision clearly, and in many different ways. They must confidently assert that not only is the transformation possible, but it is essential to the future of the business and employee growth.

Yet some of the most important communication is nonverbal. Leaders must change, too. If teams observe executives pronouncing they are Agile, while continuing to exhibit command and control leadership, optimism will be quickly replaced with cynicism. As a result, many people may decide to not participate, waiting for the change to fail. Can you blame them? Why should people change if their leaders are unwilling?

---

1. Chip Heath and Dan Heath, *Switch: How to Change Things When Change Is Hard* (Crown Publishing, 2010).
2. John P. Kotter, *Leading Change* (Harvard Business Review Press, 1996).

Empower Employees for Broad-Based Action

"Transformation of the work environment requires organizational change, and that rarely happen unless many people assist. Yet employees won't help, or can't help, if they are powerless."[3] What may seem obvious is worth a reminder from the House of Lean: *People do all the work*. Executives and change agents cannot implement specific working patterns. That's a responsibility of the people who perform the work. This means people must be

- Well-trained in the new ways of working
- Empowered to make decisions that affect how the change is implemented
- Able to take risks and experiment in implementing the change, without the fear of reprisal
- Allowed to safely challenge the elements of the status quo that impede change
- Invited to respectfully remind leaders, managers, and others when they revert to the old ways of working

Generate Short-Term Wins

Change of this magnitude is difficult. To maintain the momentum needed to continue revamping systems and behaviors, leaders need to focus on generating some quick wins. Early success will start to show benefits and speed the transformation. Success can be highlighted as examples of true progress.

That's why the first ART launch is critical. It will be highly visible and set expectations for future ARTs. Leaders should focus on the following:

- The proper training and coaching for the entire ART and key stakeholders
- Transparently defining and prioritizing the program vision, roadmap, and backlog
- Fostering an effective Program Increment (PI) planning session, including supporting the funding and logistics for face-to-face planning
- Active participation in the Inspect and Adapt (I&A) workshop
- Assisting with the formation of teams and communicating new roles and responsibilities (it should be done collaboratively with workers)

---

3. John P. Kotter, *Leading Change* (Harvard Business Review Press, 1996).

Leaders should anticipate that the first PI planning session will be chaotic; however, it will create a burst of energy and generate significant enthusiasm from the teams. After all, many of them probably have never been empowered to plan their own work. Management can leverage that excitement to encourage a positive outcome, even in the first PI.

Consolidate Gains and Produce More Wins

The positive experience of the first ART can be used as a stepping-stone to launch additional ARTs. This should establish a pattern of success, along with the roles and responsibilities of the team. The preparation for the next ART should become clearer. It's also likely that Business Owners, DevOps, system architects, and other key stakeholders may participate in multiple ARTs. Their experience can help improve the launches of future trains.

By the end of the first few PIs, improvements in quality, productivity, solution outcomes, and Business Owner satisfaction will be evident. These results will reinforce and support the direction of change.

Anchor New Approaches in the Culture

Culture eats strategy for breakfast.
—Peter Drucker

Drucker's quote is fair warning for all who attempt organizational change. As the new winning habits start to permeate the company, this momentum can erode as the inertia of the existing culture acts as an anchor to the previous ways of working. Leaders must watch for warning signs of complacency. These include the following:

- People feel too comfortable.
- Little innovation or risk-taking occurs.
- Learning slows or stops.
- New practices are disguised with the old ways of working.
- There is little or no challenge to the status quo or continuous improvement.

Leaders need to avoid this potential complacency by methodically replacing or eliminating the systems that support the old culture. This may involve the following:

- Revamping performance evaluation and incentive compensation to support a Lean-Agile environment
- Managing new initiatives as features, capabilities, and epics, instead of traditional project initiation and heavyweight business cases

- Adopting Agile procurement and contract management
- Replacing project cost accounting with Lean-Agile budgeting
- Using Agile metrics, instead of phase gates, and other progress reporting that measures conformance to plan over adapting to change

To guarantee that there's only one way of working—the new way *forward* with Lean-Agile development—leaders must communicate that these impediments will be quickly addressed and then follow through on that commitment. Leaders should make a Big Visible Information Radiator (BVIR), like a kanban board to show the backlog of impediments and their progress.

With these transparent protocols in place and Lean-Agile leaders engaged, the enterprise will begin to establish a new culture, one that increases employee engagement and masters the habit of *delivering value in the shortest sustainable lead time.*

Know the Way and Emphasize Lifelong Learning

The second piece of guidance challenges leaders to create an environment that truly values and promotes continuous learning. It encourages the scientific method of experimentation that involves trial and error, tolerates failure, and allows people to take risks and learn.

Know the Way

Leaders initiate the journey. As a result, they first need to understand the new values, principles, and practices of Lean-Agile development. Further, they need to exhibit them with new behaviors. For most, that usually involves taking *Leading SAFe*, a two-day class for leaders that has proven effective in helping management gain the knowledge needed to effectively lead the change.

Emphasize Lifelong Learning

The bodies of knowledge behind SAFe—Agile development, systems thinking, and Lean product development—are well expressed in hundreds of books and white papers, many distilling a lifetime of expertise into a few hundred pages. While the SAFe bibliography contains more than 100 references, the following is a short list of recommended books.

We encourage leaders, SPCs, and knowledge workers to read them all and continue their learning journey. The list focuses on the books most relevant to the values and principles that describe SAFe, and the list changes as new works become available. Here are our current favorites as of this writing:

- *Principles of Product Development Flow*, Don Reinertsen
- *The Lean Machine*, Dantar Oosterwal
- *Lean Product and Process Development*, Allen Ward and Durward Sobek II
- *SAFe 4.0 Reference Guide*, Dean Leffingwell
- *The Goal*, Eliyahu Goldratt
- *Out of the Crisis*, W. Edwards Deming
- *Agile Software Requirements*, Dean Leffingwell
- *The Five Dysfunctions of a Team*, Patrick Lencioni
- *Leading Change*, John P. Kotter
- *Leading SAFe 4.0 LiveLessons* (Video Training), 2nd Edition, Dean Leffingwell
- *The Rollout: A Novel about Leadership and Building a Lean-Agile Enterprise with SAFe*, Alex Yakyma

In addition, leaders can facilitate ongoing learning by doing the following:

- Sponsoring and participating in book clubs
- Hosting lunch-and-learns
- Benchmarking with other companies
- Supporting outside conferences and educational opportunities

Develop People

In the book *Managing for Excellence*,[4] Bradford and Cohen describe three different leadership styles. They are "leader as expert," "leader as conductor," and "leader as developer of people." Before we go further, it's important to note that there is no perfect leadership style. Each of these styles can be effective depending on the situation and context. They work best when a leader knows when to apply each of them.

---

4. David L. Bradford and Allan R. Cohen, *Managing for Excellence* (John Wiley & Sons, 1997).

Leader as Expert

The leader as expert is technically proficient in one or more knowledge areas or domains. Using this style, the expertise of the leader is used to define tasks and select a particular course of action. That may make sense when the leader knows more about the work at hand than the follower. Figure 4-1 highlights some of the characteristics and challenges of this model.

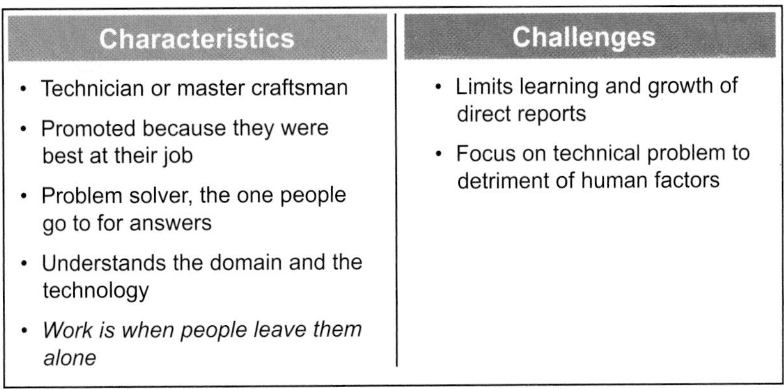

Characteristics
• Technician or master craftsman
• Promoted because they were best at their job
• Problem solver, the one people go to for answers
• Understands the domain and the technology
• Work is when people leave them alone
Challenges
• Limits learning and growth of direct reports
• Focus on technical problem to detriment of human factors

Figure 4-1. Leader as expert

The leader as expert is a common role in the high-tech industry. Most engineering managers grew through the ranks based on their technical or scientific expertise. They were promoted into management to provide technical competence and to help assure that solutions were technically and economically viable. That makes sense. Who wants a manager who doesn't know what they're talking about?

However, as Figure 4-1 illustrates, there's a serious downside as well. The leader as expert may think of work as "when people leave me alone" or that "my work is to define a technical course of action for others." That limits the growth and empowerment of the direct reports. After all, according to Peter Drucker's definition, "Workers are knowledge workers if they know more about the work they perform than their bosses" (principle #8 in chapter 5, "SAFe Principles"). Does the leader as expert really scale in our particular industry, meeting our particular challenges? Probably not.

Leader as Conductor

The leader as conductor doesn't provide the technical solution but instead orchestrates the activities of the organization to achieve the desired objectives. This is a sensible leadership style as well. The leader may have influence beyond the local team, may better understand the organization and its politics, and can let others focus on the technical tasks at hand. It's particularly effective when coordination is a prerequisite for maximum performance. However, this leadership style has challenges as well, as Figure 4-2 illustrates.

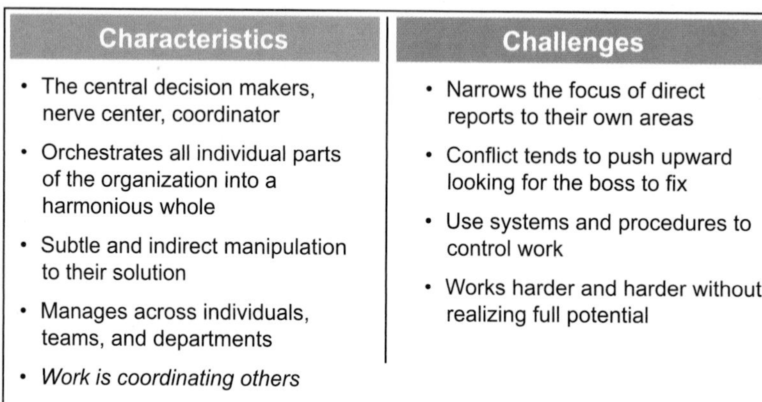

Characteristics
The central decision makers, nerve center, coordinator
Orchestrates all individual parts of the organization into a harmonious whole
Subtle and indirect manipulation to their solution
Manages across individuals, teams, and departments
Work is coordinating others
Challenges
Narrows the focus of direct reports to their own areas
Conflict tends to push upward looking for the boss to fix
Use systems and procedures to control work
Works harder and harder without realizing full potential

Figure 4-2. Leader as conductor

The leadership style has a significant disadvantage: If this leader's work *is to coordinate others,* how do their direct reports gain their own experience in getting things done?

Leader as Developer of People

The goal of the leader as developer of people is to help teams realize their fullest potential. In other words, their *work is to develop other's knowledge, skills, and experience.* The behaviors and benefits of this style appear in Figure 4-3.

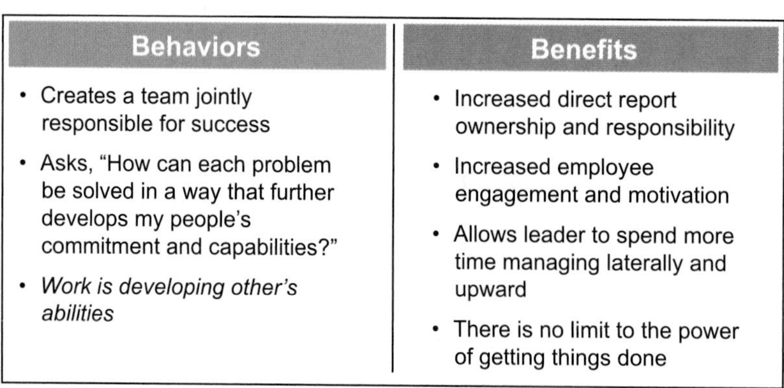

Behaviors
Creates a team jointly responsible for success
Asks, "How can each problem be solved in a way that further develops my people's commitment and capabilities?"
Work is developing other's abilities
Benefits
Increased direct report ownership and responsibility
Increased employee engagement and motivation
Allows leader to spend more time managing laterally and upward
There is no limit to the power of getting things done

Figure 4-3. Leader as developer of people

This leadership style is more favorable to knowledge workers, who typically need a high degree of collaboration and coordination with others. These leaders do the following:

- Create a team jointly responsible for success
- Let others design the solution and coordinate activities as necessary to bring it to market
- Give credit for successes to the team and shoulder responsibility when things go wrong
- Show empathy and support when the team makes mistakes
- Create a learning culture that enables people to continually develop their knowledge and skills and to pursue their passions
- Encourage and help individuals leave their comfort zone to solve challenging problems and take on new opportunities
- Foster an environment that rewards risk-taking and innovation, absent of fear

This leadership style allows each direct report to reach their potential, increasing productivity and engagement. It maximizes both the personal and professional benefits of their relationship with management. As Lean-Agile leaders, we have no greater responsibility or opportunity.

The Future of Leadership?

The previous section offers a view of three common leadership styles, each of which can be effective in certain situations. Understanding and knowing when to apply these styles is an integral part of becoming an effective leader. But perhaps this, in itself, represents a traditional view, one that assumes that leaders and managers are people who are born—or groomed—to be leaders. As we have seen in this book, organizing around value is a fairly fluid process. Value moves, and our organizations must evolve quickly to support it. Traditional organizational structures—whether functional or line of business—may not have the agility needed to compete in the digital economy, nor can they necessarily provide the business environment in which this next generation of knowledge workers and millennials can thrive.

For an arrestingly different view of leadership, we refer to a Harvard Business Review article "Leadership in Online Labs,"[5] by Reeves, Malone, and O'Driscoll. In this article, the authors present a potentially more futuristic view, based on their studies from the

5. https://hbr.org/2008/05/leaderships-online-labs

field of on-line gaming. In their studies, they observed the following behaviors that "create the right environment" for high-performing teams in online gaming:

- *Leaders switch roles.* One of the most interesting aspects was the way in which people naturally change roles, from leading a guild in one instance to following orders the next. "Leadership is a task, not an identity—a state that a player enters and exits rather than a personal trait that emerges and thereafter defines the individual." The decision about who should lead occurs naturally during the course of the game, often based on someone volunteering to lead, rather than hierarchy. This frequent switching of roles helps people become better leaders and followers.
- *Hyper-transparency of information.* The gaming world provides rich data that is available to everyone, not just a few select leaders. This data includes a wide variety of information about individual and team performance. The transparency of information helps leaders make quick, real-time decisions; governs the assignment of roles and rewards; and provides the basis for a fair and honest system.
- *Nonmonetary incentives.* Rewards are provided through nonmonetary incentives, such as virtual points and digital badges. The purpose is to provide motivation via peer recognition and feedback, rather than cash. This larger trend of nonmonetary incentives is evidenced today in many popular apps (for example, Fitbit, HabitRPG, Waze, Candy Crush Saga). The authors even suggest that "selective gamification of the work environment" may be beneficial.

The authors conclude that perhaps what the industry needs is "more fluid workforces, self-organized and collaborative work activities, and decentralized, nonhierarchical leadership." In many ways, this is a parallel description of Lean-Agile management patterns. And finally, as one of the gamers noted, "If you want better leadership ... why not change the game instead of trying to change the leaders?" Fair point.

Inspire and Align with Mission. Minimize Constraints

The Principle of Mission: Specify the end state, its purpose, and the minimal possible constraints.[6]

—Don Reinertsen

This principle clearly defines the primary responsibility of leadership in the Lean enterprise: Define the mission, but create only the minimum boundaries and

6. Don Reinertsen, *The Principles of Product Development Flow* (Celeritas, 2009).

conditions for teams to address it. *Ba*,[7] a Japanese word for the energy of a self-organizing team, makes this equally clear.

- Ba is energized by intentions, vision, interest, and mission.
- Leaders provide autonomy, variety, trust, and commitment.
- The team is challenged to question the way they work and improve every aspect of what and how they do things.

Leaders should communicate the broad strategic goals but avoid constraining teams with outdated work rules or ways of planning. The mission simply communicates the *what* and the *why*, not the *how*. The teams have the autonomy to develop the best solution and the freedom to pivot quickly, as new ways arise to meet the mission.

In addition, leaders need to eliminate demotivating policies and procedures, especially those that promote unhealthy competition, encourage favoritism, or cause busywork.

Decentralize Decision-Making

Most experts in Lean practices reach the same conclusion: Decentralized decision-making is critical to delivering value in the shortest sustainable lead time. After all, a decision postponed is a decision delayed, which increases the cost of undelivered value. In addition, escalated decisions land on the desks of managers who may have broader decision authority but also less local context on which to reach the best conclusions. And that's why Reinertsen and others recommend decentralizing decision-making as a principle of product development flow. That brings us to SAFe Lean-Agile principle *#9—decentralize decision-making*.

Of course, that's a bold demand, and the arguments on both sides are obvious. This isn't to say that all decisions should be decentralized. That could incite anarchy or gridlock over what gets built. What are needed are decision-making guidelines to help those determining who decides. Reinertsen suggests that an enterprise should do the following:

- Centralize decisions that are infrequent, are long-lasting, and have significant economies of scale
- Decentralize all others, including those that are frequent and time critical and those that require local information

7. Hirotaka Takeuchi and Ikujiro Nonaka, *Hitotsubashi on Knowledge Management* (2004, 2009).

We'll discuss this further in the next chapter, when we review SAFe Lean-Agile principle #9—*decentralize decision-making.*

Unlock the Intrinsic Motivation of Knowledge Workers

Workers are knowledge workers if they know more about the work they perform than their bosses.

—Peter Drucker

The work of Drucker,[8] Daniel Pink,[9] and others—along with Lean's endorsement of empowered problem solving—leads us to SAFe Lean-Agile principle #8—*unlock the intrinsic motivation of knowledge workers*. This is described more fully in chapter 5, "SAFe Principles." But for a preview of what to expect, Drucker further notes the following:

- Workers themselves are best placed to make decisions about how to perform their work.
- To effectively lead, the workers must be heard and respected.
- Knowledge workers have to manage themselves. They need autonomy.
- Continuing innovation has to be part of their work and is the responsibility of "knowledge workers."

Clearly, this describes a new talent contract between management and employees, one that recognizes the needs of a knowledge worker and challenges Frederick Taylor's "scientific" industrial principles of management." Taylor's is the twentieth century model, where "management plans the work and the workers actually perform the tasks."[10] As you'll see in chapter 5, "SAFe Principles," the new management charter includes these values:

- Leveraging the systems view
- Understanding the role of compensation

8. Peter Drucker, *The Effective Executive* (Harper Business, Revised Edition, 2006).
9. Daniel Pink, *Drive, The Surprising Truth About What Motivates Us* (Riverhead Books, 2011).
10. https://en.wikipedia.org/wiki/Frederick_Winslow_Taylor

- Providing autonomy with purpose, mission, and minimum possible constraints
- Creating an environment of mutual influence

In short, leaders need to create the right culture, where empowerment, mutual influence, and trust flourish.

Evolve the Development Manager Role

By applying the principles of Lean-Agile development, SAFe emphasizes the values of nearly autonomous, cross-functional teams and ARTs. It supports a leaner management infrastructure, with more empowered teams and faster, local decision-making. Traditional daily employee instruction and activity management are no longer required.

Development management, however, is still necessary. Employees need managers to help them with career growth, compensation, and general personnel-related responsibilities. Managers are also required to help build systems by providing the mission and systematically addressing impediments and bottlenecks.

And of course, management still has final accountability for effective delivery of value.

> **DEVELOPMENT MANAGER**
> In this context, "development manager" is a proxy title for those who are traditionally responsible for managing the people who build the solutions. Typical titles include development manager/director/vice president, delivery manager, information technology (IT) manager, chief technology officer, quality assurance (QA) manager, and program manager.

Many of these responsibilities traditionally fall to development managers, and adopting Lean-Agile development does not rescind their responsibilities.

However, these "managers as Lean-Agile leaders" will evolve from a command-and-control style to a new servant-leadership approach. That said, they will still have the following responsibilities in the Lean-Agile enterprise.

Recruiting and Retaining Talent

- Attract, recruit, and retain capable individuals. Build high-performance teams, and teams of teams.
- Participate in defining and administering compensation, benefits, and promotions.
- Listen to and support teams in problem identification, root-cause analysis, and decision-making. Eliminate impediments, and advance systems and practices in support of Lean-Agile development.
- Use subtle control in assigning people to teams, address issues that teams cannot solve, and make personnel changes when necessary.
- Serve as an Agile coach and advisor. Remain close enough to the team to add value and be a competent manager; stay far enough away to let them problem-solve on their own.

Provide Alignment

- Define and communicate the mission and vision.
- Establish and support ART organizations. Work with Release Train Engineers (RTEs), Value Stream Engineers (VSEs), and stakeholders to help ensure alignment and effective execution of strategic themes.
- Work with the System Architect/Engineer, Product Managers, and Product Owners to establish clear content authority.
- Help ensure the engagement of Business Owners, Shared Services, and other stakeholders

Support Built-in Quality

- Understand, support, and apply SAFe's built-in quality practices.
- Teach problem-solving skills and corrective action techniques.
- Foster formal and informal learning groups, such as CoPs.

Provide Transparency

- Create an environment where the facts are always friendly and transparent. Avoid behaviors and measures that cause information hiding, because no one can manage a secret.

- Communicate openly and honestly with all stakeholders. Keep backlogs and information radiators fully visible to all. Value productivity, quality, transparency, and openness over internal politics.

Assist with Program Execution

- Help teams build Agile milestones and roadmaps, as well as the plans that enable them. Develop, implement, and communicate the economic framework.
- Participate in I&A workshops. Protect teams from distractions and unrelated or wasteful work.
- Assist the RTEs and VSEs with PI readiness and planning activities. Participate in key ART events, such as PI planning, system demos, and the I&A workshop.
- Provide other resources as necessary for teams and ARTs to successfully execute their vision and roadmap.
- Build partnerships with suppliers, consultants, subcontractors, and internal and external stakeholders.

Evolve the System. Eliminate Impediments

- Systematically help remove organizational impediments to the flow of work.
- Clearly define roles and responsibilities in SAFe and adjust reporting structures, where necessary.

Adopt a Servant Leadership Approach

A mindset change is often required for development managers in the transition from directing and managing activities to acting as a servant leader. Servant leadership is a philosophy and set of practices that enriches the lives of individuals, builds better organizations, and ultimately creates a more just and caring world.[11] Robert Greenleaf, author of *The Power of Servant Leadership*, discusses the following nine characteristics that embody servant leaders:

1. *Listening.* Listen receptively to what is being said and support teams in problem-solving and decision-making.
2. *Empathy.* Understand and empathize with others.

11. https://www.greenleaf.org/what-is-servant-leadership/

3. *Healing.* Support teams both physically and mentally and take steps to help them be happy and engaged.
4. *Self-awareness.* Get to know yourself and understand your strengths and weaknesses. Think deeply about your emotions and behavior and consider how they affect the people around you.
5. *Persuasion.* Use persuasion rather than their authority to encourage people to take action. Strive to build consensus so that everyone supports decisions.
6. *Conceptualization.* Create mission and vision statements. Help your teams understand how their work ties into the aim of the enterprise.
7. *Foresight.* Use tools like SWOT analysis to help predict what's likely to happen in the future by learning from past experiences, identifying what's happening now, and understanding the consequences of your decisions.
8. *Stewardship.* Take responsibility for the actions and performance of your team, and be accountable for the role team members play in your organization.
9. *Commitment to the growth of people.* Be committed to the personal and professional development of your teams. Build a sense of community within your organization by providing opportunities for people to interact with one another across the company.

Summary

This chapter discussed the roles and responsibilities of Lean-Agile leaders and managers in SAFe.

The key takeaways from this chapter are as follows:

- In SAFe, Lean-Agile leaders take responsibility for enterprise success. They understand and teach Lean-Agile behaviors to their people.
- The ultimate responsibility for adoption, success, and ongoing improvement of Lean-Agile development lies with managers, leaders, and executives.
- There are eight behaviors leaders must focus on to ensure a successful adoption of SAFe.

    1. Exhibit the Lean-Agile mindset.
    2. Lead the change.

3. Know the way and emphasize lifelong learning.
4. Develop people.
5. Inspire and align with mission. Minimize constraints.
6. Decentralize decision-making.
7. Unlock the intrinsic motivation of knowledge workers.
8. Evolve the role of the development manager.
    - SAFe takes its cues for leading successful change management from John Kotter, author of *Leading Change*. He offers these eight keys to successful change:
        1. Establish a sense of urgency.
        2. Create a powerful guiding coalition.
        3. Develop the vision and strategy.
        4. Communicate the vision.
        5. Empower employees for broad-based action.
        6. Generate short-term wins.
        7. Consolidate gains and produce more wins.
        8. Anchor new approaches in the culture.

- SAFe supports a leaner management infrastructure, with more empowered individuals and teams. This enables faster decision-making by teams that are closer to the work and have better information. Traditional, daily employee instruction and activity direction is no longer required.
- Agile team members still need managers to assist them with career development, setting and managing expectations, and providing the active coaching they need to advance their skills and career goals.
- A mindset change is often required for development managers in the transition from directing and managing activities to acting as a servant leader. Servant leadership is a philosophy and set of practices that enriches the lives of individuals, builds better organizations, and ultimately creates a more just and caring world.

5

SAFe Principles

The impression that "our problems are different" is a common disease that afflicts management the world over. They are different, to be sure, but the principles that will help to improve the quality of product and service are universal in nature.

—W. Edwards Deming

Why Focus on Principles? 61
Principle #1: Take an Economic View 62
Principle #2: Apply Systems Thinking 70
Principle #3: Assume Variability; Preserve Options 74
Principle #4: Build Incrementally with Fast, Integrated Learning Cycles 76
Principle #5: Base Milestones on Objective Evaluation of Working Systems 79
Principle #6: Visualize and Limit WIP, Reduce Batch Sizes, and Manage Queue Lengths 80
Principle #7: Apply Cadence; Synchronize with Cross-Domain Planning 83
Principle #8: Unlock the Intrinsic Motivation of Knowledge Workers 87
Principle #9: Decentralize Decision-Making 89
Summary 91

Why Focus on Principles?

The Scaled Agile Framework (SAFe) is based on Lean-Agile principles—the core beliefs, truths, and economic values that drive effective roles and practices. Principles are enduring; they stand the test of time and can be applied universally, no matter what the situation. But they're not the same as practices. A practice is a specific activity, action, or way of accomplishing something. A practice that works in one situation may not necessarily apply or work in another.

A Lean-Agile transformation will deliver substantial benefits. However, it is a significant change, and every implementation is somewhat different. Fortunately, SAFe is a scalable and configurable framework, allowing each organization to apply it to its own business model.

Therefore, before an enterprise can effectively apply SAFe practices, an understanding of the underlying principles is required. This chapter describes nine SAFe Lean-Agile principles.

#1 **Take an economic view**

#2 **Apply systems thinking**

#3 **Assume variability; preserve options**

#4 **Build incrementally with fast, integrated learning cycles**

#5 **Base milestones on objective evaluation of working systems**

#6 **Visualize and limit WIP, reduce batch sizes, and manage queue lengths**

#7 **Apply cadence, synchronize with cross-domain planning**

#8 **Unlock the intrinsic motivation of knowledge workers**

#9 **Decentralize decision-making**

Principle #1: Take an Economic View

While you may ignore economics, it won't ignore you.

—Don Reinertsen, *Principles of Product Development Flow*

Achieving the goal of Lean—the *sustainably shortest lead time, with best quality and value to people and society*—requires a fundamental understanding of the economics of building systems. Without such an understanding, even a technically competent system may cost too much to develop, take too long to deliver, or have manufacturing or operating costs that cannot be sustained.

Leadership, management, and knowledge workers must all understand the economic impact of their decisions. Therefore, SAFe's first Lean-Agile Principle is to *take an economic view.* Two primary aspects are:

- To deliver incrementally, early, and often
- To sequence jobs for maximum benefit

In addition, Reinertsen identifies a supporting set of economic principles. These are as follows:

- Do not consider money already spent.
- Understand economic trade-off parameters.
- Make economic decisions continuously.
- Use decision rules.

Each of these is discussed in this chapter.

Deliver Incrementally, Early, and Often

The Agile economic imperative and primary benefit of SAFe is that solutions are developed iteratively and incrementally. Each increment reduces risk and uncertainty and produces value. As shown in Figure 5-1, this is in stark contrast to a single-pass, phase-gate, waterfall development approach.

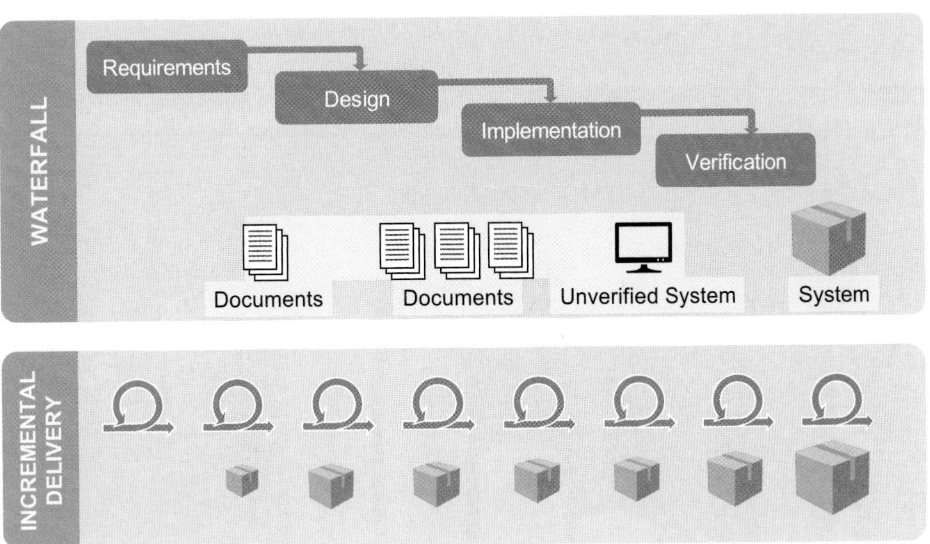

Figure 5-1. Moving to early and continuous delivery of value

Each increment (the little boxes in Figure 5-1) delivers value to the customer much earlier in the development process, as shown in Figure 5-2.

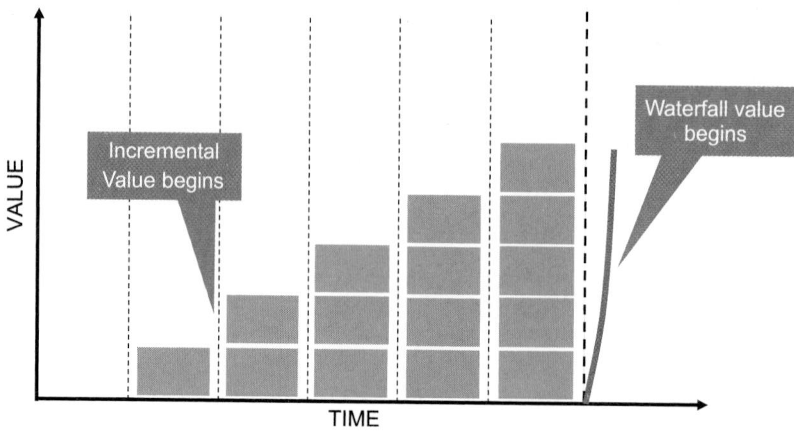

Figure 5-2. Incremental delivery accelerates value

Moreover, the value of each increment persists over time, and the accumulated value delivers substantial benefits even early in the solution life cycle. In contrast, *all* the value for waterfall delivery must wait until the end (and that's only if it's delivered on time!), when all the features are completed.

In addition, there is a compounding economic factor: New features or solutions delivered early to market are typically more valuable than those delivered later, as shown in Figure 5-3.

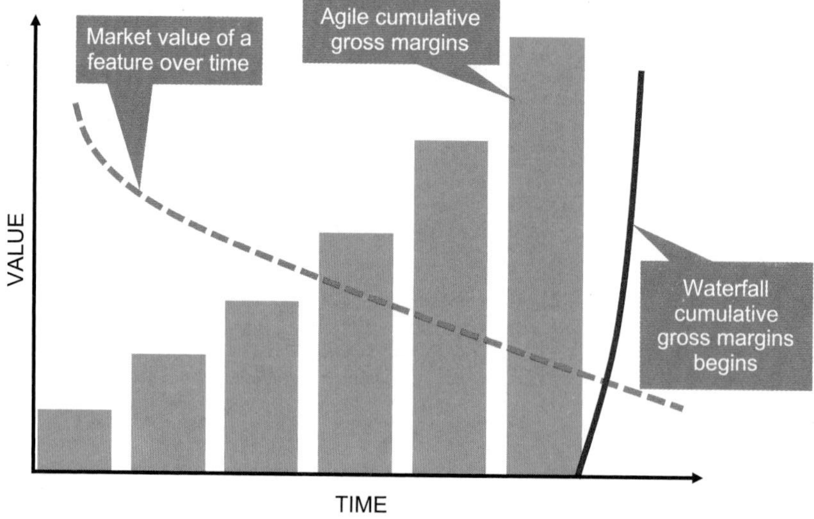

Figure 5-3. Market value of a feature is higher earlier

This means that a solution delivered early—even with a set of minimum viable features—provides more total economic value than a theoretically more complete product delivered later. Early and often is simply better economically. That is the Agile economic imperative.

Sequence Jobs for Maximum Benefit

Earlier, we mentioned the important role that Reinertsen's *Principles of Product Development Flow* plays in providing many of the primary underpinnings for SAFe. After all, SAFe is a *flow-based* system, designed to provide a continuous flow of value to the customer. This is a critical difference from traditional systems development, which tends toward large, infrequent releases.

In turn, this triggers a fundamentally different requirement for prioritization of work. In a flow-based system, work must be reprioritized continuously, based upon the economic and technical facts known at that time. Understanding how to *sequence jobs* is critical to achieving the best economic outcomes.

Reinertsen describes an algorithm for job sequencing called Weighted Shortest Job First (WSJF). WSJF is calculated by dividing the Cost of Delay (CoD) for a job (value not achieved while waiting) by the duration of the job.

$$\text{WSJF} = \frac{\text{Cost of Delay}}{\text{Duration}}$$

The job with the highest WSJF is the next most important job, as it delivers the most value in the least amount of time. WSJF can be applied at any level of SAFe.

For further understanding of WSJF, refer to Reinertsen's original work[1] and the SAFe article[2] by that name. In the context of SAFe, we still need to establish mechanisms for determining CoD and duration so teams can calculate WSJF.

1. Donald Reinertsen, *The Principles of Product Development Flow: Second Generation Lean Product Development* (Celeritas, 2009).
2. http://dev.scaledagileframework.com/wsjf/

Calculating the Cost of Delay

In SAFe, "jobs" are the epics, features, and capabilities that deliver value. SAFe describes these three primary parameters that contribute to the CoD:

- *User and/or business value.* This item represents the net value to the user and/or business of the particular job. Do the users prefer this over that? What is the revenue impact?
- *Time criticality.* This value captures the time-sensitivity of the job. Does timing of delivery matter? Is there a fixed deadline? Will the customers wait or move to another solution?
- *Risk reduction and/or opportunity enablement.* This value represents some of the important intangibles. What else does this do for our business? Does it reduce the risk of this or a future delivery? Will this feature open up new business opportunities?

The sum of these parameters is the total CoD for the job.

Cost of Delay = User Business Value + Time Criticality + Risk Reduction and/or Opportunity Enablement

To establish the value, it isn't necessary to attempt to establish absolute metrics for these parameters. Instead, Agile teams use relative estimating to estimate work, and this technique applies well to the CoD parameters. In other words, teams just compare jobs to each other and rank each parameter relative to other jobs.

Duration

Next, teams need to estimate job *duration*. That can be somewhat difficult, as at the time of prioritization, it may not be possible to know what people are available, which affects the duration of the job. Fortunately, all other things being equal, bigger jobs take longer to do, so *job size* is a good proxy for duration. Relative estimating can be used here, too, to quickly establish the *job size*. Agile teams get pretty good at estimating relative job size.

Calculate Weighted Shortest Job First

With that data, jobs can then be compared to each other via a reasonably straightforward calculation, using the worksheet illustrated in Figure 5-4.

$$WSJF = \frac{COD}{\text{Job duration}} = \frac{\text{User-business value + Time criticality + RR | OE}}{\text{Job size}}$$

Job name	User/ Business Value	Time Criticality	RR | OE Value	CoD	WSJF
	PARAMETERS			CALCULATED	

1. Rate each parameter using the same scale: 1, 2, 3, 5, 8, 13, 20.
2. Do each parameter one at a time. Start with the smallest item in each column and give it a "1".
3. Compare each job relative to the "1".
4. Calculate the CoD and WSJF, the largest WSJF number has the highest priority.

Figure 5-4. WSJF formula and worksheet for comparing jobs

Teams enter the job name and the individual parameters relative to other jobs and then calculate the result. The jobs with the highest WSJF are the next highest priority. This serves as a fairly straightforward, fast, and effective prioritization technique, which allows stakeholders for ARTs, value streams, or the portfolio to pick the next most important job to work on.

There are other advantages to this technique as well.

- Because of the job size denominator, WSJF favors smaller jobs. Therefore, larger jobs must be broken down into smaller ones to obtain a higher priority. That encourages incremental development.
- Since the updated job size estimates include only the work remaining, frequently reprioritizing automatically eliminates consideration of money already spent ("sunk costs," another consideration that we will discuss in this chapter).

Supporting Economic Principles

Delivering incrementally and sequencing jobs are two essential aspects for achieving better business outcomes. However, Reinertsen describes a number of additional economic principles as well, including the following:

- Do not consider money already spent.
- Understand the economic trade-off parameters.
- Make economic choices continuously.
- Use decision rules to decentralize economic control.

Do Not Consider Money Already Spent

While it might seem obvious, it's important to note that money already spent is a "sunk cost." It's gone, it isn't coming back, and it should never enter into an economic choice about future priorities.

Managers, however, often face the pressure of continuing investment in projects, influenced by the amounts of money already spent. After all, no one wants to "lose the investment," and/or face the political consequences of killing a project. It just looks bad, even when it's the right thing to do. So, often cash continues to pour into projects that will not deliver intended benefits, hoping somehow that it will all work out in the end.

When deciding whether to pivot or persevere with further investment, *ignore sunk cost.* Instead, fully examine whether the incremental effort will justify the remaining value. After all, there may be other, potentially higher WSJF jobs, waiting to be implemented.

Understand Economic Trade-Off Parameters

Reinertsen notes that "understanding economics requires understanding of the interaction amongst multiple variables." Figure 5-5 illustrates five parameters that can be used as an analysis tool to improve economic decision-making for developing new products and services.

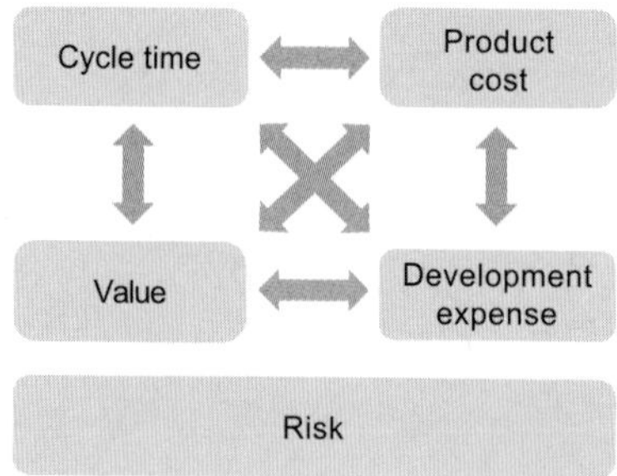

Figure 5-5. Five primary economic trade-off parameters

1. *Development expense* is the cost of labor and materials required to implement a capability.
2. *Cycle time* measures the period from the beginning to the end of a process.
3. *Product cost* is the manufacturing expense and/or deployment and operational costs.
4. *Value* is the economic worth of the capability to the customer.
5. *Risk* is the uncertainty of the technical or business viability of the solution.

Sometimes the absolute value of these numbers cannot be easily determined. But most generally, this is a thinking tool, and these trade-offs do not necessarily require knowing the precise monetary value of each parameter. The following insights from our students serve as good examples of how this analysis can be applied in the real world:

- Delayed performance testing increases cycle time, increases development expense, and diminishes the value of features.
- Test automation decreases cycle time, reduces risk, and reduces overall development expense.
- Late defect fixing increases development expense and increases cycle time and risk.

Make Economic Choices Continuously

In flow-based systems, the timing and frequency of economic choices is not a one-time, up-front event. Instead, choices must be made continuously. The following are just a few examples of how this applies:

- Portfolio epics are continually re-prioritized as they go through the various steps of the kanban system.
- The program and value stream backlogs are continually refined and re-prioritized at PI boundaries.
- Set-based design keeps multiple requirements and design choices open for longer periods of time.
- System demos provide frequent integration points that inform design choices and decisions as to when to release value.
- Teams continuously prioritize their backlog of user stories, defects, spikes, and refactors.

Use Decision Rules to Decentralize Economic Control

The path to Lean success doesn't just begin and end at the top of the organization, where a handful of people make all the decisions. Indeed, "as you move lower in a decision network, the number of small decisions being made increases in number, making it possible for the combined value of these small choices to exceed the value of the larger decisions."[3]

Decision rules establish the economic logic and reasoning behind a decision. They support decentralized, and better, decision-making. Good decision rules enable teams to make the right decisions faster, by doing the following:

- Aligning economic choices made within and across programs
- Reducing risk and enabling more decisions to be decentralized
- Reducing the effort required to make good decisions
- Providing transparency into the economic logic for decisions

Ultimately, teams execute strategy via implementing the solutions necessary to accomplish strategic intent. In so doing, they make many decisions every day. Management helps teams make better decisions by developing decision rules that help teams make better economic choices.

Principle #2: Apply Systems Thinking

A system must be managed. It will not manage itself. Left to themselves, components become selfish, independent profit centers and thus destroy the system. ... The secret is cooperation between components toward the aim of the organization.

—W. Edwards Deming

Chapter 1, "Business Need for SAFe," briefly introduced systems thinking as one of the three foundational bodies of knowledge in SAFe. Systems thinking takes a holistic approach to solution development. It incorporates all aspects of a system and its environment into the design, development, deployment, and maintenance of the system itself.

Figure 5-6 illustrates the primary aspects of systems thinking. Understanding these aspects helps leaders and teams navigate the complexity of solution development, the organization, and the larger picture of total time to market.

3. http://www.decision-making-solutions.com/small-decisions.html

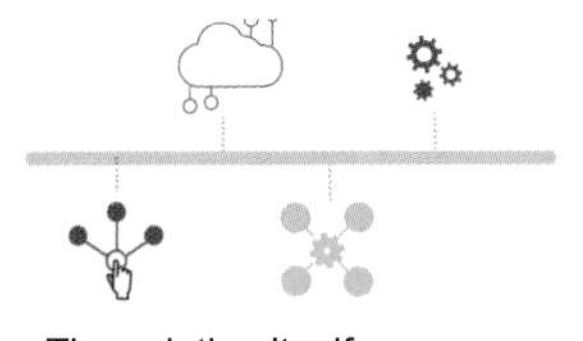
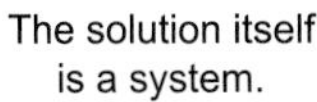
The solution itself is a system.

The enterprise building the system is a system too.

Optimize the full value stream
A system must be managed.

System Arch/Eng

Lean-Agile Leaders

Figure 5-6. Aspects of systems thinking

The Solution Is a System

Solution

SAFe provides guidance for the development and deployment of complex software and systems. SAFe calls this the solution and is the output of each value stream. Applications, satellites, medical devices, and websites are all examples of solutions. When it comes to such systems, Deming's guidance that "a system must be managed" leads to a number of critical insights.

- The boundaries of the system, what it is, and how it interacts with the environment and systems around it must be clearly understood.
- Optimizing a component does not optimize the system. When developing systems, it's important to assure that the components do not become selfish and hog the resources—computing power, memory, electrical power, whatever—that other elements need.
- For the system to behave well as a system, an understanding of the intended system behavior and some higher-level understanding of its architecture (how the components work together to accomplish its aims) are necessary. The intentional design of a system is fundamental to systems thinking.
- The value of a system passes through its interconnections. Those interfaces—and the dependencies they create—are critical elements to providing ultimate value. Continuous attention to those interfaces and interactions is vital.
- A system can evolve no faster than its slowest integration point. The faster the full system can be integrated and evaluated, the faster the actual knowledge of the system grows.

The Enterprise Building the System Is a System, Too

The second aspect to systems thinking—the people, management, and processes of the organization that builds the system—is also system. The understanding that *systems must be managed* applies here as well, and all of these roles apply here, too. Otherwise, the components of the organization building the system will optimize locally and become selfish, limiting the rate and quality of the overall value delivery. This leads to another set of systems thinking insights.

- Building complex systems is a social endeavor. Therefore, leaders must facilitate the creation of an environment where people can collaborate on the best way to build better systems.
- Suppliers and customers are integral to the value stream. They must be treated as partners, based on a long-term foundation of trust.
- Optimizing a component does not optimize the system here either. Locally optimizing teams or functional departments does not optimize the flow of value through the enterprise.
- Value crosses organizational boundaries. Accelerating value delivery requires eliminating functional silos and creating virtual cross-functional organizations, such as an Agile Release Train (ART).

Understand and Optimize the Full Value Stream

The entire SAFe portfolio is considered to be a collection of value streams, each of which delivers one or more solutions to the market. As illustrated in Figure 5-7, each development value stream consists of the sequence of steps necessary to implement a new concept, which is integrated and deployed via a new or existing system.

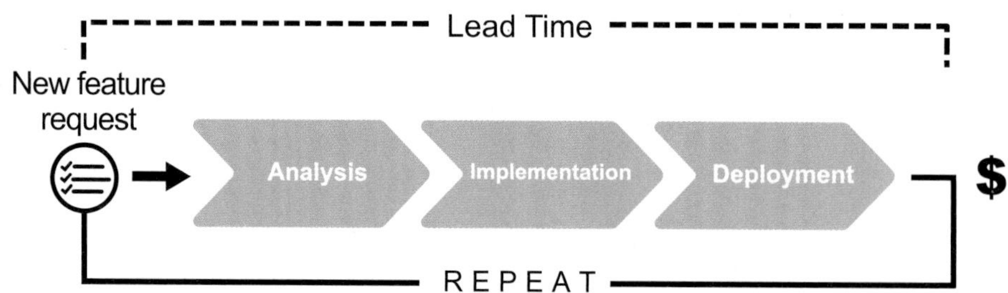

Figure 5-7. The solution development value stream

This third aspect of systems thinking—understanding and optimizing the full value stream—is the only way to reduce the total time it takes to go from "concept to cash.[4] Systems thinking mandates that leaders and practitioners understand and continuously optimize the full value stream, especially as it crosses technical and organizational boundaries.

To address this challenge, value stream mapping provides a systematic way to look at all the steps required to produce value. In so doing, one quickly recognizes that the actual value added steps—the creation of code and components, deployment, validation and so on—consume only a small portion of the total time to market. It then becomes obvious to focus on eliminating or reducing delays between steps to improve cycle time. Figure 5-8 provides an example of a value stream map. In this example, almost all the time between feature request and deployment is wait time—resulting in a highly inefficient process.

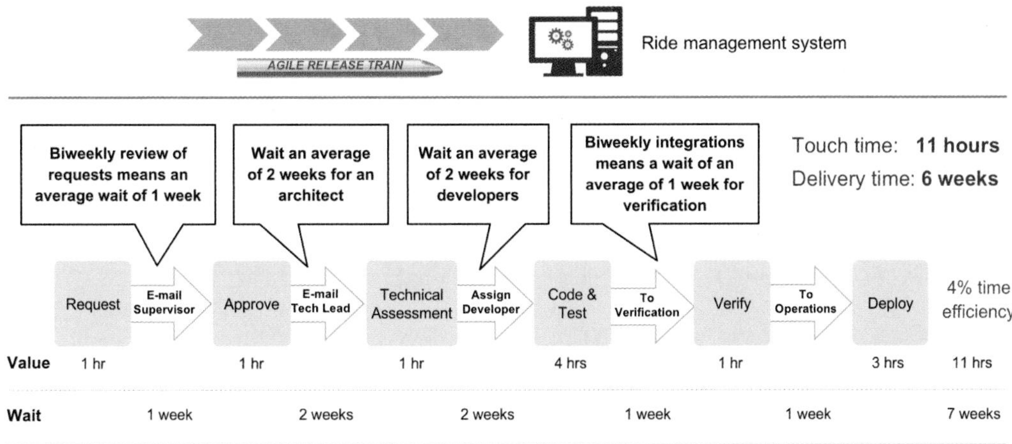

Figure 5-8. Value stream mapping example: Most of the time is wait time

Only Management Can Change the System

Everyone is already doing their best; the problems are with the system ...
only management can change the system.

—W. Edwards Deming

This Deming quote prepares us for a final set of insights: Systems thinking requires a new approach to management as well, a perspective where managers are problem solvers, take the long view, proactively eliminate impediments, and

4. Mary Poppendieck and Tom Poppendieck, *Implementing Lean Software Development* (Addison-Wesley, 2006).

lead the organizational changes necessary to improve the systems that limit performance. These Lean-Agile leaders do the following:

- Exhibit and teach systems thinking and Lean-Agile values, principles, and practices
- Constantly engage in problem-solving, eliminating roadblocks and improving ineffective internal processes and systems
- Apply and teach root-cause analysis and corrective action techniques
- Collaborate with the teams to reflect at key milestones, and identify and address shortcomings
- Take a long-term view, investing in enabling capabilities such as infrastructure, practices, tools, and training, which provides the foundation for faster value delivery and higher quality and productivity

Understanding these systems thinking aspects helps leaders and teams truly comprehend *what* they are doing, *why* they are doing it, and the *impact* on those around them. In turn, this leads to a leaner and smarter enterprise, one that can better navigate the organization and solution development complexities, leading to better business outcomes.

Principle #3: Assume Variability; Preserve Options

Generate alternative system-level designs and subsystem concepts. Rather than try to pick an early winner, aggressively eliminate alternatives. The designs that survive are your most robust alternatives.

—Allen C. Ward, *Lean Product and Process Development*

Solution development can be described as the "process of converting uncertainty to knowledge."[5] Development happens in the midst of tremendous variability. Technology and market uncertainty are ever present. But variability is inherently neither bad nor good, as it drives both risk and opportunity. Rather, it's the type and timing of variability that determines economic value.

Attempting to eliminate variability too soon may result in poor economic outcomes and a risk-adverse culture, which cannot innovate. (Examples are freezing requirements and design early in the timeline and a culture where every "project" must be a success.)

5. Dantar Oosterwal, *The Lean Machine* (Amacom, 2010).

On the other hand, unnecessary variability from routine work should readily be addressed (for example, automated code deployment that eliminates error-prone manual processes). What's left is the remaining, inherent variability of technology uncertainty.

Set-Based Design

The fundamental understanding that variability is ever present drives teams to develop more effective development practices. One such example is *set-based design*.

Traditional development practices tend to drive teams to select a single design option quickly and then modify that design until it eventually meets the system intent. "This can be an effective approach, unless of course one picks the wrong starting point; then subsequent iterations to refine that solution can be very time-consuming and lead to a suboptimal design."[6]

This can be described as a "point-based" approach, as shown at the top of Figure 5-9. Here, a single option chosen up front often results in significant rework and delays that are typically discovered at the end. And the later those problems are discovered, the costlier they are to fix. And the bigger and more technically innovative the system is, the higher the odds are that you chose the wrong starting point!

A better approach is *set-based design*, as shown in Figure 5-9.

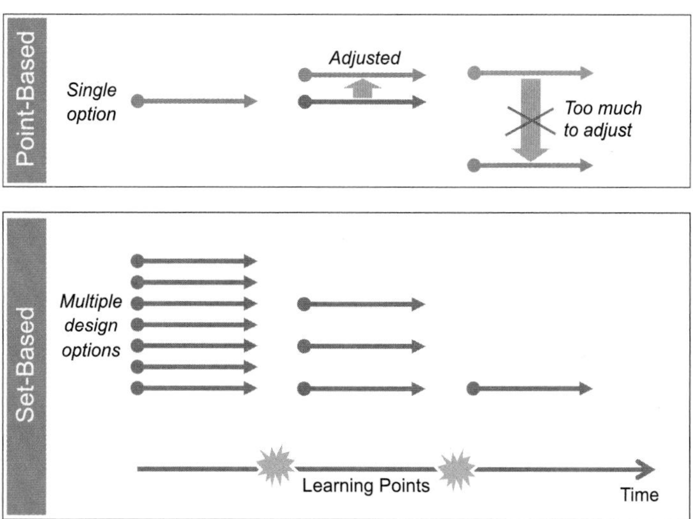

Figure 5-9. Point-based vs. set-based design

6. Marco Lansiti, "Shooting the Rapids: Managing Product Development in Turbulent Environments" (*California Management Review* 38, 1995).

Set-based design recognizes that *requirements* must be flexible to accommodate economic *design* choices, and *designs* must be flexible to support emerging knowledge.

Set-based design manages risk better by considering multiple design options at the start. Thereafter, teams continuously evaluate economic and technical trade-offs—typically as exhibited by objective evidence presented at integration *learning points*. They then eliminate the weaker options over time and, finally, converge on a final design, based on the knowledge that has been gained to that point.

This process keeps design options open for as long as possible, converges as and when necessary, and produces more optimal technical and economic outcomes.

Principle #4: Build Incrementally with Fast, Integrated Learning Cycles

The epiphany of integration points is that they control product development and are the leverage points to improve the system. When timing of integration points slip, the project is in trouble.

—Dantar P. Oosterwal

This fundamental principle of both Lean and Agile is pivotal to describing the basic mechanism for a new approach to building systems.

In traditional, phase-gate development, investment cost begins immediately and accumulates until a solution is delivered. Often, there is little to no actual value delivered until all the committed features are available or the program runs out of time or money. During development, it is difficult to get any meaningful feedback because the process isn't designed for it, and the system isn't designed or implemented in such a way that incremental capabilities can be delivered. The risk remains in the program until the deadline, and even into deployment and initial use.

This process often results in loss of trust between the teams building the solution and the customer. In an attempt to adjust for this, customers and teams try even harder to define the requirements and select "the best" design up front. They also typically implement even more rigorous phase gates. Each of these solutions actually *compounds* the underlying problem.

The principles of taking an economic view, applying systems thinking and set-based design, informs us that a better approach is to *build incrementally, with fast integrated learning cycles*. This leads us to the next set of insights.

Integration Points Create Knowledge from Uncertainty

By focusing development on *integration points*, the Lean-Agile team develops incrementally. The knowledge gained from integration points establishes continuous technical viability. In addition, many integration points can serve as Minimum Viable Products (MVPs) or prototypes that can be released for testing the product in the market, establishing usability, and gaining objective customer feedback. Where necessary, these fast feedback points allow teams to "pivot" to an alternate course of action, one that should better serve the needs of the intended customers.

> **INTEGRATION POINTS**
>
> Integration points are events where a significant cross-functional group of people pulls aspects of the system together and helps ensure that ARTs and suppliers are creating an integrated and tested solution that is fit for its intended purpose. Figure 5-10 shows an example of multiple teams integrating the various components of the system (for example, hardware, operating system, and drivers). After integration is complete, the solution is demoed for stakeholders to evaluate the system.

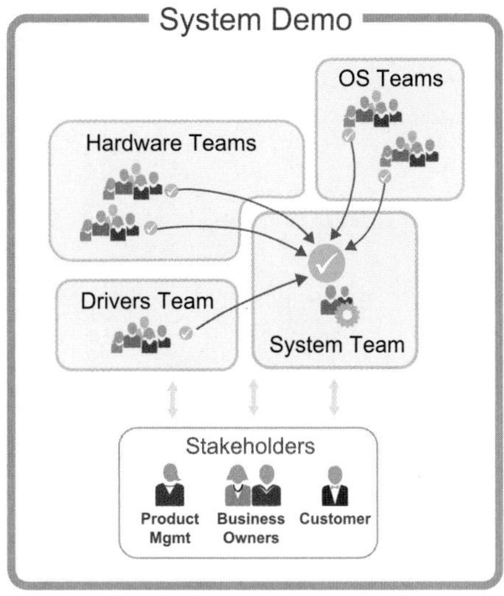

Figure 5-10. A system demo is an example of a significant integration point

Integration Points Occur by Intent

Cadence-based integration points become the primary focus of the ART, via both a development process and a solution architecture designed for that purpose. Each integration point is a "pull event" that gathers the various solution elements into an integrated whole, even though it might address only a portion of the system intent. Integration points align stakeholders as well.

Routine synchronization helps assure that the evolving solution addresses the real and current business needs, as opposed to assumptions established at the beginning of the process. Each integration point delivers its own value by converting uncertainty into new knowledge. For example, knowledge of the technical viability of the current design choice and solution is based on objective evaluation of the integrated solutions.

Faster Learning through Frequent PDCA Cycles

Figure 5-11 illustrates how integration points reinforce the basic Plan-Do-Check-Adjust scientific learning cycle developed by Shewhart.[7] As we described, these integration points serve as the primary mechanism for controlling the variability of solution development. The system, like science, advances one cycle at a time.

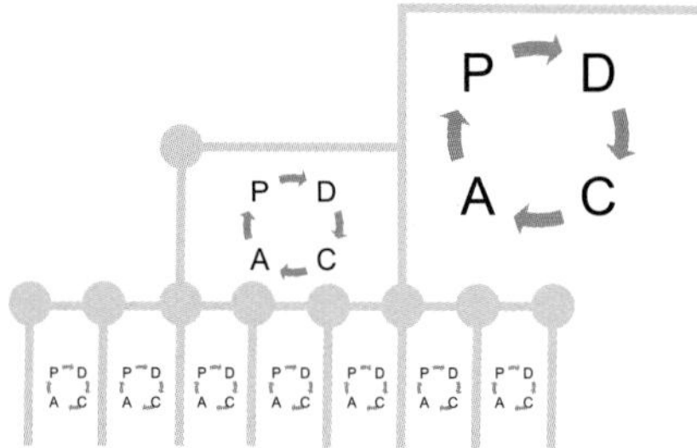

Figure 5-11. Nested, harmonized integration points occur by intent using a fixed cadence

Moreover, *the more frequent the integration points, the faster the learning.*

In complex systems, local integration points assure that each element, component, or capability is meeting its responsibilities to the overall solution intent. Local integration points for features or components must then be integrated at the next higher system level. The larger the system, the more such integration levels exist. The top-level, least-frequent integration point (for example, a solution in SAFe) provides the only true measure of solution progress.

---

7. Walter Andrew Shewhart, *Statistical Method from the Viewpoint of Quality Control* (New York: Dover, 1939).

When the timing of integration points slip, it's a sure sign of problems and a likely delayed schedule. Even then, this timely knowledge helps facilitate recovery via changes to technical approach, scope, cost, or delivery timing.

Principle #5: Base Milestones on Objective Evaluation of Working Systems

There was in fact no correlation between exiting phase gates on time and project success ... the data suggested the inverse might be true.
—Dantar P. Oosterwal, *The Lean Machine*

The Problem with Phase-Gate Milestones

Building today's large-scale systems requires substantial financial investment. Therefore, stakeholders must collaborate to ensure that the proposed return on investment will be achieved throughout the development process versus hoping everything will be okay in the end.

They have to measure progress, too. However, many companies rely on a sequential, phase-gated development process. Progress and control of investments rely on review and approval of completed milestones—discovery, requirements, design, development, test, and delivery.

But there's an inherent flaw in this model. In most cases, there isn't a working solution available at the gates to demonstrate the actual progress and solution viability. As a result, true progress isn't known until the end, when the solution is integrated and tested. Figure 5-12 shows that late discovery of problems is a significant and common problem with the phase-gate approach.

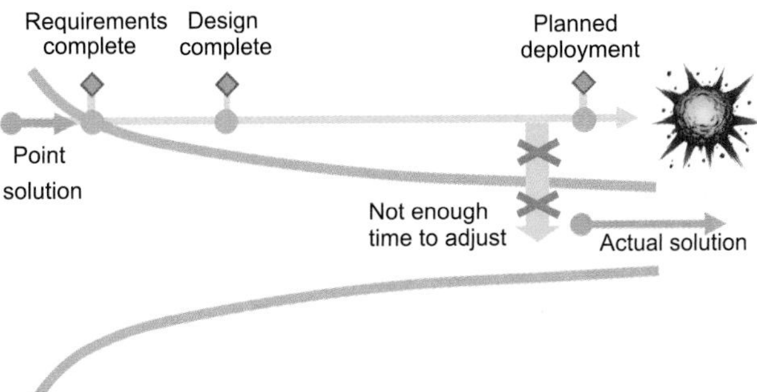

Figure 5-12. The problem with one-pass, phase-gate milestones

Moreover, as we described earlier, the attempt to define the systems via a point solution early tends to eliminate better design alternatives. Perhaps this is why Oosterwal notes, "the inverse might be true."

PI Milestones Provide Objective Evidence

Unlike phase-gate development, SAFe PI development milestones include all the steps in the development process—requirements, design, development, and testing—together producing an increment of value. This is done routinely, on a fixed cadence, as illustrated in Figure 5-13.

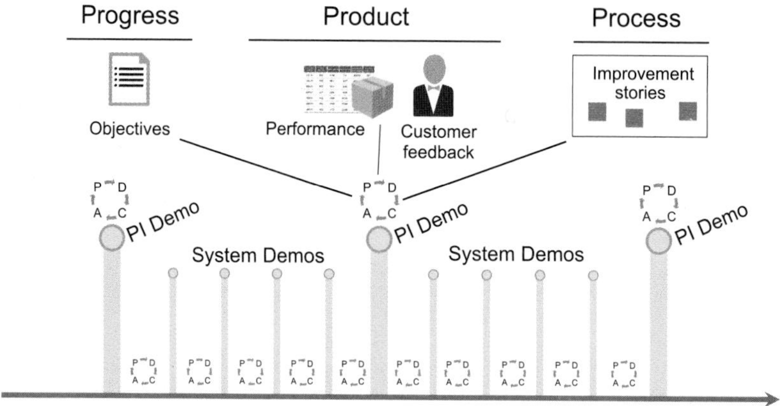

Figure 5-13. PI milestones replace phase-gate milestones

These PI milestones are used to provide objective evidence as to the viability of the solution in process. The milestones are also used to assess the overall progress against the nearer-term objectives and the roadmap to evaluate the solutions and to inspect and adapt the development process itself.

Principle #6: Visualize and Limit WIP, Reduce Batch Sizes, and Manage Queue Lengths

Operating a product development process near full utilization is an economic disaster.
—Donald Reinertsen

To achieve the shortest sustainable lead time, teams must implement a continuous flow model, allowing new system capabilities to move quickly from concept to deployment.

This requires eliminating the project-based funding and organizational model, along with any phase gates that impede flow and can falsely indicate progress.

The three primary keys to implementing flow are

1. Visualize and limit Work-in-Process (WIP)
2. Reduce the batch sizes of work
3. Manage queue lengths

Visualize and Limit WIP

Having too much work in the system causes multitasking and frequent context switching. It overloads the people doing the work and reduces focus, productivity, and throughput. This results in increased wait times for new functionality and unhappy people.

The first step is to make the current WIP visible to all stakeholders. An example is shown in the kanban board of Figure 5-14.

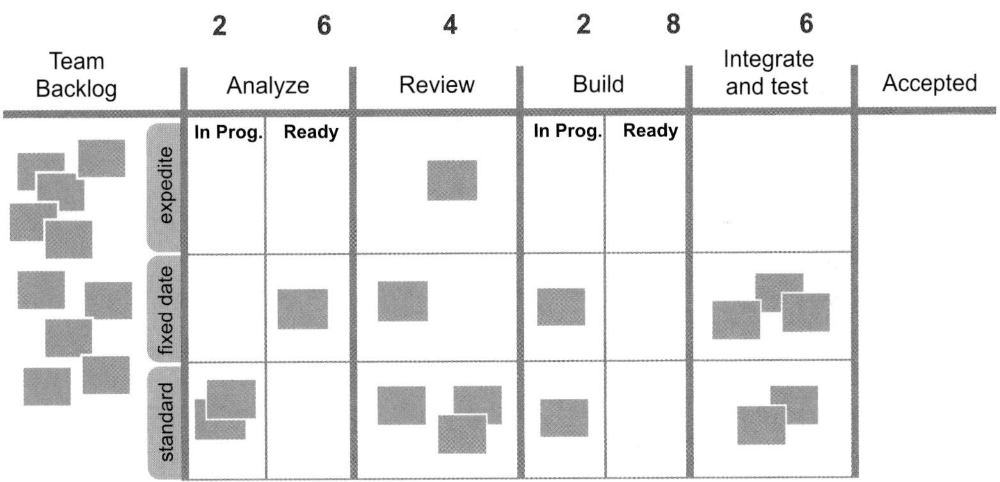

Figure 5-14. Example kanban board

The kanban board shows the total amount of work at each development step and helps identify bottlenecks. In some cases, simply visualizing the current work allows developers to address the systemic problems of too much work starting and not enough flowing and finishing.

The next step is to establish WIP limits and thereby balance the work against the available capacity. When any step reaches its WIP limit, no new work is started until the bottleneck is cleared. Flow increases measurably.

Reduce Batch Size

Another way to improve flow is to decrease the batch sizes of the work. Small batches go through the system faster and with less variability in completion times. That fosters faster learning and faster value delivery.

As Figure 5-15 illustrates, the economically optimal batch size is dependent upon both the holding cost (the cost of inventory and for delaying feedback and value) and the transaction cost (the cost of planning, implementing, and testing the batch).

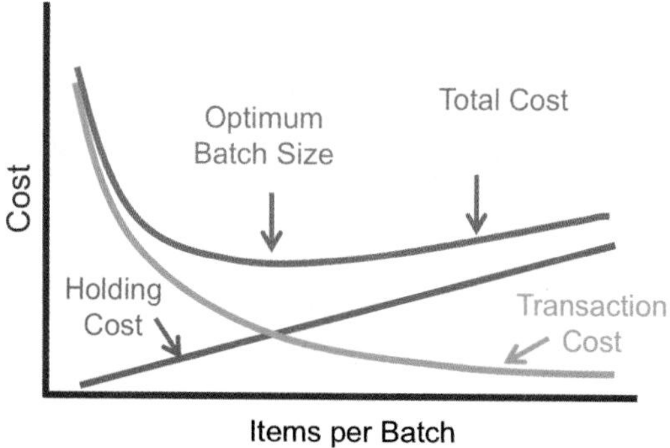

Figure 5-15. Total cost for a batch of work is the sum of the transaction cost and holding costs

To improve the economics of handling smaller batches and increase throughput and reliability, it's essential to reduce the transaction costs associated with any batch. This typically involves increasing investment on infrastructure and test automation, including practices such as continuous integration, test-driven development, and DevOps.

Manage Queue Lengths

The last method to achieve flow is to manage—and generally reduce—queue lengths. Long queues of work are just bad. They create the following:

- *Longer cycle times.* There's a longer wait for new items entering the queue.
- *Increased risk.* The items in the queue, such as requirements, decay over time.

- *Increased variability*. Each item has some variability, and the more items, the more total variability.
- *Lower motivation*. A really large queue of work lowers the sense of urgency.

In contrast, reducing queue length decreases delays, reduces waste, and increases quality and predictability of outcomes.

Decreasing Wait Times

Little's law, the fundamental law of queuing theory, tells us that the *average wait time is equal to the average queue length, divided by the average processing rate*. (Even the line at Starbucks teaches us that the longer the queue, the longer the wait.)

This also tells us that there are only two options to decrease wait times: reduce the length of the queue or increase the processing rate. Increasing the processing rate—doing things faster—is indeed beneficial, but improvements in processing rates have limitations before impacting quality.

The *fastest* way to reduce wait times is to reduce the *length of the queue*. This can be accomplished by keeping backlogs short and largely uncommitted. Visualizing the backlog helps immensely.

In summary, to increase overall throughput, combining the three elements of *visualizing and limiting WIP*, *reducing batch sizes*, and *managing queues* can spark measurable improvements in throughput, quality, customer satisfaction, and employee engagement.

Principle #7: Apply Cadence; Synchronize with Cross-Domain Planning

Cadence and synchronization limit the accumulation of variance.

—Donald Reinertsen

Solution development is an inherently uncertain process. This uncertainty conflicts with the business's need to manage investment, track progress, and plan and commit to a longer-term course of action. The Lean-Agile approach strives to balance this inherent *variability* with the *certainty* needed to enable the business to plan and operate effectively. When it comes to R&D, it's a balancing act, to be sure.

The primary means to achieve this balance is to use *cadence* and *synchronization*, supported by *cross-domain planning*.

- Cadence transforms unpredictable events into predictable ones. It makes routine that which can be routine. Cadence provides a rhythmic pattern—the dependable heartbeat of the development process.
- Synchronization causes multiple events to happen at the same time. If done on a cadence, it allows multiple development perspectives to be understood, resolved, and integrated simultaneously, thereby limiting deviation from plan to a single time interval.

Figure 5-16 highlights many aspects of cadence and synchronization.

Cadence	Synchronization
• Makes waiting times for new work predictable • Supports regular planning and cross-functional coordination • Limits batch sizes to a single interval • Controls injection of new work • Provides scheduled integration points	• Facilitates cross-functional tradeoffs of people and scope • Aligns all stakeholders • Provides for routine dependency management • Supports integration and assessment of full system • Provides feedback from multiple perspectives

Figure 5-16. Aspects of cadence and synchronization

Applying Cadence in SAFe

The SAFe "develop on cadence" mantra illustrates how critical cadence is to the development process. The following are examples:

- Agile teams use a fixed (typically two weeks) cadence for iterations; ARTs and value streams apply a fixed cadence (eight to twelve weeks) for PIs.
- Event calendars are established well in advance. This includes PI planning, system demos, Inspect and Adapt (I&A), and team-level events. This lowers the cost of those events and facilitates planning.
- System and solution integration are frequent and programmatic.

However, Reinertsen also notes that delivering on cadence is another matter entirely, and that requires scope or capacity margin. This means programs need to be careful about planning to meet date-based commitments, including Program Increments (PIs) and other milestones. Some scope or capacity margin (buffer) is required, and you'll see that in many elements of the SAFe planning and commitment processes.

Applying Synchronization in SAFe

Cadence-based synchronization is applied routinely in SAFe. The following are examples:

- Teams align their iterations to the same schedule to support communication, coordination, and system integration.
- Events such as Scrum of Scrums help manage dependencies.
- ARTs in a value stream align PIs for the same reason.
- System and solution demos integrate components of the system to routinely assess overall viability.
- Routine, cross-functional planning aligns the development teams, business, customers, and suppliers to a common mission and context.

Taken together, cadence and synchronization—and the associated activities—help reduce uncertainty and manage the variability inherent in research and development.

Synchronize with Cross-Domain Planning

Future product development tasks can't be pre-determined. Distribute planning and control to those who can understand and react to the end results.

—Michael Kennedy, *Product Development for the Lean Enterprise*[8]

As Kennedy notes, and as decentralized decision-making (principle #9) implies, centralized planning for significant solution initiatives is problematic. Simply, the complexity is too great, and the facts change too quickly for a centralized planning function to be effective. In its place, SAFe provides for routine, *cross-domain*, face-to-face planning. This is the glue that holds the entire process together.

There is an additional benefit as well. The most visible example of this is PI planning, where teams and stakeholders from different functional areas gather to plan the work for an upcoming PI, as illustrated in Figure 5-17.

8. Michael Kennedy, *Product Development for the Lean Enterprise* (Oaklea Press, 2003).

Figure 5-17. Face-to-face, cross-domain PI planning

This event is immutable in SAFe. (If you aren't doing PI planning, you aren't doing SAFe). PI planning (and in a like manner, pre- and post-value stream planning) is used to do the following:

- Continuously align all stakeholders to a common technical and business vision. Based on the current state, business and technology leaders refine the mission. This aligns all stakeholders to a common mission that describes both near- and longer-term goals.
- Plan and commit to the next program increment. The distribution of planning and control empowers teams to create, within the given constraints, the best possible plans to achieve the best possible solution. But it isn't just a planning session, as systems requirements and design are continually evolved as well.

There is one additional and significant benefit to this process, which is that *periodic planning limits variance from plan to a single time interval*, as Figure 5-18 illustrates.

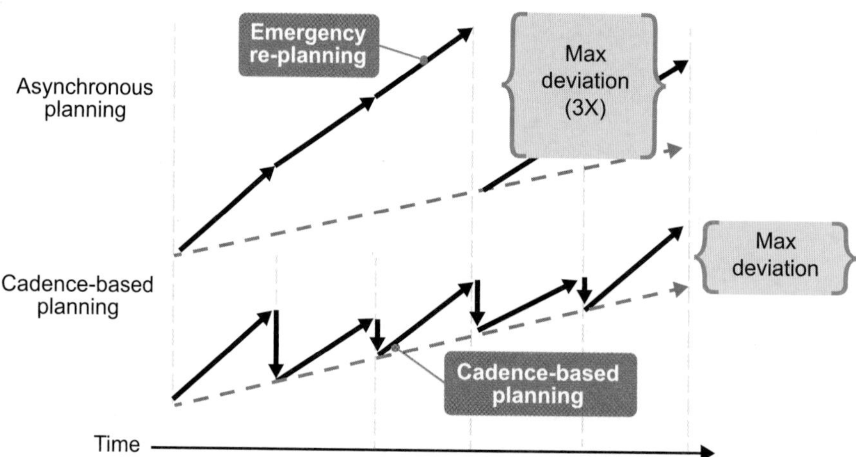

Figure 5-18. Periodic planning limits deviation from plan to a single time interval

In turn, this means the business has a continuing and updated plan on which they can take the appropriate action.

The development of large-scale systems is fundamentally a social activity, and this planning event provides a continuous opportunity to build and improve the social network that builds the solution. This is such an important topic, that chapter 7, "Planning a Program Increment," is devoted entirely to the value and mechanisms of PI planning.

Principle #8: Unlock the Intrinsic Motivation of Knowledge Workers

Knowledge workers are people who know more about the work they perform than their bosses.

—Peter Drucker[9]

Drucker's definition of a knowledge worker is a wake-up call for many. With this definition, how can any manager seriously attempt to supervise and coordinate the technical work of people who know more about the work than they do? Indeed, they cannot. Instead, what they can do is to *unlock the intrinsic motivation of knowledge workers*. Tips for accomplishing this include the following:

- Leveraging systems thinking
- Understanding the role of compensation
- Creating an environment of mutual influence
- Providing autonomy, mastery, and purpose

Leveraging Systems Thinking

Leveraging systems thinking allows knowledge workers to communicate across functional boundaries, make decisions based on economics, and achieve fast feedback about the viability of their solution. They now can participate in continuous, incremental learning and mastery, and they can contribute to a more productive and fulfilling solution development process.

9. Peter F. Drucker, *The Essential Drucker* (Harper-Collins, 2001).

Understanding the Role of Compensation

Many organizations still embrace assumptions about human potential and individual work performance that are outdated. Despite mounting evidence that such measures don't work and often do harm, they continue to pursue short-term incentive plans and pay-for-performance schemes.

Authors as varied as Pink[10] and Drucker[11] have each highlighted the fundamental paradox of compensation for knowledge workers: If you don't pay people enough, they won't be motivated. But after a certain point, *money no longer motivates*. In fact, specific monetary incentives can have the opposite effective for knowledge workers.

Lean-Agile leaders understand that neither money nor the reverse—threats, intimidation, or fear—inspire ideation, innovation, and deep workplace engagement. Most specifically, incentive-based practices, such as individual Management by Objectives (MBOs), cause internal competition and can destroy the cooperation necessary to achieve the larger aim. These should be eliminated.

Creating an Environment of Mutual Influence

To effectively lead, the workers must be heard and respected.
—Peter Drucker

An environment of mutual influence fosters motivation and empowerment. Leaders create an environment of mutual influence by giving honest feedback supportively, by showing willingness to become more vulnerable, and by encouraging others to do the following:[12]

- Disagree with respect and where appropriate.
- Advocate for the positions they believe in.
- Make their needs clear and push to achieve them.
- Enter into joint problem solving, with management and peers.
- Negotiate, compromise, agree, and commit.

---

10. Daniel Pink, *Drive: The Surprising Truth About What Motivates Us* (Riverhead Books, 2011).
11. Peter F. Drucker, *The Essential Drucker* (Harper-Collins, 2001).
12. David L. Bradford and Allen Cohen, *Managing for Excellence: The Leadership Guide to Developing High Performance in Contemporary Organizations* (John Wiley & Sons, 1997).

Providing Autonomy, Mastery, and Purpose

It appears that the performance of the task provides its own intrinsic reward ... this drive ... may be as basic as the others....

—Daniel Pink, *Drive: The Surprising Truth About What Motivates Us*

Daniel Pink's work, and the work of many others, helps us understand that there are three primary factors in establishing deep workplace engagement: *autonomy, mastery,* and *purpose.*

- Autonomy is the desire to self-direct, to manage one's own life. Simply, when it comes to knowledge work, self-direction is better.
- Mastery is the inherent need for people to grow in their careers and acquire new skills that allow them to provide ever higher levels of contribution.
- Purpose is the need to make a connection between the aim of the enterprise and the worker's daily activities. This makes the work more meaningful and links the worker's personal goals to the company mission.

Lean-Agile leaders need to understand these paradigms and strive to continuously create an environment where knowledge workers can do their best work.

In summary, we live in an age where knowledge workers outnumber management, are as smart or smarter, and have more local context. Unlocking their intrinsic, raw potential is a significant factor in improving the lives of those doing the work, as well as providing better outcomes for customers and the enterprise.

Principle #9: Decentralize Decision-Making

Knowledge workers themselves are best placed to make decisions about how to perform their work.

—Peter F. Drucker

Delivering value in the shortest sustainable lead time requires decentralized decision-making. Any decision that must be escalated to higher levels of authority introduces a delay in delivery. In addition, escalated decisions can decrease the effectiveness of decisions because of the lack of local context, plus changes to facts that occur during the waiting period.

Simply, decentralized decision-making reduces delays and improves product development flow and throughput. It enables faster feedback, more innovative solutions, and higher levels of empowerment.

Centralize Strategic Decisions

This is not to say, however, that *all* decisions should be decentralized. Some decisions are strategic, have far-reaching impact, and are largely outside of the team's responsibility. After all, leaders still have accountability for outcomes. And they have the market knowledge, longer-range perspectives, and understanding of the business and financial landscape necessary to steer the enterprise.

This leads us to an understanding that some decisions should be centralized. Generally, these decisions are as follows:

- *Infrequent.* These decisions aren't made often and typically are not urgent. Deeper consideration is appropriate. (Examples are product strategy and international commitments.)
- *Long lasting.* Once made, these decisions are unlikely to change. (Examples are a commitment to a standard technology platform and a commitment to organizational realignment around value streams.)
- *Provide significant economies of scale.* These decisions provide large and broad economic benefit. (Examples are a common way of working, standard development languages, standard tooling, and offshoring.)

Leadership is charged with making these types of decisions, supported by the input of those impacted by the decisions.

Decentralize Everything Else

The vast majority of decisions do not reach the threshold of strategic importance. Therefore, *all other decisions should be decentralized.* These types of decisions are typically as follows:

- *Frequent.* These decisions are frequent and common. (Examples include team and program backlog prioritization and response to defects and emerging issues.)
- *Time critical.* A delay in these types of decisions comes at a high cost. (Examples include point releases, customer emergencies, and dependencies with other teams.)

- *Require local information*. These decisions need specific local context, whether it be technology, organization, or specific customer or market impact (Examples include a decision to ship a release to a specific customer, resolve a significant design problem, and self-organization of individuals and teams to an emerging challenge.)

The workers who have better local context and detailed knowledge of the technical complexities of the current situation should make these decisions.

A Lightweight Thinking Tool for Decision-Making

Understanding how decisions are made is a key factor in empowering knowledge workers. Leadership's responsibility is to establish the rules for decision-making (including, for example, the economic framework) and then largely empower others to make them. Figure 5-19 provides a simple tool and exercise for thinking about whether decisions should be centralized or decentralized.

1. Consider the three significant decisions you are currently facing.
2. Rate each item using the table below.
3. Would you centralize or decentalize?

Decision	Frequent? Y=2 N=0	Time Critical? Y=2 N=0	Economies of Scale? Y=0 N=2	Total

Scale: 0 to 2 (low to high)

Then add the total: **0 to 3 = Centralize** | **4 to 6 = Decentralize**

Figure 5-19. A simple decision-making framework and exercise

Summary

This chapter described SAFe's principles, which are the core beliefs, truths, and economic values that drive effective Lean-Agile roles and practices.

The key takeaways from this chapter are as follows:

- Principles are enduring. They stand the test of time and can be applied universally no matter the situation.
- A practice is a specific activity, action, or way of accomplishing something. A practice that works in one situation may not necessarily apply or work in another. That's why we need principles.
- SAFe is based on nine Lean-Agile principles:
    1. *Take an economic view.*
    2. *Apply systems thinking.*
    3. *Assume variability; preserve options.*
    4. *Build incrementally with fast, integrated learning cycles.*
    5. *Base milestones on objective evaluation of working systems.*
    6. *Visualize and limit WIP, reduce batch sizes, and manage queue lengths.*
    7. *Apply cadence; synchronize with cross-domain planning.*
    8. *Unlock the intrinsic motivation of knowledge workers.*
    9. *Decentralize decision-making.*
- Before you can effectively apply SAFe, you need a deep understanding of the principles to know how and why SAFe works.
- The principles themselves are a system, and the whole is greater than the sum of the parts.

Part III

Program and Team Level

Nothing beats an Agile team ... except a team of Agile teams.

—The Authors

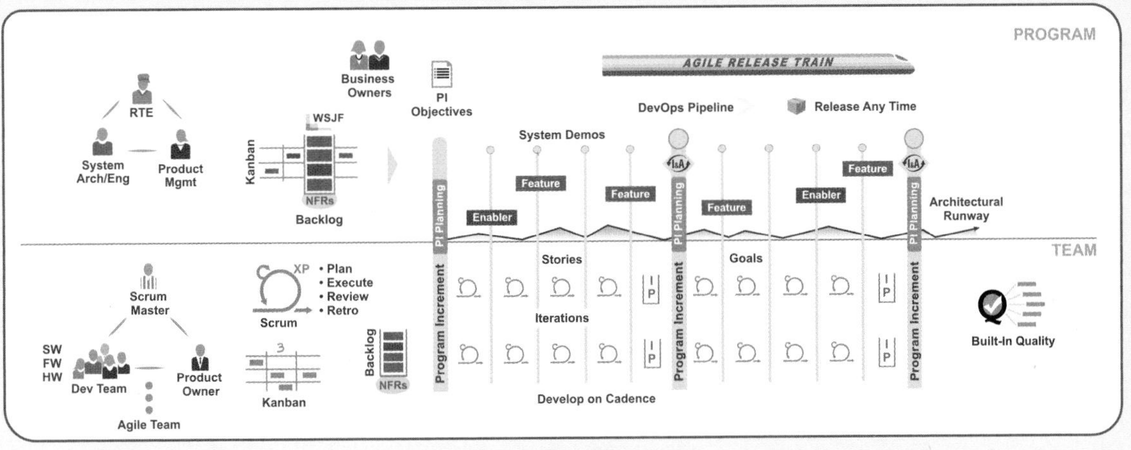

• Chapter 6 – The Agile Release Train
• Chapter 7 – Planning a Program Increment
• Chapter 8 – Executing a Program Increment
• Chapter 9 – Inspect and Adapt

6

The Agile Release Train

The more alignment you have, the more autonomy you can grant.
The one enables the other.

—Stephen Bungay, Author and Strategy Consultant

Overview 95
ART Organization 97
Develop on Cadence. Release Any Time 100
Vision 102
Features 103
Program Backlog 104
Roadmap 104
Agile Teams Power the Train 105
User Stories and the Team Backlog 107
Summary 111

Overview

The Agile Release Train (ART) is a long-lived, self-organizing, team-of-Agile-teams and other stakeholders (approximately 50–125 people total) that defines new functionality and plans, commits, executes, and delivers solutions together. ARTs are cross-functional and have all the capabilities—software, hardware, firmware, and other—needed to define, implement, test, and deploy new system functionality. An ART operates continuously, with a goal of delivering continuous product development flow, as shown in Figure 6-1.

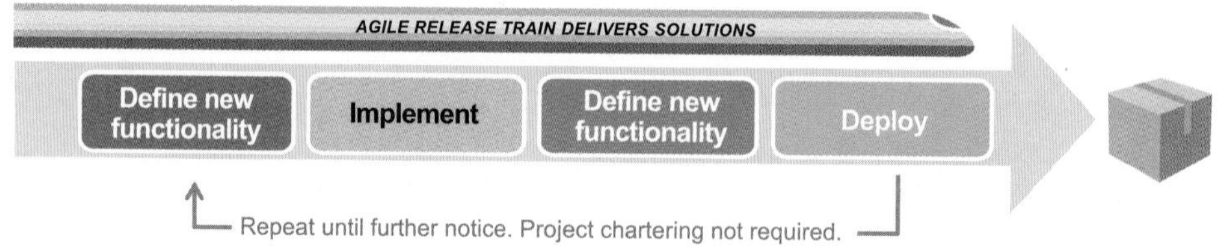

Figure 6-1. The long-lived Agile Release Train

The ART aligns teams to a common mission and helps manage the inherent risk and variability of solution development. Each operates on a set of common principles:

- The "train" departs the station on a known, reliable schedule, as determined by the chosen Program Increment (PI) cadence. If a feature misses a train, it can catch the next one.
- Each train delivers a new increment of value every two weeks. The system demo provides a mechanism for evaluating the working system, which is an integrated increment from all the teams.
- The PI timebox is fixed (typically eight to twelve weeks). All teams on the train are synchronized to the same iteration start/end dates and duration (two weeks by default). ARTs can release value any time.
- The train has a known velocity. Each train can reliably estimate how much cargo (new features) it can deliver within each PI.
- All "cargo"—including prototypes, models, software, hardware, and documentation—goes on the train.
- Agile teams power the train and build the solution. Teams embrace the Agile Manifesto and the values and principles of the Scaled Agile Framework (SAFe). They apply Scrum, Extreme Programming (XP), kanban, and built-in quality practices.
- Most people needed by the ART are dedicated full-time to the train, regardless of their functional reporting structure. Time and quality are fixed. Scope is varied as necessary to meet the PI timebox.
- The ART plans and commits to their work through periodic, face-to-face PI planning.
- Innovation and Planning (IP) iterations provide a guard band (buffer) for estimating, as well as dedicated time for PI planning, innovation, continuing education, and infrastructure work.

Additionally, in larger value streams, multiple ARTs collaborate to build larger solution capabilities. In such cases, some ART stakeholders participate in value stream events, including the solution demo and pre- and post-PI planning.

ART Organization

ARTs are typically virtual organizations that have all the people needed to define and deliver value. This breaks down the traditional functional silos that may exist prior to implementing SAFe, as shown in Figure 6-2.

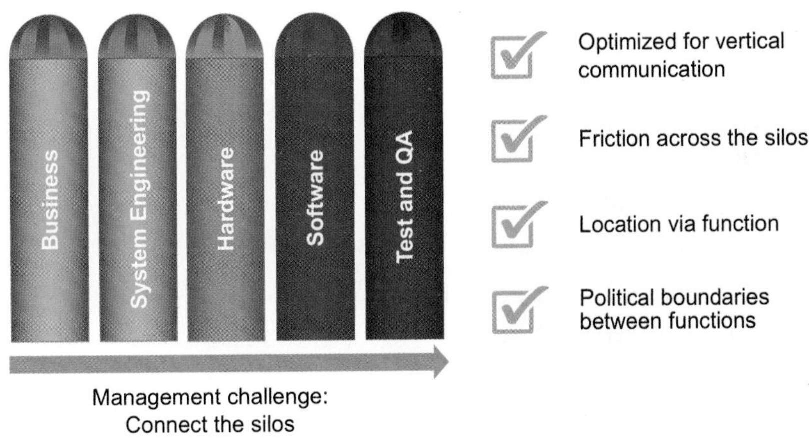

Figure 6-2. Traditional functional organization

In the prior functional organization, developers work with developers, testers work with other testers, and architects and systems engineers work with each other. While there are reasons why organizations have evolved that way, value doesn't flow easily, as it must cross all the silos. The daily involvement of managers and project managers is necessary to move the work across the silos. As a result, progress is slow, and handoffs and delays rule.

Instead, the ART takes a systems view and builds a cross-functional organization that is optimized to facilitate the flow of value from ideation to deployment, as Figure 6-3 illustrates.

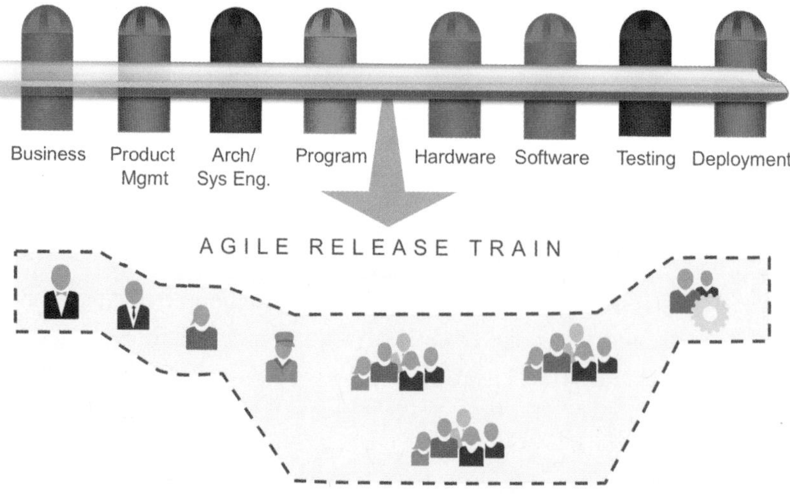

Figure 6-3. Agile Release Trains are fully cross-functional

Likewise, Agile teams within the ART are cross-functional, as shown in Figure 6-4.

Figure 6-4. Agile teams are cross-functional

Each Agile team has the skills and people needed (designers, developers, testers, and so on) to effectively deliver a feature or component with a minimum number of dependencies on others.

Together, this fully cross-functional organization—whether physical (direct organizational reporting) or virtual (line of reporting is unchanged)—has everyone and everything it needs to define and deliver value. It is self-organizing and self-managing at the team *and* program levels. This creates a far leaner organization, one where traditional daily task and project management is no longer required. Value flows more quickly, with a minimum of overhead. That is the purpose of the ART.

Agile Release Train Roles

In addition to the Agile teams, three primary roles help ensure successful execution of the ART, as illustrated in Figure 6-5.

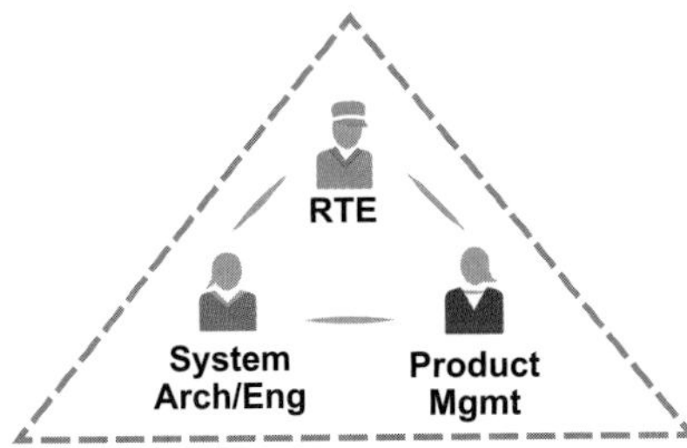

Figure 6-5. Program leadership, product management, and architecture triad

- *Release Train Engineer (RTE)* is the servant leader who facilitates program-level processes and execution and escalates impediments. They also facilitate risk and dependency management and continuous improvement.
- *Product Management* is responsible for "what gets built," as defined by the vision, roadmap, and new features in the program backlog. They work with customers and Product Owners to understand and communicate their needs, and they also participate in solution validation.
- *System Architect/Engineer* is an individual or team that defines the overall architecture for the system. They work at a level of abstraction above the teams and components and define Nonfunctional Requirements (NFRs), major system elements, subsystems, and interfaces.

In addition to these three primary functions, the following roles play an important part in ART success:

- *Business Owners* are key stakeholders of the ART and have ultimate responsibility for the business outcomes of the train.
- *Customers* are the ultimate buyers of the solution.
- A *System Team* typically provides assistance in building and maintaining the development and test environments. This includes continuous integration and test automation, as well as integrating assets from Agile teams and performing any end-to-end solution testing the teams can't perform.
- *Shared Services* are specialists—for example, data security, information architects, Database Administrators (DBAs), technical writers—that are necessary for the success of an ART but cannot be dedicated to a specific train.

Develop on Cadence. Release Any Time

ARTs also address one of the most common problems with traditional Agile development: that teams working on the same solution operate independently and asynchronously. That makes it extremely difficult to routinely integrate the full system. In reality, while the teams work in short iterations, the result is that the *system itself* may not be iterating at all. This increases the risk of late discovery of issues and problems, as shown in Figure 6-6.

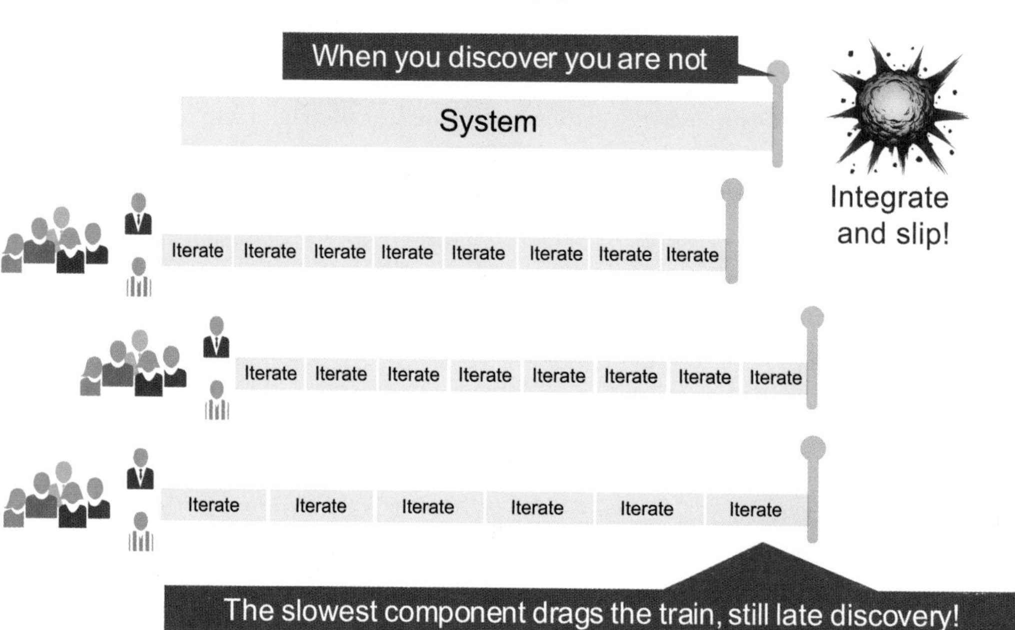

Figure 6-6. Asynchronous Agile development

Instead, the ART applies *cadence* and *synchronization* to assure that the *system is iterating (sprinting) as a whole*, as shown in Figure 6-7.

Cadence and synchronization assure that the focus is constantly on the evolution and objective assessment of the full system, rather than its individual elements. The system demo, which occurs at the end of the iteration after the team demos, provides objective evidence that the system is iterating.

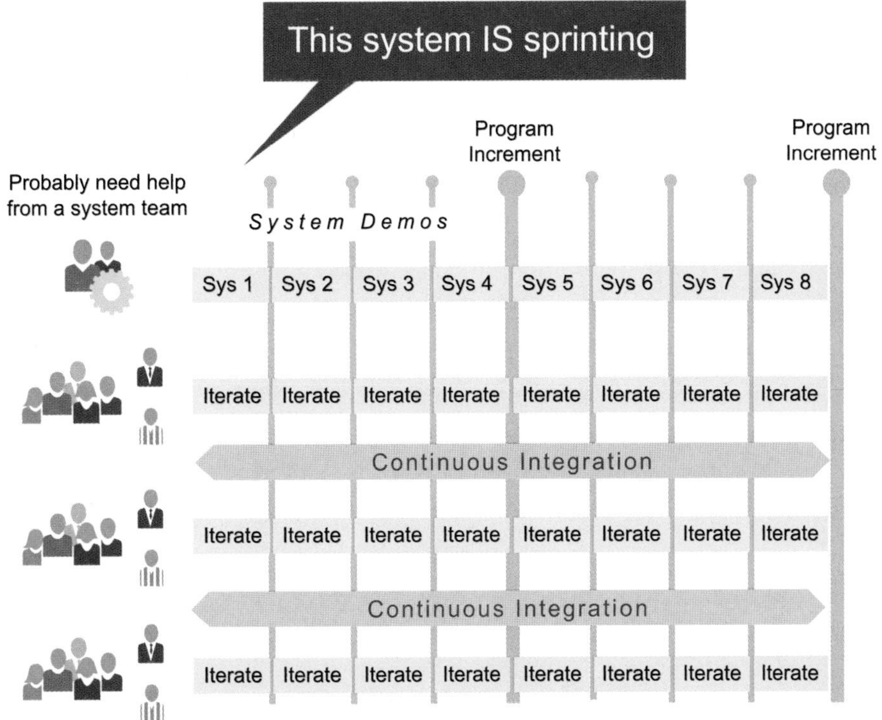

Figure 6-7. Aligned development; this system is sprinting

Separating Development and Release Concerns

As we described in principle #1, the rate of solution delivery is a key economic driver for the enterprise. More frequent delivery of solutions usually results in better economic outcomes.

Indeed, for many, *continuous delivery* of solutions represents an ideal end state. For other enterprises, however, that may not be practical or desirable. This may be because of reasons of security, requirements for high availability, risk management, or regulations for safety critical or financial systems. Moreover, the customer's operational environment (for example, deployment infrastructure, access to test labs) or business (for example, customer buying seasons) may not be well suited to continuous deployment.

To provide maximum flexibility to the business, the development and release cadence is often decoupled. On the Big Picture, this concept is called *develop on cadence* and *release any time*.

As we described, the development cadence provides the reliable heartbeat for ARTs. Releasing, however, is a different concern. In practice, we observe different patterns for releasing.

1. *Releasing on the PI cadence.* It can be convenient for the enterprise to release at the end of each PI, in which case PI planning, Inspect & Adapt (I&A), and release are all coordinated during the Innovation and Planning (IP) iteration. This may also include final verification, validation, and release documentation. In this case, release dates are predictable and can be known far in advance.
2. *Releasing less frequently.* In many cases, however, releasing on the PI cadence may not be feasible or desirable. For example, deployed systems may constitute critical infrastructure for a customer's operating environment. In other cases, the timelines for systems that contain both software and hardware—such as mobile phones or satellites—are driven by long lead times. In these cases, releasing on PI cadence is not an option, and release cycles are necessarily longer.
3. *Releasing more frequently.* In some cases, highly frequent (and even continuous) release is appropriate. Here, the PI provides the cadence, synchronization, and alignment the enterprise needs to plan for larger value delivery, aggregate customer and stakeholder feedback, and routine inspection and adaption.

Further, in larger and more complex value streams, the previous release patterns are overly simplistic, as each of these cycles may be in effect for various systems or components. After all, building really big systems is complicated; not all the components of the solution will be releasable at the same time. Each ART and value stream must determine the most economically efficient and effective release cycle for their own situation. As we said: *Develop on cadence. Release any time.*

Vision

Lean-Agile development typically decreases dependencies on documentation, especially up-front requirements specifications. In its place, Product Management provides the ART with a program *vision* that communicates the ongoing direction for the solution. The vision answers the following types of questions:

- What will this new solution do?
- What problems will it solve?

- What features and benefits will it provide?
- For whom will it provide them?
- How will it create differentiation?
- What system qualities (NFRs) will it deliver?

The vision should inspire and motivate people to come along on the journey, in alignment with the business objectives. While there are many ways to express this vision, the vision must be communicated and translated into a set of upcoming *features* at each PI Planning session.

Features

Features are used to describe larger systems behaviors that fulfill the user's needs. Features, along with their benefits, are expressed in plain, readily understood language in a Feature and Benefit (FAB) matrix. Figure 6-8 shows an example.

- *Feature.* A short phrase with a name and context
- *Benefit.* A brief description of the benefit to the user

Feature	Benefit
In-service software update	Significantly reduced planned downtime
Hardware VPN acceleration	High-performance encryption for secure WAN
Traffic congestion management	Improved overall quality of service across different protocols
Route optimization	Improved quality of service due to faster and more reliable connectivity

Figure 6-8. Features and benefits matrix example for a network router

Features are sized so they can be delivered in a single PI. Like user stories, acceptance criteria are created for features, which are used to determine whether the implementation is correct and should result in delivering the business benefits. Figure 6-9 shows an example.

Feature:
In-service software update

Acceptance Criteria:
- Nonstop routing availability
- Automatic and manual update support
- Rollback capability
- Support through existing admin tools
- All enabled services are running after the update

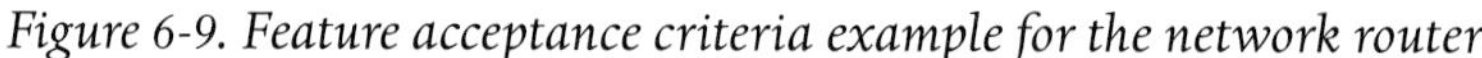

Figure 6-9. Feature acceptance criteria example for the network router

Program Backlog

Product Management has the responsibility for identifying, prioritizing, and sequencing features, which are the keys to the economic success of the ART. Features arise from various stakeholders—customers, Business Owners, Product Management, and Architects. They may originate from the local context of the ART, or they may arise as a result of splitting larger epics or capabilities.

Features are developed and managed through the program kanban. Those that are approved are maintained in the program backlog and are prioritized for implementation using Weighted Shortest Job First (WSJF).

The program backlog also includes enabler features that advance learning and build the architectural runway. The runway ensures that sufficient architecture exists to support the implementation of near-term features, without excessive redesign and delays.

Roadmap

The solution advances incrementally, one PI at a time. But a longer-term view is typically required. The roadmap consists of a series of planned PIs with features and other milestones, as shown in Figure 6-10.

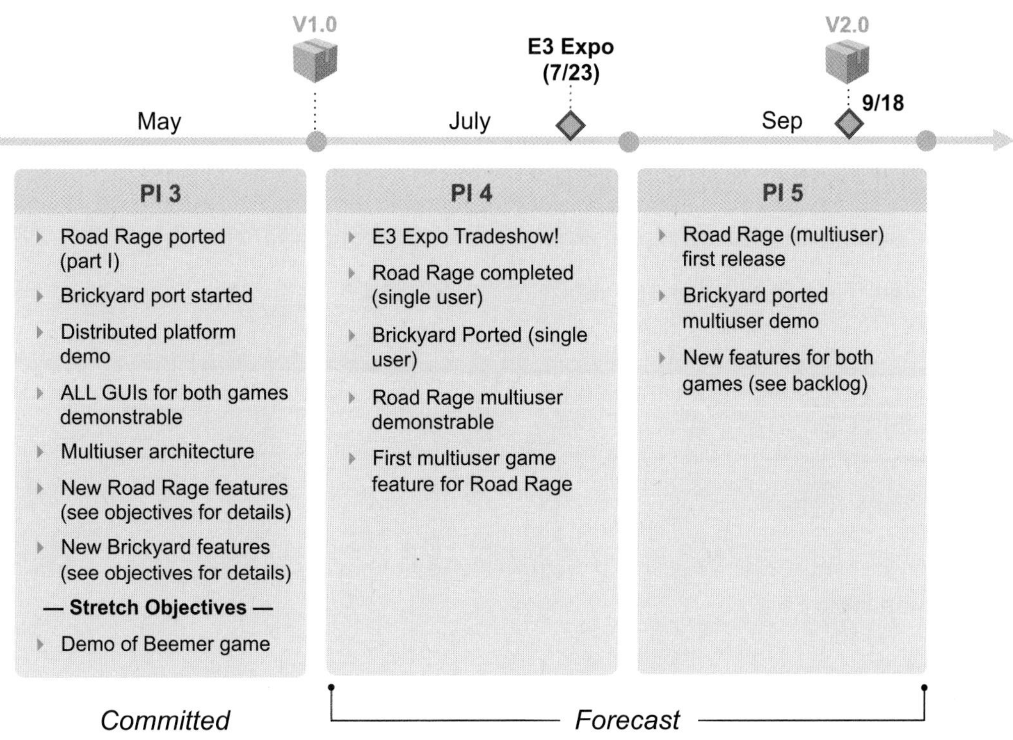

Figure 6-10. An example of a roadmap for a gaming company

The roadmap shows the deliverables for the current committed PI and offers visibility into the next two PIs. This provides enough detail to run the business yet offers a short enough time frame to keep long-term commitments from interfering with the flexibility to adapt to changing business priorities. The roadmap is developed and updated by Product Management as the vision and delivery strategy evolve.

Agile Teams Power the Train

Agile teams define, build, and test features and components. They use various Agile practices, based primarily on Scrum, XP, and kanban.

Each Agile team has dedicated individual contributors, covering all the roles necessary to build a quality increment of value for an iteration. Teams can deliver software, hardware, firmware, and any combination.

Each Agile team does the following:

- Estimates and manages their own work
- Determines the technical design in their area of concern, within architectural and user experience guidelines
- Commits to the work it can accomplish in an iteration timebox
- Continuously improves process and deliverables

By moving work to teams and trains instead of bringing people to the work, enterprises help create stable, long-lived teams and ARTs that relentlessly improve their ability to deliver solutions.

Agile Team Roles

Each Scrum team consists of three primary roles that help ensure successful execution, as shown in Figure 6-11.

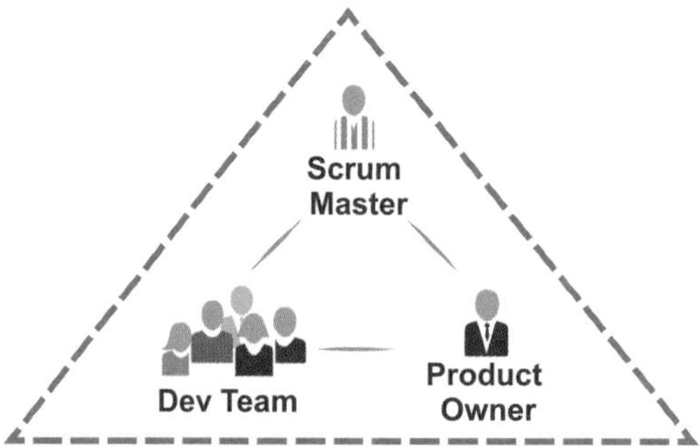

Figure 6-11. Agile team structure

- *Scrum Master.* The Scrum Master is the servant leader for the team, facilitating team meetings, fostering Agile behavior, helping remove impediments, and maintaining the team's focus. They also help build a high-performing and self-managing team.
- *Product Owner.* The Product Owner owns the team backlog, acts as the customer for developer questions, prioritizes the work, and collaborates with Product Management to plan PIs and to deliver the larger scope of value.

- *Development Team*. The Development Team has three to nine dedicated individual contributors, covering all the roles necessary to build a quality increment of value for an iteration. Developers, testers, and various specialists create and refine user stories and acceptance criteria; they define, build, test, and deliver stories in support of features.

Team kanban roles are less rigorously defined, though many SAFe kanban teams implement the Scrum roles as well.

User Stories and the Team Backlog

User Stories

During PI planning, features are broken down into smaller *user stories*. As defined in XP, user stories are negotiable expressions of intended system behavior. They are not requirements; instead, they are short, simple descriptions of a small piece of desired functionality, told from the user's perspective.

Stories provide just enough information for the intent to be understood by both business and technical people. They are a "promise for a conversation," intended to serve as a focal point for a more thorough discussion of the intended behavior and impact. Details are deferred until the story is ready to be implemented.

Stories are often described in terms of *a user story voice* format, as shown in Figure 6-12.

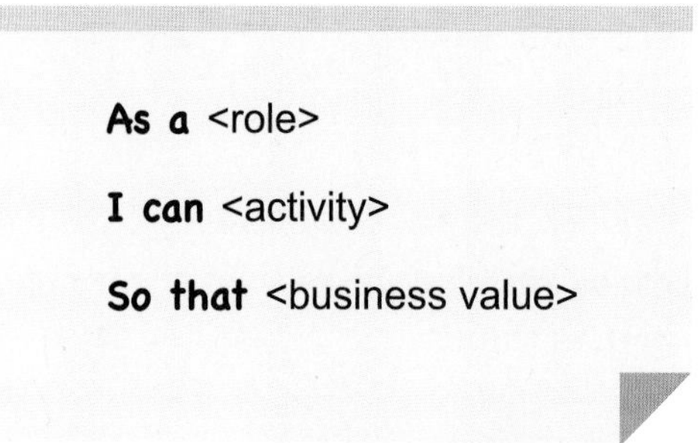

Figure 6-12. User story voice format

The user story voice has three main parts:

1. *User role.* The person performing the action
2. *Activity.* The action the user does with the system
3. *Business value.* The value the user receives from the action

Through conversations and acceptance criteria, stories get elaborated as they are implemented, helping to ensure system quality. Acceptance criteria can be captured and automated in acceptance tests. These tests confirm that the functionality has been implemented properly, both when the story is written, and later, as the solution evolves. This is a critical element of built-in quality practices.

While the user story voice is the common case, not every system interacts with an end user. Sometimes the "user" is a device (for example, mobile phone) or other system (for example, transaction server). In this case, the role in the user story can be the device or system (for example, as the park operations system, I log all activities in the Baja Park ride so they are available for safety audits).

Enabler stories are another type of story. These lay the foundation for the development of future user stories. They may express any of the following:

1. *Infrastructure.* These are used to build development and testing frameworks that enable a faster and more efficient development process.
2. *Architecture.* These build the architectural runway, which enables smoother and faster development.
3. *Exploration.* These stories help build a better understanding of what is needed by the customer and of prospective solutions, and they evaluate alternatives.

Estimating Stories

Agile teams use story points to estimate their work. A story point is a singular number that represents a combination of things:

- *Volume*—How much is there?
- *Complexity*—How hard is it?
- *Knowledge*—What's known?
- *Uncertainty*—What's not known?

Story points are relative to each other; they are not connected to any specific unit of measure. The size (effort) of each story is estimated relative to the smallest story, which is arbitrarily assigned a size of 1. A modified Fibonacci number sequence (1, 2, 3, 5, 8, 13, 20, 40, 100) is used to reflect the inherent uncertainty in estimating, especially large numbers (for example, 20, 40, 100, and so on).

Two good techniques for sizing stories are "estimating (planning) poker" and "white elephant sizing." You can find more information about these techniques on www.tastycupcakes.org, a community-run website that provides Agile games, techniques, and approaches.

The number of story points a team can achieve in an iteration is the team's *velocity*. A team's current velocity is used to estimate the amount of work that can be done in an iteration; it is not a measure of team performance. Velocity varies from team to team and is also dependent on the type of work. The ART's velocity is determined by adding all the team's velocities for the PI, which, again, is used to help plan future work.

Teams estimate their work in a standard way, using story points. In this way, features that require the work of multiple teams can be estimated in standardized story points, as a basis for meaningful economic decisions.

Team Backlog

User stories are maintained in the *team backlog*. There are several important concepts behind this apparently simple construct.

- It truly contains all things. If a thing is in there, it might get done. If it isn't, there's no chance it will be completed.
- It's a list of "want to do" items, not a commitment. Items can be estimated (preferable) or not, but neither case implies a specific time commitment as to when any of them will be done.
- It contains user stories and enablers, as well as improvement stories, which capture the results of the team's iteration retrospective.
- It has a single owner—the team's Product Owner. This protects the team from the problem of multiple stakeholders, each with potentially differing views of what's important.

The team backlog helps manage some of the complexity of Agile at scale by having a single source of work for each team. Figure 6-13 illustrates a view of the team backlog, with its three primary input sources.

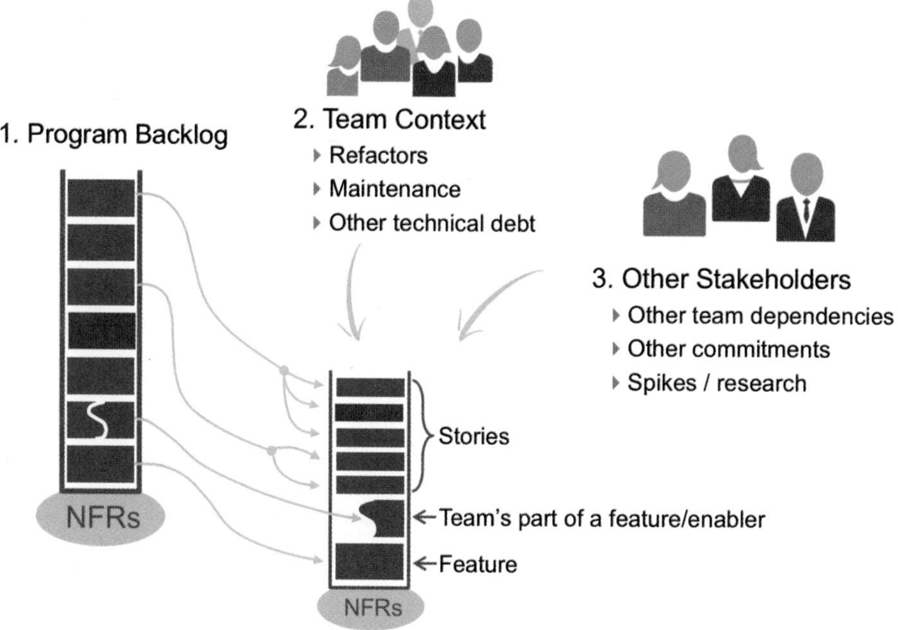

Figure 6-13. Expanded view of the team backlog

Balancing Types of Work with Capacity Allocation

Every team faces the problem of how to balance the backlog of internally facing work—maintenance, refactors, and technical debt—with the new user stories that deliver more immediate business value.

A total focus on new functionality may work for a bit, but this will be short-lived, as delivery velocity will be eventually slowed by a crushing load of technical debt.

This complicates the challenge of sequencing work, as the Product Owner is constantly trying to compare the value of unlike things, including defects, refactors, and new user stories.

To solve this problem, *capacity allocation* is used to determine how much effort should be applied to each type of activity for a given period, as Figure 6-14 illustrates.

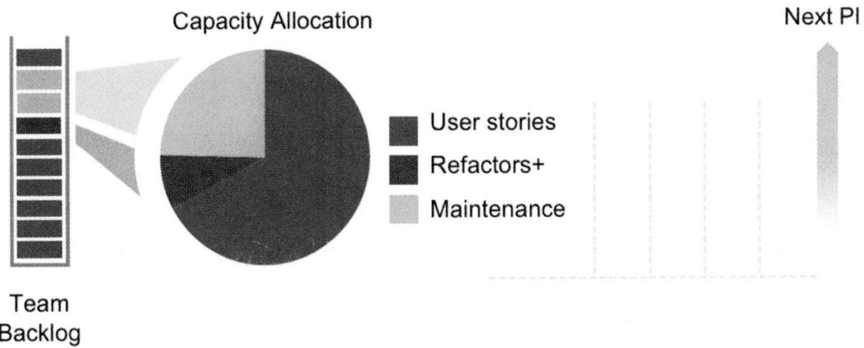

Figure 6-14. Team backlog capacity allocation

Capacity allocation helps alleviate velocity degradation due to technical debt, while keeping existing customers happy with a stream of new functionality. It can be applied flexibly by changing allocations at iteration or PI boundaries. Capacity allocation is also used for program and value stream backlogs.

Summary

This chapter gave an overview of the ART, which is a long-lived, self-organizing, team-of-Agile-teams and other stakeholders that defines new functionality and plans and delivers solutions together.

The key takeaways from this chapter are as follows:

- ARTs are typically virtual organizations that have all the people needed to define and deliver value. This breaks down the traditional functional silos that may exist prior to implementing SAFe.
- Agile teams power the train and use various Agile practices, based primarily on Scrum, XP, and kanban. Teams can develop software, hardware, or any combination needed.
- There are primary roles that help ensure successful execution of the ART: RTE, Product Management, and System Architect/Engineer.
- ARTs develop on cadence, which provides the rhythm for the train. However, releasing is a separate concern, and trains can release solutions at any time, such as on the PI boundary or more or less frequently than the PI cadence.

- Product Management provides the ART with a program vision that communicates the ongoing direction for the solution.
- Features are used to describe larger systems behaviors that fulfill the user's needs and are expressed in plain language in the Feature and Benefits (FAB) matrix. Features are developed and managed through the program kanban. Those that are approved are maintained and prioritized in the program backlog using Weighted Shortest Job First (WSJF).
- During PI planning, features are broken down into smaller user stories. As defined in XP, user stories are negotiable expressions of intended system behavior.
- The roadmap provides a longer-term view of what is required for the solution. It consists of a series of planned PIs with features and other milestones.

7

Planning a Program Increment

Future product development tasks can't be predetermined. Distribute planning and control to those who can understand and react to the end results.

—Michael Kennedy, *Product Development for the Lean Enterprise*

Overview 113
Preparation for the PI Planning Event 115
Day 1—Create and Review Draft Plans 118
Day 2—Finalize Plans and Commit 125
Summary 133

Overview

There is no magic in SAFe ... except maybe for PI planning.

—The authors

There is no other, more powerful event like PI planning in the Scaled Agile Framework (SAFe). It is the cornerstone of the Program Increment (PI)—which provides the cadence, or rhythm, for the Agile Release Train (ART).

It's amazing how much alignment and energy are created when there are 100 or so people all working together toward a common mission, vision, and shared purpose. Gaining that alignment in just two days can save weeks, if not months, of delays waiting on decisions, getting ahold of the right people, and coming to agreement via a flurry of emails.

More importantly, this event represents a critical and cultural milestone for the implementation of SAFe.

- This is the event where the teams come together periodically to better *define* and *design* the system that fulfills the vision and commit to near-term PI objectives.
- This is the event the ART uses to create, foster, and sustain a sense of shared mission, responsibility, cooperation, and collaboration.
- This is the event where the responsibility for planning moves from central authority to the teams who do the work. This sends a signal of true change from management that the teams are now empowered.
- This is the event that builds the social network that the ART depends on. After all, building large-scale, complex solutions is a social endeavor.

As shown in Figure 7-1, PI planning is a significant event, which occurs either face-to-face in a single location or in multiple face-to-face locations at the same time.

In Figure 7-1, there are teams in the United States planning at the same time with remote teams in India, using video conferencing. Leads from teams in Eastern Europe are attending the US event in person and are collaborating with their teams remotely. US-based Business Owners are sitting at the table in the middle, being accessible to everyone. Product Owners are with their teams in India.

Figure 7-1. A multisite PI planning event

Whenever possible, attendees include all members of the ART. After all, they are the ones doing the work, so they are the only ones who can design the system, plan, and then commit to the plan. Led by a facilitator (Release Train Engineer [RTE] or other), PI planning takes place over two days and occurs within the Innovation and Planning

(IP) iteration. That prevents the planning meeting from affecting the PI timebox or the capacity of other iterations in the PI.

When value streams have multiple ARTs, pre- and post-PI planning meetings are held to coordinate across individual ART planning sessions. For more information, refer to chapter 12, "Coordinating ARTs and Suppliers."

Preparation for the PI Planning Event

Such a significant event requires preparation, coordination, and communication. Product Management, Agile teams, System and Solution Architect/Engineering, the System Team, Business Owners, and other stakeholders must be well prepared.

Preparation for a successful event is required in three major areas:

1. Organizational readiness
2. Content readiness
3. Facility readiness

Organizational Readiness

Prior to planning, it's important to ensure that programs have reasonable strategic alignment among participants, stakeholders, and Business Owners. In other words, they all must agree on exactly what they are building. To address this, preparedness questions include the following:

- *Planning scope and context.* Is the scope of the planning process—product, system, or technology domain—understood?
- *Business alignment.* Is there reasonable agreement on priorities among the Business Owners?
- *Agile teams.* Does each team have dedicated developer and test resources and an identified Scrum Master and Product Owner?

For more on organizational readiness, see chapter 17, "Implementing Agile Release Trains."

Content Readiness

PI Planning starts with leadership providing shared vision and context. Presentation elements include the following:

- *Executive briefing.* A briefing by a senior executive or line-of-business owner, which defines the current business context.
- *Product/solution vision briefing.* Briefings prepared by Product Management, including the vision and top 10 features in the program backlog. To be ready, Product Managers develop acceptance criteria that can be used to establish that the feature meets its Definition of Done (DoD).
- *The architecture vision briefing.* The briefing prepared by the CTO, Enterprise Architect, and/or System Architect/Engineering communicates architectural strategy, as captured by new enablers and nonfunctional requirements.

Facility Readiness

Securing the physical space and technical infrastructure necessary to support the large number of attendees isn't trivial either, especially if there are remote participants. Considerations include the following:

- *Facility.* The planning venue must be large enough for all attendees. If there is not sufficient space for the teams to plan, breakout rooms—if close by—may be appropriate.
- *Technical and communications support.* Support people need to be identified and available during setup, testing, and the event itself.
- *Communication channels.* For distributed planning meetings, primary and secondary audio, video, and presentation channels must be available.

Role of the Facilitator

The PI planning event represents an alignment singularity—the point at which all must agree on what should and can be accomplished in the upcoming PI. As such, it can be a politically charged session, where stakeholders see the work physics of what they are asking for and teams objectively determine what they can do. Since imagination and market opportunity is largely unlimited, that means most ARTs are overloaded with expectations and excess Work in Process (WIP), which must be flushed out of the system. Bringing those expectations into alignment with reality can be a bit traumatic for many stakeholders.

To this end, the importance of an effectively facilitated event cannot be understated. Someone has to run an objective process such that the facts are surfaced and addressed.

That responsibility falls to the role of the facilitator. The facilitator organizes and guides PI planning to ensure that the group's objectives are met effectively, with good participation and full buy-in from everyone involved. The RTE may be a good candidate to be the facilitator. Often, they have experience as a program manager and may have the skills needed to plan and facilitate this type of event. In other cases, the RTE may bring in someone else to facilitate the event. This allows the RTE to focus on the teams and their needs and enables someone else to be committed to managing the timing and progress of the event, free of distraction and without a vested interest in the outcome.

The secret of good facilitation is an effective group process that flows—and with it flows the ART's ideas, solutions, and decisions. An agreed-to agenda helps. Over time, SAFe has evolved a standardized agenda, which works in most contexts, as shown in Figure 7-2.

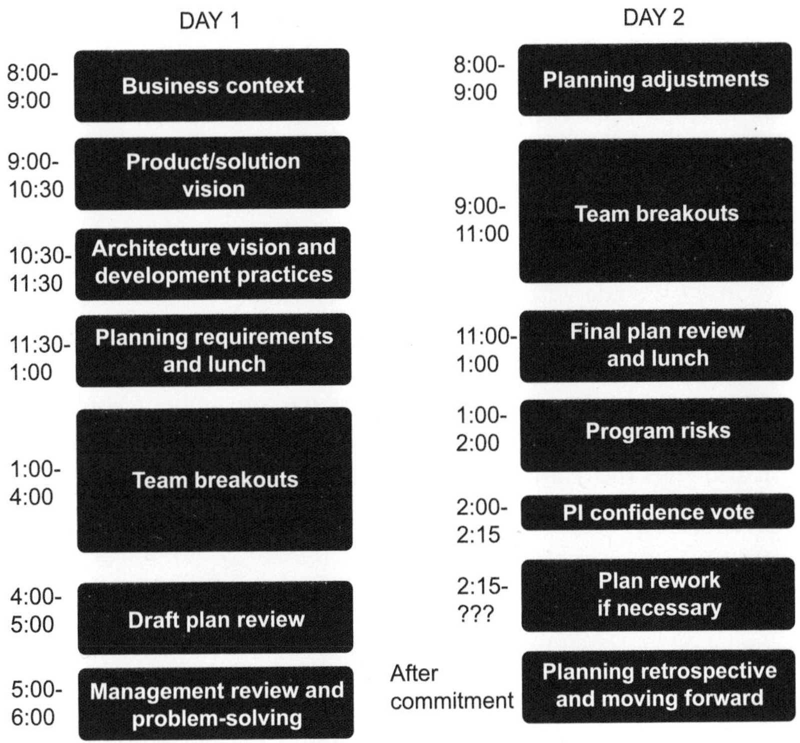

Figure 7-2. Standard PI planning meeting agenda

Day 1—Create and Review Draft Plans

Day 1 of the event begins with the facilitator reviewing the objectives and agenda, working agreements, planning rules and expectations, and other logistics. The facilitator also presents the upcoming calendar of events, including the iteration and release cadence, future PI planning dates, scheduled releases, holidays, milestones, or other events that may affect planning objectives or team capacity.

Business Context

Next, a senior executive or line-of-business owner provides the business context for the planning session. This may include the following:

- Discussions of current business performance and strategy
- Measures of customer satisfaction
- Organizational developments and updates to operating plans
- Strengths, Weaknesses, Opportunities, Threats (SWOT) analysis

This discussion *sets the tone* for the PI planning session and can drive the motivation and enthusiasm for the PI and the solution being developed. It's a chance to share success stories, understand the market risks, and rally the troops around a set of challenges to overcome.

The presenter may conclude with an overview of strategic themes and business objectives for the upcoming periods.

Since this is an opportunity to align all development teams under a common vision, meeting organizers should reach as high into the organization as possible for this opening speaker. It also gives the teams a chance to meet and interact with a senior executive who drives the business vision.

Product/Solution Vision

Next, Product Management presents the current vision, the objectives for the upcoming PI, and feature priorities. If there are multiple product managers, each may need some time to present the vision and top features for their particular area of the solution.

Architecture Vision and Development Practices

In this session, the System Architect/Engineering presents the vision for the architecture. This may include descriptions of new architectural epics for common infrastructure, any large-scale refactors under consideration, and system-level Nonfunctional Requirements (NFRs).

In addition, as Agile puts extreme pressure on development practices and infrastructure, a technical leader usually guides the discussion about changes to standard development practices, and new tools and techniques for built-in quality practices for the Definition of Done (DoD).

Team Planning Breakouts

The next session is the longest and most critical of the event. At this point, the teams break out into separate meetings and draft their initial plan to achieve the objectives of the PI. In this session, the teams iterate through a process that proceeds roughly as follows:

- Meet with product managers and other stakeholders to better understand features and their priorities.
- Estimate the velocity the teams will have during each iteration.
- Brainstorm and identify all the stories needed to meet the input objectives and prioritized features of the PI. (Note: There's no time for story elaboration or acceptance criteria. Too much detail bogs down the process and creates false precision and excessive WIP.)
- Understand the impact of architectural initiatives on the plan, and identify stories for those initiatives as well.
- Incorporate improvement backlog items that came out of previous team retrospectives and the PI's Inspect and Adapt (I&A).
- Identify dependencies within the team and on other teams.
- Estimate the stories and place them on iterations in order until capacity is exhausted.
- Capture a backlog of things that can't be accomplished in the time period and will have to be postponed.

During this process, teams will consult with Product Managers, System Architect/ Engineering, the System Team, User Experience, and other teams. Their goal is to understand the scope and priorities necessary for infrastructure development, resolve dependencies, and understand the potential for reuse of common code. *It's an intense and active time.*

Plans are created using flipchart paper and story cards (or stickies) so that they're visible for all to see. Teams create one sheet per iteration, another for team PI objectives, and one to capture program risks and impediments. A standard plan might appear as shown in Figure 7-3.

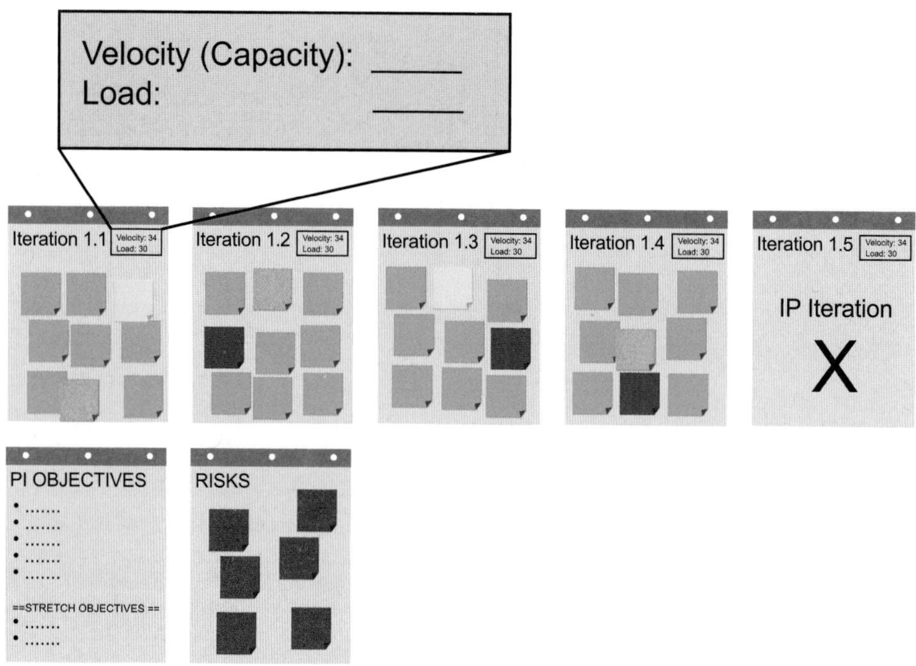

Figure 7-3. Team PI planning deliverables

Note that the IP iteration should not contain any user stories, even though the teams may identify other stories dedicated to such specialty tasks as load and performance testing, system documentation, and other activities.

As shown in Figure 7-4, teams use color-coded sticky notes to provide visibility into the number of backlog items dedicated to certain activity types, such as user stories, maintenance, and enablers.

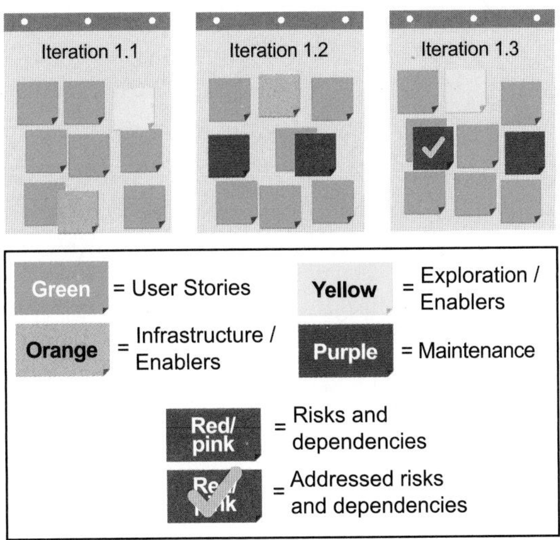

Figure 7-4. Color-coded stickies categorize work items

Starting Fast with Capacity-Based Planning

In the first PI planning session, many teams will not have used Scrum in the past and will, therefore, not have a starting velocity to plan with. In this case, teams simply start with eight points per iteration for each full-time technical contributor. They then identify a story that will take about one day of work, and estimate it at one story point. Other stories are estimated relative to that one. Teams split any story larger than eight points.

This accomplishes two things.

1. Assures that most teams have a reasonable number of right-sized stories in an iteration
2. Normalizes estimation across teams. This is important for feature and epic-level estimating and for conversion into cost estimates where necessary

Note: If teams already have velocities, a quick check will probably discover that they are already mostly normalized. Small teams will have about 30, really big teams 50–60. If this is not the case, the facilitator may want to have some teams adjust accordingly so that program velocities make sense. While there may be some emotion around the adjustment, just remind the teams that they are unit-less numbers, so there can be no harm in making an adjustment to make it easier to manage the economics of the program.

Hourly Planning Checkpoints

During the team breakouts, the facilitator holds an hourly Scrum of Scrums (SoS) checkpoint to keep the planning on track. In this short stand-up meeting, the RTE and the Scrum Masters from each team meet to review planning status using a checklist. Figure 7-5 shows an example. The SoS is often followed by a "meet after" for any problems that need more discussion.

	A	B	C	D	E	F	G	H	I	J	K	L
3	**Scrum of Scrums Check-In** **PI Planning Radiator**	Team 1	Team 2	Team 3	Team 4	Team 5	Team 6	Team 7	Team 8	Team 9	Team 10	Team 11
5	**Day 1, Check-In 1: Getting Started**											
6	Do you understand the planning requirements?	y	y	y	y	y	y	y				
7	Do you know who your team is for the whole PI?	y	y	y	y	y	y	n				
8	Is your working space setup?	y	y	y	y	y	y	y				
9	Do you have a Product Owner & Scrum Master?	y	y	y	y	y	y	n				
10	Do you have access to the team members and stakeholders you need?	n	y	y	y	y	y	n				
11	Do you understand (and can you find) the vision that drives your backlog?	y	y	y	y	y	y	y				
12	Have you identified the velocity for each Iteration in your PI?	n	n	y	n	n	y	y				
13	Do you understand the architectural context, and who to go to for questions?	y	n	y	y	y	y	y				
14	Do you understand which resources are shared (e.g., UX, Training, and Documentation) and who to go to for questions?	y	y	y	y	y	y	y				
15	Do you understand the role of the System Team and DevOps, and who to go to for questions?	y	y	y	y	y	y	n				
16	**Day 1, Check-In 2: Iteration Planning Progress**											

Radiator Day 1 | Radiator Day 2 | Distributed Team Check-In Times

Figure 7-5. Example Scrum of Scrums planning radiator

Draft Plan Review

At the designated time, the group reconvenes in the plenary session to review each of the plans. Many plans will be incomplete. However, the review is still held on time so that the groups can see the planning process and take an initial look at the assumptions, dependencies, and objectives that their counterpart teams are working on. Each team presentation is strictly timeboxed at five to ten minutes per team, based on the size of the ART. Business Owners should be present throughout.

In addition, other executives, managers, and key stakeholders in the company may be invited to this portion of the event. This allows program visibility and a shared business and development context. Managers may have input or adjustments to the plan based on their contribution and perspective. In turn, the development teams may also have dependencies on these functions, for example, marketing, sales, customers, distribution, deployment, and IT.

Each team presents using the agenda shown in Figure 7-6.

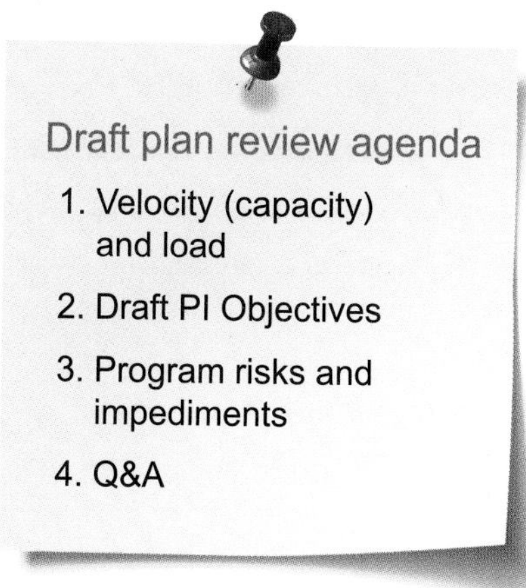

Figure 7-6. Sample draft plan review agenda

Typically, there will be a few minutes left for Questions and Answers (Q&A), in which the facilitator has to walk the line between abruptly cutting off important discussions about dependencies, trade-offs, and misunderstandings to keep the sessions within the allotted timebox.

The session proceeds until all teams have presented their draft plans, even at the risk of exceeding the time allocated. For most attendees, this is the end of day 2.

Management Review and Problem-Solving Meeting

Some attendees, however, remain for additional, important work. Specifically, management and some team leads meet to make adjustments to scope and objectives based on the first day of planning. It's likely that there will be far more work than the teams can possibly accomplish in the PI timebox. Many programs are over-scoped by 50–100 percent, and that will be obvious now. Resource constraints, bottlenecks, excessive dependencies, and team dynamics may also pose problems.

If these issues are allowed to persist into the second day, day 2 may come out badly for one of these two reasons:

1. The process will not converge on agreed-to PI objectives because of these unresolved issues.
2. Convergence will appear to happen, but the PI is at great risk because real, underlying problems have not been addressed.

To this end, some set of managers, Business Owners, Product Managers, System Architects/Engineers, Product Owners, and Scrum Masters must meet to address the larger challenges identified in the draft review session. Figure 7-7 shows some common questions asked by the facilitator.

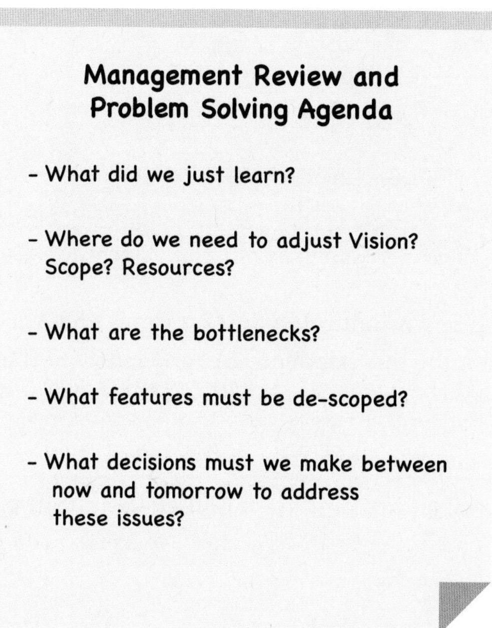

Figure 7-7. Common questions during the management review meeting

The facilitator keeps key stakeholders together as long as necessary to make the decisions needed to increase the likelihood of a successful PI. Resolving these issues may involve cuts to scope, rethinking prior commitments and accepting that some critical milestones will not be met. It may become necessary to rethink team assignments or move entire features from one team to another. Any final decisions should be carefully and clearly summarized, as they will inform the next day's planning session.

Day 2—Finalize Plans and Commit

In the opening session of day 2, the facilitator reviews the agenda and the objectives. Figure 7-8 shows a more detailed version of the day 2 agenda.

8:00-
9:00
Planning adjustments
Planning adjustments made based on previous day's management meeting
9:00-
11:00
Team breakouts
1 2
3 4
Teams develop final plans and refine risks and impediments
Business Owners circulate and assign business value to team objectives
11:00-
1:00
Final plan review and lunch
Teams present final plans, risks, and impediments
1:00-
2:00
Program risks
Remaining program-level risks are discussed and ROAMed
2:00-
2:15
PI confidence vote
Team and program confidence vote
2:15-
???
Plan rework if necessary
1 2
3 4
If necessary, planning continues until commitment is achieved
After commitment
Planning retrospective and moving forward
Retrospective
Moving Forward
Final Instructions

Figure 7-8. Example PI planning day 2 agenda

During day 2, the program must commit to a plan of action that fits the capacity of the teams, while delivering maximum value in the next PI timebox.

Planning Adjustments

Based on the previous day's management review and problem-solving meeting, planning adjustments are discussed. Here are some examples:

- Changes to priorities
- Adjustments to plan and milestones
- Changes to scope
- Movement of people or teams

A senior manager (or perhaps the management team as a group) takes responsibility for describing the issues and planning adjustments that were agreed to during the review meeting at the end of day 1.

Team Breakouts Continue

Based on the new knowledge (and a good night's sleep), teams work to create their final plans.

- Teams finalize their iteration plans and PI objectives.
- Teams establish stretch objectives to provide the guard band (buffer) needed for predictability.
- Business Owners circulate and assign business value to PI objectives from low (one) to high (ten).
- Teams consolidate program risks, impediments, and dependencies.
- Teams ensure that the program board (covered later in the chapter) is updated with all features and cross-team dependencies.

And, as with day 1, the planning SoS convenes hourly to ensure that the teams and plans are ready for the final review.

Team PI Objectives

Toward the end of the planning session, the teams will be focused on negotiating the final PI objectives with Product Management and Business Owners.

Team PI objectives are brief summaries of what the teams are prepared to commit to during the PI, *expressed in business terms*. Many of the objectives will be based on features from the backlog, which were described in the day 1 vision briefing. Others, however, may represent infrastructure or architectural objectives the team must achieve. Still others may be a summary of a set of features, milestones, releases, or even less tangible items that remain worthy of notice and attention at this top-level output of the PI planning process.

"SAFe's use of PI objectives provides a unique tool to create an immediate feedback loop from the teams back to the business owners, allowing a quick validation of the teams' grasp of the desired outcomes. In short, we give the teams the following challenge:

"Can you concisely convey, in words the business owner understands, the essence of the value sought by implementing this set of features?"

"By asking the teams to summarize the intent and the outcomes they believe the business owner wants to achieve, we close the loop of understanding and drive crucial conversations that expose these misunderstandings. This in turn enables a much tighter form of alignment that transcends the written language of the feature to be amplified by the tacit understanding gained between the team and the business owner." [1]

Stretch Objectives

The goal of the entire session is to commit to a near-term set of objectives. But gaining a meaningful commitment can be tricky. It's R&D after all. But without it, the business can't plan, even for the short term.

Applying "stretch objectives" helps immensely by providing a guard band for the reliability of the PI. These objectives are included in the planning process (that is, stories have been defined and included in the plan for these objectives), but the stretch objectives are *not* included in the PI commitment. They also give management an early warning of objectives that the ART may not be able to deliver. The expectation is that teams will meet most of their committed objectives. This gives teams the flexibility they need to commit to a subset of the planned objectives, without too much risk in the total scope of the work.

And one must constantly keep in mind that stretch objectives are used to identify what can be variable within the scope of a plan. *Stretch objectives are not the way for stakeholders to load the teams with more work than they can possibly do.* It's simply used to identify objectives that the teams can't commit to because there is too much risk or uncertainty.

Establish Business Value

The primary evaluation tool of the ART is a predictability *measure* that tracks the percent of business value achieved for each PI objective in the plan. To execute this, the business value of each objective is set by the Business Owners toward the end of the PI planning session, as shown in Figure 7-9.

1. Eric Willeke, "The Role of PI Objectives," http://dev.scaledagileframework.com/the-role-of-pi-objectives/

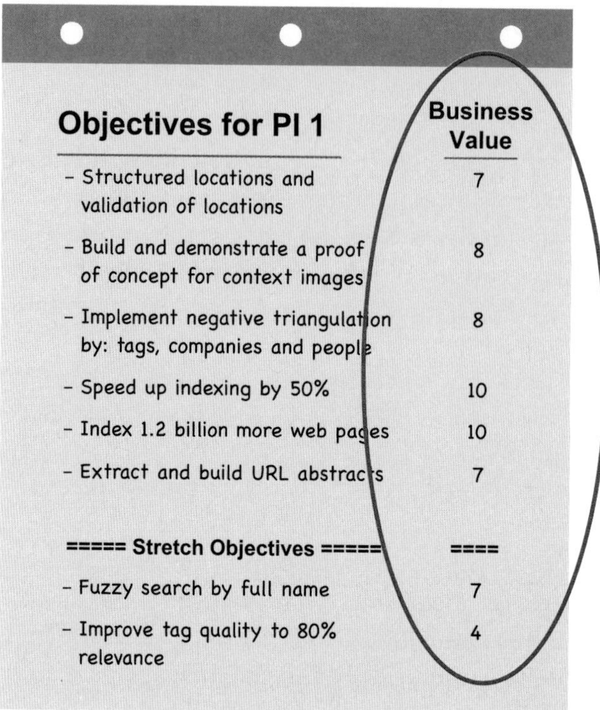

Objectives for PI 1
Business Value
- Structured locations and validation of locations
7
- Build and demonstrate a proof of concept for context images
8
- Implement negative triangulation by: tags, companies and people
8
- Speed up indexing by 50%
10
- Index 1.2 billion more web pages
10
- Extract and build URL abstracts
7
===== Stretch Objectives =====
====
- Fuzzy search by full name
7
- Improve tag quality to 80% relevance
4

Figure 7-9. Setting business value for team PI objectives

Naturally, not all objectives deliver equal value, and Business Owners are likely to assign higher numbers on externally visible objectives than they would on infrastructure accomplishments and architectural epics. That's as it should be. And yet, mature Business Owners know that these technical concerns will also increase the velocity of the teams in producing future business value. So, placing some business value on those items shows maturity and support for the teams.

As the road after PI planning takes its inevitable twists and turns, having objectives ranked by business value guides the teams to make trade-offs and minor scope adjustments in ways that deliver the maximum business value.

Program Board

Typically, a program board is created by the RTE in advance of planning and is updated by the teams during planning. The board highlights the feature delivery dates, milestones, and dependencies among teams and with other ARTs, as shown in Figure 7-10.

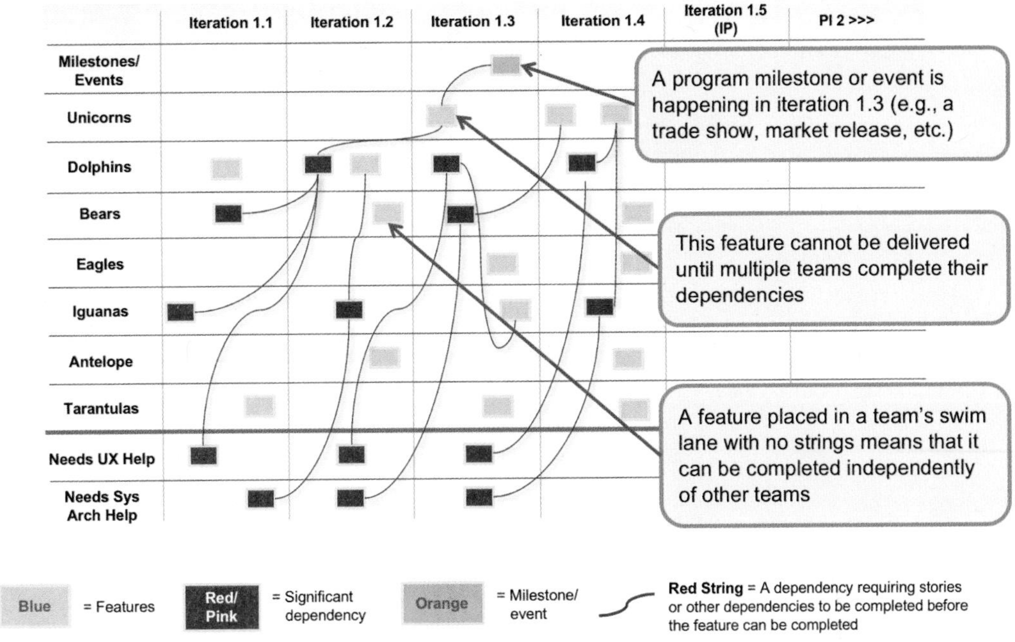
Iteration 1.1
Iteration 1.2
Iteration 1.3
Iteration 1.4
Iteration 1.5 (IP)
PI 2 >>>
Milestones/ Events
Unicorns
Dolphins
Bears
Eagles
Iguanas
Antelope
Tarantulas
Needs UX Help
Needs Sys Arch Help
A program milestone or event is happening in iteration 1.3 (e.g., a trade show, market release, etc.)
This feature cannot be delivered until multiple teams complete their dependencies
A feature placed in a team's swim lane with no strings means that it can be completed independently of other teams
Blue
= Features
Red/ Pink
= Significant dependency
Orange
= Milestone/ event
Red String = A dependency requiring stories or other dependencies to be completed before the feature can be completed

Figure 7-10. Program board example

Final Plan Review

This is a repeat of the review session from the day before, but by now, the teams will have completed their plans.

- All iterations are planned (except for the IP iteration). Work fits into the time available.
- Out-of-scope work has been identified on a backlog sheet.
- Business Owners/Product Managers have reviewed and agreed to plan and objectives.
- Teams have a final set of PI objectives (including stretch) with business value assigned by Business Owners.
- Teams have also identified all critical dates and have updated the program board with milestones and features.
- Teams have identified the key risks and impediments outside of their local control but have the potential to cause the team to fail to meet the objectives.

Figure 7-11 shows a sample agenda for the final walk-through.

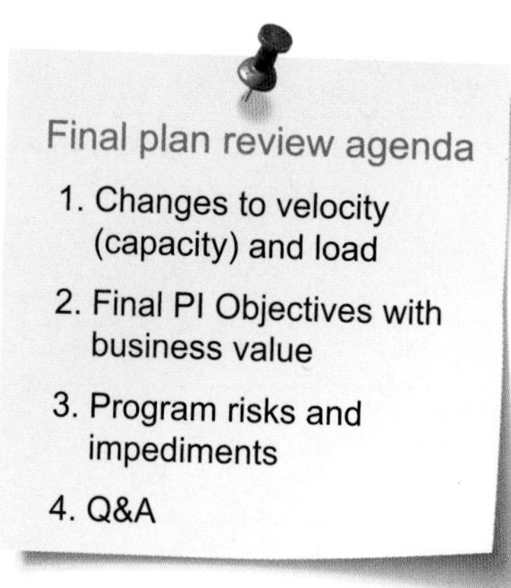

Figure 7-11. Final plan review agenda

During each team's presentation, the facilitator is looking for agreement within and across the teams, as well as among the Business Owners, on the feasibility and appropriateness of the plan. Questions from reviewers are asked and answered.

At the end of each team's time slot, each team states their remaining risks and impediments. But there is no attempt to resolve them in this brief period. If the plan is acceptable to the Business Owners, the team brings their team PI objective sheet and remaining program risks sheet to the front of the room. This allows everyone to see the summary of PI objectives unfold in real time. This process continues until all teams have presented their plans.

Addressing Program Risks and Impediments

Even though the plans are now complete, there is still work to do. During the planning, teams were asked to identify the most critical program risks and impediments—the very issues that could affect their ability to meet their agreed-to objectives. Addressing them is critical, as they typically represent things that—left unaddressed—may interfere with the success of the next PI.

ROAMing the Risks

By now, the teams will have addressed the risks that are under their local control. Otherwise, they couldn't be responsible for their own plan. The remaining risks and impediments will need to be addressed in a broader, management context. To that end, every program-level risk identified by the team will be addressed in front of the full group. Each item is discussed until it can be categorized in one of the following ROAM categories:

- *Resolved*. If, after discussion, the teams agree that an issue is no longer a material concern, it moves to resolved.
- *Owned*. If an item cannot be resolved in the course of the meeting, someone takes ownership. The item is then moved to the owned sheet, where its owner is recorded.
- *Accepted*. Some risks or impediments are potential occurrences (for example, a delayed vendor delivery, excessive emergency maintenance requirements) that must simply be acknowledged and accepted. If these actually occur, then the ART will likely not meet all elements of the commitment.
- *Mitigated*. Often, the teams can develop a plan to mitigate the impact of a risk item such that it should not materially impact the outcome. If so, a mitigation plan is identified.

The Commitment

After all risks have been moved to a ROAM category, the "backlog of risks and impediments" sheet is empty. The PI objectives are apparent and visible in the front of the group.

Now is the time to ask to ask the teams how confident they are that they will be able to meet the objectives of this PI. The teams vote using a "fist of five," where each finger represents a level of confidence.

1. No confidence; will not happen
2. Little confidence; probably will not happen
3. Good confidence; the team should be able to meet the objectives
4. High confidence; should happen
5. Very high confidence; will happen

If the average is three or more fingers, management should accept the commitment and move forward. If the average is less than three fingers, then there's still work to do. Scope and resources must be adjusted again, and planning continues—that day, into the evening, or even rolling over into the next morning—until a commitment is reached. At this point, alignment and commitment are more valuable than strict adherence to a timebox.

A Commitment in Two Parts

Achieving a reasonable commitment in the face of so many unknowns, some of which are outside the control of the teams, is not a trivial thing. After all, there is inherent risk and uncertainty in research and development. Leadership must create a culture wherein risk-taking and commitment are both part of the norm. Given this context, when teams do their confidence vote, all can interpret that as a commitment, but this commitment has two parts.

1. Teams commit to do everything reasonable to meet the agreed-to objectives.
2. In the event that, over time, facts change or new learning occurs that indicates that achieving the committed objectives is no longer achievable, teams agree to escalate immediately so that management is informed and corrective action can be taken.

In this way, teams know that they can and should take reasonable risks and also commit to an outcome, knowing that management understands and appreciates the risks and is fully supportive of the trust, transparency, and integrity that this model engenders.

Planning Retrospective

The next session is a brief retrospective of the PI planning session led by the facilitator. Figure 7-12 shows a simple format to capture the results, along with a few example comments.

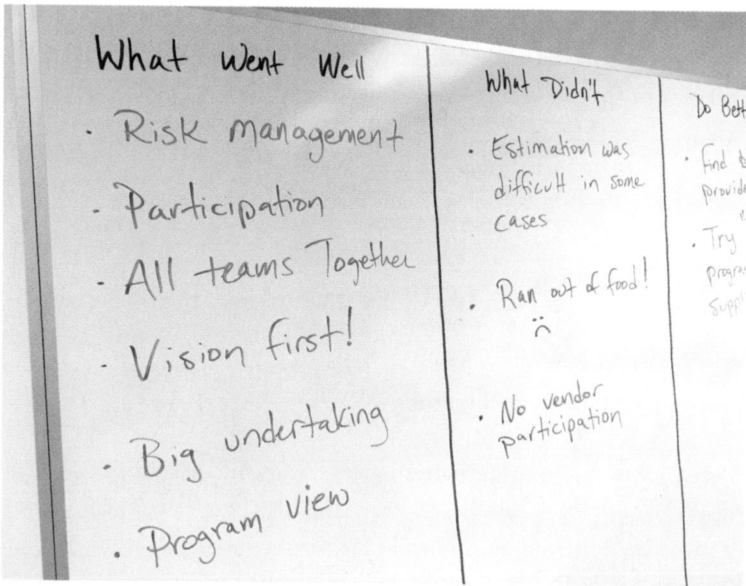

Figure 7-12. Method for capturing results during planning retrospective

This session should last no longer than 15–20 minutes. Near the end of that timebox, the facilitator may ask the teams to rank the items in the third column (what we could do better next time) to focus on process improvements that can be taken before the next planning session.

Moving Forward and Final Instructions to Teams

The last session is typically a discussion about the next steps, along with final instructions to the teams. This might include the following:

- Capturing the team PI objectives and user stories in the Agile project management tool
- Reviewing team and program calendars
- Reviewing iteration planning meeting locations

After planning is done, the RTE summarizes the individual team PI objectives into a set of program PI objectives.

Summary

This chapter provided an overview of the PI planning process, which is a cadence-based, face-to-face planning event that serves as the heartbeat of the ART. It is integral and essential to SAFe.

The key takeaways from this chapter are as follows:

- Preparation for a successful PI planning event is required in three major areas: organizational readiness, content readiness, and facility readiness.
- PI planning delivers many business benefits, which include establishing face-to-face communication, aligning development to the business and architectural vision, identifying dependencies, matching demand to capacity, and accelerating decision-making.
- The facilitator, often the RTE, organizes and guides PI planning to ensure that the ART's objectives are met effectively, with clear thinking, good participation, and full buy-in from everyone.
- The first day of planning includes establishing the business context and planning requirements, creating draft plans, and concluding with a management review and problem-solving meeting.

- The second day of planning includes discussion of planning adjustments, finalizing plans and establishing business value, ROAMing the risks, approving the final plan and committing to the PI objectives to end the session.
- The key outputs of PI planning are a program board, which highlights the feature delivery dates, milestones, and dependencies, and PI plans and a committed set of PI objectives.

8

Executing a Program Increment

Vision without execution is hallucination.

—Thomas Edison

Overview 135
The Iteration Cycle 136
Building Quality In 140
Improving Team Flow with Kanban 143
Managing ART Flow 146
System Demo 154
Innovation and Planning 154
Inspect and Adapt 156
Summary 156

Overview

The Big Picture illustrates how the Agile Release Train (ART) teams and stakeholders continuously deliver value in a series of Program Increments (PIs).

As we described in the previous chapter, each PI starts with a planning session and is followed by four (the default number)[1] execution iterations.

Each PI concludes with an Innovation and Planning (IP) iteration. During each PI, team and program activities help "keep the train on the tracks," as shown in Figure 8-1.

1. Although this is the default pattern, there is no fixed rule for how many iterations are in a PI. Experience has shown that PIs with a duration of between eight and twelve weeks work best, with a bias toward the shorter end of the range.

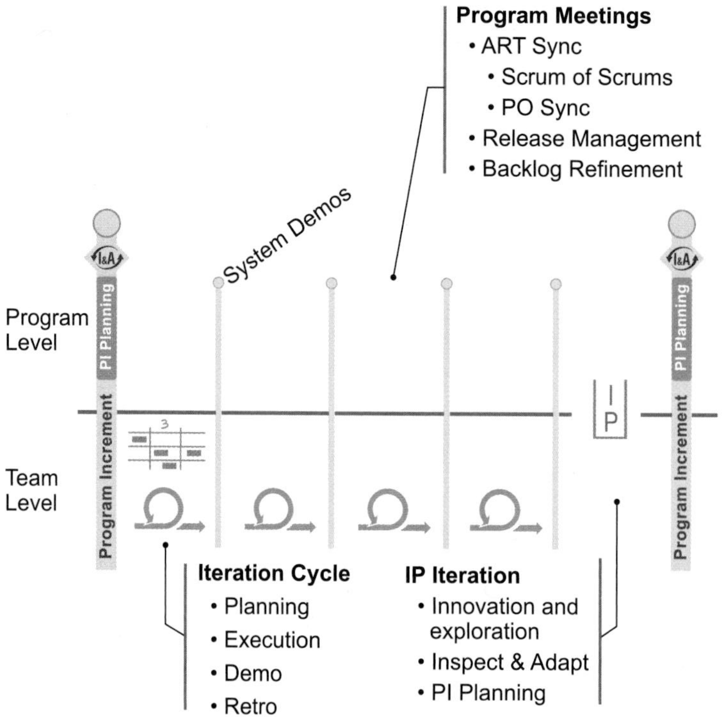

Figure 8-1. Program execution events and meetings

In this chapter, we'll describe the typical Scrum cycle first and then address how to improve flow in Scrum using kanban techniques. Then we describe the SAFe kanban model, for systems teams and others who operate with more of a response mandate. Even then, we'll apply cadence and synchronization to assure alignment and full system integration with other teams on the train. Finally, we describe the other program-level meetings and events, concluding with Inspect and Adapt (I&A).

The Iteration Cycle

Most teams use Scrum, which has a routine set of activities, including iteration planning, execution, review, and retrospective.

Iteration Planning

Iteration planning is a standard and well-defined Scrum activity. In the Scaled Agile Framework (SAFe), it also involves refining the details and adjusting the initial iteration plans that were created during the PI planning event.

Attendees include the Product Owner, Scrum Master, Development Team, and other stakeholders. The meeting is timeboxed to a maximum of four hours (for a two-week sprint). Planning inputs include the following:

- The team and program PI objectives
- Stories that were identified during PI planning
- Existing stories from the team's backlog, defects, enablers, and so on

The Product Owner presents the highest-priority stories. The team discusses implementation options, technical issues, Nonfunctional Requirements (NFRs), and dependencies. The team elaborates acceptance criteria, estimates the effort to complete the story, and puts it in the iteration backlog.

When the team reaches the limit of its velocity for that period, it summarizes the stories into a set of iteration goals and adjusts as needed to achieve the larger purpose of making progress toward the PI objectives.

The output of iteration planning includes the following:

- The iteration backlog, consisting of the stories and acceptance criteria the team committed to in the iteration
- Iteration goals—the business and technical objectives of the iteration
- A commitment to the work needed to achieve the iteration goals

Figure 8-2 shows that the team's commitment has two parts, which helps maintain a healthy balance between commitment and adaptability.

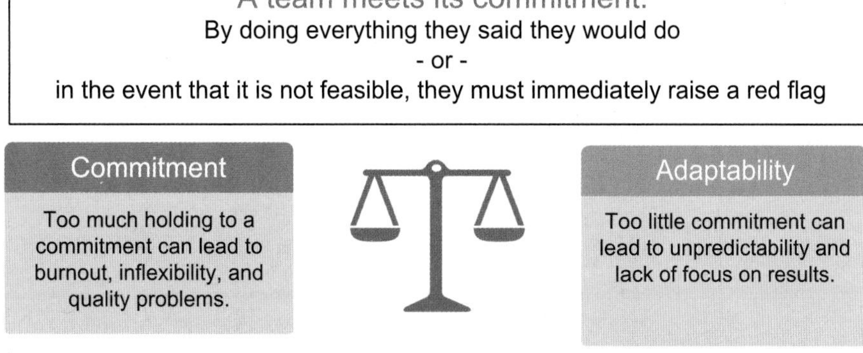

Figure 8-2. Balancing commitment and adaptability

Iteration Execution

After planning, the team starts implementing new user stories, each of which creates a new baseline of functionality. Teams avoid "waterfalling" the iteration by ensuring that they are completing full define-build-test cycles for each story, as Figure 8-3 illustrates.

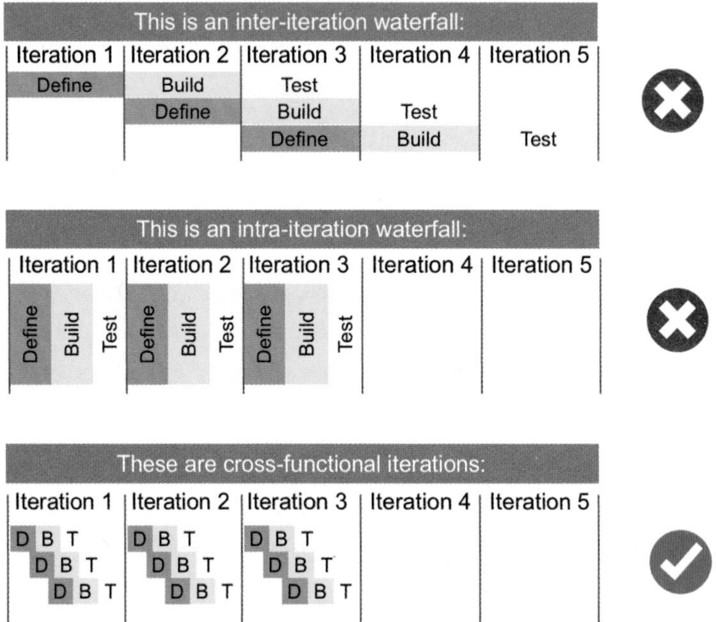

Figure 8-3. Delivering full stories serially avoids the mini-waterfall

Further, implementing stories in thin, vertical slices is the foundation for fine-grained incremental development, integration, and testing, as shown in Figure 8-4.

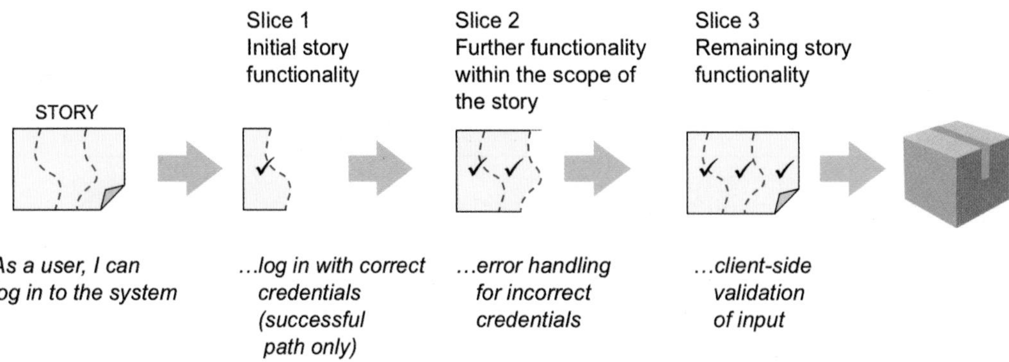

Figure 8-4. Implementing stories in vertical slices

This approach enables the shortest possible feedback cycle and allows the teams to integrate and test a small increment of the working system.

Tracking Progress

Iteration tracking provides visibility into the status of the stories, defects, and other activities that the team is working on. Most teams use a Big Visible Information Radiator (BVIR) or "storyboard" such as that illustrated in Figure 8-5.

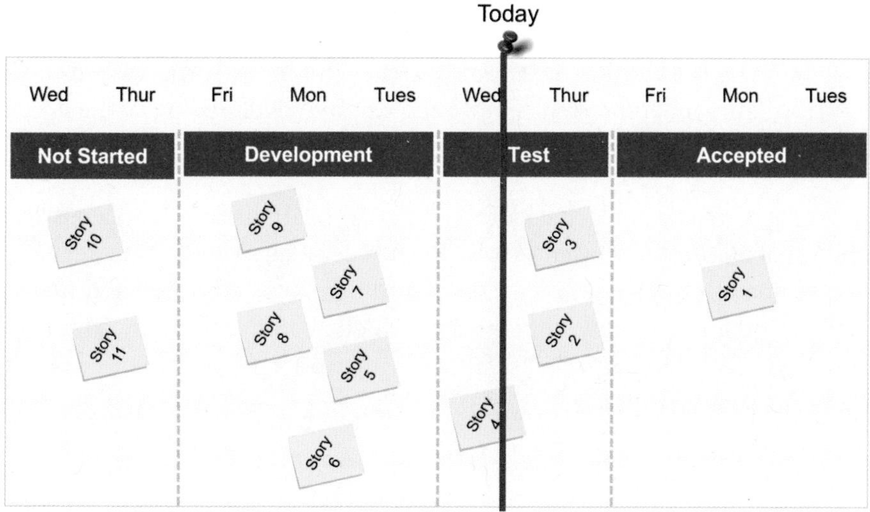

Figure 8-5. A simple storyboard

Daily Stand-Up

Each day, the team holds a Daily Stand-Up (DSU) to coordinate their work. The standard format is for each team member to speak and address the following questions:

- What stories did I work on yesterday to help the team meet the iteration goal?
- What stories will I be able to complete today?
- What is getting in my way of meeting the iteration goal?

The DSU is strictly timeboxed to 15 minutes. The meeting is most effective when held in front of a BVIR or kanban board (covered later in the chapter). The DSU is not a management reporting or problem-solving meeting. Rather, it's a tool to help team members identify issues and address dependencies. It is often followed by a "meet-after" for some attendees, whereby time is dedicated to address any issues raised.

Iteration Review

Each iteration concludes with an iteration review to demo the increment and adapt the backlog as needed. During the review, the team assesses whether it has met the iteration goals, and reviews any other metrics it has agreed to analyze, including velocity. The data provides some of the context for the retrospective that follows. Another aspect of the review is to show any working stories that have not yet been demonstrated to the Product Owner and other stakeholders and to get feedback. Teams demo every story, spike, refactor, and new NFR.

The preparation for the review begins during iteration planning, where teams start thinking about how they will demo the stories they are committing to. This facilitates planning and alignment and fosters a more thorough understanding of the needed functionality for the increment.

The review starts with a quick check of the iteration goals and then proceeds with a walk-through of all the committed stories. Each is demoed in a working, tested system. Spikes are demoed through a presentation of findings. After all completed stories are demoed, the team reflects on any stories that were not completed and why. This discussion usually uncovers impediments or risks, false assumptions, changing priorities, estimating inaccuracies, or overcommitment.

Iteration Retrospective

After the iteration review, the whole team participates in a retrospective to reflect on the work just completed and to develop a plan for improvements in the next iteration. The Scrum Master facilitates and applies tools and processes for data collection and problem-solving. The team reviews the results of improvement stories identified in the prior retrospective and identifies new stories for improvement in the next iteration. One simple format is a simple analysis of *what went well, what didn't,* and *what to do better next time.*

Building Quality In

Built-in quality is one of the four core values of SAFe. The enterprise's ability to deliver new functionality with the *fastest sustainable lead time* and to be able to react to rapidly changing business environments is dependent on solution quality. But built-in quality is not unique to SAFe. Rather, it is a core principle of the Lean-Agile mindset, where it helps avoid the cost of delays associated with recall, rework, and defect fixing.

The Agile Manifesto is focused on quality as well: "Continuous attention to technical excellence and good design enhances agility."[2]

The following sections summarize recommended practices for achieving built-in quality.

Software Practices

SAFe's software quality practices—many of which are inspired by Extreme Programming (XP)—help Agile software teams ensure that the solutions they build are high quality and adaptable to change. The collaborative nature of these practices, along with a focus on frequent validation, creates an emergent culture in which engineering and craftsmanship are key business enablers. These include the following:

- *Continuous Integration (CI).* This is the practice of merging the code from each developer's workspace into a single main branch of code, multiple times per day. This lessens the risk of deferred integration issues and their impact on system quality and program predictability. Teams perform local integration at least daily. But to confirm that the work is progressing as intended, full system-level integration should be achieved at least one or two times per iteration.
- *Test-first.* Consists of a set of practices that encourages teams to think deeply about intended system behavior before implementing code. In Test-Driven Development (TDD), developers write an automated unit test first, run the test to observe the failure, and then write the minimum code necessary to pass the test. In Acceptance Test-Driven Development (ATDD), story and feature acceptance criteria are expressed as automated acceptance tests, which can be run continuously to ensure continued conformance as the system evolves.
- *Refactoring.* Refactoring is "a disciplined technique for restructuring an existing body of code, altering its internal structure without changing its external behavior."[3] A key enabler of emergent design, refactoring is essential to Agile. To maintain system robustness, teams continuously refactor code in a series of small steps, providing a solid foundation for future development.
- *Pair work.* Some teams follow *pair programming*, but that may be too extreme for many. More generally, pair work may couple developers and testers on a story. Still others prefer more spontaneous pairing, with developers collaborating for critical code segments, refactoring of legacy code, development of interface definition, and system-level integration challenges.

---

2. http://agilemanifesto.org/principles.html
3. Martin Fowler, *Refactoring: Improving the Design of Existing Code* (Addison-Wesley Professional, 1999).

- *Collective ownership.* This practice "encourages everyone to contribute to all segments of the solution. Any developer can change any line of code to add functionality, fix bugs, improve designs, or refactor."[4] It's particularly critical as big systems have big code bases, and it's less likely that the original developer is still on the team or program. And even if they are, waiting for "someone else" to make a change is a handoff and a certain delay.
- *Agile architecture.* This is a set of principles and practices (see SAFe *Architectural Runway* and *Principles of Agile Architecture* guidance) that support the active evolution of the design and architecture of a system, *concurrent with* the implementation of new business functionality. With this approach, the architecture of a system evolves over time while simultaneously supporting the needs of current users. It avoids Big Design Up Front (BDUF) and the starting and stopping of phase-gated development.

Firmware and Hardware Practices

With respect to firmware and hardware, the quality goal is the same, but the physics and economics—and therefore the practices—are somewhat different. There, errors and unproven assumptions in firmware and hardware development can introduce a much higher cost of change and rework over time, as illustrated in Figure 8-6.

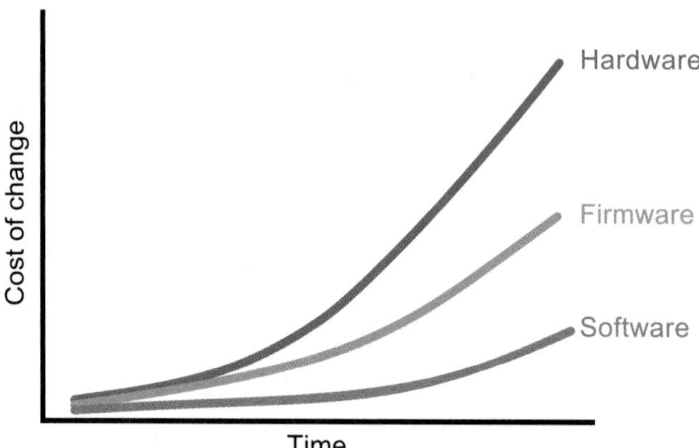

Figure 8-6. Relative cost of change over time for software, firmware, and hardware[5]

4. www.extremeprogramming.org/rules/collective.html
5. www.innolution.com/blog/agile-in-a-hardware-firmware-environment-draw-the-cost-of-change-curve

This higher cost of change drives developers of complex systems to a number of practices that assure quality during solution development.

- *Model-based systems engineering.* This is the application of modeling and tools to the requirements, design, analysis, and verification activities in solution development. It provides a cost-effective way to learn about system characteristics prior to and during development. It helps manage the complexity and cost of large-system documentation.
- *Set-based design.* This is a practice that maintains multiple requirements and design options for a longer period in the development cycle. Empirical data is used to narrow focus based on the emergent knowledge. (Set-based design was discussed further in principle #3 in chapter 5, "SAFe Principles.")
- *Frequent system integration.* For many software solutions, CI is an achievable goal. However, systems with physical components—molds, printed circuit boards, mechanisms, fabricated parts, and so on—evolve more slowly and can't be integrated and evaluated every day. However, that can't be an excuse for late and problematic integration. That is why builders of complex and embedded systems shoot for *early and frequent* integration of components and subsystems.
- *Design verification.* Even frequent integration is not enough. First, it can occur too late in the process because of the dependencies of the availability of various system components. Second, it can't predict and evaluate all potential usage and failure scenarios. To address this, builders of high assurance systems perform design verification to ensure that a design meets the solution intent. This may include specification and analysis of requirements between subsystems, worst-case analysis of tolerances and performance, Failure Mode Effects Analysis (FMEA), modeling and simulation, full verification and validation, and traceability.

Improving Team Flow with Kanban

Kanban is a method for visualizing and managing work. Kanban systems include Work in Process (WIP) limits, which help to identify bottlenecks and improve the flow of work.

Agile teams, including Scrum teams, can apply kanban to better understand their process, how work flows through their system, and how to make the development process more effective. The primary aspects of a kanban system include the following:

- Work moves through the system in a series of defined steps.
- All work is visualized, and the progress of individual items is tracked.
- Teams agree on specific WIP limits for each step and change them to improve flow.
- Teams adopt specific policies covering how work is managed (for example, entry/exit criteria for a step, classes of services).
- Work items are tracked from the time they enter the system to the time they leave, providing continuous indicators of flow, WIP, and measures of lead time.

The Kanban Board

To get started, teams typically create a graphic representation of their current process and define some initial WIP limits. Figure 8-7 shows an example of one team's initial kanban board.

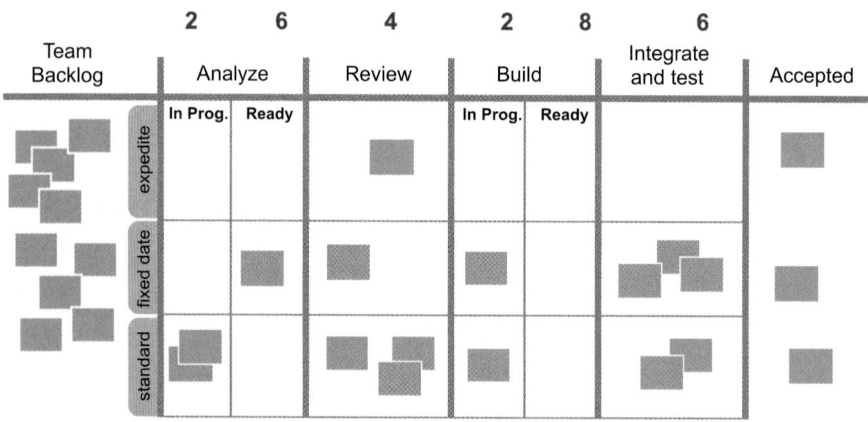

Figure 8-7. Example of a team's initial kanban board

In this case, the team has included two "ready" buffers to better manage variability of flow. One comes before the "review" step; perhaps it helps smooth the flow of review by external subject-matter experts whose availability may be uneven. The other buffer comes before "integrate and test," which, in this case, requires the use of shared test fixtures and resources. Since people on the same infrastructure also perform integration and testing, these two steps are treated as a single state.

A team's kanban board evolves over time. After defining the initial process steps and WIP limits—and executing for a while—the team's bottlenecks, resource constraints, and overspecialization will begin to surface. The team can then improve its process accordingly. As assumptions are validated, teams adjust WIP limits, and steps may be merged, split, or redefined.

Measuring Flow

To understand and improve their flow and process, kanban teams use objective measures, including average lead time, WIP, and throughput. One common method is to use a Cumulative Flow Diagram (CFD), illustrated in Figure 8-8.

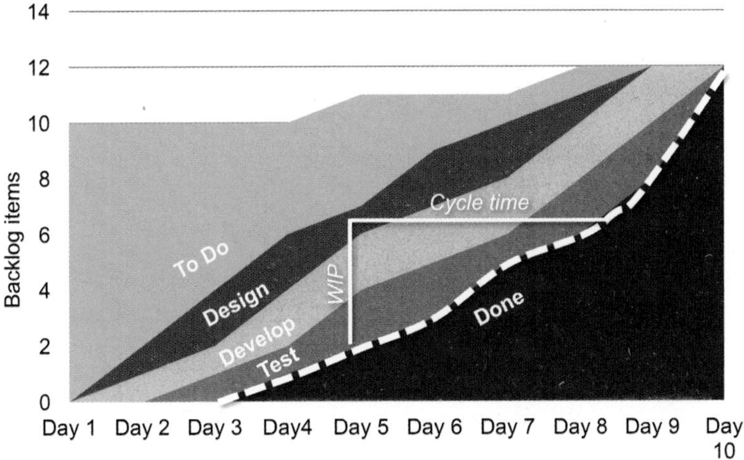

Figure 8-8. CFD shows how lead time and WIP evolve over time

The CFD also provides data for calculating current iteration throughput (average number of stories per day). It also provides visualization of trends and significant variations, which may be a result of internal impediments the team is unaware of or external forces that impede the flow.

Managing Work with Class of Service

Figure 8-7 shows "classes of service" to help teams optimize the execution of backlog items. Each class has a specific "swim lane" on the board and an execution policy for managing that type of work. Here are some examples:

- *Standard.* Normal prioritization and sequencing practices apply.
- *Fixed date.* Some items are required to meet milestones and dependencies with a predetermined date. These items are pulled into development when necessary so as to be finished on time.

- *Expedite.* These are high-priority items that must be done as soon as possible. They can be pulled into implementation even in violation of current WIP constraints. Typically, teams set a policy that there can be only one expedite item in the system at a time. Teams may swarm on that item to make sure it moves through the system quickly.

Kanban Teams Are on the Train

Some teams—often the System Team and maintenance teams—choose to apply kanban as their primary development method.

In these contexts, the uneven arrival of the work, fast-changing priorities, and the lower value of planning "what exactly will be done in the next iteration" all lead them to this choice. However, these teams are "on the train," and certain rules apply.

- *Cadence and synchronization still apply.* Kanban teams participate in ART activities and events. This includes PI planning, the all-important system demo, and Inspect and Adapt (I&A).
- *Estimating work.* Kanban teams generally do not invest as much time in estimating as most Scrum teams do. However, they must be able to estimate the demand against their capacity for PI planning and also participate in the economic estimation of larger backlog items.
- *Calculating velocity.* To plan and forecast, the teams must understand their velocity. Kanban teams use their CFDs to estimate their actual throughput in stories per iteration or simply count and average them. Teams can then calculate their derived velocity by multiplying the throughput by an average story size. In this way, both Scrum and kanban teams participate equally in the larger planning, road-mapping, and economic framework.

Managing ART Flow

ARTs are designed to be long-lived and support a continuous flow of value to the customer. Trains continuously run; they don't stop and restart. That means they must continuously pull in new work, elaborate it, analyze it, implement it, and release it. In this section, we'll describe some of the aspects of ART value flow.

Program Backlog and Kanban

Each ART delivers valuable features every PI. To do that, they must always have a small backlog of new features that are visible to everyone, have been socialized, and are ready to implement. To achieve this, ARTs use a kanban system to analyze features and get them ready for implementation. Features that are approved for implementation are maintained in the program backlog, as shown in Figure 8-9.

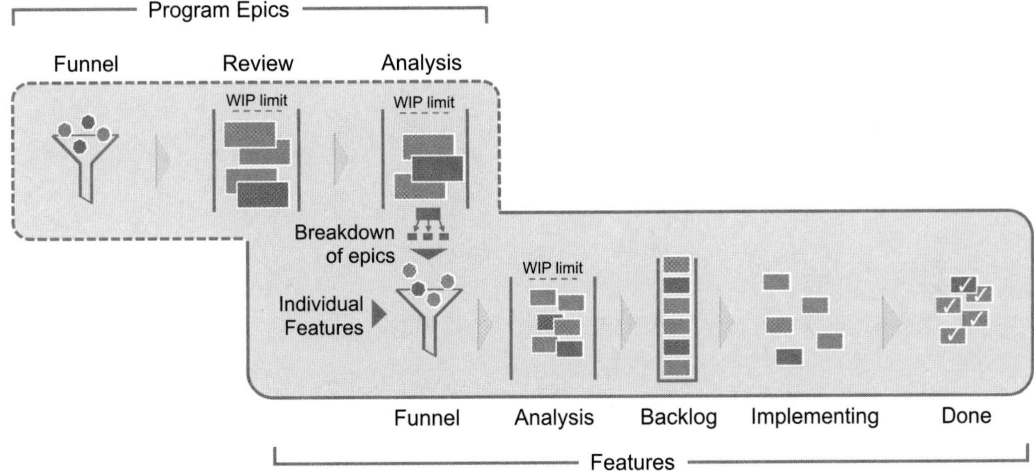

Figure 8-9. Example program kanban system

The kanban system consists of two main elements.

- *Program epic section.* This section analyzes and approves program epics and splits them into features to be further explored and implemented "downstream." The workflow follows the equivalent set of example steps in the portfolio kanban. (See chapter 13, "Portfolio Level Overview.")
- *Feature section.* This section is used to analyze, approve, and ready features (and enablers) for implementation. Many features originate locally from the ART; others are initiated by splitting portfolio or program epics. Product Management and System Architects/Engineers have content authority for features and enablers, respectively.

The following is a typical list of kanban steps for the program level:

- *Funnel.* Captures new feature ideas. These include requests for new functionality, as well as enablers needed to implement NFRs, build architectural runway, or enhance infrastructure.

- *Analysis.* Features that best align with the vision and strategic themes move to analysis for further exploration. Key attributes such as business benefit, acceptance criteria, and size are refined. Some features may require prototyping or other exploration. This step is WIP limited to assure that the right level of analysis is done and to balance the flow of new features to implementation capacity.
- *Backlog.* The highest-priority features, sufficiently elaborated and approved by Product Management, move to the program backlog, where they are prioritized with WSJF and await implementation.
- *Implementing.* At every PI boundary, the ART pulls the top WSJF features from the program backlog and moves them into implementing. WIP is limited by default, as the teams put in only what they can accomplish in a PI.
- *Done.* When implemented and accepted, they progress to done.

Sync Meetings

Keeping work moving requires frequent collaboration. To assess and manage progress and dependencies, ARTs coordinate through various "sync" meetings. These typically include the following:

- *Scrum of Scrums (SoS).* The Release Train Engineer (RTE) typically facilitates the SoS that meets to coordinate ART dependencies and to provide visibility into progress and impediments. Scrum Masters and others update their progress toward milestones and PI objectives and manage inter-team dependencies. This meeting is typically held weekly (or more frequently, as needed).
- *Product Owner (PO) Sync.* The purpose of the PO sync is to gain visibility into how well the ART is progressing toward achieving PI objectives, to discuss problems or opportunities with feature development, and to assess any scope adjustments. In addition, this meeting is often used for program backlog refinement. This meeting is also held weekly (or more frequently, as needed).

Sometimes, it makes sense to combine the SoS and PO sync meetings. This is called an "ART Sync" meeting, as illustrated in Figure 8-10.

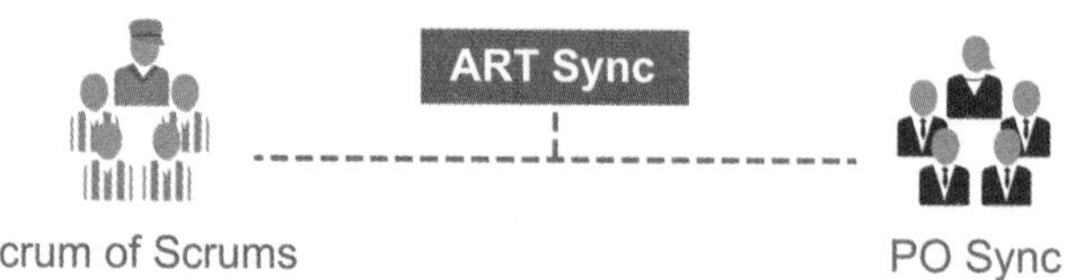

Figure 8-10. SoS and PO sync can be combined into a single meeting

Release Management

Release Management provides governance for any upcoming releases and also offers regular communication to management. This function has the authority to approve any scope, timing, or resource adjustments necessary to help ensure a quality release. Sometimes this can be handled by the teams and the trains themselves as part of their DevOps capability but, often, additional stakeholders, and some additional governance, is required. In such cases, Release Management meetings may be held with representatives that typically include:

- RTEs and Value Stream Engineers (VSEs)
- Business Owners and Product and Solution Managers
- Sales and marketing
- Internal IT, production, and deployment personnel
- Development managers, system and solution-level QA
- CTOs and/or System and Solution Architects/Engineering

Release Management may meet weekly, or as often as needed, to assess status and address current impediments. The meeting also provides senior management with regular visibility into upcoming releases and other milestones.

Enabling Flow with Architectural Runway

The concept of architectural runway provides one of the means by which Agile architecture is implemented. An architectural runway exists when the system has sufficient existing technological infrastructure to support the implementation of the highest-priority features in a near-term PI, *without* excessive redesign and delay. This runway provides the necessary technical basis for quickly implementing new features. It is a key enabler of development flow.

But as Figure 8-11 illustrates, the architectural runway is constantly consumed by new functionality. ARTs must continually invest in extending the runway by implementing enablers to support new functionality. Some of these enablers fix existing problems with the solution—for example, the need to enhance performance—while others might implement foundational technical capabilities and services that will be used by future system behaviors.

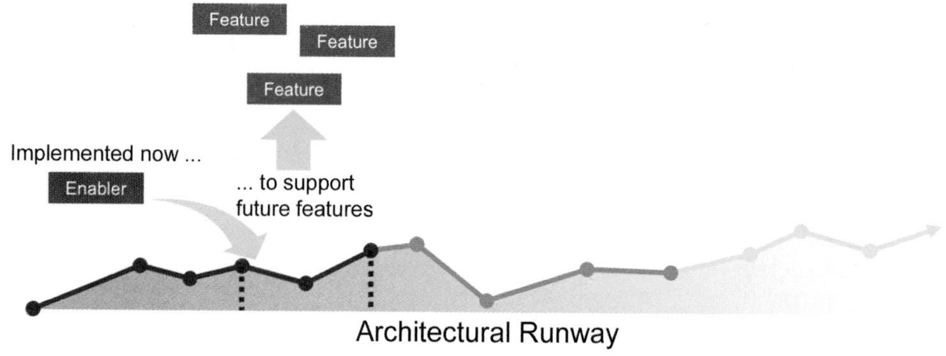

Figure 8-11. Building and consuming architectural runway

For this reason, teams need some intentional architecture—a set of planned architectural initiatives that enhance solution design, performance, and usability, and that provide guidance for cross-team design and implementation synchronization.

Together, intentional architecture and emergent design enable ARTs to create and maintain large-scale solutions. Emergent design enables fast, local control so that teams react appropriately to changing requirements without excessive attempts to future-proof the system. Intentional architecture provides the guidance needed to ensure that the system as a whole has conceptual integrity and efficacy. Achieving the right balance of emergent design and intentional architecture drives the effective evolution of large-scale systems.

Without enough investment in the architectural runway, the train will experience slow value delivery, needing to redesign for the delivery of each feature. Too much runway, however, will create architecture "inventory" that might never be used and can even clog the system. A sense of balance is required.

Lean UX

In SAFe, Lean UX is the application of lean principles to user experience design, focusing on minimizing waste in the development process and gaining fast, experiential feedback.

It uses an iterative, hypothesis driven approach to product development, through constant measurement and learning loops (build – measure – learn). In SAFe, Lean UX is applied at scale, with the right combination of centralized and decentralized user experience design and implementation.

As described below, Lean UX in SAFe adheres to its principles of Lean-Agile development at scale.

- *SAFe Principle #2: Apply systems thinking.* As Seiden and Jeff Gothelf note,[6] "Lean principles drive us to harmonize our 'system' of designers, developers, product managers, quality assurance engineers, marketers, and others in a transparent, cross-functional collaboration that brings non-designers into our design process." In addition, Lean UX in SAFe is a challenge of scale and is not strictly a local concern. Instead, designers take a system view and work to harmonize design elements across the larger solution, so that users who work across the system experience common styles, designs, and interactions.
- *SAFe Principle #3: Assume variability; preserve options.* SAFe principle #3 drives UX designers to commit to final designs only at the last responsible moment. Big up-front user experience design (just like up-front anything) is avoided. Instead, the design evolves in parallel with the solution development, with teams committed to refactoring user designs as necessary in support of new knowledge.
- *SAFe Principle #4: Build incrementally with fast, integrated learning cycles.* Perhaps this principle summarizes SAFe Lean UX best. The user experience is built incrementally, on the same basic cadence at which the system evolves. Short iterations, rapid functional prototypes, and fast user feedback drive the design to optimum efficacy. This occurs at the local (story, component) level, as well as the system (features and subsystems) level and value stream (systems and capabilities) levels.
- *SAFe Principle #5: Base milestones on objective evaluation of working systems.* And finally, how does one know when the user experience is a quality experience? Simply, local team iteration reviews and system and solution demos highlight integrated user interactions and reactions. Product Owners and Product Managers serve as proxy users to some extent throughout development. And, because end-users ultimately determine value, they are brought into the development process whenever and wherever possible to validate user experience.

Given the above, achieving Lean UX at enterprise scale often challenges traditional UX roles and responsibilities. Heroic and independent UX designers no longer create pixel perfect designs up front. Instead, constant team collaboration, experimentation, fast feedback, (and yes, some continuous UX refactoring), rule the day.

---

6. Jeff Gothelf and Josh Seiden, *Lean UX: Designing Great Products with Agile Teams* (O'Reilly Media; Kindle Edition), Kindle Locations 155–157.

DevOps Pipeline

> Most generally, readers of this book come from three industries: Independent Software Vendors (ISVs), builders of embedded and complex systems, and enterprise IT shops. While many of the same principles and practices apply across all industries, the notion of "DevOps and the continuous delivery pipeline" (DevOps pipeline, for short) is particularity relevant to IT.

Real, tangible value occurs only when the end users are successfully operating the solution in their environment. DevOps is a combination of two words, "development" and "operations," which represents the ability of an enterprise to develop and release small batches of functionality to the business or end user in a continuous flow process. The ability to do so is integral to the value stream, and therefore DevOps is integral to SAFe.

Many SAFe concepts—small batch size, short iterations, fast feedback, continuous integration, test automation, and more—support this ultimate business need. Indeed, ARTs are developed and designed in large part for this specific purpose. They are cross-functional, and include all the skills necessary (define-design-build-test and deploy) to accomplish this objective. Initially, this typically involves engaging deployment and operations personnel within an ART, as well as cross training development teams with the skills to deploy.

Over time, the distinction between development and deployment is reduced, and ARTs operate with a continuous delivery pipeline, a mechanism by which they can seamlessly define, implement and deliver solution elements to the user, without handoffs or much external production or operations support.

Technically, there are three main processes that must be automated to implement this continuous delivery pipeline:

1. Retrieving all necessary artifacts from version control, including code, scripts, tests, metadata, and the like
2. Building, integrating, deploying, and validating the code in a staging environment
3. Deploying the validated build from staging to production, and quickly validating the new system

For most traditional IT shops, this is a form of agility that takes significant time to develop. Toward that end, SAFe offers six specific, recommended practices for building the deployment pipeline:

- *Build and maintain a production-equivalent staging environment.* Implement a staging environment that has the same or similar hardware and supporting systems as production.
- *Maintain development and test environments to better match production.* Implement development and test environments to closely resemble production by taking an economic view.
- *Deploy to staging every iteration; deploy to production frequently.* Do all system demos from the staging environment, including the final system and solution demos. In that way, deployability becomes part of Definition of Done (DoD) for every user story, resulting in potentially deployable software every iteration.
- *Put everything under version control.* This includes the new code, all required data, all libraries and external assemblies, configuration files or databases, application or database servers—everything that may realistically be updated or modified.
- *Start creating the ability to automatically build environments.* In order to establish a reliable deployment process, the environment setup process itself needs to be fully automated.
- *Start automating the actual deployment process.* This includes all the steps in the flow, including building the code, creating the test environments, executing the automated tests, and deploying and validating verified code and associated systems and utilities in the target environment.

In addition, to assure continuous and reliable operations, development teams should build application telemetry into the system, so that the system itself can report on its current health and status.

And finally, the impact on application architecture should not be underestimated. Long term, the continuous delivery pipeline requires systems that were designed—at least in part—for this primary purpose.

System Demo

The primary measure of ART progress is the objective evidence provided by a working solution in the system demo. Every two weeks, the full system—the integrated work of all teams on the train for that iteration—is demoed to the train's stakeholders. (This is in addition to each team's iteration demo.) Stakeholders provide the feedback the train needs to stay on course and take corrective action.

At the end of each PI, a final system demo is held as part of I&A. That demo is a significant and somewhat more structured affair, as it demonstrates the accumulation of all the features (from all teams on the train) that have been developed over the course of the PI.

In value streams with multiple ARTs, the results of all the development efforts from multiple trains—along with the contributions from suppliers—are demoed to the customers and other key stakeholders for objective feedback and evaluation. This solution demo is in addition to each ART's PI system demo. For more information, please see chapter 12, "Coordinating ARTs and Suppliers."

Innovation and Planning

IP iterations provide a regular, dedicated, and cadence-based opportunity for teams to work on activities that are difficult to fit into standard development iterations. These can include the following:

- Full solution integration, verification, and validation; release documentation; and so on (if releasing on the PI boundary)
- Innovation and exploration, hackathons, and so on
- I&A workshop, including final PI system demo
- Program and team backlog refinement
- Work on technical infrastructure, tooling, and other systemic impediments
- Fostering continuing education
- PI planning

In addition, IP iterations fulfill another critical role by providing an estimating buffer for meeting PI objectives and enhancing release predictability. However, routinely using that time for completing the work is a failure pattern. Doing so defeats the primary purpose of the IP iteration, and innovation will suffer. Teams must take care that the estimating guard does not simply become a crutch. ARTs typically report that their overall efficiency, velocity, sustainability of pace, and job satisfaction are all enhanced by regular opportunities to "recharge their batteries and sharpen their tools." Figure 8-12 illustrates an example IP calendar.

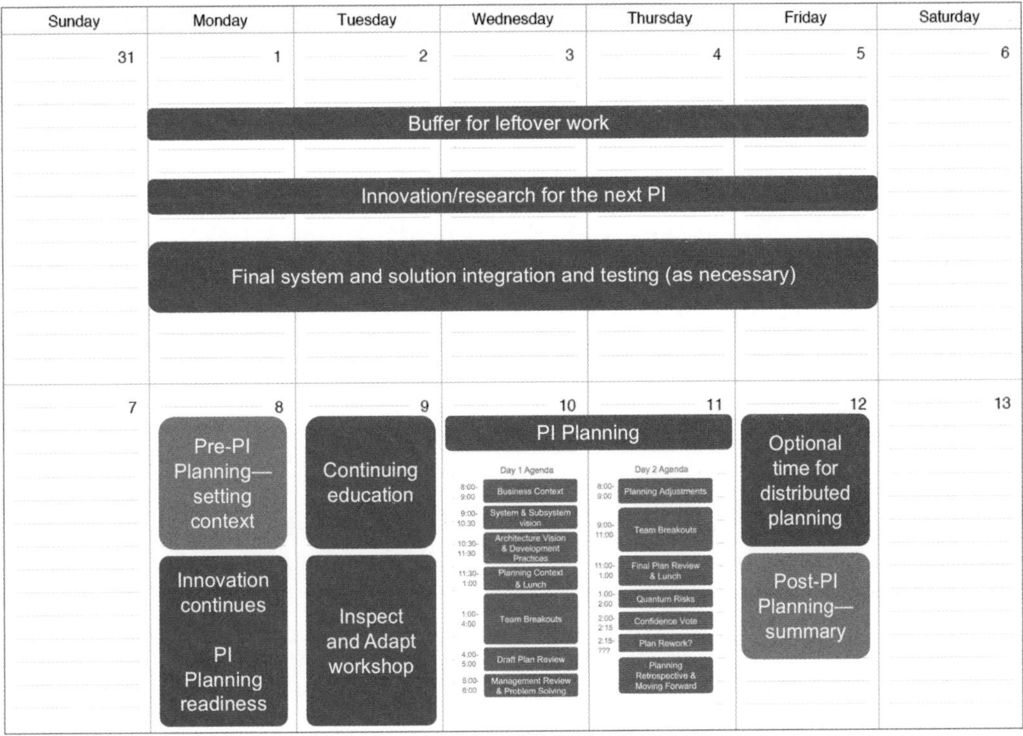

Figure 8-12. Example IP iteration calendar

Innovation

Innovation is one of the pillars of the Lean-Agile mindset. But finding time for it in the midst of urgent delivery deadlines can be difficult. To this end, ARTs use IP iterations to schedule time for research and design activities and hackathons. The rules for a hackathon can be simple.

- Team members work on whatever they want, with whomever they want.
- They demo their work to others at the end.

The insights from these activities routinely make their way into program backlogs, helping to drive innovation. Some innovations and fixes will make their way directly into the product. Automation and process improvements arising from the hackathons will be leveraged right away.

Inspect and Adapt

The I&A is held at the end of each PI and provides time to demonstrate the solution, get feedback, and then reflect, problem solve, and identify improvement actions. The improvement items can then be immediately incorporated into PI planning. This workshop has a timebox of three to four hours and has three parts.

- The PI system demo
- Quantitative measurement
- The problem-solving workshop

This is such an important event that it is the entire subject of chapter 9, "Inspect and Adapt."

Summary

This chapter gave an overview of executing the PI, which starts with a planning session and is typically followed by four execution iterations. Each PI concludes with an IP iteration.

The key takeaways from this chapter are as follows:

- The iteration cycle occurs within the PI and consists of four main activities: iteration planning, execution, demo, and retrospective.
- Built-in quality is one of the four core values of SAFe. The enterprise's ability to deliver new functionality with the fastest sustainable lead time and react to rapidly changing business environments is dependent on solution quality.
- Kanban is a method for visualizing and managing work. Agile teams, including Scrum teams, can apply kanban to better understand their process, how work flows through their system, and how to make the development process more effective.
- ARTs use a kanban system to analyze features and get them ready for implementation. Features that are approved for implementation are maintained in the program backlog.
- The architectural runway provides the necessary technical basis for quickly implementing new features. It is a key enabler of development flow.

- In IT shops, ARTs build and operate a DevOps pipeline that is used to help automate a continuous flow of small, incremental releases to end users. In some contexts, continuous delivery is an appropriate, and achievable, goal.
- ARTs apply scaled Lean UX practices based on SAFe's Lean-Agile principles. These practices support emergent knowledge via fast, objective feedback on component, feature, system, and solution-level user experience design and implementation.
- The primary measure of ART progress is the objective evidence provided by a working solution in the system demo. At the end of each PI, a final system demo is held as part of I&A. It demonstrates all the features (from all teams on the train) that have been developed during the course of the PI.
- IP iterations provide a regular, dedicated, and cadence-based opportunity for teams to work on activities that are difficult to fit into standard development iterations (for example, hackathons, PI planning, I&A).
- The I&A is a regular event, held at the end of each PI, that provides time to demo the solution, get feedback, problem solve, and identify improvement actions.

9

Inspect and Adapt

At regular intervals, the team reflects on how to become more effective, then tunes and adjusts its behavior accordingly.

—Agile Manifesto

Overview 159
PI System Demo 160
Quantitative Measurement 160
Retrospective and Problem-Solving Workshop 162
Inspect and Adapt at the Value Stream Level 166
Summary 167

Overview

The Inspect and Adapt (I&A) workshop is a significant event held at the end of each Program Increment (PI). It is the capstone of the PI.

A regular time to reflect, collect data, and solve problems, the workshop is where teams and stakeholders assess the solution in process and define and take action on the improvements needed to increase the velocity, quality, and reliability of the next PI.

All program stakeholders participate, resulting in a full understanding of the current context, along with a set of improvement stories that can be added to the backlog for the upcoming PI planning. As a result, every Agile Release Train (ART) improves every PI. Continuous improvement is assured with implementation of the identified backlog improvement items.

The I&A has three parts.

1. PI system demo. This is a demo of all features completed by the ART during the previous PI.
2. Quantitative measurement. A review of any quantitative metrics teams have agreed to collect and discuss.
3. Problem-solving workshop. A short retrospective for the PI, along with a structured problem-solving workshop, which systematically addresses the larger impediments that are limiting velocity.

For large solutions, the I&A workshop also occurs at the value stream level.

PI System Demo

The PI system demo is the first part of the workshop. But this particular system demo is somewhat different from the biweekly (every two weeks) versions that preceded it. This demo shows all the features that have been developed during the course of the PI. Also, the audience is typically broader. For example, additional customer representatives and internal stakeholders are likely to attend. The demo tends to be more formal and is staged to demonstrate and evaluate all the features that have been accomplished in the PI. It typically requires some additional preparation and some technical scaffolding to reflect all the elements of the solution.

But like any other system demo, the PI system demo should be timeboxed to an hour or less, with a level of abstraction high enough to keep the important stakeholders engaged and providing feedback.

Quantitative Measurement

In the second part of the workshop, teams review any quantitative metrics they have agreed to collect and then discuss the data and trends. In preparation for this, the Release Train Engineer (RTE) is often responsible for gathering the information, analyzing it to showcase interesting statistics and findings, and presenting the measurements.

During the PI system demo, the Business Owners, Agile teams, and other key stakeholders collaboratively rate the actual business value achieved for each team's PI objectives and record it on the *Team PI Performance Report*, as shown in in Figure 9-1. This report compares the actual business value achieved to the planned business value.

Since stretch objectives are *not* part of the commitment, they don't count in the planned value but do count in the actual score, also shown in Figure 9-1. In other words, it is possible to achieve more than 100 percent of committed objectives.

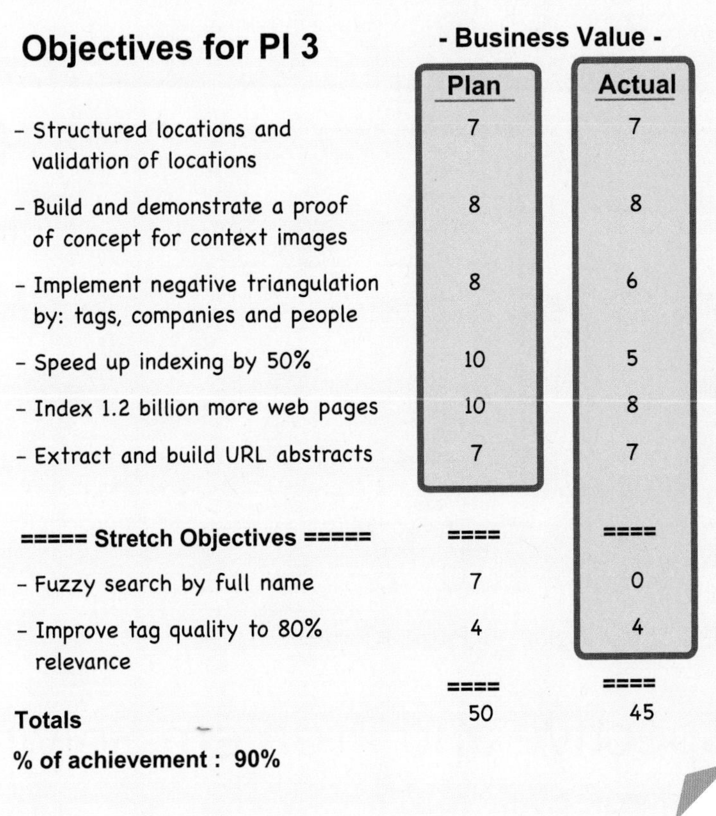

Figure 9-1. Team PI Performance Report

To assess the overall predictability of the release train, the *Team PI Performance Report* is summarized, for all teams on the train, to calculate the key *measure* of ART delivery reliability, the *Program Predictability Measure*, as illustrated in Figure 9-2.

Reliable trains should generally operate in the 80 percent to 100 percent range (highlighted by the green band in Figure 9-2), which allows the business and its internal and external stakeholders to plan effectively.

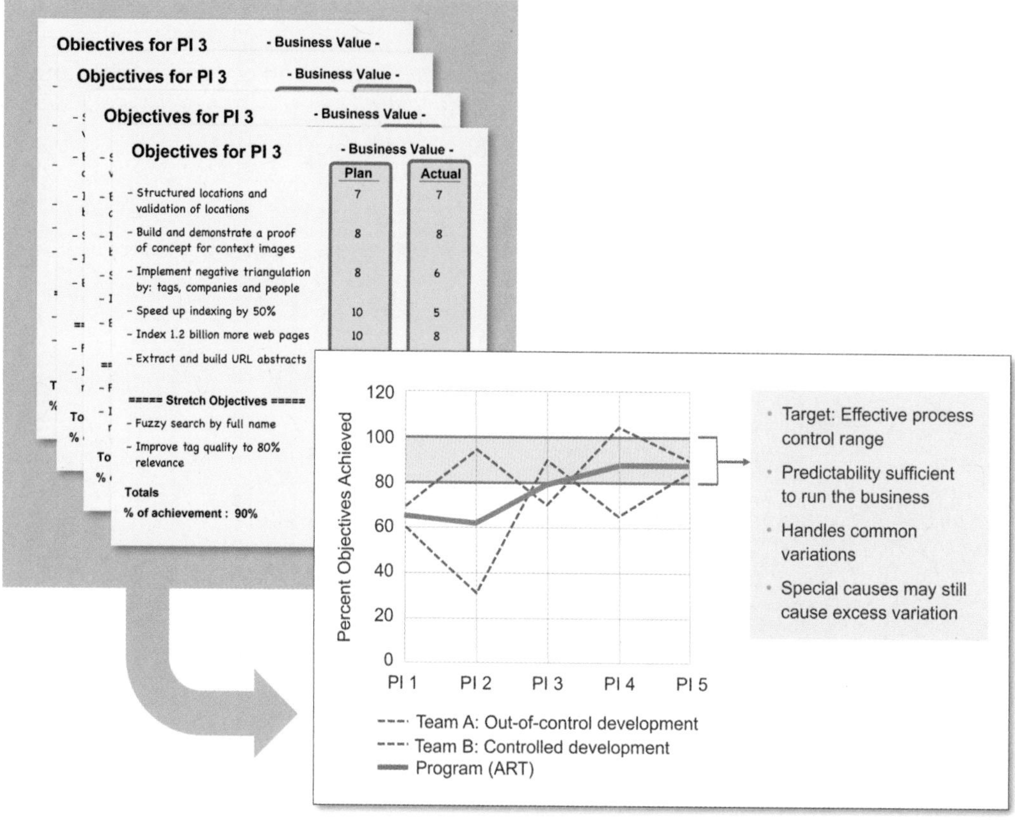

Figure 9-2. Program Predictability Measure

Retrospective and Problem-Solving Workshop

Retrospective

The teams then run a brief retrospective with the goal of identifying the larger impediments they'd like to address. This session is typically timeboxed to 30 minutes or less. There's no right way to do this, and a number of Agile retrospective formats can be used.[1] The objective of the selected format is to identify a small number of significant problems that the teams can potentially address.

1. Esther Derby and Diana Larsen, *Agile Retrospectives: Making Good Teams Great* (Pragmatic Bookshelf, 2009).

Based on attendance at the retrospective and the nature of the problems identified, the groups coordinate which items to tackle. People have a choice of resolving team-level problems or, more typically, selecting a program-level problem and joining others who want to work on the same issue. This self-selection helps provide cross-functional and differing views. It also seeds the problem-solving working group with people most likely to be affected and motivated to address the issue.

Key ART stakeholders—including Business Owners, customers, and management—join the teams in this retrospective. They're often the only ones who can unblock impediments that exist outside the team's control.

Problem-Solving Workshop

When addressing significant problems, a structured root-cause analysis and problem-solving workshop format can be effectively applied. Root-cause analysis is a set of problem-solving tools that identifies the origins of an issue, rather than simply addressing the symptoms. The steps are shown in Figure 9-3 and described in the paragraphs that follow.

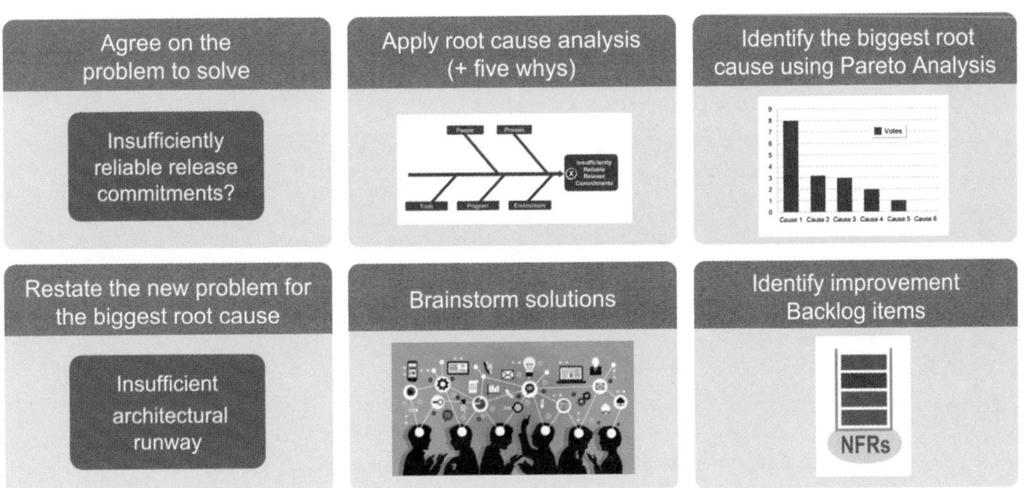

Figure 9-3. Steps in the problem-solving workshop

Agree on the Problem(s) to Solve

American inventor Charles Kettering is credited with saying "A problem well stated is a problem half solved." At this point, the teams will have selected the problem they want to work on. But do they really agree on what the problem is? Could it be that they have differing perspectives? To resolve those questions, the teams should spend a few minutes stating the problem—the what, where, when, and impact—as succinctly as they can. Figure 9-4 illustrates a Baja Ride systems engineering example.

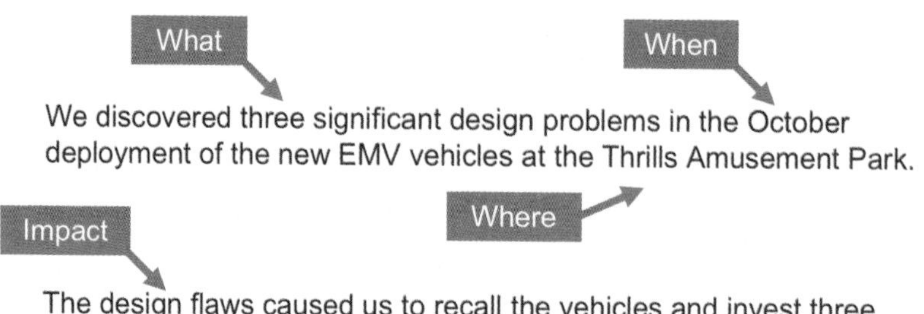

Figure 9-4. Example problem statement[2]

Perform Root-Cause Analysis

Next the working group performs root-cause analyses, using proven problem-solving tools such as fishbone diagrams and the "five whys."[3]

Also known as an Ishikawa diagram, the fishbone is a visual tool used to explore the causes of events or the sources of variation in a process. As shown in Figure 9-5, the name of the problem is written to the right at the end of the "backbone."

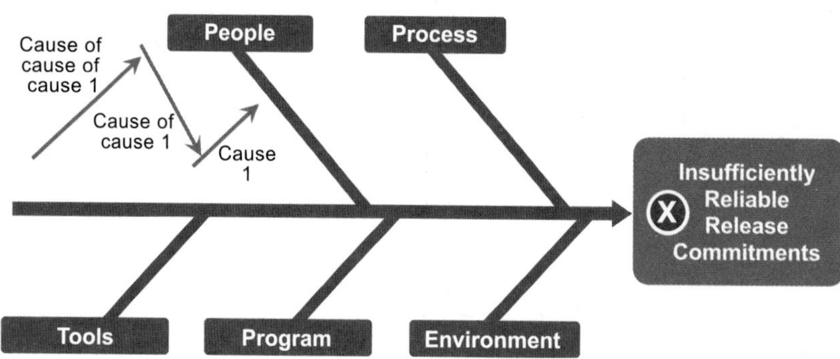

Figure 9-5. Fishbone diagram with major sources identified

2. Concept contributed to SAFe by Beth Miller.
3. Originally described by Sakichi Toyoda and Taiichi Ohno of Toyota, where it was integral to the Toyota Production System, the foundation of Lean thinking.

Causes are identified and then grouped into major categories as bones off the main bone, for example, people, process, tools, program, and environment. Team members then brainstorm factors they think contributed to the problem to be solved. Once a cause is named, its root cause is identified with the "five whys" technique. By simply asking "why," for as many as five times (just a guideline; three will often do it), each cause of a cause can be discovered and then added to the diagram.

Identify the Biggest Root Cause

Complex problems often have many contributing root causes. To address this, Pareto Analysis (also known as "the 80/20 rule") is applied as a decision-making technique used to narrow down the number of actions that produce the most significant overall effect. It applies the principle that 20 percent of the root causes may contribute to 80 percent of the problem.

Once all the possible causes of causes have been identified, team members then cumulatively vote on the item they think is the biggest factor causing the end problem. To illustrate their consensus on the largest root causes, the team then creates a Pareto chart, similar to the example in Figure 9-6.

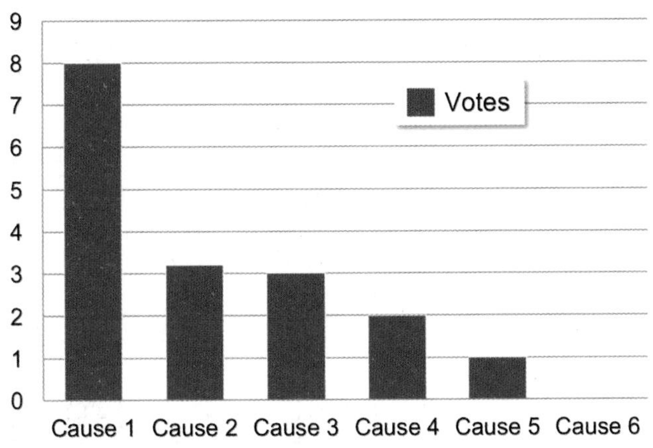

Figure 9-6. Pareto chart of probable causes

Restate the New Problem

The next step is to pick the largest cause from the list and restate it clearly as a problem. This should take only a few minutes, as the teams should now be close to the root cause.

Brainstorm Solutions

At this point, the root cause should be clear enough to start to suggest potential solutions. The working group then brainstorms as many corrective actions as they can think of, by applying these rules of brainstorming:

- Generate as many ideas as possible,
- Suspend judgment of the ideas; do not allow criticism or debate during the ideation period.
- Let the imagination soar.
- Mutate and combine ideas.

Create Improvement Backlog Items

The team then votes and identifies up to three actionable solutions. These become the improvement stories that get fed into the next PI planning session that follows. During that session, the RTE helps assure that the stories are incorporated into the iteration plans. This confirms that actions will be taken and resources allocated—they require people, resources, and visibility—just like with any other backlog item. This closes the loop on the retrospective.

With I&A, problem-solving becomes routine, and continuous improvement becomes simply habit, firmly engrained in the culture of the Lean enterprise. More tactically, team members and stakeholders can be assured that each ART is firmly on its path of improving quality, productivity, and business outcomes.

Inspect and Adapt at the Value Stream Level

The previous section describes a rigorous approach to problem-solving in the context of the ART. But many ARTs are part of a larger value stream. In that case, some value stream stakeholders may attend the ART I&A to provide feedback.

In addition, as Figure 9-7 illustrates, a value stream I&A workshop is typically required, which follows the same format as the ART I&A. Attendees include the customers and primary stakeholders of the value stream level, as well as representatives from the various ARTs and suppliers.

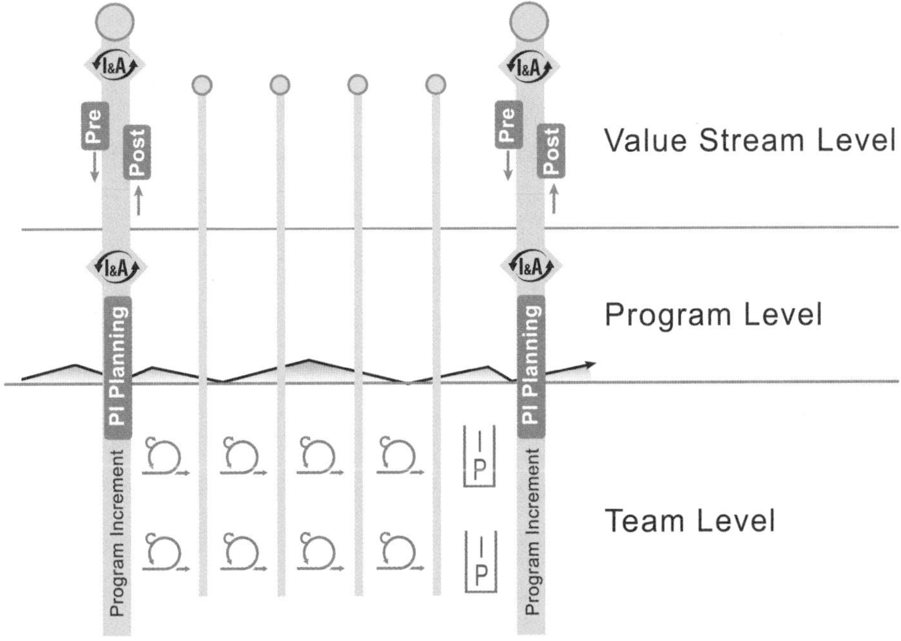

Figure 9-7. I&A may occur at both the ART and value stream levels

Summary

This chapter provided an overview of the Inspect & Adapt process, which is a regular event, held at the end of each PI, that provides time to demonstrate the solution, get feedback, and then reflect, problem solve, and identify improvement actions.

The key takeaways from this chapter are as follows:

- The I&A workshop has three parts: PI system demo, quantitative measurement, and retrospective and problem-solving workshop.
- The PI system demo, the first part of the workshop, shows all the features that have been developed over the course of the PI.
- In the second part of the workshop, teams review any quantitative metrics they have agreed to collect and then discuss the data and trends.
- In the last part, the teams run a brief retrospective with the goal of identifying the larger impediments they'd like to address. Finally, a structured root-cause problem-solving workshop is conducted to address larger significant problems.
- A value stream I&A workshop is typically required when there are multiple ARTs in a value stream. This value stream I&A typically follows the same format as the ART I&A.

Part IV
Value Stream Level

Deliver value in the sustainably shortest lead time. Best possible quality and value to people and society.

—House of Lean

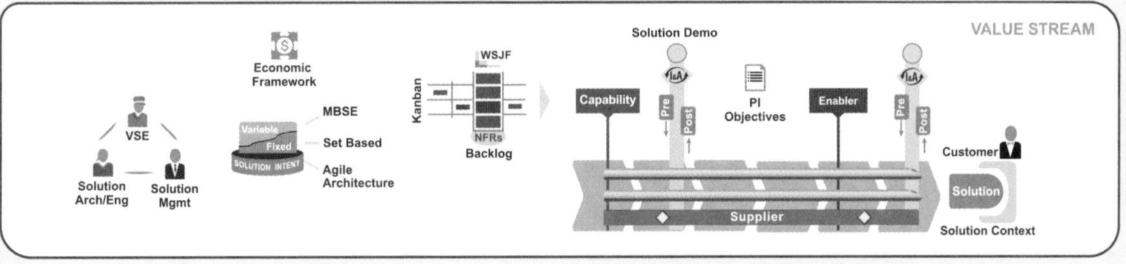

- Chapter 10 – Value Stream Overview
- Chapter 11 – Defining Large and Complex Solutions
- Chapter 12 – Coordinating ARTs and Suppliers

10

Value Stream Overview

Projects and practices fail when they optimize one part of the value stream at the expense of others or when the parts just don't fit

—Allen C. Ward

Overview 171
Economic Framework 173
Capabilities and the Value Stream Backlog 176
Value Stream Epics 177
Defining and Building the Solution 178
Value Stream Flow 179
Summary 180

Overview

The value stream level is optional and is designed to support those defining, building, and deploying the world's most important and complex systems. These solutions are so substantial that they typically require multiple Agile Release Trains (ARTs), as well as the contribution of suppliers.

An example would be an organization that builds defense systems, which have significant safety, performance, and compliance demands. Building these systems may require hundreds of mechanical, electrical, and software engineers, as well as external suppliers. These systems are often mission-critical, and failure can have serious, even life-threatening, consequences.

Enterprises that build smaller and largely independent systems may not need this level. Even then, however, some of these systems are mission- or life-critical. They are far from trivial systems, and some elements of the value stream level may still be useful. For example, solution intent, set-based design, model-based system engineering, and Agile architecture practices can be adopted without implementing the entire value stream level. This is part of the scalability and modularity of the framework.

Lean-Agile development is now replacing traditional phase-gate development approaches, which haven't scaled well to meet the challenges described here. To deliver the right business outcomes, as well as effective and safety-compliant solutions, a leaner, more Agile approach is needed. To achieve that, the value stream level offers additional practices, roles, and events to support implementation and coordination. These include the following:

- An economic framework to provide financial decision rules and boundaries for value stream decision-making
- Solution intent as a repository for intended and actual solution behavior
- Solution context, which describes the way the solution fits in the deployed environment
- Pre– and post–Program Increment (PI) planning, which helps multiple ARTs and suppliers build an aligned plan for the next PI
- Solution demo, which provides an integrated demo from multiple ARTs and suppliers
- Value stream backlog containing capabilities and enablers, which describe the larger behaviors of the solution

Similar to the program level, the value stream level is organized around PIs, providing cadence and synchronization of multiple ARTs and suppliers.

The value stream level also includes additional roles to facilitate coordination, as described next.

Value Stream Roles

Like the program level, the value stream level has its own "triad" of critical functions and roles needed to coordinate and advance the value stream solution, as Figure 10-1 shows.

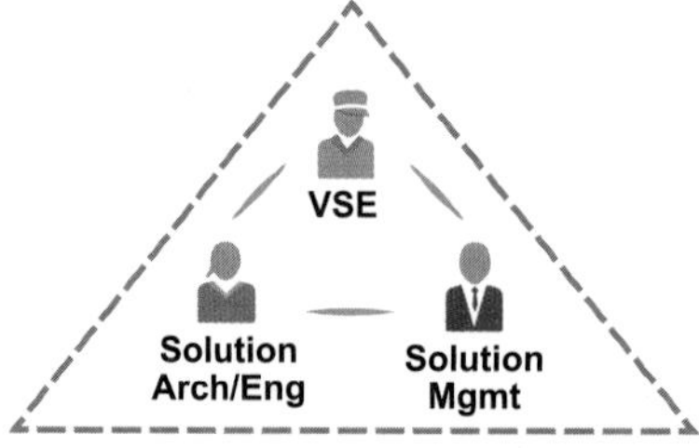

Figure 10-1. VSE, Solution Architect/Engineering, and Solution Management triad

- The *Value Stream Engineer (VSE)* is a servant leader and coach who supports and facilitates the work of all ARTs and suppliers. Similar to an RTE, the VSE is responsible for making sure that the value stream runs smoothly by identifying and resolving bottlenecks. The VSE facilitates events and meetings at the value stream level and monitors the kanban system and metrics for this level.
- *Solution Management* represents the customer's overall needs across trains, as well as communicating the strategic themes of the portfolio vision. Solution Management collaborates with Product Management to define capabilities and splits them into features. Solution Management is the primary content authority for the value stream backlog and its prioritization via Weighted Short Job First (WSJF). Solution Management also contributes to the economic framework that governs decision-making across ARTs and Agile teams.
- *Solution Architect/Engineering* collaboratively defines the technology and architecture that connects the solution across trains. It works with the train's *System* Architect/Engineering team to help guide their portion of the solution's design.

In addition to the three roles, customers are shown in the value stream level in the four-level Scaled Agile Framework (SAFe), just as they appear in three-level SAFe. Although customers are displayed just once on the Big Picture, in reality they are involved at every level of SAFe, from team to portfolio. They are part of the value stream and are thereby inseparable from the development process. Customers work closely with Solution and Product Management and other key stakeholders to shape the solution intent, the vision, and the economic framework in which development occurs. They help define and prioritize the solution's development and participate in solution planning, demos, and process improvement.

Economic Framework

The economic framework is designed to permit fast, effective decision-making, within the financial constraints of the value stream. This requires three things.

1. An understanding of the financial constraints and decision-making rules
2. Sufficient knowledge of the current local context and subject domain
3. Delegation of decision-making authority

Many aspects of the economic framework are directly embedded in various SAFe practices, including the following:

- Lean-Agile budgeting
- Epic funding and governance
- The principle of decentralized decision-making
- Job sequencing using Cost of Delay (CoD) and WSJF

Figure 10-2 illustrates where many of the decision rules and decision-making authority may occur within this framework. These four practices are briefly described in the following sections.

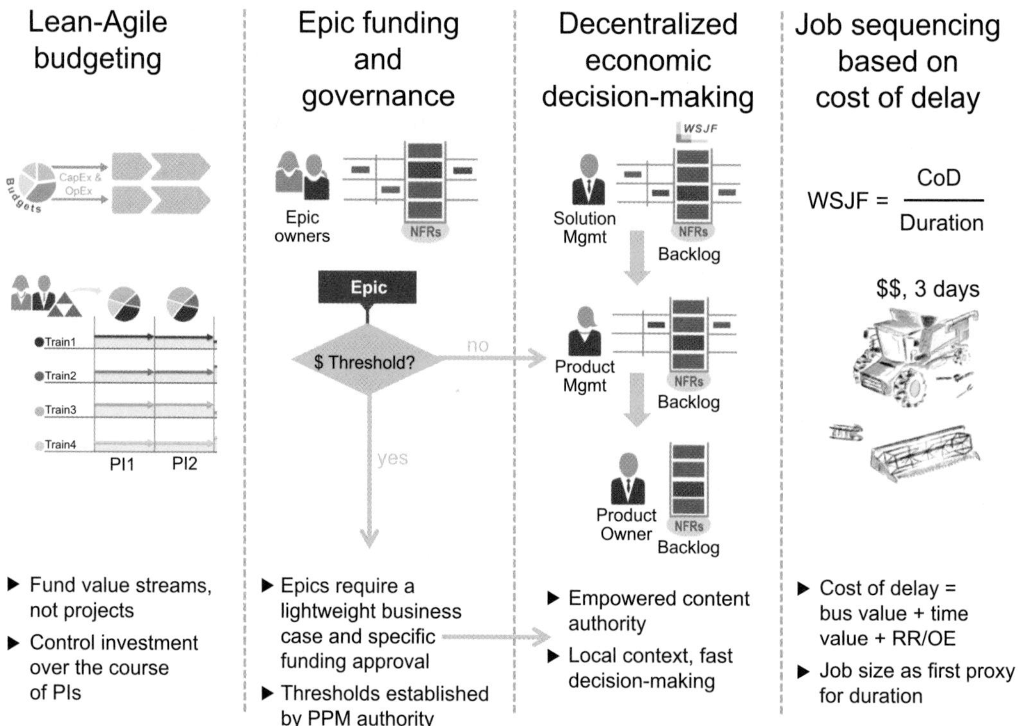

Figure 10-2. Economic framework decision rules and decision-making authority

Lean-Agile Budgeting

SAFe suggests a Lean-Agile funding model, where budgets are allocated to long-lived value streams instead of projects. Unlike projects, the cost for each PI is largely fixed, and the scope is adjusted as needed to meet the business needs of the value stream. There are no "project overruns" that must be justified with this model. Value stream budgets can be adjusted over time at PI boundaries, based on the relative value that each provides. This process is further described in chapter 14, "Lean-Agile Budgeting, Forecasting, and Contracting."

Epic Funding and Governance

Allocating funds to the value streams (and as a result to the ARTs) is all well and good. But what happens when there are substantial financial decisions to make, such as portfolio, value stream, or program epics? Spending authority comes with the responsibility to communicate any investments that are not routine. This is the role of the kanban systems at the portfolio, value stream, and program levels. Each epic requires a lightweight business case and an explicit approval process, which is described further in chapter 13, "Portfolio Level Overview."

Decentralized Economic Decision-Making

With these budget elements in place, the enterprise then empowers people to make content decisions at each level of the framework (for example, Solution Management for value streams, Product Management for ARTs, and Product Owners for teams). Of course, they don't act alone. They work with their larger stakeholder community to determine the best course of action.

Job Sequencing Based on Cost of Delay

Every significant program has a backlog of new jobs—features and capabilities—waiting to be implemented to increase the value of the solution. In a flow-based system, optimizing the sequence of jobs based on CoD produces better economic outcomes than prioritizing work by theoretical Return on Investment (ROI) or "first-come, first-served" methods. Program and value stream kanban systems and backlog staging areas are the keys to success. When capacity exists, jobs are "pulled" for implementation based on WSJF, which is the CoD weighted by job size (a proxy for duration).

Capabilities and the Value Stream Backlog

Capabilities are larger work items that appear at this level to capture and define higher-level solution behaviors. These typically span multiple ARTs.

New capabilities may arise from a local context or occur as a result of splitting portfolio epics that may cut across multiple value streams. Another potential source of capabilities is the solution context, where an aspect of the solution environment may drive needed functionality.

Capabilities have attributes and practices similar to features. Here are some examples:

- They're written using a phrase, statement of benefits, and acceptance criteria; they are structured to fit within a single PI.
- Associated enablers describe and bring visibility to all the technical work required to support effective development and delivery of business capabilities.
- They're developed and approved using the value stream kanban.
- Capabilities approved for implementation are maintained in the value stream backlog and are prioritized using WSJF.
- Acceptance criteria are used to determine when the functionality has been properly implemented.

To be executed by ARTs, capabilities must be first split into features, which then are split into user stories that are implemented by teams within an iteration timebox.

The following list provides 10 patterns for "splitting work," as described by Leffingwell in *Agile Software Requirements:*[1]

1. Workflow steps
2. Business rule
3. Major effort
4. Simple/complex

---

1. Dean Leffingwell, *Agile Software Requirements: Lean Requirements Practices for Teams, Programs, and the Enterprise* (Addison-Wesley, 2011).

5. Variations in data
6. Data methods
7. Deferring Nonfunctional Requirements (NFRs)
8. Operations
9. Use-case scenarios
10. Breaking out a spike

Figure 10-3 illustrates an example of splitting a capability into features.

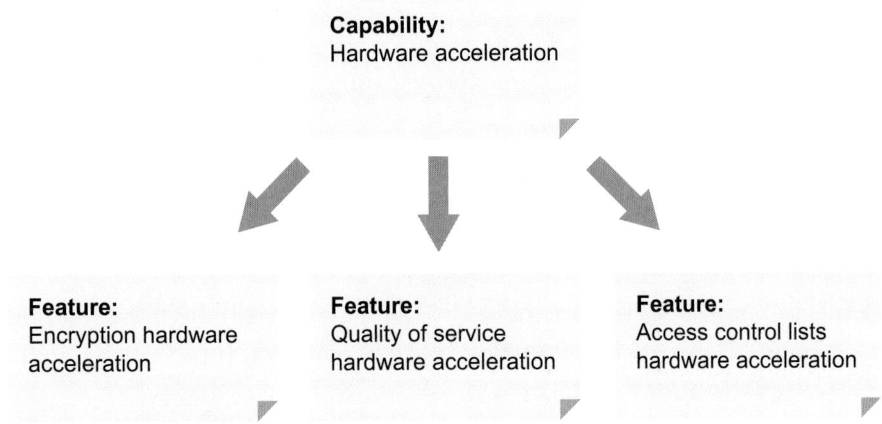

Figure 10-3. Example of a capability split into features

Value Stream Epics

Value stream epics are initiatives large enough in scope and cost to warrant analysis and a lightweight business case. Unlike capabilities that can be split to fit inside a single PI, value stream epics usually take several PIs to develop. They may arise as a result of portfolio epics, or they may occur locally as value streams plan larger initiatives.

Value stream epics are analyzed in the kanban system. Once approved, they're split into capabilities and enablers. More details about epics (for example, lightweight business case or epic value statement) are covered in the discussion of portfolio epics in chapter 13, "Portfolio Level Overview."

Defining and Building the Solution

Solution behavior and decisions are managed in solution intent, which serves both as a single source of truth and as a repository for requirements in their transition from variable to fixed intent. In addition to vision and roadmap, which also apply at this level, the development of solution intent in an adaptive manner is supported by these three additional practices:

- *Model-based systems engineering.* Describes how requirements and design elements can be developed, documented, and maintained in flexible and accessible models, as opposed to documents
- *Set-based design.* Practices that support preservation of options and the move from variable to fixed requirements over time, while deferring decisions to the last responsible moment
- *Agile architecture.* Supporting the balancing act between emergent design, which is built just in time by the Agile teams, and intentional architecture, which is created collaboratively with the senior technical leaders and the teams

A key element of the value stream level is the *solution* itself. Although the solution also appears at the program level in the three-level view, additional practices and details are described at the value stream level.

The behavior of a solution is governed by its solution context—the environment in which a deployed solution operates. Solutions are developed based on capabilities and enablers, which are used to satisfy the needs of customers and to realize the value stream vision and roadmap.

Capabilities are managed through the value stream kanban system to ensure they are evaluated and analyzed before they reach the value stream backlog. At that point, they're sequenced for implementation. The kanban system limits Work in Process (WIP) and focuses trains on getting value stream backlog items fully done, before starting on a new work. This is essential for coordinating ARTs and suppliers to deliver capabilities together.

Larger initiatives are managed as value stream epics and are broken down into capabilities during analysis. In many cases, they require suppliers who develop components, subsystems, or capabilities for the value stream. These suppliers participate in value stream–level meetings.

Value Stream Flow

The value stream kanban is used to bring visibility and analyze upcoming work, as shown in Figure 10-4. It consists of two main elements: the value stream epic and the capability sections. Value Stream Management and Solution Architects/Engineers, who have responsibility over capabilities and enablers, manage this system.

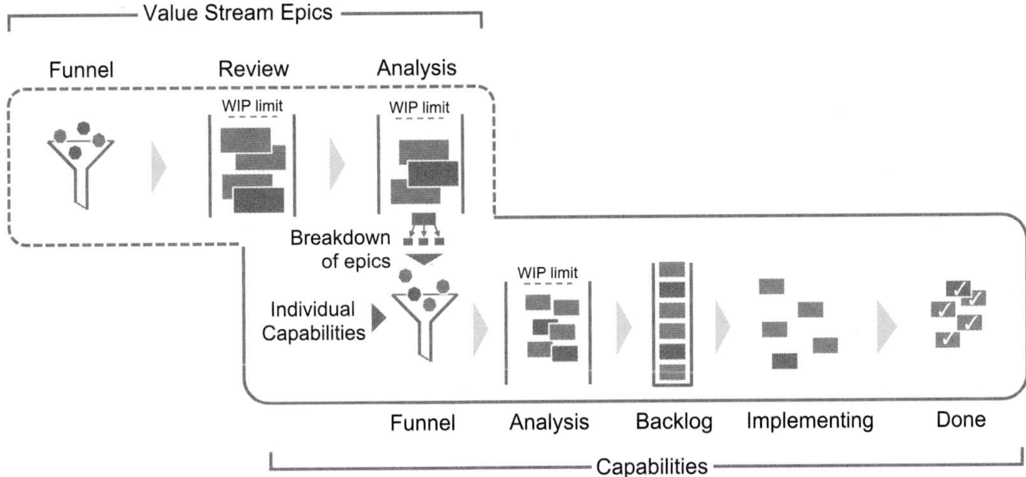

Figure 10-4. Example kanban system for the value stream level

Value stream epic section. This section is used for analyzing and approving value stream epics, as well as splitting them into capabilities to be further explored and implemented in the "downstream" capabilities portion of the value stream kanban (see Figure 10-4). Value stream or portfolio level stakeholders are generally involved in approving these epics. Depending on how frequently value stream epics occur in the local context of the value stream level, this section is not always present in the kanban. Its workflow follows the equivalent set of example steps in the portfolio kanban. See chapter 13, "Portfolio Level Overview."

Capability section. This section is used for preparation, prioritization, and implementation of capabilities. Solution Management and Architects/Engineers have full content authority for this part of the kanban. The following are typical steps for the capability section of the kanban:

- *Funnel.* All new capabilities are captured here. They may require new or enhanced functionality, including capabilities to implement system qualities or support architecture or infrastructure.

- *Analysis.* Capabilities that best align with the value stream (or portfolio) vision and support current strategic themes are moved to analysis for further exploration. This step requires refinement of the key attributes of a capability: business benefit, acceptance criteria, and size in story points. Some capabilities under analysis may require prototyping or other forms of exploration that involve Agile teams.
- *Backlog.* When sufficiently elaborated, and approved by Solution Management, the highest-priority capabilities move to the value stream backlog, where they're prioritized with WSJF.
- *Implementing.* At every PI boundary, the value stream pulls the top capabilities from its backlog and moves them to the implementing step. The transition is part of the pre-PI planning process, where selected capabilities are broken down into features and then are implemented by teams during the PI.
- *Done.* Capabilities accepted by Solution Management progress to this final step.

Summary

This chapter provided an overview of the value stream level, which is intended for builders of large and complex solutions. Such solutions typically require multiple ARTs, as well as the contribution of suppliers. The key takeaways of this chapter are as follows:

- Enterprises that build systems that are largely independent or that can be built with a few hundred practitioners may not need this level. Even then, however, those are far from trivial systems, and some elements of the value stream level may still be useful.
- The VSE is a servant leader who facilitates the work of multiple ARTs and suppliers.
- The Solution Management role represents the customer's overall needs across trains, as well as the strategic themes of the portfolio vision.
- The Solution Architect/Engineering role collaboratively defines the architecture that connects the solution across trains.
- In addition to the triad of roles (VSE, Solution Management, and Solution Architect/Engineering), customers are the ultimate buyers of every solution and are integral to the value stream.

- The economic framework permits fast, effective decision-making, within the scope of the value stream budget. This requires three things: an understanding of the rules for decision-making; knowledge of the current local context, or domain; and delegating relevant decision-making authority.
- Capabilities are similar to features; however, they account for higher-level behaviors of the solution, which often span multiple ARTs.
- Value stream epics are initiatives large enough to warrant analysis and a lightweight business case but are constrained to a single value stream.
- The value stream kanban is used to manage the flow of value stream epics and the capabilities.

11 Defining Large and Complex Solutions

It isn't that they can't see the solution. It is that they can't see the problem.

—Gilbert K. Chesterton

Overview 183
The Solution 184
Solution Intent 186
Fixed and Variable Solution Intent 187
Developing Solution Intent 188
Documenting Solution Intent 191
Solution Context 192
Summary 196

Overview

Building large-scale and complex systems is one of the most difficult and challenging endeavors today. In addition, many such large systems have an unacceptably high cost of failure. This has created a barrier to Agile adoption, as the need for a more rigorous definition and validation of solution behavior may appear to conflict with the Agile Manifesto's value of "working software over comprehensive documentation."[1] Clearly, builders of systems need both.

In addition, the engineering of these complex and highly reliable solutions requires and creates large amounts of technical information, resulting in far more "comprehensive documentation." Much of this information reflects the intended behavior of the solution.

1. http://agilemanifesto.org

Here are some examples:

- Capabilities, features, stories, and Nonfunctional Requirements (NFRs)
- System architecture, domain-level models, and designs (for example, electrical and mechanical)
- Application Programming Interfaces (APIs), physical interfaces, customer specifications, tests, test data, and results

Other relevant information records some of the key decisions and findings about the system. This may include information from trade studies, results of experiments, the reasons for design choices, and more. In many cases, this information and traceability between artifacts must become part of the official record, whether out of necessity or regulation.

To manage the complexity and intensity of this information, the following concepts are described in this chapter:

- *Solution.* The products, systems, or services
- *Solution intent.* The knowledge repository that stores the previously mentioned information
- *Solution context.* The broader ecosystem in which the solution operates

While these concepts are critical for developing large-scale and complex systems, they can also be useful in developing systems that are smaller in scope but require more rigorous definition.

The Solution

A *solution* is the set of final products, systems, or services delivered to the external customer or that enables the work of an operational value stream within the organization. Although solution development is the subject of both the program and value stream levels, the building of large and complex systems is the entire purpose of the value stream level. And building such systems typically requires a number of core practices and elements, as shown in Figure 11-1, which is followed by a brief description of each.

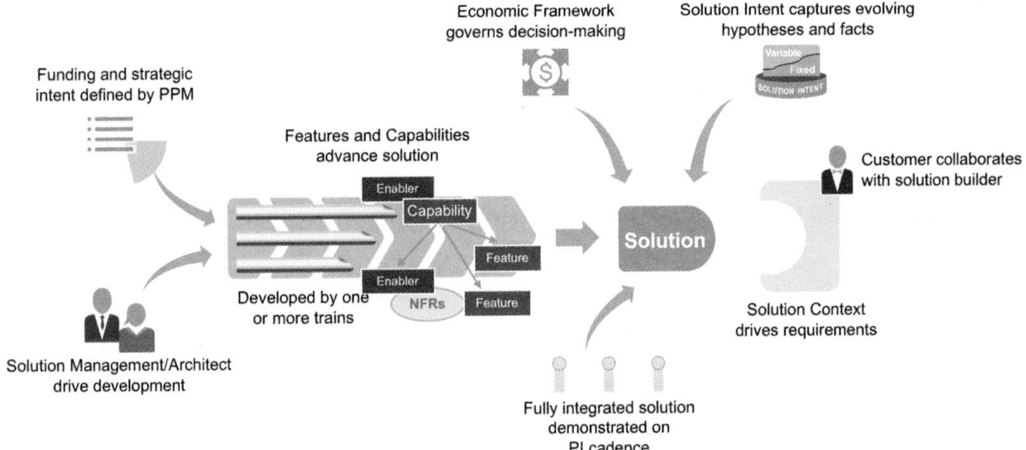

Figure 11-1. Overview of solution development

- *Solution.* At the center of the figure is the solution, which is delivered by multiple Agile Release Trains (ARTs) and suppliers collaborating in a value stream.
- *Solution intent.* The solution intent captures the goal and behavior of the solution and allows for exploring and defining fixed and variable requirements and designs.
- *Customer.* The customer collaborates with the teams to clarify the intent, validate assumptions, and review progress. Customers are part of the value stream and play a critical role in defining solution intent and context.
- *Solution context.* The solution context provides the additional information that determines operational requirements and constraints.
- *Solution demo.* Solution increments are fully integrated and evaluated in the solution demo, which occurs at least once every Program Increment (PI).
- *Solution Management/Architects.* These people help drive development and have the primary responsibility for solution definition and architecture, respectively. They establish scope and priority decisions and manage the flow of features, capabilities, and enablers that advance the solution.
- *ARTs and suppliers.* These trains apply common cadence and synchronization to build the solution in increments, described by features, capabilities, enablers, and NFRs.

- *Program Portfolio Management (PPM).* PPM provides funding allocation and alignment for the value stream.
- *Economic framework.* The economic framework governs development and provides for decentralized decision-making.

Managing Multiple Solutions in the Portfolio

A portfolio typically contains multiple value streams, each of which delivers a solution. Some value streams, and thereby solutions, are largely independent, while others may have a number of crosscutting concerns and dependencies, as shown in Figure 11-2.

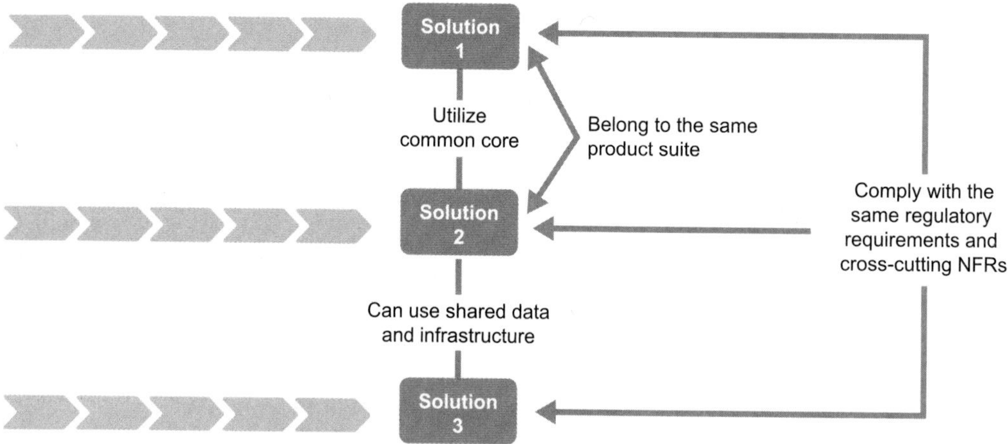

Figure 11-2. An example of crosscutting solution concerns in a portfolio

Sometimes these crosscutting concerns provide enhanced capabilities that deliver strategic differentiation. But other times, they're just dependencies that must be addressed as part of the solution. In either case, coordination across value streams is required.

Solution Intent

Solution intent is a knowledge repository used to define, store, manage, and communicate "what is being built" and "how it will be built," as shown in Figure 11-3. It serves many purposes, including the following:

- Provides a single source of truth for solution behavior
- Records requirements, design, and architecture decisions

- Facilitates exploration and analysis activities
- Aligns customers, teams, and suppliers to a common understanding
- Supports compliance and contractual obligations

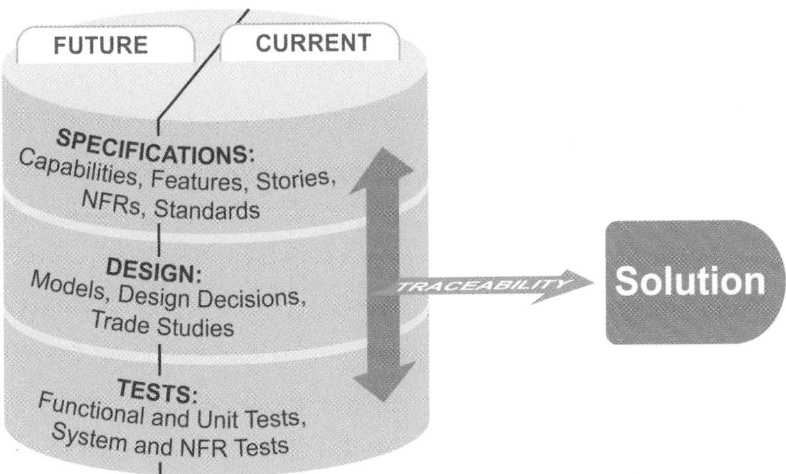

Figure 11-3. Anatomy of solution intent

As Figure 11-3 illustrates, builders of large and complex systems must constantly know two things about the solution.

- *Current state.* What, exactly, the current system does at any point in time
- *Future state.* What changes are intended for the future state

Knowledge of both the current and future states can be captured in any form suitable to the teams, but it includes these three primary elements:

1. *Specifications.* Capabilities, features, stories, NFRs, and standards
2. *Designs.* Models, prototypes, drawings, and trade studies
3. *Tests.* Functional and unit tests and system and NFR tests

Fixed and Variable Solution Intent

As mentioned earlier, teams use solution intent for a variety of purposes. None of these, however, mandates creating fully defined up-front "point-solution" specifications.

"Such early decisions restrict exploration of better economic alternatives and often lead to waste and rework."[2] Fixed and variable solution intent supports this adaptive approach, as described here:

- *Fixed intent.* This represents required and/or known solution behaviors. They might be nonnegotiable or may have emerged during the course of development. Here are a few examples:
  - *Performance specifications*: "The pacemaker waveform must operate in the following range. ..."
  - *Compliance standards*: "Comply with all PCI credit card compliance requirements."
  - *Core capabilities that define the solution*: "The Baja Adventure Ride holds four adult riders."
- *Variable intent.* These are solution behaviors that allow the teams to explore the economic trade-offs of requirements and design alternatives that could meet the need. Once established, these new agreements will eventually become fixed requirements (for example, "The ride vehicle has a maximum passenger load of 400kg").

Developing Solution Intent

The Scaled Agile Framework's (SAFe's) Lean-Agile approach to developing system knowledge differs from the traditional waterfall approach. Figure 11-4 illustrates the artifacts and processes used to develop solution intent using an emergent method.

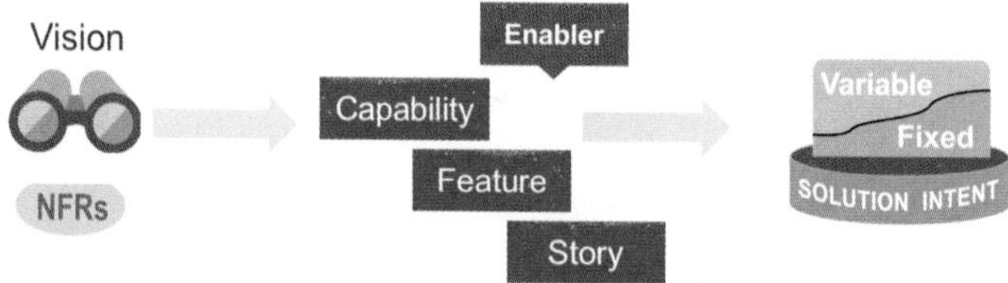

Figure 11-4. Developing solution intent

Solution intent begins with a vision. It describes at a high level the purpose and key capabilities of the intended solution, as well as the critical NFRs. This knowledge, along

2. Allen C. Ward and Durward Sobek II, *Lean Product and Process Development* (Lean Enterprise Institute, 2014).

with an emerging roadmap and critical milestones, can provide sufficient guidance to the teams for initial PI planning and execution. Capabilities, features, stories, and enablers are used to further define and realize the solution behavior.

Collaborating on Solution Intent

Although solution intent is shown at the value stream level in the Big Picture, it doesn't only arise there. ARTs help define solution intent and build the capabilities and subsystems that support it. This requires collaboration between the customer, Architecture/Engineers, and Solution and Product Management, as shown in Figure 11-5.

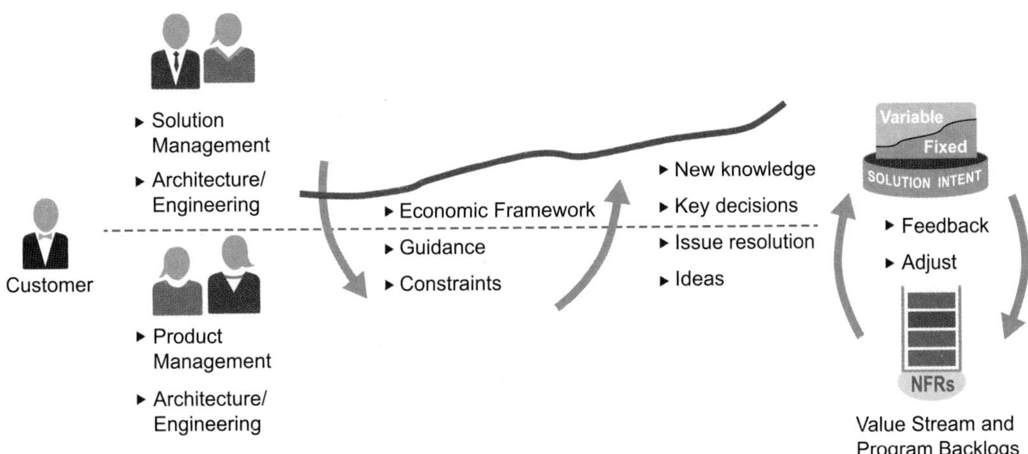

Figure 11-5. The collaboration that develops solution intent

Typically, the Solution Architect and Systems Engineering team drive the highest-level, system-wide decisions. This could include system decomposition, interfaces, and allocations of requirements to various subsystems and capabilities. In turn, required solution behaviors are allocated to the ARTs where they influence the program backlogs.

Solution Engineering also establishes how solution intent is structured and may define where information is managed to support analysis and compliance needs.

Moving from Variable to Fixed Solution Intent

Building and deploying a solution requires moving from variable to fixed intent. This process entails exploring options and keeping them open for as long as possible—within the constraints of the economic framework. As more information becomes known, the teams implement new features, and more requirements become fixed, as Figure 11-6 illustrates.

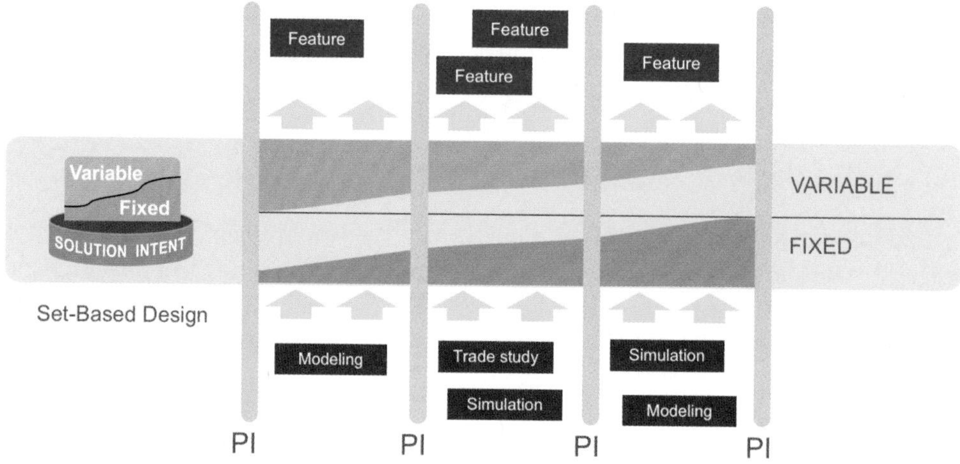

Figure 11-6. Moving from variable to fixed solution intent

System of Systems Solution Intent

A system's solution intent doesn't always stand alone. Many solutions are systems that participate in a higher-level system of systems. In those cases, other systems, as well as suppliers, provide teams with unique knowledge and solution elements that accelerate development. Suppliers, for example, will often have separate and independent requirements, designs, and other specifications for their subsystem or capability. From their perspective, that's their solution intent. The top-level solution intent must, therefore, include the relevant supplier knowledge and information to communicate decisions, facilitate exploration, align teams, and support compliance. Figure 11-7 shows this chain of requirements and design decisions.

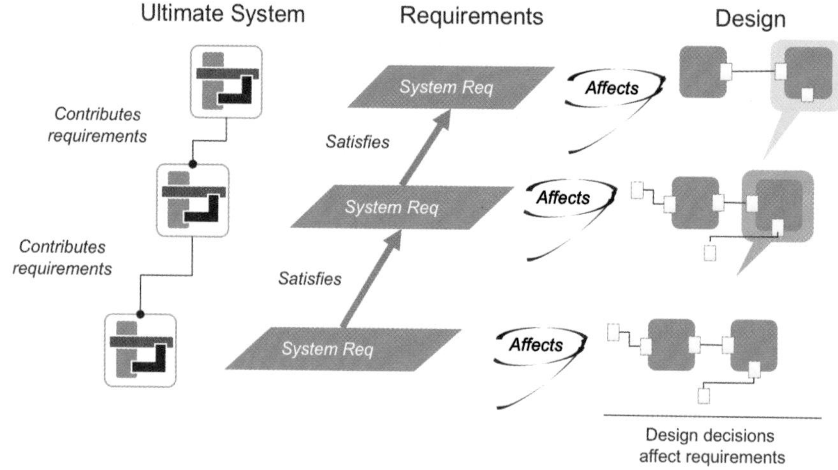

Figure 11-7. Solution intent hierarchy

> *System of systems* is a collection of task-oriented or dedicated systems that pool their resources and capabilities to create a new, more complex system, which offers more functionality and performance than simply the sum of the constituent systems.[3]

Documenting Solution Intent

Solution intent is a means to an end—a means to guide builders of systems to communicate decisions and demonstrate compliance. Planning content, organization, and documentation strategies should begin with the end in mind. But more is not necessarily better. SAFe recommends keeping design and architecture documentation lightweight. Best practices include the following:

- *Favor models over documents.* An environment of continuous change challenges a document-centric approach to organizing and managing solution intent. Model-based systems engineering provides an easier way to maintain and manage this information.
- *Solution intent is a result of collaboration.* Solution intent is not the exclusive domain of the Product and Solution Managers, Architects, and Engineers. Many team members participate in the creation, feedback, and refinement of solution intent.
- *Keep options open.* Defer decisions to local teams, and make them at the last responsible moment. Set-based design practices help avoid committing to design and requirements too early.
- *Maintain a single source of truth.* Record any requirements and design decisions in only one place, a single source of truth.
- *Communicate at a high level.* Describe system behavior with solution intent, at the highest possible level. Don't over-specify. Provide a range of acceptable behaviors. Decentralize requirements and design decision-making authority.
- *Keep it simple.* Record only what is needed. Solution intent is a tool to help build a product and meet compliance and contractual obligations. Less can be more.

3. https://en.wikipedia.org/wiki/System_of_systems

Solution Intent in High Assurance Environments

Complex and/or regulated environments may require substantially more investment in solution intent documentation. Compliance may mandate the creation of standards-based or other technical specifications. Some even require recording the results of exploration and decisions. Others mandate traceability to support analysis, feasibility, and demonstration of solution compliance to approved requirements.

In these cases, some elements of solution intent will be formally documented. However, this documentation can be "compiled" during solution development, rather than defined in an "up-front" mandate.

Traceability connects the artifacts of solution intent to each other and to the components of the systems that realize the full system behavior.

Solution Context

Builders of systems rarely build just for themselves. Often, a system is developed, deployed, installed, and maintained in an environment that is unlike the one in which it was created. An understanding of solution context is integral to the solution's ability to produce the desired result. The solution context helps identify critical aspects of the target solution environment and its impact on usage, installation, operations, support, and even marketing, packaging, and selling.

Here are a few examples:

- System of systems (for example, avionics system as part of the aircraft) or product suite (word processor as part of an office suite)
- Production infrastructure (for example, cloud environment where solution is deployed)
- Other applications or systems the target solution is integrated with

Understanding and aligning solution intent with solution context requires continuous interaction with the customer, as shown in Figure 11-8. Customers understand the vision and have the required decision-making authority. The degree of interaction depends on the level of connection between the solution and its environment.

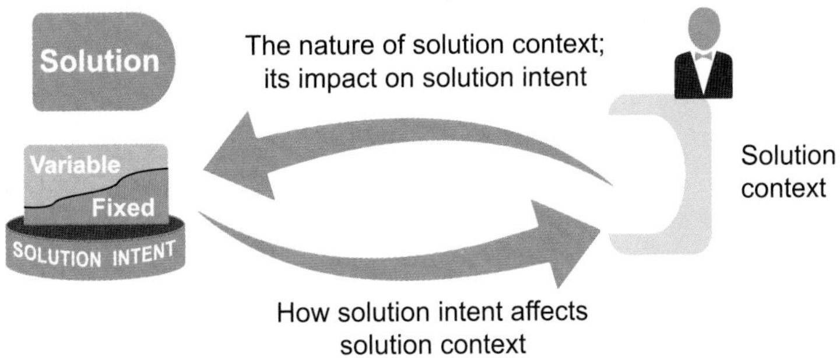

Figure 11-8. Solution intent and solution context inform each other

To ensure this alignment, the customer participates in the pre- and post-PI planning meetings and solution demos as frequently as possible. The customer also regularly integrates the solution in their context. This regular cadence of interaction and integration provides validation of the result within the customer's environment.

Solution Context for a System of Systems

The solution supplier-to-customer relationship in large system-of-systems contexts is a unique and cascading thing, as Figure 11-9 shows.

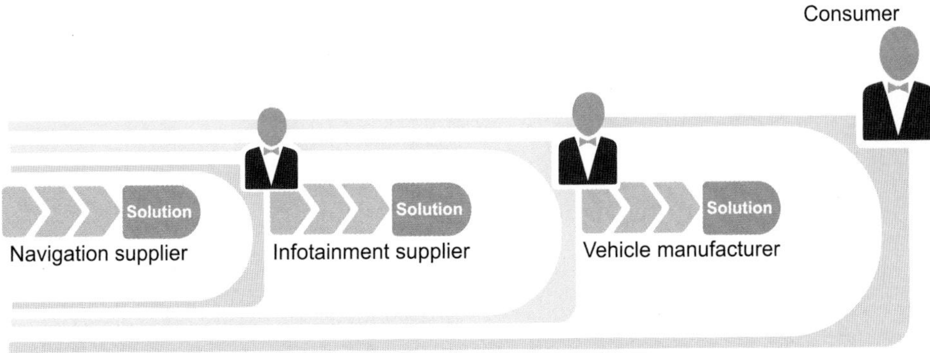

Figure 11-9. Solution contexts wrap in a system of systems

Each organization in the supply chain delivers its solution to the customer's context, which specifies how the solution is packaged, deployed, and integrated. That customer, in turn, provides a solution in context to their customer, and so on. In Figure 11-9, for example, a vehicle navigation system supplier first operates in the infotainment supplier's context, then in the vehicle manufacturer's context, and finally in the consumer's context. Because each organization has the ability to determine the success of the solution, one must be aware of the full value chain.

Solution Context for IT Deployment Environments

Even when the software being developed is for an internal customer, the solutions for the production environment still require context. Deployment must consider specific interfaces, deployed operating systems, firewalls, APIs to other applications, and hosted or cloud infrastructure, as Figure 11-10 shows.

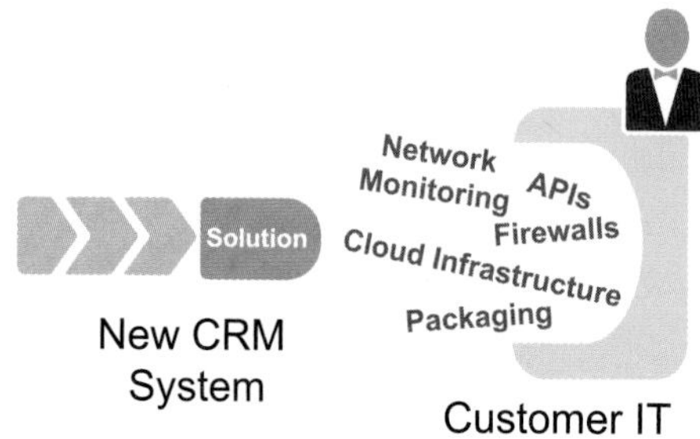

Figure 11-10. Solution contexts for internal IT deployment

In this example, the new Customer Relationship Management (CRM) system should reflect the required interfaces, as well as how the application is packaged, released, hosted, and managed in the end environment.

Solution Context Includes Portfolio-Level Concerns

There is one final consideration. Generally, the products and services of a business must work together to accomplish its larger business objectives. These solutions do not stand alone and are part of a larger solution portfolio and thus are also a portfolio-level concern. As such, emerging initiatives (typically in the form of portfolio epics) also drive solution intent and affect the solution's development and deployment.

For internally hosted systems, compatibility with other solutions is also often required, further extending the solution context. For example, larger operational value streams often use solutions from multiple development value streams, as Figure 11-11 illustrates.

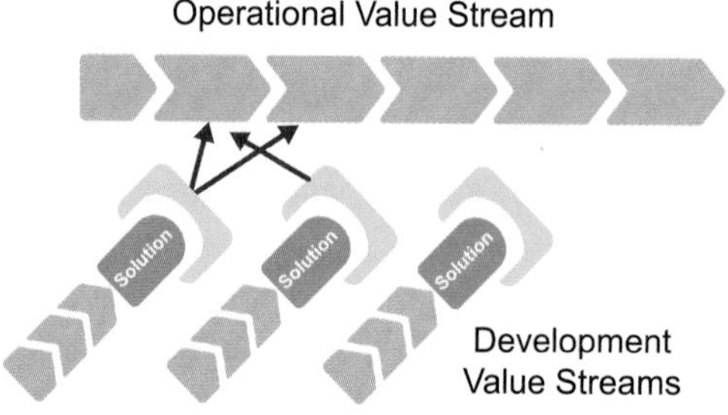

Figure 11-11. Solutions work together to support the full operational value stream

To provide a seamless, end-to-end solution to the operational value stream, each of these solutions must collaborate and integrate.

Continuous Collaboration Ensures Fitness for Use

Ensuring that a solution will work correctly in its context requires continuous feedback. Cadence-based development frequently integrates the entire system-of-systems value stream to demonstrate progress toward the top-level context's milestone and release commitments. Continuous collaboration ensures that the solution can be deployed in the customer's context.

Here are some examples:

- The customer raises and discusses context issues during PI planning and solution demos.
- Solution Management and the customer continually ensure that the vision, solution intent, roadmap, and value stream backlog align with the solution context.
- Issues discovered in the customer's context run through the value stream kanban system for analysis and resolution.
- Teams and the customer share relevant context knowledge, environment, and infrastructure—such as interface mock-ups, test and integration environments, and test and deployment scripts.
- Solution Architect/Engineering ensures technical alignment with solution context, including interfaces and constraints.

Consequently, there are many collaboration points between the builders of systems and the customer organization. A number of SAFe roles carry that responsibility, along with their customer counterparts, as shown in Figure 11-12.

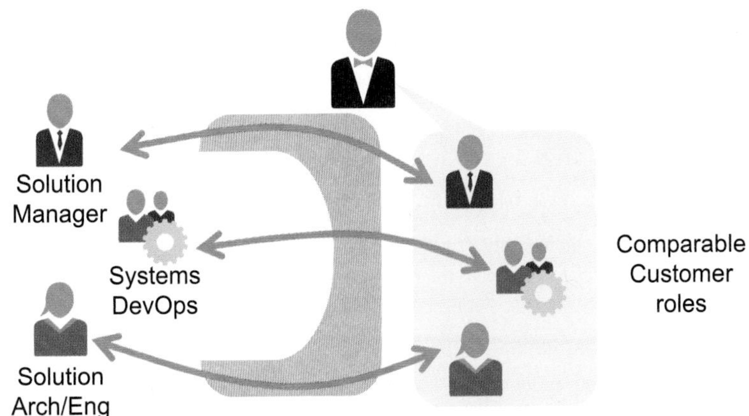

Figure 11-12. Collaboration between builders of systems with customer roles

Summary

This chapter discussed defining large-scale and complex solutions that typically require multiple ARTs, as well as the contribution of suppliers.

The key takeaways of this chapter are as follows:

- The engineering of complex and highly reliable solutions requires and creates large amounts of technical information. Much of this information reflects the intended behavior of the solution and is recorded in the solution intent.
- Solution intent is a critical knowledge repository to store, manage, and communicate "what is being built" and "how it will be built."
- Solution intent captures the goal of the solution and allows for exploring and defining fixed and variable requirements and designs, derived in part from the solution context.
- Building and deploying a solution requires moving from variable to fixed intent. This process entails exploring options and keeping them open for as long as possible—within the constraints of the economic framework.
- A lean approach to developing large and complex systems means that design and architecture documentation is kept as lightweight as possible. For example, models are favored over documents to maintain a single source of truth.
- Complex and/or regulated environments require substantially more investment in solution intent documentation. Compliance may mandate the creation of standards-based or other technical specifications.
- The customer's solution context drives requirements and constrains design and implementation decisions that are described in the solution intent.
- The solution context helps identify critical aspects of the target solution environment and its impact on usage, installation, operations, support, and even marketing, packaging, and selling.
- Cadence-based development frequently integrates the entire system-of-systems value stream to demonstrate progress toward the top-level context's milestone and release commitments.

12

Coordinating ARTs and Suppliers

Every science consists in the coordination of facts; if the different observations were entirely isolated, there would be no science.

—Auguste Comte, founder of sociology

Overview 197
Value Stream PI Planning 198
ART PI Planning 200
Value Stream Post-PI Planning 201
Frequent Solution Integration 204
Value Stream Sync 206
Solution Demo 206
Value Stream Inspect and Adapt 207
Summary 207

Overview

In part III of this book, we discussed planning and executing a Program Increment (PI), as well as the Inspect and Adapt (I&A) event for a single Agile Release Train (ART). But as covered in the previous chapter, when it comes to building really big systems, a single ART is only part of the story. In these larger value streams, execution requires the coordination of multiple ARTs and suppliers, and there are additional roles, responsibilities, and activities as well.

In this chapter, we will describe *coordinating ARTs and suppliers,* and cover the following topics:

- Value stream pre-PI planning
- ART PI planning in a value stream context
- Value stream post-PI planning

- Frequent solution integration
- Value stream sync
- Solution demo
- Value stream I&A

Figure 12-1 illustrates these value stream execution activities.

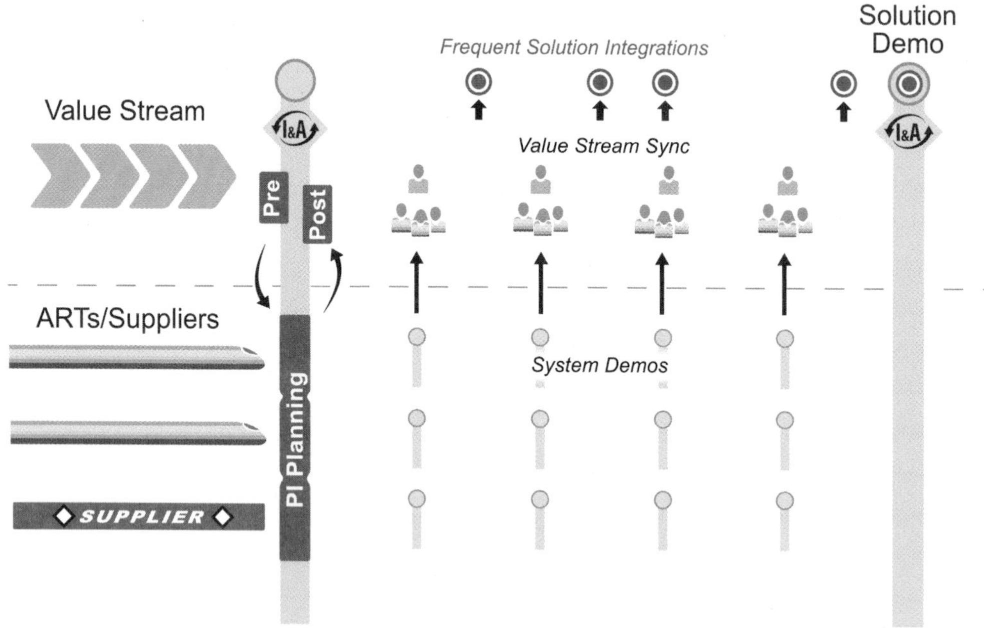

Figure 12-1. Value stream execution events

Value Stream PI Planning

The first element on the left of Figure 12-1 is value stream pre-PI planning. The purpose of this event is to establish the larger value stream context and goals for the ART PI planning meetings that follow. Inputs to pre-planning include the value stream vision and roadmap, context from the most recent solution demo, any updates to solution intent, and the highest-priority capabilities from the value stream backlog. Attendees at this event typically include the following:

- Customers and customer representatives
- Value Stream Engineer (VSE), Solution Management, and Solution Architect/ Engineering

- Solution-level System Team and Release Management
- Key representatives from all the ARTs and suppliers, usually Product Management, System Architect/Engineering, Release Train Engineers (RTEs), and engineering managers

The pre-PI planning meeting is used to build the context that allows the ARTs and suppliers to effectively create their plans during their individual PI planning sessions. There is no prescribed format for such a meeting, and it may occur as a single event or multiple sessions over time. But for simplicity's sake, let's assume a single event and suggest the agenda shown in Figure 12-2.

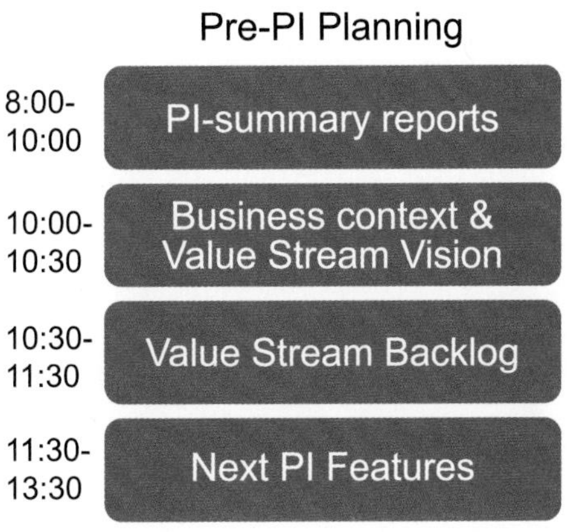

Figure 12-2. Example pre-PI planning meeting agenda

PI Summary Reports

Each ART and supplier briefly reports on the accomplishments of the previous PI. This discussion does not replace the need for the solution demo, but rather it summarizes what has been achieved to date.

Business Context and Value Stream Vision

A senior executive presents a briefing about the current state of the value stream and the larger context of the full portfolio. Solution Management presents the current value stream vision and highlights changes from the previous PI. They may also present a roadmap for the upcoming three PIs, as well as milestones that occur during that period, to ensure that they are known and addressed.

Value Stream Backlog

Solution Management reviews the top capabilities for the upcoming PI. Solution Architect/Engineering will discuss upcoming enabler capabilities and epics.

Next PI Features

Each ART's Product Management will present the feature backlog they have prepared for the upcoming PI and discuss any known dependencies with other trains and the potential impact on the solution.

ART PI Planning

The next sequential step in this process is where the individual ARTs perform their PI planning (the entire topic of chapter 7, "Planning a Program Increment"), as illustrated in Figure 12-3.

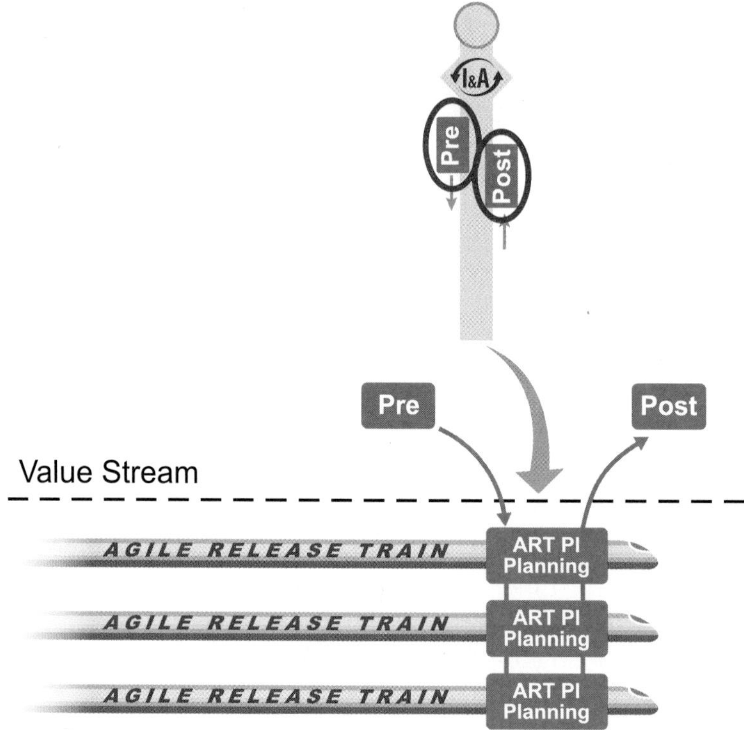

Figure 12-3. ART PI planning follows value stream pre-PI planning

With this sequence, ART Product Managers will have had an opportunity to review their initial plans at the pre-PI planning meeting and made whatever adjustments are necessary. Product Management, along with the RTE and System Architect, will have a better understanding of the value stream context and will be more prepared to fulfill their mission.

Value stream stakeholders will attend as many of the ART PI planning sessions as they can. However, the practical logistics of large value stream planning may limit value stream stakeholder participation. However, it's important that key ART stakeholders—particularly Solution Management, VSE, and Solution Architect/Engineering—take part in as many of the ART PI planning sessions as is possible.

In many cases, ART planning sessions are concurrent, and value stream stakeholders participate by circulating among the ART PI planning sessions. Suppliers and customers play a critical role as well and must also be represented.

Value Stream Post-PI Planning

The post-PI planning meeting occurs after the ARTs have run their respective PI planning sessions, and it is used to synchronize the ARTs and create the overall solution plan and roadmap. Participants include value stream and key ART stakeholders. Figure 12-4 shows a sample agenda, followed by a description of each agenda item.

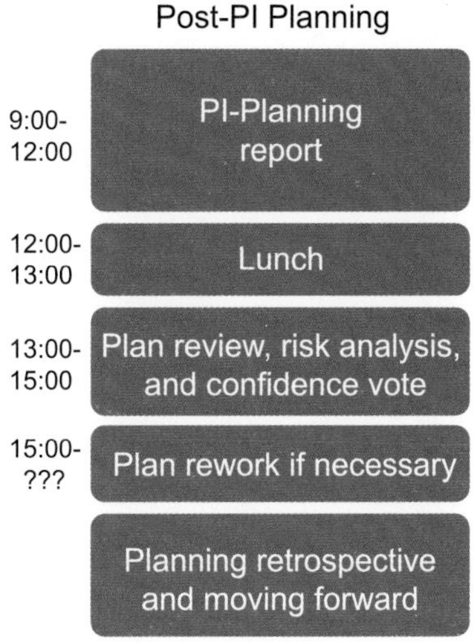

Figure 12-4. Example post-PI planning meeting agenda

PI Planning Report

Each ART's Product Management presents the plans devised at their individual PI planning meetings, explaining the ART PI objectives and when each is expected to be available. The VSE works with RTEs to build the value stream board and discuss dependencies with other ARTs and suppliers, as shown in Figure 12-5.

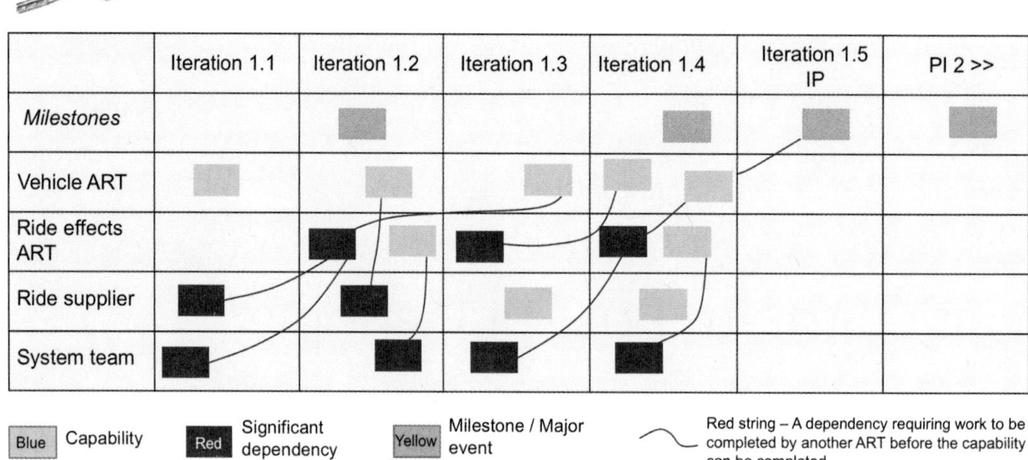

Figure 12-5. Example of a value stream board

Value Stream PI Objectives

Once the ART PI objectives have been discussed and the value stream board has been built, deliverables, milestones, and ART objectives can be summarized into the value stream objectives, as Figure 12-6 illustrates.

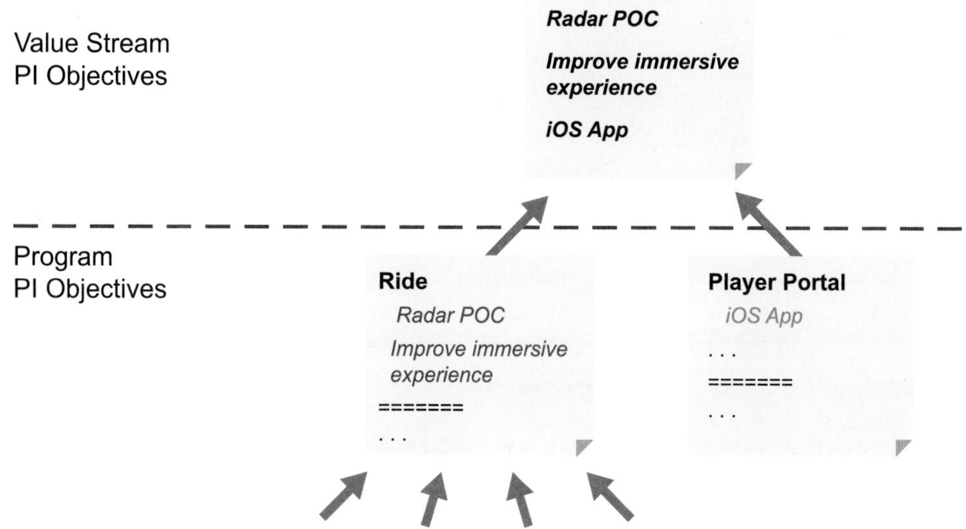

Figure 12-6. ART PI objectives summarized into value stream PI objectives

Plan Review, Risk Analysis, and Confidence Vote

All the participants review the complete plan. During PI planning, the ARTs have identified critical risks and impediments that could affect their ability to meet their objectives. Relevant risks are addressed in a broader value stream context in front of the full group. One by one risks are addressed and "ROAMed," meaning they are organized into one of the following categories: resolved, owned, mitigated, or accepted. (See chapter 7, "Planning a Program Increment," for more information on "ROAMing" risks.)

Once all risks have been addressed, the group votes on its confidence in meeting the value stream PI objectives. The team conducts a "fist-of-five vote." If the average is three or four fingers, then management should accept the commitment. If the average is fewer than three fingers, then planning adjustments are made, and plans are reworked. Any person voting two fingers or fewer should be given time to voice their concern, which might add to the list of risks.

Plan Rework If Necessary

If necessary, the group revises its plans for as long as it needs to reach commitment. This could cascade into follow-up meetings in the ARTs, as teams will need to be involved in any change to the plans.

Planning Retrospective and Moving Forward

Finally, the VSE facilitates a brief retrospective meeting to capture "what went well," "what didn't," and "what could be done better next time." Following this, next steps are discussed, including capturing objectives, using project management tooling, and finalizing the schedule of upcoming key activities and events.

Value Stream Planning Outputs

A successful event delivers three primary artifacts.

1. *A set of value stream objectives.* Solution Management, Solution Architect/ Engineering, and customers set business value and objectives. This may include stretch objectives and goals built into the plan but not committed to by the solution.
2. *A value stream planning board.* A value stream planning board, which highlights the objectives, anticipated delivery dates, and any other relevant milestones, is created by summarizing the data from the ART's program boards, as illustrated by Figure 12-6.
3. *An agreed set of value stream PI objectives.* A confidence vote is held to demonstrate the group's support and agreement for meeting these objectives.

Thereafter, the value stream roadmap is updated based on the objectives for the planned PI.

Frequent Solution Integration

When it comes to value stream execution, frequent solution integration—across multiple ARTs and suppliers—is critical to development success.

System integration at the ART level happens frequently, driven by the system demo, at every *iteration* boundary. That's not a trivial feat, and ARTs invest in substantial infrastructure and automation to enable frequent system-level integration.

But clearly that isn't enough for large value streams. However, it is typically significantly more difficult to integrate across multiple ARTs and suppliers, especially when building multidiscipline, large, complex systems. As shown in Figure 12-7, an integrated solution demo happens at the PI boundary. That mitigates the larger risk of a solution being developed for months and never fully integrated.

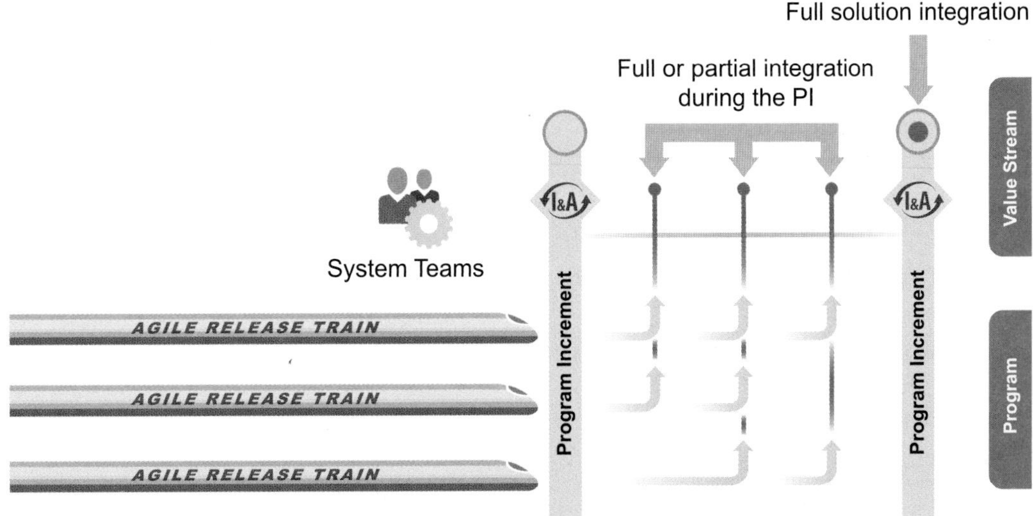

Figure 12-7. Frequent solution integration is the real measure of progress

To achieve integration across multiple trains and suppliers, however, you can't just wait until the end of the PI. Instead, the recommendation is to integrate multiple times during PI execution; otherwise, solution development will suffer from too much variability, late discovery, and rework. Integrating multiple times per PI helps the value stream "fail fast"—fast enough to effectively adjust the course of action for the PI.

Initially, defining solution integration points requires some careful planning, given the capacity needed for all activities involved. Later, the value stream may choose to gravitate toward a specific solution-level integration cadence. For example, integrate every iteration, every other iteration, and so on.

Because of the disparity of environment and the physically distributed nature of these large systems, a value stream–level system team is most likely required to perform some of this work. But the integration process must directly involve ARTs; otherwise, they may produce an incompatible solution increment, which adds waste into the process.

Enabling full-fledged, frequent solution integration across multiple ARTs and suppliers requires proper planning, tooling, test equipment, and significant integration infrastructure. However, it is the only way to assure the fastest possible development of these large-scale or complex systems.

Value Stream Sync

The VSE typically facilitates a once per iteration (or more frequently, as conditions require) meeting to continuously coordinate work across multiple ARTs and to provide visibility into progress and impediments.

The VSE, Solution Management, Release Train Engineers, System/Solution Architect/Engineer, and others (where appropriate) meet to update their progress toward milestones, program PI objectives, and dependencies among the ARTs. The meeting is often timeboxed to less than 60 minutes and is followed by a "meet-after" to solve problems identified.

This team is also responsible for keeping other value stream stakeholders informed as required.

Solution Demo

The solution demo is a major event in the life of the solution. The entire value stream demos a fully integrated solution, showing the accomplishments of the previous PI. It provides a regular opportunity for senior managers and high-profile stakeholders to review the progress and evaluate the fully integrated solution.

Usually coordinated by Solution Engineering, value stream stakeholders (who include Solution Management and the VSE) will typically attend. The insights learned from the demo inform these stakeholders of the current objective assessment of solution progress, performance, and potential fitness for customer use.

While the timing of the solution demo will vary based on value stream and solution context, it provides critical context for the pre- and post-PI planning meetings.

Value Stream Inspect and Adapt

In chapter 9, "Inspect and Adapt," we covered the I&A process at the program level. In larger value streams, however, an additional I&A workshop is required, following the same format as the program I&A.

The participants in the value stream I&A include the primary stakeholders of the value stream level (VSE, Solution Management, Solution Architecture/Engineering, and Business Owners), as well as representatives from the various ARTs and suppliers.

Summary

In this chapter, we discussed the general flow of events for coordinating multiple ARTs and suppliers to execute the work in a large value stream.

The key takeaways of this chapter are as follows:

- Pre- and post-PI planning events align the ARTs and suppliers to a common value stream vision and roadmap.
- The pre-PI planning meeting is used to set context for the upcoming ART PI planning sessions.
- Pre-PI planning is followed by the individual ART PI planning sessions, which occur on a common cadence. Value stream stakeholders attend as many of the ART PI planning sessions as possible.
- The post-PI planning event is used to synchronize the ARTs and create the overall solution plan and roadmap. Some adjustments to the ART plans are often required as a result of this additional planning.
- At the end of the post-PI planning meeting, there should be an agreement on a set of value stream PI objectives to be implemented in the PI and to be demonstrated at the next solution demo.
- ART system demos serve as excellent sync points for periodic value stream sync meetings, but these can be held whenever necessary.
- Frequent solution-level integration is the primary, objective measure of progress and serves to mitigate risk throughout development.

- The solution demo is to the value stream what the system demo is to the ART: objective evidence of real solution progress. It is the most significant event of the value stream level.
- While the timing of the solution demo will vary based on value stream and solution context, it provides critical context for the pre- and post-PI planning meetings.
- In a manner similar to the ART I&A, a comparable event is held each PI for, and by, value stream stakeholders. This closes the loop on relentless improvement at the value stream level.

Part V
Portfolio

To succeed in the long term, focus on the middle term.

—Geoffrey A. Moore

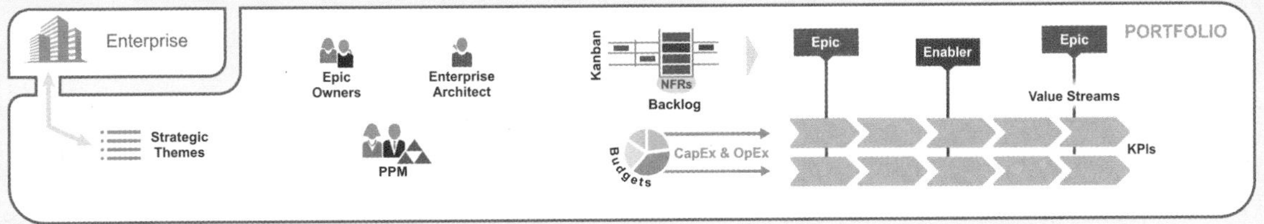

- Chapter 13 – Portfolio Level Overview
- Chapter 14 – Lean-Agile Budgeting, Forecasting, and Contracting

13

Portfolio Level Overview

Do our innovation investments focus on leveraging our crown jewels, or are we spreading ourselves too thin and failing to achieve genuine competitive separation?

—Geoffrey Moore

Overview 211
Connecting the Portfolio to the Business 213
Defining Strategic Themes for a Portfolio 213
Influence of Strategic Themes 214
Measuring Progress Against Strategic Themes 215
Portfolio Roles 215
Lean-Agile Program Portfolio Management 218
Advancing Solution Behavior with Portfolio Epics 221
Establishing Enterprise Value Flow 223
Coordinating Value Streams 225
Summary 228

Overview

The portfolio level describes the principles, practices, and roles needed to govern investments for a set of development value streams. These include the following:

- Identifying value streams and organizing teams and programs around them
- Communicating the enterprise strategy with strategic themes
- Empowering decision makers with Lean-Agile budgeting
- Program Portfolio Management (PPM), which provides portfolio strategy and investment funding, common program management elements, and governance

- Epic Owners, who facilitate the analysis of business epics through the kanban system
- Enterprise Architects, who work with business stakeholders and Solution and System Architects to drive holistic technology implementation across value streams
- Portfolio backlog and kanban system, which provide visibility, prioritization, and governance of crosscutting initiatives (epics)
- Coordinating work across multiple value streams

Aligning Scaled Agile Framework Instances to the Enterprise Portfolio

Each portfolio contains a set of value streams and provides funding and governance for the products, services, and solutions needed to fulfill some aspect of the enterprise strategy.

In the small-to-midsize enterprise, one portfolio can typically be used for the entire technical solution set. In the larger enterprise (typically those with more than 500 to 1,000 technical practitioners), multiple portfolios will likely be required—one for each line of business—as shown in Figure 13-1.

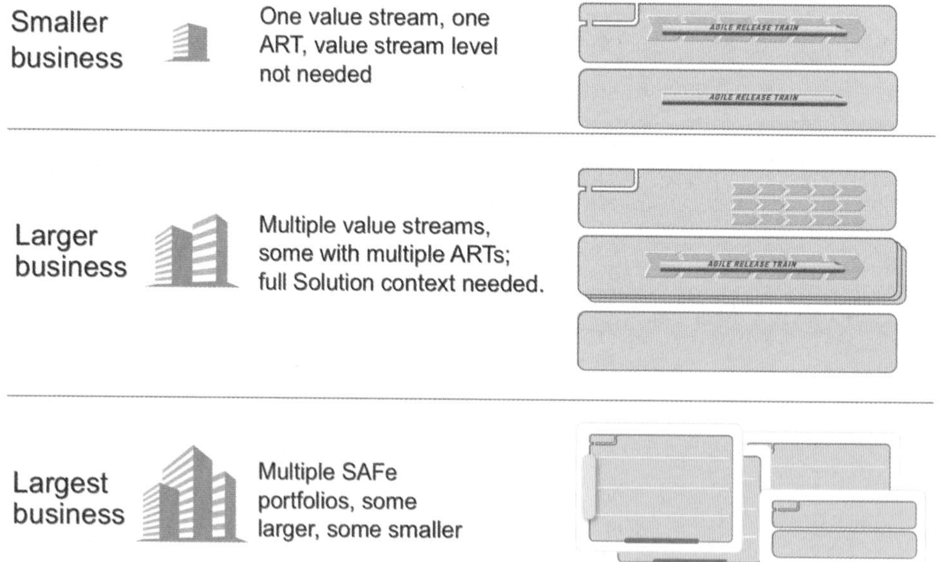
Smaller business
One value stream, one ART, value stream level not needed
AGILE RELEASE TRAIN
AGILE RELEASE TRAIN
Larger business
Multiple value streams, some with multiple ARTs; full Solution context needed.
AGILE RELEASE TRAIN
Largest business
Multiple SAFe portfolios, some larger, some smaller

Figure 13-1. Portfolio and value stream structure for different sized enterprises

In all cases, the portfolio is not the entire business, and it's important to ensure that the portfolio's solutions evolve to meet the changing needs of the enterprise. Guidance for identifying the enterprise value streams and then designing Agile Release Trains (ARTs) to deliver this value is given in part VI, "Implementing SAFe."

Connecting the Portfolio to the Business

Each portfolio exists for a single reason: to fulfill its contribution to the overall enterprise strategy. This is accomplished by aligning each portfolio's vision to the enterprise strategy. The primary mechanisms for this are the following:

- Value streams
- Overall portfolio budget
- Strategic themes
- Constant feedback through Key Performance Indicators (KPIs)

Defining Strategic Themes for a Portfolio

Strategic themes are differentiated business objectives, which help guide value streams to deliver specific, valuable business results. They help simplify the communication of the strategy by aligning the portfolio vision to the evolving enterprise business strategy.

Some examples of strategic themes are as follows:

- Implementing product and operational support for trading FOREX securities (securities company)
- Lowering warehouse costs (online retailer)
- Establishing single sign-on from portfolio applications to internal enterprise apps (independent software vendor)

Defining the portfolio budget and strategic themes is part of a strategy formulation process and requires extensive collaboration of enterprise executives, as well as portfolio stakeholders, as illustrated in Figure 13-2.

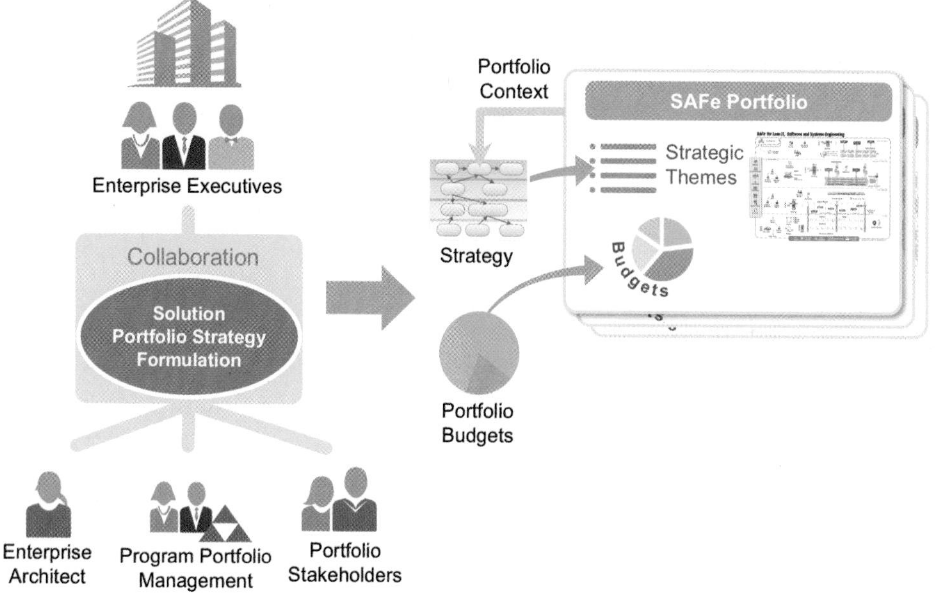

Figure 13-2. Strategic themes collaboration

Influence of Strategic Themes

Most generally, strategic themes define "what needs to be new and different" from the current state. As such, they heavily influence many aspects of the Scaled Agile Framework (SAFe), as illustrated in Figure 13-3. Each of these aspects is described in the list that follows.

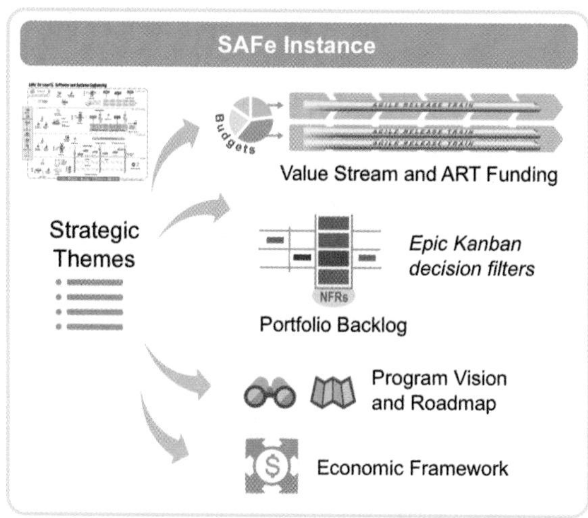

Figure 13-3. Influence of strategic themes

- *Value stream funding.* Strategic themes heavily influence value stream budgets, which provide the money, resources, and people necessary to accomplish the portfolio vision.
- *Portfolio kanban decision filters.* Strategic themes provide decision-making filters in the portfolio kanban system, influencing the content of the portfolio backlog.
- *Program vision and roadmap.* Value streams and programs operate fully within the context of the portfolio vision, so evolving strategic themes may directly impact their backlogs.
- *Economic framework.* Strategic themes may have a significant impact on the economic framework, where they can affect any of the major parameters, including cycle time, product cost and value, development expense, and risk.

Measuring Progress against Strategic Themes

While strategic themes communicate differentiated intent for the enterprise, success criteria provide a tool for understanding progress toward the intent.

However, many desirable measures associated with the accomplishment of strategic intent are *trailing* indicators. Factors such as Return on Investment (ROI) and new markets penetrated can take a long time to achieve. In their place, the enterprise needs feedback through *leading* indicators, many of which are not financial. Lean enterprises apply innovation accounting[1] to address this challenge. Innovation accounting offers thoughtful looks at which early indicators are likely to produce the desired long-term results.

Portfolio Roles

These three main roles support the portfolio level:

- Program Portfolio Management (PPM)
- Epic Owners
- Enterprise Architects

Each is described in the following paragraphs.

---

1. Eric Ries, *The Lean Startup: How Today's Entrepreneurs Use Continuous Innovation to Create Radically Successful Businesses* (Crown Business, 2011).

Program Portfolio Management

PPM represents the individuals who have the primary responsibility for strategy and investment funding, common program management practices, and governance within a specific portfolio, as illustrated in Figure 13-4.

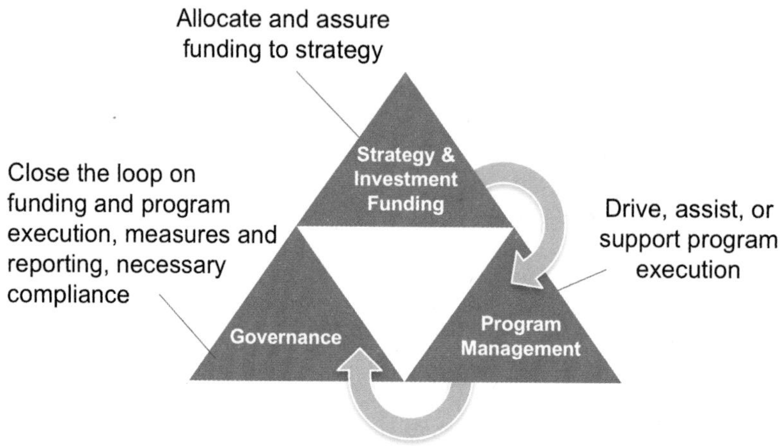

Figure 13-4. Strategy and investment funding

Epic Owners

Epic Owners are responsible for driving individual portfolio business epics from identification through the analysis process of the portfolio kanban system. They're also tasked with presenting the merits of the epic to PPM for a go/no-go approval decision.

The Epic Owner role may be assumed by anyone who has the domain knowledge and skills required to facilitate the epic through the kanban. Typically, Product Managers, Enterprise Architects, program managers, or business analysts fulfill this role. An Epic Owner usually works with one or two epics at a time, which falls within their area of expertise and the current business mission.

After approval, Epic Owners may work with Product and Solution Management to assist them with splitting the epic into value stream epics, program epics, or features. They may also help prioritize these items in the appropriate backlogs.

An Epic Owner can be effective only through close collaboration with other key stakeholders. Figure 13-5 highlights the key participants in the collaboration.

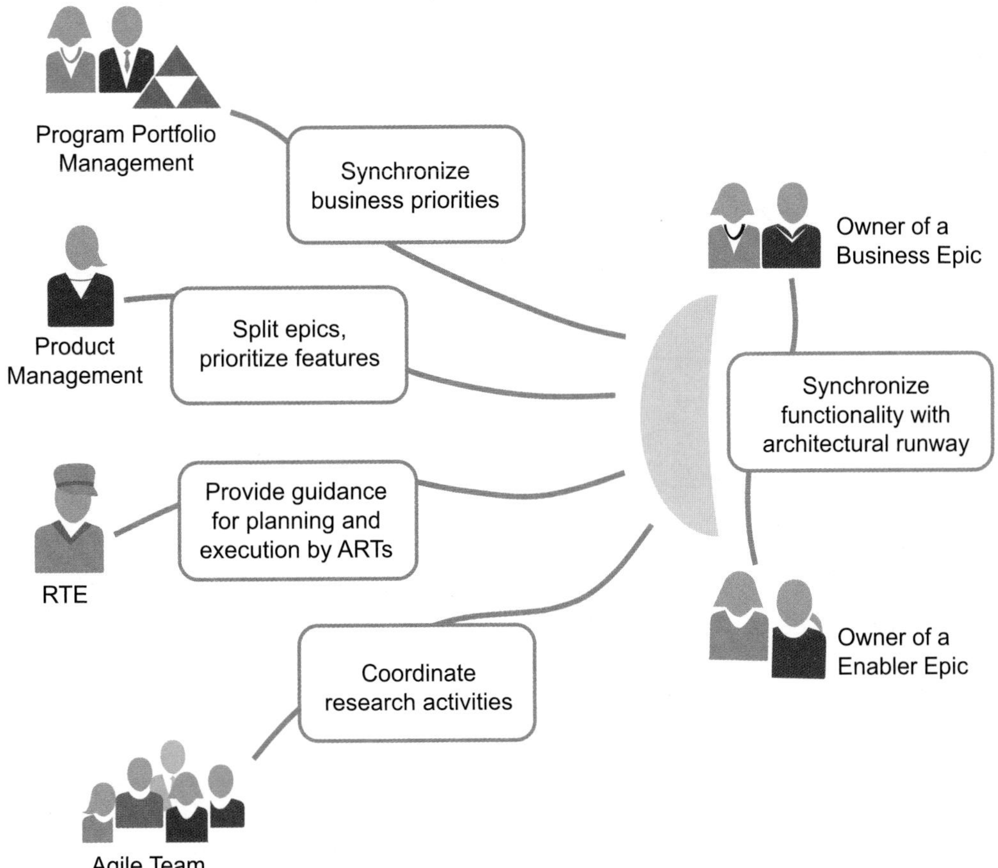

Figure 13-5. Collaborative nature of the Epic Owner role

Enterprise Architects

Enterprise Architects work with business stakeholders and Solution and System Architects to guide holistic technology implementation across value streams. The Enterprise Architect relies on continuous feedback, fosters adaptive design and engineering practices, and drives collaboration of programs and teams around a common technical vision. Their key responsibilities include the following:

- Act as the Epic Owner for portfolio enabler epics and participate in business epic analysis where applicable.
- Participate in the strategy for building and maintaining the enterprise architectural runway.

- Understand and communicate strategic themes and other key business drivers for architecture to system architects and nontechnical stakeholders.
- Influence common modeling, design, and coding practices.
- Collect, generate, and analyze innovative ideas and technologies that are applicable across the enterprise.
- Facilitate the reuse of ideas, components, and proven patterns.

In addition to these roles, an Agile Program Management Office (PMO) often assists PPM to fulfill their duties.

Lean-Agile Program Portfolio Management

Traditional mindsets can severely handicap the move to enterprise agility. To that end, SAFe provides seven transformational patterns that can be used to move the organization to "Lean-Agile PPM," as illustrated in Figure 13-6.

	From Traditional Approach		To Lean-Agile Approach
#1	Centralized control	➡	Decentralized decision-making
#2	Project overload	➡	Demand management; continuous value flow
#3	Detailed project plans	➡	Lightweight, epic-only business cases
#4	Centralized annual planning	➡	Decentralized, rolling-wave planning
#5	Work breakdown structure	➡	Agile estimating and planning
#6	Project-based funding and control	➡	Lean-Agile budgeting and self-managing Agile Release Trains
#7	Waterfall milestones	➡	Objective, fact-based measures and milestones

Figure 13-6. Lean-Agile program portfolio transformational patterns

These transitions help you better understand how to fulfill the primary PPM responsibilities—strategy and investment funding, program management, and governance—in a more effective Lean-Agile fashion. Each is further described in the following sections.

Strategy and Investment Funding

The purpose of strategy and investment funding is to support the implementation of the business objectives through programs that develop and maintain value-added products and services. In accordance with business strategy and current strategic themes, investment funding is allocated to value streams, which are identified, fostered, monitored, and continuously improved. Additional Lean practices help the enterprise meet its economic objectives, as outlined here:

- *Lean-Agile budgeting.* Each value stream has its own budget, which is typically updated twice annually.
- *Demand management and continuous value flow.* If demand isn't managed at the portfolio level, the invisible killer of "too much Work in Process (WIP)" will limit velocity and quality, causing teams and individuals to thrash from one initiative to another.
- *Epics and lightweight business cases.* To provide visibility and economic justification for upcoming, crosscutting work, epics must be defined and responsibly analyzed, each supported by a lightweight business case.

Program Management

PPM helps support successful program execution. While this responsibility lies primarily with the ARTs, the PPM function can help develop, harvest, and apply successful program execution patterns across the portfolio. Regardless of reporting structure, however, Agile program management replaces the customary functions with more effective processes, including the following:

- *Self-managing ARTs.* Self-organizing and self-managing ARTs take the place of traditional project and program chartering and management activities.
- *Decentralized, rolling-wave planning.* Centralized planning is replaced with decentralized, rolling-wave PI planning.
- *Agile estimating and planning.* Detailed project plans, lengthy business cases, and too-early requirements definition are replaced by Agile estimating and planning and lightweight business cases.

Governance

Governance functions still exist in Agile. Otherwise, there would be no portfolio-level feedback on investment spend and program reporting or any means to communicate and validate important standards and requirements for security, regulations, quality, and releasing. The governance function provides for portfolio context and life-cycle governance, as described here:

- *Portfolio context.* The portfolio context includes quantitative measures, such as ROI, market share, customer net promoter score, innovation accounting, and more. It also includes qualitative data, such as Strengths, Weaknesses, Opportunities, and Threats (SWOT) analysis. Most important, it represents the accumulated solution, taking into account the market and business knowledge of the portfolio stakeholders.
- *Life-cycle governance.* Principle #4 (build incrementally with fast, integrated learning cycles) and principle #5 (base milestones on objective evaluation of working systems) encourage and facilitate incremental development and fast customer feedback. In place of traditional phase-gated milestones, Agile milestones include Program Increments (PIs) and incremental releases, as illustrated in Figure 13-7.

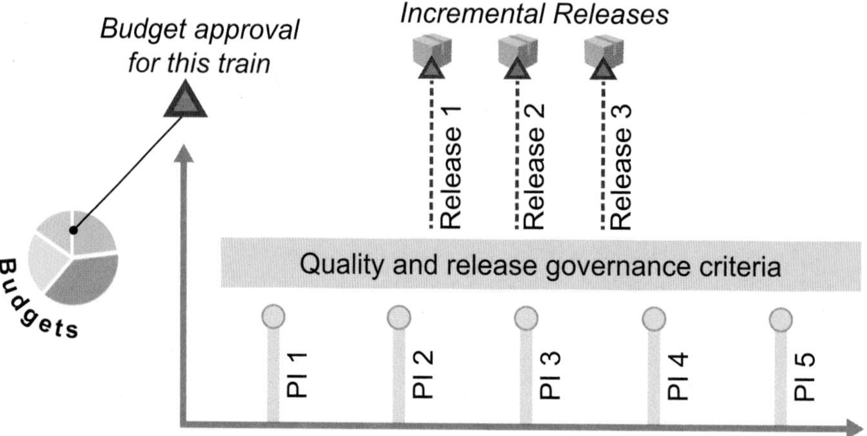

Figure 13-7. Agile milestones include PIs and frequently releasable solutions

By far, the most meaningful internal milestones are the previously mentioned releases and PIs. They are supported by frequent customer feedback and metrics within each iteration of the PI and Inspect and Adapt (I&A) retrospective cycle.

Advancing Solution Behavior with Portfolio Epics

Portfolio epics capture the largest initiatives that occur within a portfolio. Typically, these epics are crosscutting, meaning that they affect more than one value stream and ART. There are two types, as listed here:

- Business epics directly deliver customer and end-user value.
- Enabler epics are used to evolve the architectural runway to support upcoming business epics.

Epics are initially documented as a simple phrase and then elaborated into an epic value statement, as shown in Figure 13-8.

Forward-Looking Position Statement	
For	<customers>
who	<do something>
the	<solution>
is a	<something - the "how">
that	<provides this value>
Unlike	<competitor, current solution, or non-existing solution>
our solution	<does something better - the "why">
Scope	
Success criteria:	• •
In scope:	• •
Out of scope:	• •
NFRs:	• •

Figure 13-8. Epic value statement

Portfolio epics are initially captured in the portfolio kanban and move through this system under WIP limits. As they move from the left to the right of the kanban, more effort is expended to elaborate and analyze them. This aids time management, allowing responsible analysis that prevents wasting effort on epics not worthy of this level of attention. Epics that make it to the analysis step are elaborated in greater detail, using a lightweight business case, which is applied for analysis and approval. Figure 13-9 shows an example.

SCALED AGILE

Lightweight Business Case

Epic Name: (Short name for the Epic)	Funnel Entry Date: (Date the Epic ent	Epic Owner:
Epic Description: (A description of the Epic; consider using the Epic Value See http://www.scaledagileframework.com/epics/)		
Success Criteria: (Describe how the success of the Epic will be measured Availability increases from 93% to 99.9%, etc.)		
In Scope: • ... • ... • ...	Out of Scope: • ... • ... • ...	
Sponsors: (List key business sponsors who will be supporting the		
Users and Markets Affected: (Describe the user community of the solution and any		
Products, Programs, Services Affected: (Identify products, programs, services, teams, departm		
Impact on Sales, Distribution, Deployment: (Describe any impact on how the product is sold, distri		

SCALED AGILE

Lightweight Business Case

Analysis Summary: (Brief summary of the analysis that has been formed to create the business case.		Go / No-Go: (Go, or No-Go recommendation)
Estimated Investment	Estimated Story Points: (Estimated story points for the Epic)	Estimated Monetary Cost: (Example: Estimated story points * cost per story point)
Weighted Shortest Job First: (WSJF relative to other Epics in the analysis queue)	Type of Return: (Market share, increased revenue, improved productivity, new markets served, etc.)	Estimated Revenue: (Revenue, Return on Investment, or other applicable financial metrics)
In-house or Outsourced Development: (Provide recommendations for where the Epic should be developed)		
Estimated development Timeline	Start Date: (Estimated start date)	Completion date: (Estimated calendar date or estimated number of PIs)
Incremental Implementation Strategy: (Epics are defined as a single whole, but each epic undergoes incremental implementation. Visit http://www.scaledagileframework.com/implementation-strategies-for-business-epics/ for details on potential strategies. Many parts of this guidance can be applied to Architectural Epics)		
Sequencing and Dependencies: (Describe any constraints for sequencing the Epic and identify any potential dependencies with other Epics)		
Milestones or Checkpoints: (Identify potential milestones or checkpoints for reevaluation of the Epic)		
Attachments: (Other supporting documentation, links to other data, feasibility studies, models, market analysis, etc., that were used in the creation of the business case)		
Other Notes and Comments: (Any additional miscellaneous Information)		

Figure 13-9. Lightweight business case template

Approved epics are maintained in the portfolio backlog, where they await implementation capacity from one or more ARTs.

The portfolio kanban system helps manage expectations for reasonable scoping and time frames to implement new business ideas. This will be discussed in further detail in the next section.

Establishing Enterprise Value Flow

Enterprise Kanban System

A set of kanban systems facilitates the flow of work from the portfolio to the program, as shown in Figure 13-10. These kanban systems help do the following:

- They increase visibility into the flow of work.
- They ensure continuous refinement of new system intent and acceptance criteria.
- They foster role collaboration about the new work across disciplines, functions, and levels of SAFe.
- They initiate economic decision-making.

The value stream and program kanban systems are connected to the portfolio kanban. Together they provide a scalable content governance system that accounts for the most significant decisions about what gets built. As they progress, capabilities and value stream epics get split into features, and program epics are loaded into the program kanban, as shown in Figure 13-10.

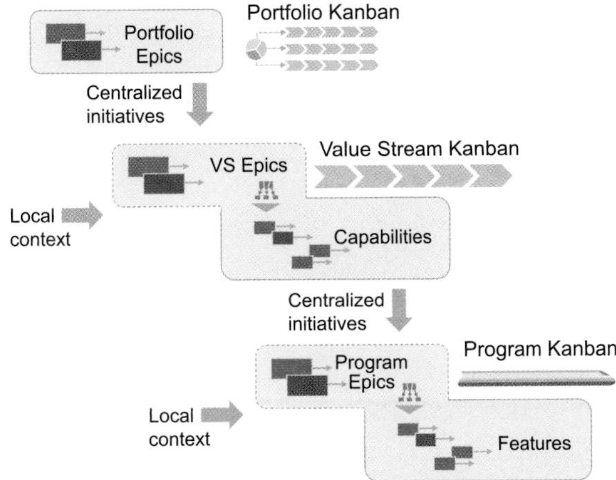

Figure 13-10. Enterprise flow of value through kanban systems

It's important to note that the kanban described earlier is *not* a strict linear or hierarchical, top-down system. That is, epics can originate at the portfolio, value stream, or program level. Likewise, capabilities, features, and stories are most typically driven from the local context, without requiring a "parent" work item above it.

Portfolio Kanban

The portfolio kanban is the highest-level kanban system in SAFe. As all kanban systems are designed for a specific purpose, the portfolio kanban is made to capture, analyze, approve, and track portfolio epics and enablers. Figure 13-11 shows an example system.

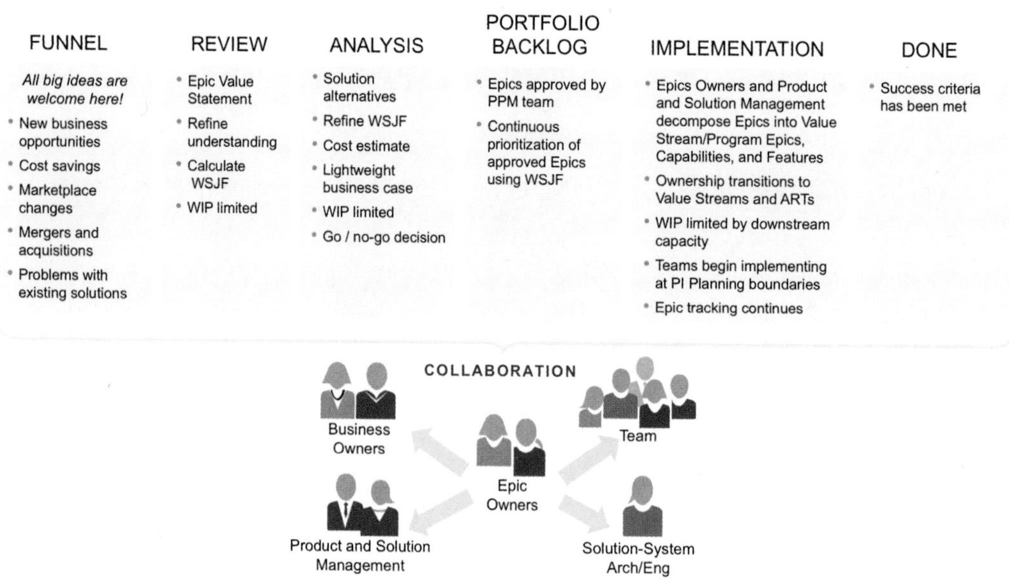

Figure 13-11. Portfolio kanban system and typical collaborators

This portfolio kanban system describes the steps an epic passes through on its way to implementation (or rejection), as well as the collaboration that is required for each step.

- *Funnel.* This is the capture stage, where all new "big" ideas are welcome.
- *Review.* In this stage, the preliminary estimates of opportunity, effort, and cost of delay are established.
- *Analysis.* This is where the lightweight business case is developed along with more thorough work to establish viability, measurable benefit, development and deployment impact, and availability of resources. At the end of this step, the epic is approved or rejected.

- *Portfolio backlog.* Epics that have made it through the portfolio kanban with "go" approval wait in the portfolio backlog until one or more trains have the capacity to begin implementation.
- *Implementation.* Once capacity becomes available, epics transition to the relevant program and value stream kanban to begin implementation. The epic progress measure and epic burn-up chart provide a means to track epics at the portfolio level.
- *Done.* The epic is done when it has met its success criteria. However, because of the scope of epics, "completion to original intent" is not always the desired case. In either case, once the epic reaches its most effective economic state, this marks the exit timing for the Cumulative Flow Diagram (CFD), if applied at this level.

Coordinating Value Streams

The portfolio level is where development value streams are represented, funded, and guided to the larger aim of the enterprise. Often the value streams within a portfolio are independent. For example, a hardware or software company may sell a number of products and services, whose technologies operate independently. More likely, however, there are dependencies between these solutions. And although we often think of dependencies as problematic, systems thinking informs us that enhanced customer value flows through these dependencies, which provide unique and differentiated capabilities. As a result, the enterprise can offer a set of solutions that cannot be easily matched by competitors.

Achieving this requires an understanding of how to coordinate value streams within a portfolio, as illustrated in Figure 13-12.

The primary aspects of cross-value stream coordination include the following:

- Portfolio cadence and synchronization
- Starting new portfolio-level work
- Program management, content management, and enterprise architecture
- Portfolio roadmap
- Deployment and release

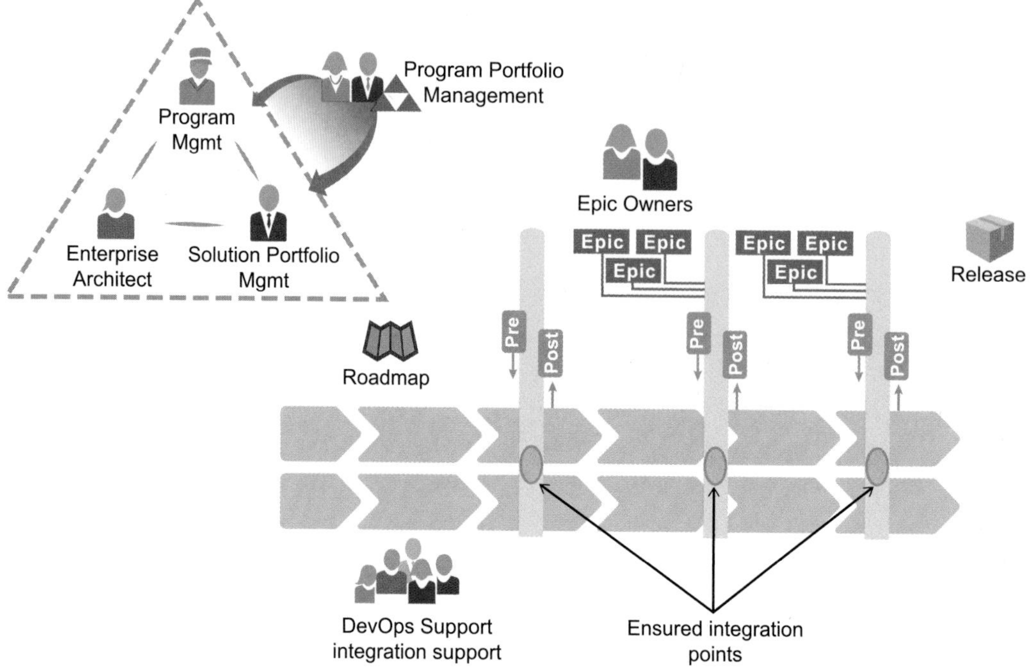

Figure 13-12. Cross-value stream coordination

Portfolio Cadence and Synchronization

Figure 13-12 depicts how the principles of cadence and synchronization apply equally well to the portfolio level as to the value streams and programs. The merits are the same: making events routine, thereby lowering the transaction costs associated with change and synchronizing the solution development of multiple value streams.

Common cadence enables the portfolio-level solution (via business epics) to progress through routine planning and integration points. Each point provides an opportunity for objective evaluation of the combined solution and is the only true measure of portfolio progress and velocity. The more frequent the points, the faster the learning and the shorter the time to market.

Starting New Portfolio-Level Work

Figure 13-12 also illustrates another key concept: The portfolio cadence determines the rate and timing of starting new portfolio-level work.

During the course of each PI, the value streams and ARTs are necessarily "heads down," focusing on achieving their committed objectives. Clearly, if new work enters the system in the interim, it causes interruptions, task switching, realignment, and movement of people and other resources to the newly revised objectives. Since teams obviously can't incorporate new and unplanned work and hope to meet their prior commitments, this portfolio PI cadence provides a steady rhythm for introducing new portfolio work. It helps the programs achieve the predictability that the enterprise depends on.

This portfolio cadence also provides regular mechanisms for managing epics through the portfolio kanban system. Any epic that's not ready prior to PI planning must wait for future service, even though resources may otherwise have been available. This also helps limit WIP for starting new and substantial initiatives.

Cross-Value Stream Program Management, Content Management, and Enterprise Architecture

As noted earlier, in many large portfolios, value streams are not stand-alone entities. Indeed, the largest measure of value often occurs when value streams coordinate to deliver strategic intent. Not surprising, this coordination requires three additional specialty roles, as illustrated in Figure 13-13. This "triad" parallels comparable roles at the program and value stream levels. It provides the primary functions necessary to ensure successful execution of portfolio initiatives.

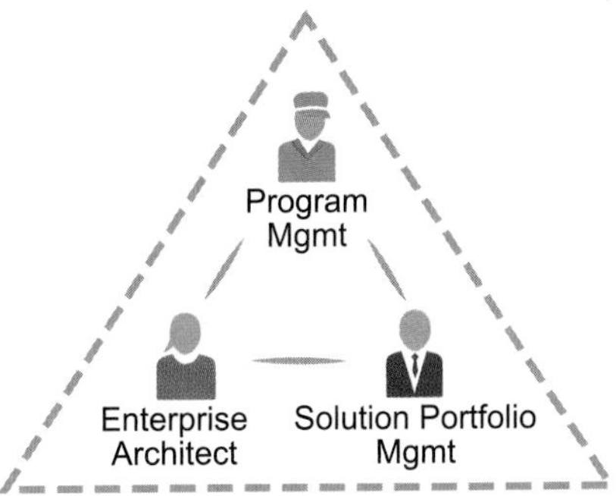

Figure 13-13. Cross-value stream program management, content management, and architecture triad

- *Cross-value stream program management.* Given the deeper coordination that is required, an additional role for cross-value stream coordination is required. In this case, a program manager—or program management function with comparable skills and experience, facilitates the execution of the strategic intent at the portfolio level. This role directly parallels the coordination responsibilities of a Value Stream Engineer (VSE) and Release Train Engineer (RTE) at their respective levels.

- *Solution portfolio management.* Someone must also steer the integrated portfolio solution set to the larger intent. These responsibilities lie with a *solution portfolio manager* role, which directly parallels the Solution Management and Product Management roles.
- *Enterprise Architect.* The Enterprise Architect fosters adaptive design and engineering practices and drives strategic architectural initiatives for a portfolio. They facilitate the reuse of ideas, components, and proven patterns across solutions. This avoids unnecessary duplication of assets and effort.

To support cadence and synchronization and decentralized planning, these roles—along with other portfolio stakeholders—may also participate in pre- and post-PI planning, as previously discussed in chapter 12, "Coordinating ARTs and Suppliers."

Portfolio Roadmap

A portfolio roadmap is a useful artifact to highlight how new content, primarily in the form of epics, contributes to the plan of intent. This higher-level roadmap also provides an opportunity to integrate aspects of lower-level roadmaps, and their associated milestones, into a more comprehensive view. This helps communicate the larger picture to enterprise stakeholders.

Deployment and Release

While DevOps pipeline capabilities are illustrated at the program-level whereby each ART has the ability to deliver somewhat independently, those local ART capabilities may not be all that's needed. Releasing integrated value may depend on effective DevOps pipeline capabilities at the portfolio level, accounting for the value streams and dependencies. In other cases, additional portfolio considerations require special treatment. For example, there may be dedicated or shared services and systems teams needed to help integrate the solution into a portfolio-level release.

Summary

This chapter discussed the portfolio level, which organizes the Lean-Agile enterprise around the flow of value through one or more value streams. Each value stream develops the systems and solutions necessary to meet the strategic intent of the portfolio.

The key takeaways of this chapter are as follows:

- Each portfolio contains a set of value streams and provides funding and governance for the products, services, and solutions that are needed to fulfill some aspect of the business strategy.
- Strategic themes help organize related business objectives that work together to deliver a specific, differentiated business result. They serve as filters for decision-making, influencing investments in value streams and epics.
- PPM represents the function that has the primary responsibility for strategy and investment funding, common program management elements, and governance within a specific portfolio.
- Epic Owners are responsible for driving individual portfolio business epics from identification through the analysis process of the portfolio kanban system.
- The Enterprise Architect works with business stakeholders and Solution and System Architects to drive holistic technology implementation across value streams.
- Portfolio business and enabler epics capture the largest initiatives that occur within a portfolio. These epics typically are crosscutting—meaning that they affect more than one value stream and ART.
- An enterprise kanban system guides the flow of value throughout the portfolio, value stream, and program levels. This kanban is not a strict linear or hierarchical, top-down system. That is, epics can originate any level without having a parent work item above it.
- Epics are initially documented as a simple phrase, elaborated into a value statement, and then expressed as a lightweight business case to analyze, review, and approve.
- The primary aspects of value stream coordination include portfolio cadence and synchronization; starting new portfolio-level work; portfolio program management, content management, and enterprise architecture; portfolio roadmap; and deployment and release. When this is necessary, additional roles may be required.

14

Lean-Agile Budgeting, Forecasting, and Contracting

Agile software development and traditional cost accounting don't match.

—Rami Sirkia and Maarit Laanti

Introduction 231
Lean-Agile Budgeting 231
Lean-Agile Planning and Forecasting 235
Lean-Agile Contracting 237
Agile Capitalization Strategies 243
Summary 247

Introduction

Many enterprises discover that applying Lean-Agile development to improve business agility directly conflicts with traditional methods for project-based budgeting and cost accounting, planning and forecasting, supplier contracting, and strategies for managing capitalization of software development. As a result, the potential benefits of the move to SAFe may become compromised. This chapter describes SAFe's Lean-Agile approach to each of these important business capabilities.

Lean-Agile Budgeting

The first of these challenges is the move away from traditional project-based work and project cost accounting to a Lean-Agile budgeting and program execution paradigm. To begin, as we described in chapter 13, "Portfolio Level Overview," the larger SAFe enterprise will typically have multiple portfolios. Each will have its own overall budget and strategic themes, as Figure 14-1 illustrates.

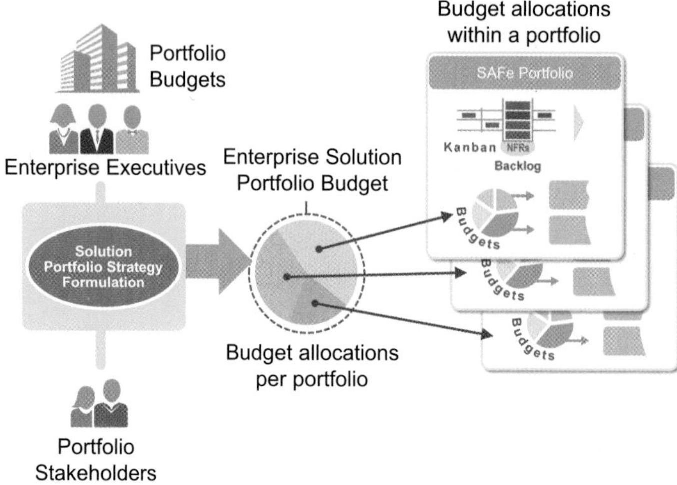

Figure 14-1. SAFe portfolio budgeting overview

Each portfolio exists for a purpose: to realize some set of technical solutions that enable the business strategy. Therefore, each must execute within an approved operating budget, as the costs for solution development are a key factor for better business outcomes. So far, so good.

Thereafter, however, things start to be very different. As we have described, centralized planning for how to *spend* the budget doesn't work effectively. Moreover, traditional project-based planning, resource allocation, budgeting, and cost accounting add immense friction to the process and slow down the delivery of value. Instead, the enterprise needs to transition from the use of projects as the primary financial and organizational mechanism toward Lean-Agile budgeting, as summarized in Figure 14-2.

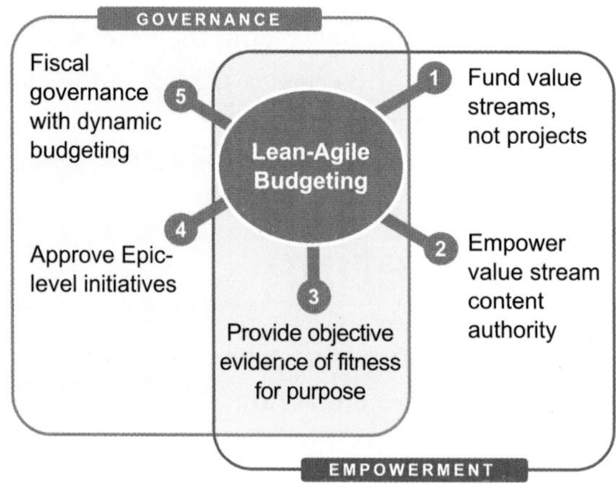

Figure 14-2. Empowerment and governance with Lean-Agile budgeting

With this new model, the enterprise has control of development spending, yet programs are empowered for rapid decision-making and flexible value delivery. In this way, companies can have the best of both worlds: a development process that is far more responsive to market needs, along with professional and accountable management of technology spending. That's a bold claim, so a more detailed description of each element follows.

Step 1: Fund Value Streams, Not Projects

In a sense, traditional project-based funding creates "temporary work for temporary people" and is in direct contradiction to long-lived teams and the need for persistent knowledge acquisition. In addition, project cost accounting requires significant administrative overhead, defense of cost overruns for unforeseen technical challenges, constant personnel reassignments, and more.

Therefore, the first step is to eliminate projects (features serve as the containers for what was project work), increase empowerment, and decrease overhead by allocating budgets to each value stream, enabling ordinary spending decisions to be made by the people who are closest to the solution. Value streams, and the ARTs that constitute them, serve as "knowledge pools" ("resource pools" in lean manufacturing) of dedicated people. This means the individuals and teams in the ART can flex to the work, swarming on critical features as necessary, controlling investment in maintenance and upgrades, and, most generally, simply doing whatever makes the most sense based on the changing flow of work. There is no need for individual project charters, along with its inevitable stop-start-stop delays.

Step 2: Empower Value Stream Content Authority

The elimination of projects is a huge step. However, there must still be a way to assure that the value streams are building the right thing at the right time. This is accomplished by empowering Product and Solution Management with content authority over features, capabilities, and enablers.

In support of this, all upcoming work is maintained and prioritized in the solution and program backlogs to provide visibility, as well as transparency of decision-making. Further, work is pulled from the backlogs based on Weighted Short Job First (WSJF) economic prioritization. Business Owners are included in this process, with a special focus prior to Program Increment (PI) planning. This assures that there is sound economic reasoning behind these critical decisions and that the right stakeholders are involved.

Step 3: Provide Objective Evidence of Fitness for Purpose

Once budgets are allocated to value streams, it's important to ensure that these investments are on track to deliver the needed solutions. This is accomplished by assessing progress every two weeks, and every PI, via the system and solution demos, respectively. Any stakeholder can participate in these demos to verify that the right thing is being built in the right way and that it's meeting the business needs of the customer, one PI at a time.

Step 4: Approve Epic-Level Initiatives

Epics are containers for larger initiatives that may cost millions of dollars and can impact multiple value streams and Agile Release Trains (ARTs). They are not routine, localized work. This is why epics require additional review and approval through the kanban system, including a lightweight business case, whether they arise at the portfolio, value stream, or program level.

Upon approval, however, epics are typically funded within the existing individual value stream's budget. (On occasion, however, additional portfolio funding may be provided.) In other words, epics are large enough to require both strategic and financial analysis and decision-making. That's what makes an epic an "epic" and a key part of the governance model.

Step 5: Exercise Fiscal Governance with Dynamic Budgeting

Finally, although value streams are largely self-organizing and self-managing, they do not create or fund themselves. Rather, Program Portfolio Management (PPM) has the authority to set and adjust the value stream budgets within the portfolio. To respond to change, funding will vary over time based on business dynamics.

Nominally, these budgets can be adjusted twice annually. If adjusted less frequently, spending is fixed for too long a time, limiting agility. If it's more frequently, the enterprise may seem to be very Agile, but people are standing on shifting sand. That creates too much uncertainty and an inability to commit to any near-term course of action.

Together, these five steps can substantially improve the flow of value through the portfolio while minimizing overhead and friction. For a deeper view of this topic, see www.scaledagileframework.com/budgeting.

Lean-Agile Planning and Forecasting

Agile has an intense focus on near-term value delivery. It also moves away from detailed longer-term plans, which—while providing some comfort to the enterprise stakeholders—also decrease the ability of the enterprise to respond to new opportunities. However, that doesn't mean planning and forecasting have no value, as the enterprise, its partners, and its customers need a near-term roadmap. Here are some examples:

- Marketing needs to understand when new product and features will be released to support demand generation.
- Sales needs to forecast anticipated revenue and plan activities to ensure it can meet the plan.
- Supply chain managers need forecasts to make timely purchasing requests, evaluate capacity, and develop logistics for production.
- Accounting needs to prepare financial plans, track capital spending, and report earnings expectations.
- Technical enablement must prepare pre-sales and marketing for the introduction of new and upgraded products and services.
- Customer and partners need to plan the implementation of new releases of the solution.

Clearly, the ability to do effective forecasting is a key economic driver and an essential ability of a Lean-Agile enterprise. We just have to do it differently.

Estimating

Of course, you can't forecast work without estimating the work. As described in chapter 13, "Portfolio Level Overview," epics represent the largest initiatives, and they must be estimated before approval. Such estimates must do the following:

- They must be fast, efficient, and as reasonably accurate as possible.
- They must support "what if" analysis of various incremental implementation scenarios.

But the traditional bottom-up, task-level estimating "work breakdown" structures require far too much specificity and, worse, tend to cause teams to revert to waterfall practices. That must be avoided. Instead, epics are split into potential features during the portfolio kanban analysis stage. These can be estimated in story points and then aggregated back into the total epic estimate.

The next question becomes, how are features estimated? Fortunately, this is something that the ART has the expertise to do.

Product Managers and System Architects—working with Product Owners and teams wherever appropriate—can use historical data to fairly quickly estimate the size of features in story points. And whenever the economics justify further investment in estimating, teams can break larger features into stories to get a more granular estimate.

Further, feature estimates—which are identified during the kanban analysis step—can then be rolled up into epic estimates in the portfolio backlog so that the economics of a potential epic can be understood before implementation begins.

Forecasting

Finally, given knowledge of program velocities, portfolio managers and other planners can use capacity allocation to estimate how long a portfolio epic might take under various scenarios. This provides a reasonable model for longer-term planning and forecasting. Given knowledge of epic estimates and ART velocities, and by applying capacity allocation, epic delivery can be forecasted over a near-term time line, as illustrated in Figure 14-3.

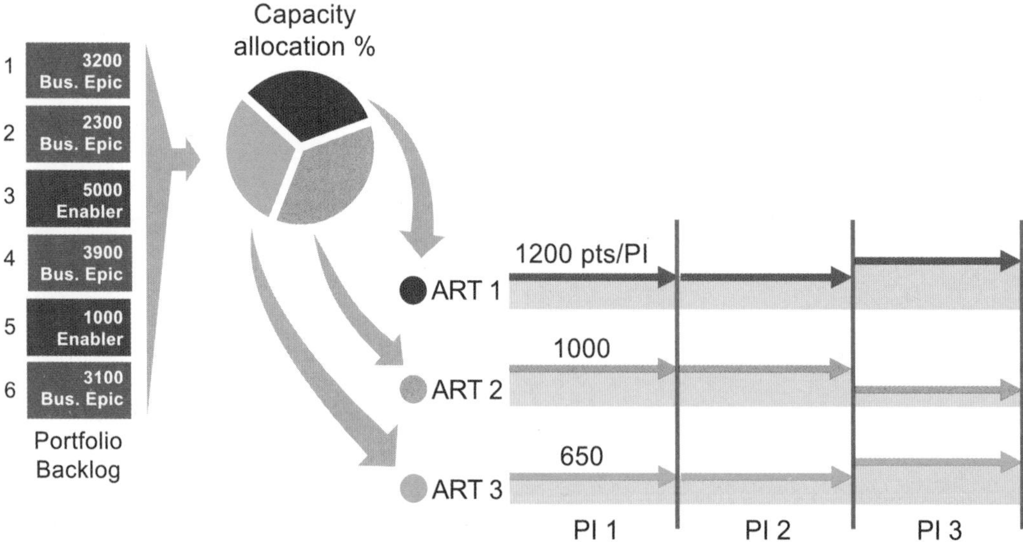

Figure 14-3. Portfolio forecasting with epic size estimates, capacity allocation, and program velocities

Agile or not, there is no crystal ball for estimating work on large-scale programs. However, SAFe provides mechanisms for estimating and planning that have been proven to be more reliable than waterfall methods.

Lean-Agile Contracting

Enterprises have used a variety of approaches to work with vendors in the outsourced procurement of complex systems or subsystems. Traditionally, there is a continuum of approaches that range from "firm fixed price" to "time and materials," with almost every variation in between. Figure 14-4 describes four points on the continuum and the means by which risk is shared among the parties.

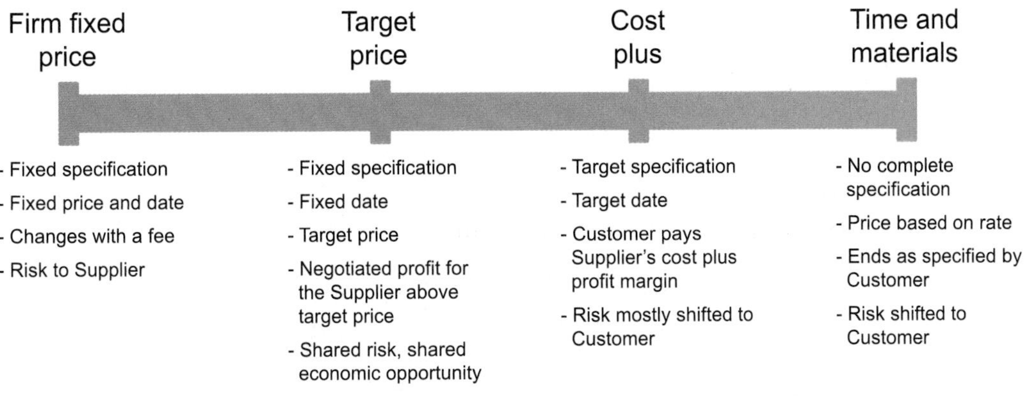
Firm fixed price
Target price
Cost plus
Time and materials
- Fixed specification
- Fixed price and date
- Changes with a fee
- Risk to Supplier
- Fixed specification
- Fixed date
- Target price
- Negotiated profit for the Supplier above target price
- Shared risk, shared economic opportunity
- Target specification
- Target date
- Customer pays Supplier's cost plus profit margin
- Risk mostly shifted to Customer
- No complete specification
- Price based on rate
- Ends as specified by Customer
- Risk shifted to Customer

Figure 14-4. A range of traditional contract types

Clearly, there's a wide range. In general, however, there is almost certainly an understanding that none of these deliver the best overall economic value, as discussed in the following sections.

Firm Fixed-Price Contracts

On the left end of the scale are firm fixed-price contracts, common in industry today. The convenience of this approach is the assumption that buyers will get exactly what they want and are willing to pay for it, as Figure 14-5 illustrates.

That makes sense on the surface. In addition, it provides an opportunity for competitive bids, which may be required in many cases. Competitive bids can potentially provide economic advantages, as the bid should go to the supplier with the highest degree of competence and efficiency.

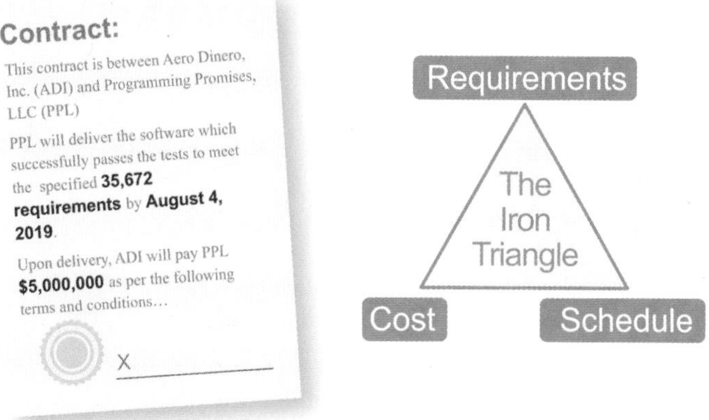

Figure 14-5. Firm fixed-price contracts create the "iron triangle" contract

However, there are many downsides to this approach:

- It assumes that the buyer's needs are well known far in advance of implementation.
- Those needs must be reflected in requirement specifications and early design details. This triggers Big Design Upfront (BDUF), waterfall-based development, and contracts.
- The contract is typically awarded to the lowest-cost bidder. That may not be the best long-term economic value for the buyer.

Moreover, to get a fixed bid, critical decisions are made prior to the start of the initiative—*when the uncertainty of information is highest.* The parties enter into the "iron triangle" of fixed scope, schedule, and cost. But as facts change, both the buyer's and supplier's hands are tied to the contract, which now defines a thing no one wants to build or buy exactly as stated. And much of the rest of the time is spent negotiating contract changes, adding waste or delay to the process.

Worst of all, once the agreement is entered into, each party has an *opposing* economic interest.

- It's in the *buyer's* best interest to get as much out of the supplier as possible in the short term, for as little money as possible.
- It's in the *supplier's* best interest to deliver the minimum value necessary to meet the contractual obligations.

The result is that this type of contract often sets up a win-lose scenario, which thereafter influences the entire business relationship between the parties, typically to the detriment of both. That's not lean thinking, and it doesn't further the long-term economic interest of either party.

Time and Materials Contracts

Given the previously mentioned issues with firm fixed-price agreements, it's clear why many in the industry want to move to the right of the spectrum. But the time and materials contract—which might appear to be extremely Agile on the surface—has its challenges as well. The buyer has only trust to count on.

Trust is a precious commodity indeed, and we rely on it in Lean. But misunderstandings, changes in market or technical conditions, and changes in buyer or supplier economic models can force trust to take a backseat. After all, it's in the supplier's best economic interest to keep being paid for as long as possible. This can drag out contracts for longer than necessary. Coupling this approach with a stage-gated process, where real progress can be known only at the end, compounds the problem.

Challenges can exist on the buyer's side as well. For example, when interviewed during a project postmortem, Stephen W. Warren, executive in charge and CIO of the Department of Veterans Affairs Office of Information and Technology, noted that, according to the project manager, "the project was never in crisis" since they were spending the entire budget every year and thus were able to renew their funding for the next year. Their measure of success, in other words, was simply whether the project would continue to get funding, rather than whether it was delivering the necessary functionality.[1]

A Collaborative Approach to Agile Contracts

Since neither end point in Figure 14-4 provides much assurance, perhaps the range in the middle is the sweet spot? Perhaps so, but even then, the biases of traditional contracts will likely creep into these agreements and expectations. What's needed is a different approach, one that "trusts and verifies" that the suppliers are building the right thing in the right way. This provides regular and objective governance for the buyer yet allows suppliers to have confidence in their customers, as well as in implied future economic commitments.

Characteristics of an Agile contract type would include the ability to do the following:

- Optimize the economic value for both parties in the long and short term.
- Exploit variability, using fixed versus variable solution intent, and adaptive response to new knowledge.
- Provide complete and continuous visibility and objective evidence of solution fitness.

1. Jason Bloomberg, "Fixing Scheduling with Agile at the VA," *Forbes* (October 23, 2014).

- Provide a measured approach to investment that can vary over time and stops when sufficient value has been achieved.
- Provide the supplier with near-term confidence of funding and sufficient notice when funding winds down or stops.
- Motivate both parties to build the best solution possible within agreed-to economic boundaries.

SAFe Managed-Investment Contracts

Given all the previously mentioned reasons, the industry can benefit by moving toward a more Agile contract paradigm, one that optimizes economic benefits for both the buyer and the supplier. We call one such approach a *SAFe managed-investment contract*, which is described next.

Pre-commitment Phase

Prior to engaging in any significant investment contract for developing a complex system with many unknowns, some due diligence is required. In this case, the customer and supplier work together to agree on terms for the basis of the contract. This is the pre-commitment phase, illustrated in Figure 14-6.

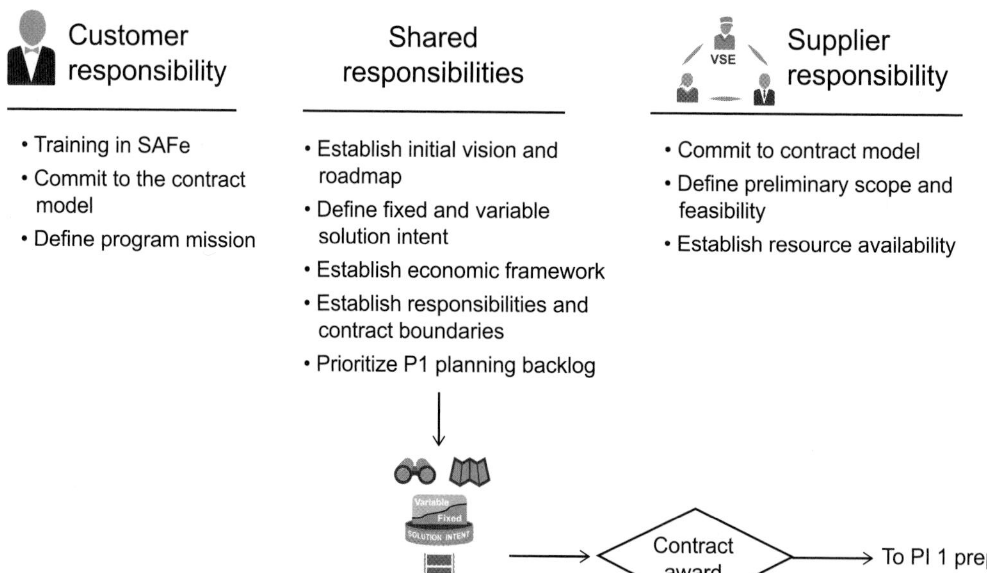

Figure 14-6. SAFe managed-investment contract pre-commitment phase

During this phase, the customer has specific responsibilities, including understanding the basic constructs and responsibilities of this form of Agile contract, as well as defining and communicating the larger program mission statement to the supplier (or potential suppliers).

The supplier must do some initial homework as well. This often includes a first analysis of potential feasibility and assurance that the supplier's core competence aligns with the buyer's needs. It also demands some understanding of the potential resources that will be required over the initial contract periods and maybe even a rough cost estimate. However, these responsibilities are largely routine.

The shared responsibilities in the middle, however, start the customer and supplier down a path to a more measured investment, supported by continuous objective evidence of fitness for use. These responsibilities include the following:

- Establishing the initial vision and roadmap
- Defining the initial fixed and variable solution intent
- Prioritizing the initial program backlog for PI planning
- Establishing execution responsibilities
- Establishing the economic framework, trade-off guideline, the PI funding commitment (number of PIs committed), initial funding levels, and other contractual terms

Regarding the PI funding commitment, in some cases the supplier may need to provide a preliminary estimate. In other cases, a pay-as-you-go approach may be suitable. Based on the agreements, the customer will agree to fund the supplier at certain rates for the early PIs. This is the initial commitment period. The length is based on context, but two PIs or so (16–24 weeks) may be a reasonable starting point.

Depending on context, the customer may have these discussions with multiple potential suppliers. If significant technical feasibility is involved, this can often be done under a separate contract, which compensates the supplier for the efforts to get to commitment. Alternately, this may be simply business as usual for the supplier, with these pre-commitment investments a part of the normal pre-sales process. At some point, however, the customer can move on to award the contract.

Contract Execution

At this point, development begins, as illustrated in Figure 14-7.

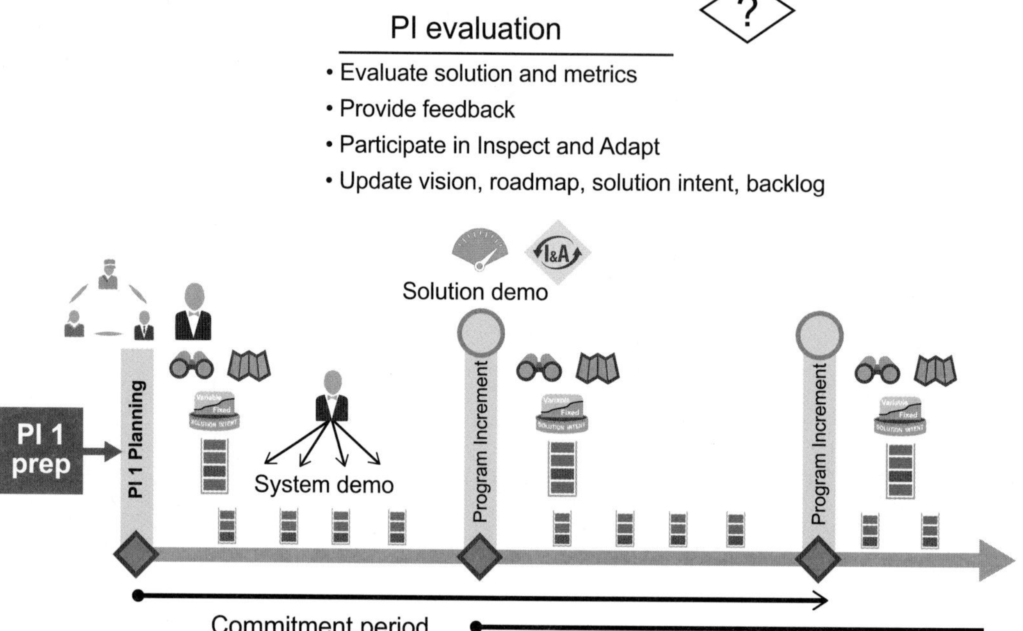

Figure 14-7. SAFe managed-investment contract execution phase

A description of the activity timeline follows:

- *PI 1 preparation.* Both the supplier and customer will invest some time and effort in preparing content and logistics for the first PI planning session. (Note: In some cases, it might be suitable that PI 1 planning is part of the pre-commitment phase, although this route clearly requires significant investment by both parties.)
- *PI 1 planning.* The first PI planning event is critical to the program. The customer and supplier stakeholders plan the first PI in iteration-level detail.
- *PI 1 execution.* Depending on context, customers participate at various levels in iteration execution. At a minimum, however, direct customer engagement is usually required for each system demo. For large value streams requiring multiple ARTs,

it might make sense for ART-level system demos to be replaced by a more fully integrated solution demo, which can occur more frequently than at PI boundaries.

- *PI evaluation*. Now each PI marks a critical milestone for both the customer and supplier, when the solution demo is held and is evaluated. Agreed-to metrics are compiled and analyzed, and decisions for the next PI are made.

The Inspect and Adapt (I&A) session is used to assess progress and to plan improvements for the upcoming PI. Based on whether sufficient value has been achieved, the customer may decide to keep funding steady, increase it, or begin winding down investment. The scope of the next PI will be determined by this decision.

This process continues until the solution has delivered the value the customer requires. At this point, the customer and supplier collaborate to reduce the scope and funding commitments in accordance with their agreement.

Agile Capitalization Strategies

Finally, there is one last financial topic to be discussed. In accordance with varying accounting rules across industries and regions, many enterprises capitalize some part of the cost of software development for approved and substantial initiatives. Historically, triggers for capitalization have been based on waterfall, phase-gate assumptions, so we'll use a different approach here, too.

In any case, portfolio stakeholders must understand both capital and operating expenses so that they are included as part of the economic framework for each value stream. Otherwise, money may be spent in the wrong categories, and the financial results will not be as intended. Here are some examples:

- Mistakes and inconsistencies in reporting of capital expenses may result in penalties, lower profit, or—even worse—restatement of earnings.
- Expensing all activities can result in overpaying taxes, understating the company's value and profits, and reducing borrowing power.

A budget for a SAFe portfolio may include both capital and operating expense elements.

- Operating expenses record the ongoing costs of running a product, business, or service. These costs are recorded and expensed in the period in which they occur.

- Capital expenses most typically reflect the monies required to purchase, upgrade, or enhance tangible physical assets, such as computing equipment, machinery, or other property. In this case, the cost of purchase is put on the balance sheet as an asset and then expensed on the income statement over the useful life of that asset.
- In some cases, some of the labor costs associated with development of intangible assets, such as patents and software, may also be subject to capital expense recording. In this case, capital expenses may include salaries and direct burden, contract labor, materials, supplies, and other items directly related to the solution development activities.

Capitalization of Software Development

This process and tracking for capitalizing of software can be challenging for companies moving to Agile development. For example, many U.S. companies are subject to U.S. Financial Accounting Standards Board (FASB) regulations, which require that a product must meet the following criteria in order to begin capitalizing software development costs:[2]

- The product has achieved technical feasibility.
- Management has provided written approval to fund the development effort.
- Management has committed the resources to development.
- Management is confident that the product will be successfully developed and delivered.

Similar accounting rules exist for other countries.

Before capitalization of software can begin, finance departments typically require documented evidence that the previous activities have been completed. Once these criteria are met, further development costs may be subject to capitalization, as described in Figure 14-8.

2. Disclaimer: The authors have no formal training or accreditation in accounting. The treatment of software costs and potential for capitalization treatment varies by country, by industry (for example, while many companies in the United States are subject to one set of rules, suppliers to the U.S. federal government have an entirely different set of rules), and even by individual company policy. Some companies choose not to capitalize software development costs at all.

Expense	Capitalize
Costs associated with establishing feasibility of a program, including: • Feasibility research and prototyping • Analysis and formulation of alternatives • High-level architectural work in support of decision-making • Training • Production maintenance and support	Costs associated with committed new projects, upgrades and enhancements that increase functionality of existing software (including major revisions of third-party products), which may include detailed design activities for committed new functionality, including: • Salaries • Cost of materials • Contract labor • Burden, including some directly associated indirect labor, and interest Excluded: General and administrative costs and overhead

Figure 14-8. Categories of expensed and potentially capitalized costs

Capitalization Triggers in Waterfall Development

Historically, capitalization has been applied in the context of waterfall development. Waterfall development has a well-defined "up-front phase" during which requirements are created, the design is produced, and feasibility is established. For those projects that receive management approval to proceed, the requirements and design milestones often serve as phase gates for starting capitalization.

Agile Development Capitalization Strategies

In Agile, however, requirements and design emerge continuously, so there is no formal gate to serve as an official prelude to capitalization. However, the majority of the work of most ARTs is usually focused on building and extending software assets that are past the point of feasibility analysis. They usually do this by developing new features for the solution. Since features "increase the functionality of existing software," the stories associated with those features constitute much of the work of the ART personnel. Therefore, feature development costs may be subject to potential capitalization.

The ARTs are also directly involved with establishing the business and technical feasibility of the various portfolio initiatives (epics) that work their way through the portfolio kanban.

This type of work does not meet the previous criteria and is expensed up until the "go" recommendation, at which time new feature development begins.

This means that both types of work may be present in any program increment (and, by extension, any relevant accounting period). Much of this work is "new feature work," which increases the functionality of existing software. Other work includes innovation and exploration efforts. These may be initiated from the portfolio kanban—as part of the research and feasibility for potential new portfolio-level epics—or it may arise locally. In addition, maintenance, infrastructure work, and so on, also occur during the period. Figure 14-9 illustrates these concepts.

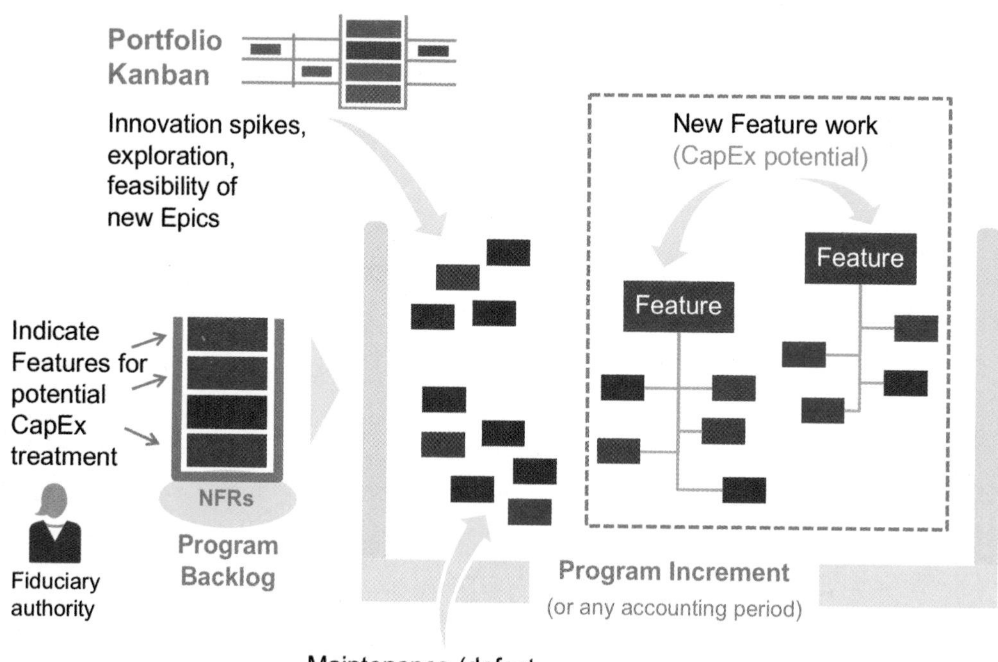

Figure 14-9. Many types of work occur within a given a PI

Categorization of Features for Capital and Operating Expenses

The work of implementing new projects and enhancing existing products is part of creating new features for the solution, which, by their very definition, enhance functionality. This work can be easily identified and tracked for potential capital expense treatment. To do so, accounting fiduciaries work with Product Management to identify such features in the program backlog. Those selected are "typed" for potential capital expense treatment, which creates the basic tracking mechanism for effort. Thereafter, teams associate new stories with those features and perform the essential work of realizing the behavior of the features by implementing stories in the new code base.

Using Stories for Operating Expense and Capital Expense Treatment

Most stories contribute directly to new functionality of the feature; the effort for those stories may be subject to capital expense treatment. Other stories, such as enabler stories for infrastructure, exploration, defects, refactors, and any other work, may not be. Agile Lifecycle Management (ALM) tooling can support the definition, capture, and work associated with implementing stories. By associating stories with features when applicable (typically called *parenting*) in the tooling, the work related to feature development can be identified for potential capital expense treatment. Various query facilities in the ALM tool can help automate the needed summary calculations.

More information on capitalizing and expensing software can be found at: http://www.scaledagileframework.com/capex-and-opex

Summary

This chapter explained why the motivation to increase business agility using Lean-Agile development is often in inherent conflict with traditional methods for budgeting, forecasting, contracting, and software capitalization. As a result, the benefits of business agility are compromised or, worse, simply unachievable. The industry needs new approaches, which were defined in this chapter.

The key takeaways are as follows:

- Lean-Agile budgeting provides strategies that directly address the challenges of traditional project funding and eliminates unnecessary waste and overhead.
- The enterprise, its partners, and customers need to forecast and plan for a near-term roadmap. Enabling effective, Agile forecasting and estimating is a key capability the Lean-Agile enterprise needs.
- Given the knowledge of program velocities, portfolio managers and other planners can use ART-level capacity allocation to estimate how long a portfolio epic might take under various scenarios. This provides a simple model for longer-term planning and forecasting.

- Enterprises have used a wide range of contract approaches, from "firm fixed price" to "time and materials," to procure complex systems from external suppliers. Since none delivers the best overall economic value, a new Agile approach is needed: the SAFe managed-investment contract.
- The SAFe managed-investment contract aligns the buyer's and supplier's economic interests, building the best solution with the least amount of waste and overhead.
- Portfolio stakeholders must understand both capital and operating expenses so that they are included as part of the economic framework for each value stream. Otherwise, money may be spent in the wrong categories, and the financial results will not be as intended.
- In some circumstances, companies may choose to capitalize certain software development costs. The development of new features that enhance solution functionality can be readily identified and tracked for potential capital expense treatment.

Part VI
Implementing SAFe

Many leaders pride themselves on setting the high level direction and staying out of the details. It's true that a compelling vision is critical. But it's not enough. Big picture, hands off leadership isn't likely to work in a change situation, because the hardest part of change—the paralyzing part—is in the details. Any successful change requires a translation of ambiguous goals into concrete behaviors. In short, to make a switch, you need to script the critical moves.

—Chip Heath and Dan Heath, *Switch: How to Change Things When Change Is Hard*

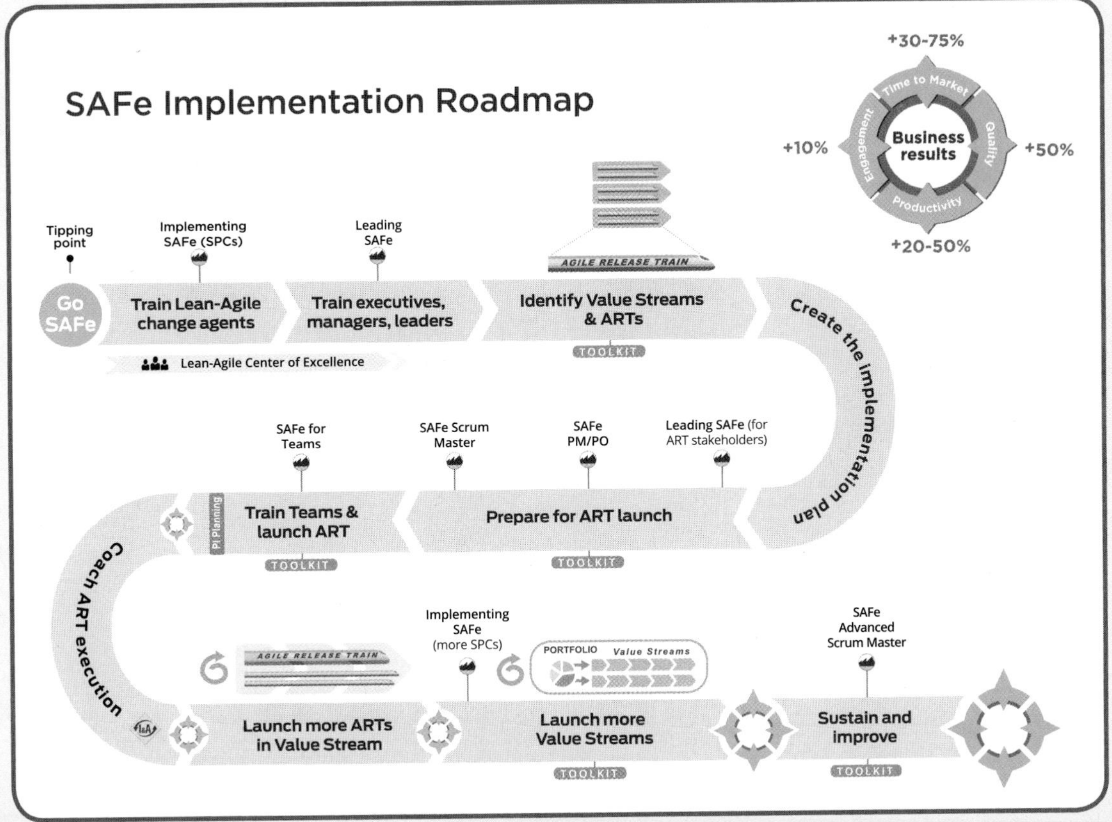

- Chapter 15 – The Guiding Coalition
- Chapter 16 – Design the Implementation
- Chapter 17 – Implementing Agile Release Trains
- Chapter 18 – Sustain and Improve
- Chapter 19 – Essential SAFe

15 The Guiding Coalition

A strong guiding coalition is always needed. One with the right composition, level of trust, and shared objective.

—John Kotter

Introduction 251
The Implementation Roadmap 252
Reaching the Tipping Point 253
The Need for a Powerful Coalition 255
Train Lean-Agile Change Agents 255
Train Executives, Managers, and Leaders 256
Charter a Lean-Agile Center of Excellence 257
Summary 258

Introduction

Throughout this book, we've described the values, principles, and practices of the Scaled Agile Framework (SAFe). Our intention has been to inform the reader on how a SAFe enterprise operates and how it achieves the business benefits that only Lean-Agile development at scale can provide. Faster time to market and higher productivity, quality, and employee engagement all await the enterprise that successfully implements SAFe. Those are worthy goals.

However, what we have not yet done is describe *how* an enterprise implements SAFe. That's where the real work begins. Part VI, which contains the final five chapters of this book, is dedicated to this purpose. The last chapter, chapter 19, "Essential SAFe," provides guidance on the minimum viable elements of SAFe. If you start with these elements, you are on the right track to begin your Lean-Agile journey.

The Implementation Roadmap

Embracing a Lean-Agile mindset, understanding and applying Lean-Agile principles, and effectively implementing Agile Release Trains (ARTs), value streams, and a Lean-Agile portfolio all come before realizing the full business benefits of SAFe. And, of course, the culture must evolve, too.

To achieve the right change, leadership must "script the critical moves."[1] Fortunately, hundreds of the world's largest enterprises have already gone down this path (see www.scaledagileframework.com/case-studies), and successful adoption patterns have become clear. Figure 15-1 shows one such pattern, the SAFe "implementation roadmap."

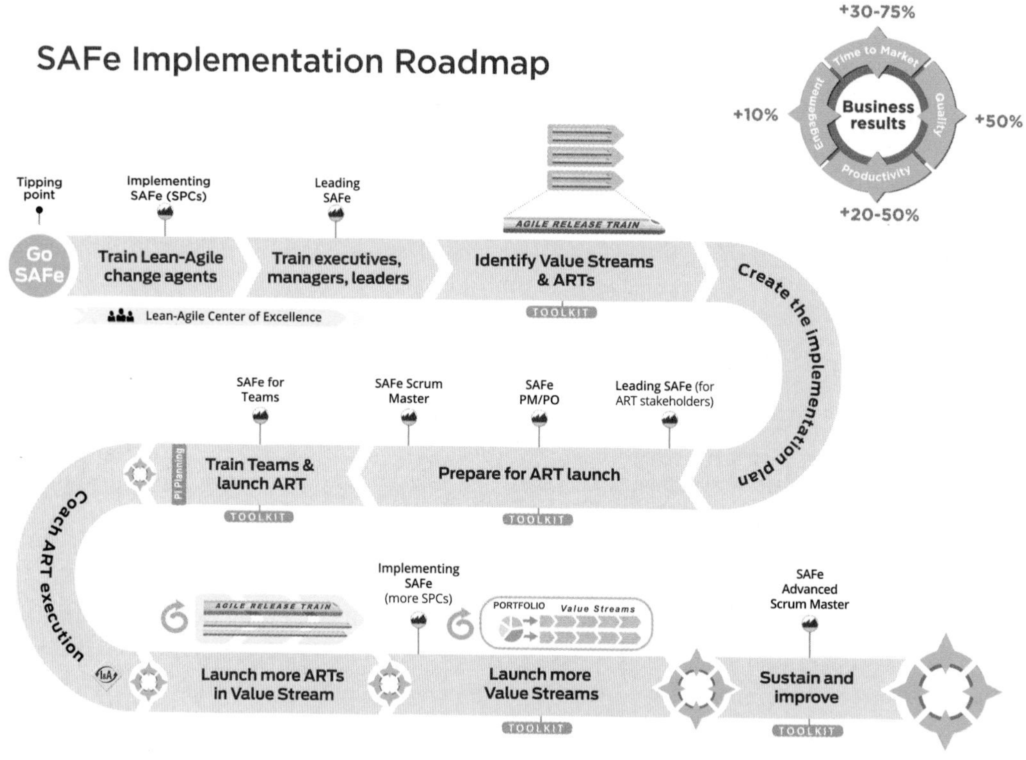

Figure 15-1. SAFe implementation roadmap

1. Chip Heath and Dan Heath, *Switch: How to Change Things When Change Is Hard* (Crown Business, 2010).

The roadmap includes the following steps:

- Reach the tipping point.
- Train Lean-Agile change agents.
- Train executives, managers, and leaders.
- Charter a Lean-Agile Center of Excellence.
- Identify value streams and ARTs.
- Create the implementation plan.
- Prepare for ART launch.
- Train teams and launch ART.
- Coach ART execution.
- Launch more ARTs in the value stream.
- Launch more value streams.
- Sustain and improve.

In this chapter, we'll provide guidance for the first four steps of this journey.

Reaching the Tipping Point

Changing the way of working—the habits and culture of a large development organization—is hard. Many report that implementing SAFe was one of the toughest yet most rewarding change initiatives that they have ever been involved in. But there has to be a reason for such a change—a reason so compelling that the status quo becomes simply unacceptable.

It has to be a reason so compelling that change becomes the only reasonable path to future success. In other words, the enterprise must reach its *tipping point*[2]—the point at which the organization's imperative is to achieve the change rather than resist it.

2. Malcom Gladwell, *The Tipping Point: How Little Things Can Make a Big Difference* (Little, Brown and Company, 2006).

We've observed two primary reasons that cause an organization to tip to SAFe.

1. *A burning platform.* Sometimes the need to change a product or service is obvious. The company is failing to compete, and the existing way of doing business is obviously inadequate to achieve a new solution within a survivable time frame. This is the easier case. While there will always be those who resist change, they are likely to be swamped by the wave of energy that drives mandatory change through the organization.
2. *Proactive leadership.* Here, the Chief Executive Officers (CEOs) and senior leaders drive the need for change by "taking a stand" for a better, future state, or simply a constant paranoia about the existing state, as in the Toyota management concept "there is a constant sense of danger."[3] This may well be the harder challenge, as the people in the trenches may not see or feel the sense of urgency necessary to do the hard work of change. In this case, senior leadership must constantly impress the need for change on others, making it clear that maintaining the status quo is simply unacceptable.

Take an Economic View

Whether reactive or proactive, the only reason to drive change in an organization is to realize the business benefits that it's intended to deliver. SAFe's principle #1 reminds us to always "take an economic view." In this context, the leaders should articulate the goal of the change in terms everyone can understand. Dozens of case studies show that enterprises can expect to see benefits in four major areas, as Figure 15-2 illustrates.

Figure 15-2. SAFe business benefits

3. Fujio Cho, chairman of Toyota, 2006–2013

Change leaders should communicate the intended benefits as part of the vision for the change. In addition, leaders should describe any other specific, tangible objectives they hope to accomplish. This will provide the fuel necessary to escape the inertia of the status quo.

The Need for a Powerful Coalition

As covered in chapter 4, "Lean-Agile Leaders," a "sufficiently powerful coalition"[4] of stakeholders is needed to create change in the organization. To be effective, this coalition requires the following:

- Leaders who can set the vision, show the way, and make blocking the change difficult
- Practitioners, managers, and change agents who can implement specific process changes
- Sufficient organizational credibility to be taken seriously
- The expertise needed to make fast, intelligent decisions

Experience has shown that there are three primary elements to achieving an effective SAFe coalition for change.

1. Train a number of Lean-Agile change agents as SAFe Program Consultants (SPCs) to provide the knowledge needed to implement the change.
2. Train executives, managers, and other leaders who can sponsor the change and support the implementation.
3. Charter a Lean-Agile Center of Excellence (LACE) to serve as an energy source and focus for the change management activities.

Train Lean-Agile Change Agents

The first step in the process is to develop change agents with the knowledge and skills needed to successfully implement SAFe. In most enterprises, they are sourced both internally and externally. They may be business and technology leaders, portfolio/program/project managers, architects, analysts, process leads, and many others.

4. John P. Kotter, "Leading Change: Why Transformation Efforts Fail" (*Harvard Business Review*, 1995).

One path to success is to take the "Implementing SAFe with SPC Certification" class. This four-day course is designed to prepare SPCs or change agents to lead the transformation. Attendees learn how to effectively apply the principles and practices of SAFe, organize and train and coach Agile teams, identify value streams and ARTs, launch ARTS, and help build and manage an Agile portfolio.

In addition, scaling Agile across the enterprise, or any material change for that matter, requires training *all* the people who do the work. To make it practical and cost effective, the makers of SAFe, Scaled Agile, Inc. (SAI), support a "train the trainer" fan-out model, which licenses SPCs (either partner personnel or enterprise employees) to teach SAFe courses inside the enterprise. This provides economic leverage as well as provisions the people needed to initiate and implement the change.

Train Executives, Managers, and Leaders

As change agents, SPCs can ignite transformation within an enterprise. But they alone do not necessarily constitute a sufficiently powerful coalition. For that, other stakeholders and senior executives must step in, step up, and lead. In W. Edwards Deming's words, "they must know what it is they must do."

Some of these key stakeholders will primarily provide ongoing executive sponsorship. Others will be directly involved in implementing SAFe, managing others who do, and participating directly in ART execution. Still others will work at higher levels of the organization to eliminate impediments that arise in the company, as well as in its existing processes, governance, culture, and practices. All of these stakeholders need the knowledge and skills to lead—rather than follow—the implementation.

The "Leading SAFe: Leading the Lean-Agile Enterprise with the Scaled Agile Framework" class is designed for this purpose. This two-day course teaches leaders the SAFe Lean-Agile mindset, principles, and practices, as well as the most effective leadership values in managing the new generation of knowledge workers. Attendees will also learn the following:

- How to support Agile teams
- How to execute and release value through ARTs
- How to participate in Program Increment (PI) planning
- How to apply the specific practices of SAFe needed to build really large systems and implement a Lean-Agile portfolio

Charter a Lean-Agile Center of Excellence

The previously mentioned training can help the organization reach the tipping point for change and also seed the enterprise with knowledgeable and active leaders who are prepared to guide it.

Most of these people, however, have full-time jobs in their current roles. And while a significant portion of their time can perhaps be devoted to the change, a smaller, dedicated group of people is typically required. These groups go by different names (such as Agile Center of Excellence, Agile Working Group, or Lean-Agile Transformation Team), but they are staffed with people for whom *implementing the change* is the primary task. The responsibilities of a Lean-Agile Center of Excellence (LACE) may include the following:

- Developing the implementation plan and managing the transformation backlog
- Establishing the metrics
- Conducting source training and coaching
- Identifying value streams and ARTs, helping launch ARTs, and providing coaching and training to ARTs and teams
- Fostering SAFe Communities of Practice (CoPs)
- Implementing Lean-Agile focus days, guest speakers, and internal case studies
- Benchmarking and connecting with the external community
- Promoting continuing Lean-Agile education
- Initiating Lean-Agile practices throughout the company, in areas such as budgeting, Program Portfolio Management, contracts, and Human Resources (HR)

The LACE operates like an Agile team and typically applies the same iteration and PI cadences as the ARTs. This allows the LACE to plan and Inspect and Adapt (I&A) in harmony with the ARTs. It also serves as an exemplar for Agile team behavior. As a result, similar roles are needed.

- The Product Owner works with stakeholders to prioritize the team's transformation backlog. A senior leader acts as the team's Product Manager.
- The Scrum Master facilitates the process and helps remove common roadblocks.
- Other members of the cross-functional team address necessary backlog items related to people, culture, development process, and technology.

The LACE may be a part of an emerging Lean-Agile Program Management Office (Agile PMO), or it may exist as a stand-alone unit. In either case, it serves as a focal point of activity, a constant source of energy that can help power the enterprise through the changes necessary. In addition, since the evolution to a Lean-Agile enterprise is a journey, not a destination, the LACE often evolves into a permanent center for continuous improvement.

Summary

This chapter introduced how an enterprise implements SAFe and covered the first four steps of the SAFe implementation roadmap.

The key takeaways from this chapter are as follows:

- Changing the way of working—the habits and culture of a large development organization—is hard. Enterprises must reach the tipping point so that the status quo becomes simply unacceptable and change is the only reasonable path to future success.
- The two primary reasons that cause an organization to tip to SAFe are a burning platform and proactive leadership.
- Leaders should communicate the intended benefits of the change as part of the vision for the change. These typically include faster time to market, increased quality and productivity, and higher employee engagement.
- Experience has shown that there are three primary elements to achieving an effective SAFe coalition for change: train a number of Lean-Agile change agents (SPCs); train executives, managers, and other leaders in leading SAFe; and charter a LACE.
- The LACE often evolves into a permanent center for continuous improvement.

16

Design the Implementation

Break down barriers between departments.

—W. Edwards Deming

Introduction 259
Create the Implementation Plan 265
Summary 268

Introduction

In the previous chapter, we described how the first four steps of the implementation roadmap create the critical mass of informed and dedicated people necessary to initiate SAFe. They are as follows:

- Reach the tipping point.
- Train Lean-Agile change agents.
- Train executives, managers, and leaders.
- Charter a Lean-Agile Center of Excellence (LACE).

In this chapter, we describe the next two steps:

- Identify value streams and Agile Release Trains (ARTs).
- Create the implementation plan.

Identify Value Streams and ARTs

As we have described, value streams are the primary Scaled Agile Framework (SAFe) construct for understanding, organizing, and delivering value. ARTs are the people and other resources that build the solutions to realize this value. Identifying enterprise value streams, and forming ARTs to create and deliver value, is the next critical step.

As a reminder, each value stream is a long-lived series of steps used to create value from a concept or an order to deliver a tangible result for the customer, as illustrated in Figure 16-1.

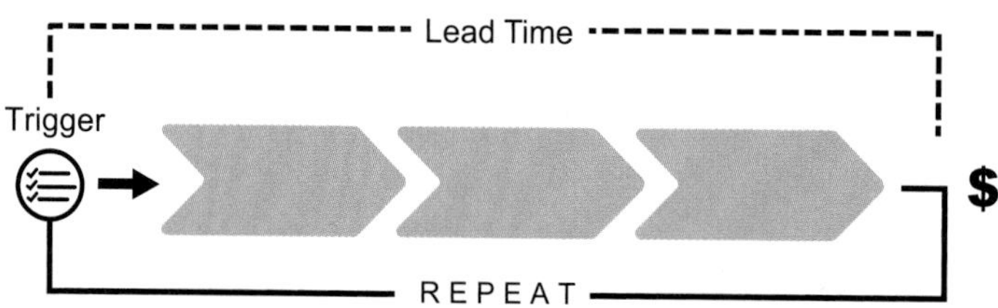

Figure 16-1. The anatomy of a value stream

The flow of value is triggered by some important event, perhaps a customer purchase order or new feature request. It ends when some value has been delivered—a shipment, a purchase, or a solution deployment. The steps in the middle are the activities the enterprise uses to accomplish this feat.

Types of Value Streams

In the larger enterprise, there are typically two types of value streams.

- *Operational value streams.* These are the steps used to provide goods or services to an internal or external customer.[1] Examples might include manufacturing a medical instrument or processing a vendor payment.
- *Development value streams.* These are the steps used to develop new products, systems, solution, or services.

Sometimes these are the same, as when a solution provider develops a product for sale. An example would be a Software as a Service (SaaS) company, such as Salesforce.com.

1. Allen C. Ward, *Lean Product and Process Development* (Lean Enterprise Institute, 2007).

SAFe concerns itself primarily with development value streams, as those are the only type of value streams represented in a SAFe portfolio. However, understanding both types of value streams, particularly in the context of the large Information Technology (IT) shop, is critical. For example, internal solution providers need to understand the operational value streams in order to build development value streams that support them, as illustrated in Figure 16-2.

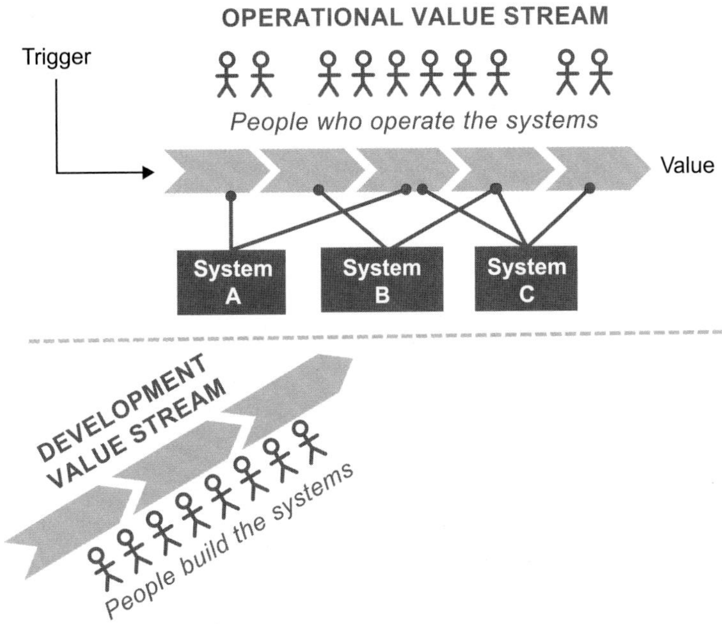

Figure 16-2. Development value streams build the systems that operational value streams use

Identifying Value Streams

For some organizations, identifying value streams is an easy task. Many are simply the products, services, or solutions the company develops and sells.

As the enterprise grows, however, the task becomes more complicated. Value flows through various applications, systems, and services, across many parts of the distributed organization to many internal and external customers.

In these cases, identifying the value streams is an important analytical activity that provides the most basic foundation for a transformation. Figure 16-3 provides a set of questions that help identify value streams.

General questions	• What are the larger software, system, or solution-based objectives that differentiate the business in the market? • How do external customers describe or perceive the flow of value they receive? • What current initiatives have a significant number of developers and testers working together now?
Questions for the independent software vendor	• What products, systems, services, applications, or solutions does the enterprise sell?
Questions for builders of embedded and cyber-physical systems	• What products and systems does the enterprise sell? What are the larger subsystems or components? What key system operational capabilities are being enabled? • What critical Nonfunctional Requirements (NFRs) are being implemented or enhanced?
Questions for IT	• What key business processes are enabled? • What internal departments are supported? • What internal or external customers do those departments serve? How do those departments describe the value they receive from IT? • What key process, cost, KPI, or business improvement initiatives are targeted?

Figure 16-3. Questions to help identify value streams

Development Value Streams Cross Boundaries

Once the value streams are identified, the next step is to form ARTs to accomplish them. In the process, it becomes obvious that development value streams cross many boundaries, as Figure 16-4 illustrates.

This means that many of the value streams—and thereby the ARTs—will be geographically distributed rather than colocated. While that complicates things, it is a reality and doesn't change the basic operating model. ARTs have a variety of techniques—including multi-location face-to-face PI planning—that can mitigate this challenge. Although we've observed that a SAFe implementation provides opportunities to evolve more geographically colocated development practices, companies simply have to start where they are at the time of initial implementation.

Identifying the value streams is a critical milestone in the implementation process. After all, achieving this requires a fundamental understanding of SAFe and the reasoning behind the changes necessary to organize around value.

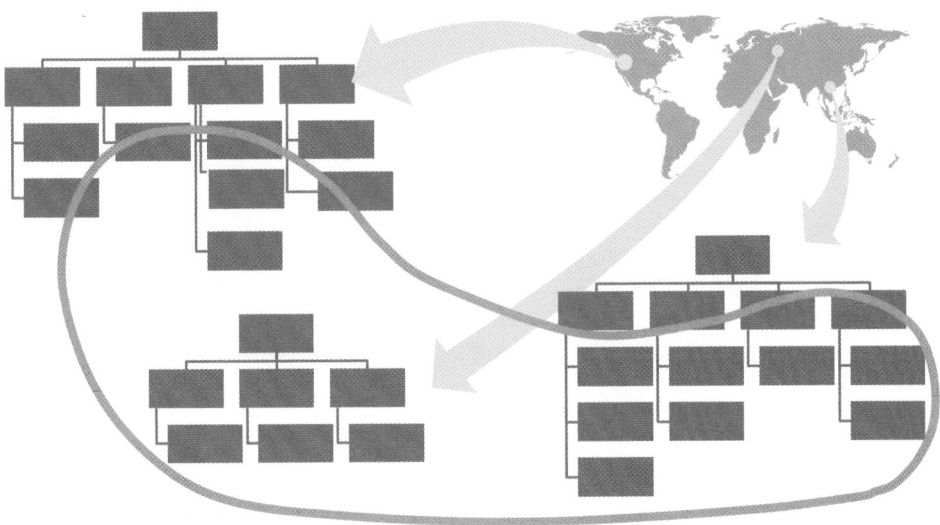

Figure 16-4. Value flows across functional, organizational, and geographic boundaries

Realize Value Streams with ARTs

A value stream is a helpful thinking tool. But it's intangible. It's simply a construct to help understand how value flows through a business. Conversely, ARTs are tangible. They're made up of real people, real teams, and real systems—with key stakeholders, customers, and users. Once an opportunistic value stream has been selected, the next question is how best to organize ARTs to most efficiently deliver the value. This determines who will be planning and working together, as well as what products, services, features, or components the train will deliver.

The next consideration is the size of the value stream. Given the 50- to 125-person ART recommendation, there are three ways to organize an ART, as shown in Figure 16-5.

1. *Multiple small value streams can fit within a single ART.* When several products or solutions can be produced with a relatively small number of people, a single ART may deliver multiple value streams. This is an easy case for ART design, as all the stakeholders required to build all the value streams can participate in one ART.
2. *A single value stream can fit within an ART.* This fairly common model is probably an example of Dunbar's number at work, the social theory that asserts that an individual can form effective relationships with only 100 or so other people. This is an easy case to organize as well, as all the stakeholders in value stream participate in the one ART.

3. *Multiple ARTs are required to create a large value stream.* This case is common for people building big solutions. A value stream that requires more than 100 people or so will probably need to be split into multiple ARTs.

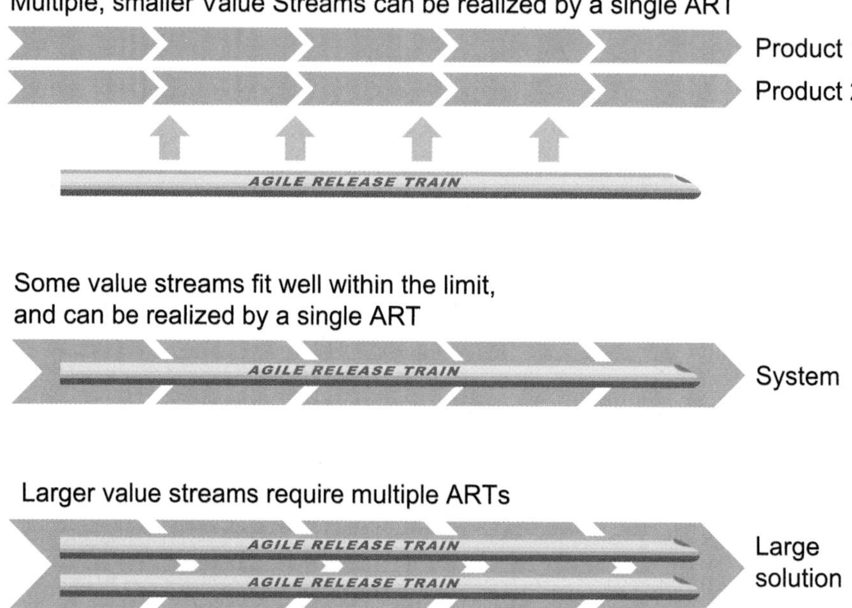
Multiple, smaller Value Streams can be realized by a single ART
Product 1
Product 2
AGILE RELEASE TRAIN
Some value streams fit well within the limit,
and can be realized by a single ART
AGILE RELEASE TRAIN
System
Larger value streams require multiple ARTs
AGILE RELEASE TRAIN
AGILE RELEASE TRAIN
Large
solution

Figure 16-5. Organizing ARTs based on value stream size

Splitting Large Value Streams into Multiple ARTs

Splitting large value streams is more "art" than science. It requires some understanding of social and organizational factors, as well as significant technical considerations. Normally, trains should be focused on a single, primary product or solution objective. In addition, teams with features and components that have a high degree of interdependency work best when they can plan and work together in a single ART.

This brings us to a common pattern, which is organizing ARTs around either capabilities or subsystems, as illustrated in Figure 16-6.

- *Capability (or feature area) ARTs are optimized for flow and speed.* This is why they're generally preferred. But care must be given to subsystem governance to keep the system architecture from decaying and ultimately reducing velocity.
- *Subsystem ARTs (applications, components, platforms, and so on) are optimized for architectural robustness.* The flow in this scenario, however, creates many dependencies, and significant coordination is required across ARTs.

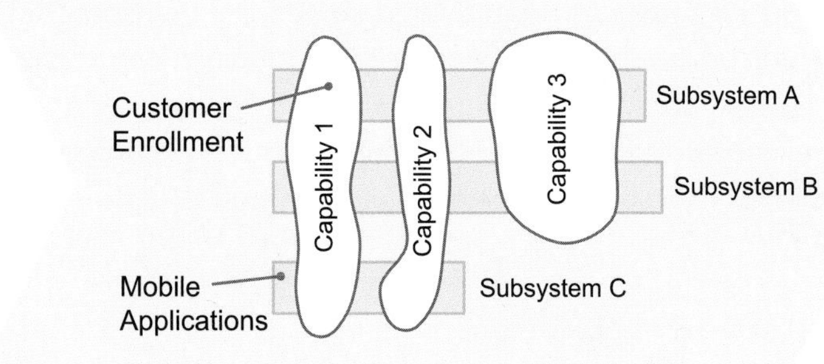

Figure 16-6. ARTs can be organized by capabilities and/or subsystems

Large value streams typically require both types of ARTs. There are other design and optimization factors as well, including geography, spoken language, and cost centers, but these are generally *far* less desirable for organizing an ART, as they usually do not optimize flow.

Create the Implementation Plan

The next step is to plan for implementing SAFe in each value stream. In a smaller portfolio, there may be only one value stream of interest, in which case the target is obvious. In the larger enterprise, some additional analysis is required, and leadership often needs to pick the first value stream to be addressed. In this case, we've observed two different patterns for implementing value streams, as Figure 16-7 illustrates.

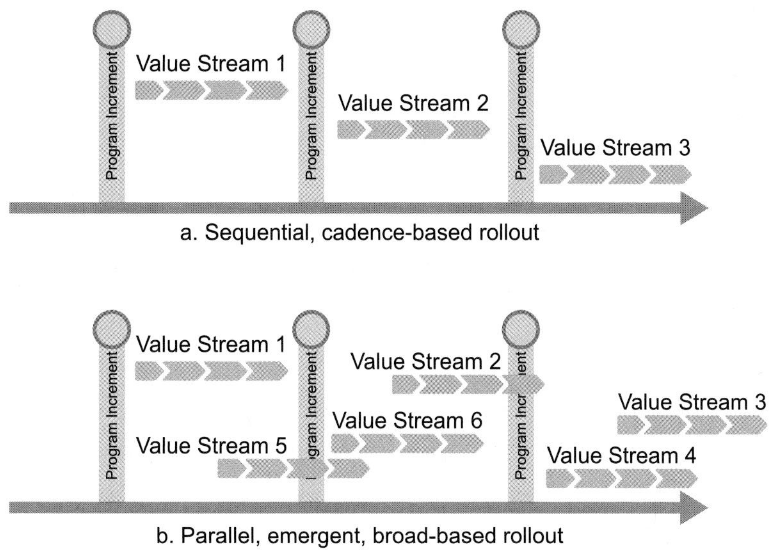

Figure 16-7. Two common rollout patterns for value streams

The top of Figure 16-7 illustrates a rollout that is planned and sequential. The reasons for doing this may include limited availability of the LACE and SAFe Program Consultants (SPCs) and the depth and breadth of leadership support. Some enterprises need to pilot or prove the new way of working, before moving ahead with a more widespread implementation. In this case, it can be convenient to plan around Program Increment (PI) boundaries.

- Scheduling the first PI planning meeting creates the timebox in which to force preparation.
- This facilitates integration and management of dependencies between value streams at future, common PI boundaries.

However, if the portfolio is large and the enterprise is already committed to SAFe, then the sequential approach can represent a high Cost of Delay (CoD) for value streams sequenced later. In this case, an approach like the bottom of Figure 16-7 may be more appropriate, where multiple value streams are launched in a parallel, overlapping manner. This is reminiscent of Kotter's "empower employees for broad-based action." After all, if there are responsible leaders and executives on each value stream, they will be keen to start experiencing the benefits of this new way of working.

> In one large enterprise business unit, we initially trained 160 managers and leaders around the world in SAFe. The plan was to provide the orientation and then come back around to the various regions with support for coaching, training, and providing other LACE types of assistance. Interestingly, the second part of the plan was never needed. Instead, the regional leaders assumed the full responsibility and successfully implemented their value streams without much further help.

Select the Initial Value Stream

You have to start somewhere. It's typical for the organization to focus initially on one value stream (and correspondingly, the first ART). This can create an initial success and gain institutional knowledge that can be applied to other value streams. To start, many companies look for a first "opportunistic" value stream, one that can be found at the intersection of the factors illustrated in Figure 16-8.

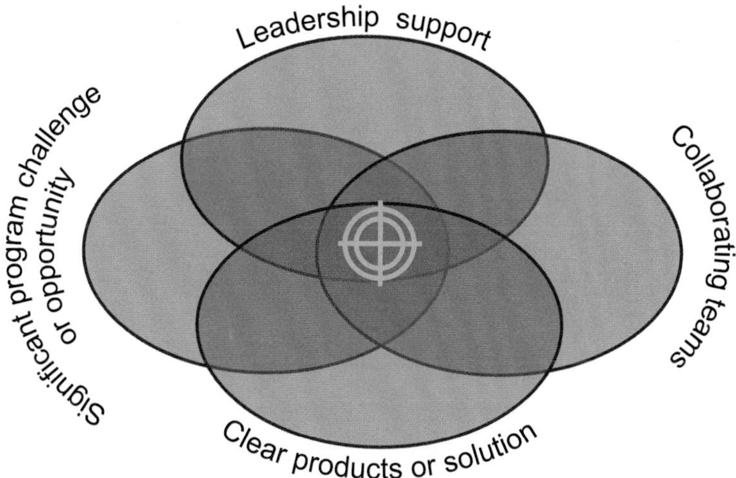

Figure 16-8. Finding an opportunistic value stream to start the transformation

The "target" is a value stream that best meets the following criteria:

- *Leadership support.* Some line-of-business managers or senior leaders already have Agile or change management experience or awareness and are anxious to put SAFe to work.
- *Clear products or solutions.* It's easiest when the solution target is clear and tangible, something the company sells directly or values highly, rather than a more abstract internal business process or capability.
- *Collaborating teams.* Somewhere in the enterprise there are already teams collaborating on building a larger solution. They may or may not be Agile, but given the need and the challenge of collaboration, the teams may be ready to embrace this change.
- *Significant challenge or opportunity.* Change is hard. Select a subject that is truly worthy of the effort, somewhere there is a large, existing challenge or a new opportunity. Creating a "short-term win" for this scenario will produce immediate benefits and facilitate faster and broader adoption.

Once the value streams are identified, the enterprise can move on to implementing ARTs in each one, which is the subject of the next chapter.

Summary

This chapter discussed the process to identify value streams and ARTs, as well as creating the implementation plan.

The key takeaways from this chapter are as follows:

- Value streams are the steps used to develop new products, systems, solutions, or services. There are two types of value streams: operational value streams and development value streams.
- Identifying enterprise value streams, and forming ARTs to create and deliver value, is a critical step in designing the implementation.
- For some organizations, identifying value streams is an easy task. Many are simply the products, services, or solutions the company develops and sells.
- In the larger enterprise, some additional analysis is required, and leadership often needs to pick the first value stream to be addressed.
- The "target" value stream is one that best meets the following criteria: leadership support, clear products or solutions, collaborating teams, and a significant challenge or opportunity.
- Given the 50- to 125-person ART recommendation, there are three ways to organize an ART: Multiple small value streams can fit within a single ART, a single value stream can fit within an ART, and multiple ARTs are required to create a large value stream.
- Large value streams must be split into smaller ones. Two common patterns are to organize ARTs around capabilities or subsystems.
- Capability (or feature area) ARTs are optimized for flow and speed. Subsystem ARTs (applications, components, platforms, and so on) are optimized for architectural robustness. Most value streams have a combination of both.
- Select value streams that are targets of opportunity. In a smaller portfolio, there may be only one value stream of interest, in which case the target is obvious. In the larger enterprise, some additional analysis is required, and leadership often needs to pick the first value stream to be addressed.
- The creation of the implementation plan usually involves selecting between two common patterns: a sequential, cadence-based rollout or a parallel, emergent, broad-based rollout.

17 Implementing Agile Release Trains

Train everyone and launch trains.

—SAFe advice

Introduction 269
Prepare for the ART Launch 270
Train Teams and Launch the ART 277
The Quick-Start Approach to ART Launch 280
Coach ART Execution 281
Launch More ARTs in the Value Stream 282
Launch More Value Streams in the Portfolio 284
Summary 285

Introduction

In the previous chapter, we described steps 5 and 6 of the implementation roadmap, specifically:

- How to identify value streams and Agile Release Trains (ARTs)
- How to create the implementation plan

In this chapter, we'll cover the next four steps in the transformation, including the most important part, which is organizing around value and by launching the ARTs in a value stream. The steps described here include how to do the following:

- Prepare for the ART launch.
- Train teams and launch the ART.
- Launch more ARTs in the value stream.
- Launch more value streams in the portfolio.

In addition, we'll describe an accelerated, one-week "quick-start" approach to ART launch, which—after some preparation—is the fastest way to get an ART structured, started, and delivering value.

Prepare for the ART Launch

At this stage, the enterprise or business unit will have identified the value streams and established a plan for implementation. It will have a rough outline for the first ART to launch in the target value stream. This is a pivotal moment, as plans now move toward implementation. From a change-management perspective, the first ART is very important, as it is the first material change to the way of working and will generate the initial "short-term wins" that help the enterprise build momentum for the rest of the rollout.

SAFe Program Consultants (SPCs) often lead the implementation of each ART and are supported by ART stakeholders and members of the Lean-Agile Center of Excellence (LACE). The major steps in preparing the launch include the following:

- Set the launch date and cadence calendar.
- Train the ART leaders and stakeholders.
- Establish the Agile teams that will constitute the ART.
- Determine who will play the individual ART roles.
- Train Product Managers and Product Owners.
- Train the Scrum Masters.
- Assess and evolve launch readiness.
- Prepare the program backlog.

Each is described in the following sections.

Set the Launch Date and Cadence Calendar

Setting the date for the first Program Increment (PI) planning session creates a forcing function for the launch. The launch date helps focus all stakeholders on the necessary preparation and allows them to set their calendar for the first PI planning event. It also defines the planning timeline for the necessary preparation work.

The cadence calendar, consisting of the iteration length (two weeks by default) and PI length (eight to twelve weeks, including the Iteration Planning [IP] iteration), must also be determined.

Once the cadence is established, the ART calendar of events can be set for up to a year in advance. This includes PI planning meetings, as well as the schedule for system demos and Inspect and Adapt (I&A) workshops. Given the scope of PI planning, this advanced notice minimizes travel and facility costs and helps assure the presence of all stakeholders. Once the ART calendar is set, team calendars can also be set, with each team defining the time and place for their planning meetings, demos, and retrospectives.

Train the ART Leaders and Stakeholders

Depending on the scope and timing of the rollout, there may be a number of ART stakeholders who have not attended a Leading SAFe training session. It is important that these key stakeholders understand and support the model, as well as their role. In that case, SPCs will arrange a two-day Leading SAFe training specifically for that purpose. This is often followed by a one-day planning workshop, where newly trained stakeholders and SPCs can create the specifics of the launch plan. After all, it is their ART, and only they (key ART stakeholders and ART SPCs) can plan for the best outcomes. Essentially, this is the handoff of primary responsibility for the change from the LACE to the newly formed ART's stakeholders.

Establish the Agile Teams That Will Constitute the ART

The next step is to establish the Agile teams that will constitute the ART. There is no one right way to do this; common patterns are 1) where the teams are largely self-organizing and self-selecting, 2) one that is more directly management designed, and 3) something in between. Something in between seems to be a common and effective pattern. But in any case, prior to PI planning, all practitioners must become part of a cross-functional Agile team. The team roster template[1] shown in Figure 17-1 is a simple tool that can help bring clarity and visibility to the team design. It can also determine whether there are real people who can be dedicated to a single team and are actually available to do the work.

1. The team roster is available in the SPC implementation toolkit.

Team #	Team name	Role	Team member name	Geographic location
1	Team A	Scrum Master	LastName, FirstName	City, Country
2	Team A	Product Owner	LastName, FirstName	City, Country
3	Team A	Developer		
4	Team A	Developer		
5	Team A	Developer		
6	Team A	Tester		
7	Team A	Tester		
8	Team A	<role>		
9	Team A	<role>		

Figure 17-1. Template for Agile team roster

The simple act of filling out the roster can be quite informative, as it starts to make concrete the more abstract concepts of Agile development. After all, the structure of an Agile team is fairly well defined, and the question of who is on the team and the nature of the specialty roles can lead to interesting discussions. Even the apparently simple act of assigning an individual to be dedicated to one Agile team can be an eye-opening experience. But there's no going back. These rules of Agile are fairly clear.

The geographic location column is often interesting, as it defines the level of colocation and distribution for each team. Of course, colocation is always better, but there may be cases where one or more individuals are not with the others. That may or may not evolve over time (most typically it does). But at least with the roster everyone understands where the current team members reside, so they can start thinking about Daily Stand-Up (DSU) times and how they will manage other team events.

Organizing Agile Teams

The next logical question is how to organize the Agile teams with respect to the solution purpose. As with the ARTs themselves, the patterns are similar, as teams can be organized around the following:

- *Features.* Feature teams are focused on user-centered functionality. This is the preferred approach, as each is capable of delivering end-to-end user value. They also facilitate the growth of "T-shaped" (multifaceted) individual skills. Feature teams are optimized for *velocity*.

- *Components.* Component teams should be used only when there are significant reuse opportunities, high technical specialization, and critical Nonfunctional Requirements (NFRs). Component teams are *optimized for system robustness and component reuse.*

Most ARTs have a mix of feature and component teams. However, ARTs should generally avoid organizing teams around technical system infrastructure (architectural layer, programming language, middleware, user interface), as this creates many dependencies, impedes the flow of new features, and leads to brittle designs.

Determine the Individual ART Roles

ARTs work only when the right people fulfill the right responsibilities. In a microcosm, the ART organization is *a system*, and all the necessary responsibilities of system definition, building, validation, and deployment have to be achieved for the system to work. To that end, the individual roles on the ART must also be filled. The program roster[2] shown in Figure 17-2 can serve as a simple template for facilitating discussions, highlighting missing responsibilities, and determining initial assignments.

Role	Team member name	Geographic location
Release Train Engineer	LastName, FirstName	City, Country
Product Manager		
Product Manager		
Business Owner		
Business Owner		
System Team		
System Team		
System Team		
DevOps		
DevOps		
DevOps		
System Arch/Eng		
UX		

Figure 17-2. Template to capture ART role assignments

2. The program roster is available in the SPC implementation toolkit.

With respect to the program roster, special care must be taken to understand who the Business Owners are. While they clearly include internal and external customers and/or their Product Management proxies, "taking a systems view" means that others (for example, VPs of development/technology, data center managers, and security architects) should be included. The right set of Business Owners is needed to assure alignment and agreement across the differing organizational responsibilities and perspectives. Only together can they assure alignment and fitness for use.

Train Product Managers and Product Owners

SAFe is based on a number of specialty roles. As we have described, Product Managers and Product Owners hold the "steering wheel" of content authority. These teammates must typically be trained in the new way of working and how to best fulfill their specific responsibilities on the ART.

SAI's two-day Product Manager/Product Owner course is designed specifically for this purpose. The course teaches prospective Product Owners and Product Managers (and Solution Managers and Epic Owners) how to drive the delivery of value in the SAFe enterprise. Attendees get an overview of SAFe's Lean-Agile mindset and principles and an in-depth exploration of role-specific practices. Attendees learn how to write epics, capabilities, features, and user stories; how to establish the relevant kanban systems to manage the flow of work; and how to manage and prioritize backlogs using Weighted Shortest Job First (WSJF).

Train the Scrum Masters

SAFe is based, in large part, on the servant leadership capabilities and Agile prowess of the Scrum Master. It's a specialty role that includes traditional Scrum team leadership responsibilities, as well as responsibilities to the larger team-of-Agile-teams that constitute the ART.

SAI's two-day SAFe Scrum Master course introduces prospective Scrum Masters to this important role. It teaches Scrum fundamentals and also explores the role of Scrum in the context of SAFe. It prepares Scrum Masters for how to facilitate team iterations, how to successfully plan and execute the PI, how to participate in ART events, and how to measure and improve the flow of work through the system using kanban. SAFe Scrum Masters will also learn how to build high-performing Agile teams by being a servant leader and coach and how to coach those teams to deliver the maximum business value.

Assess and Evolve Launch Readiness

Training individual role players to their new responsibilities is a key part of ART readiness. Since SAFe is based on the empirical I&A (Plan-Do-Check-Adjust) model, there is no such thing as perfect readiness for launch. Attempting to achieve such a state is a fool's errand, as the experience of the first PI planning, first PI, and I&A will drive rapid improvement. In addition, trying to reach too mature a state at the start is a recipe for delay of the transformation and its benefits.

However, a certain degree of readiness helps assure a more successful first planning event. Figures 17-3 and 17-4 provide a checklist for some of the further ART readiness assessment and activities. Most would agree that most of the items in Figure 17-3 are required for a successful launch. The items in Figure 17-4 are certainly desirable, but they can also be easily addressed over the first few PIs.

Area	Question
Planning scope and context	Is the scope (product, system, technology domains) of the planning process understood? Have we identified our value stream(s) and ARTs?
Release Train Engineer (RTE)	Have we identified the RTE? Does the RTE understand the scope of the role in preparing the organization and prepping for the PI planning meeting?
Planning time frame, iteration, and PI cadence	Have we identified the PI planning dates, the iteration cadence, and the PI cadence?
Agile teams	Does each feature/component team have an identified Scrum Master and Product Owner?
Team makeup / commitmert	Does every team have dedicated team members?
Agile team attendance	Are all team members present in person or are arrangements made to involve them remotely?
Executive, Business Owner participation	Do we know who will set the business context (Business Owners) and who will present the product/ Solution vision (typically Product Management)?
Business alignment	Is there reasonable agreement on priorities among the Business Owners and Product Management?

Figure 17-3. ART readiness checklist: Mandatory items

Area	Question
System Team	Has the System Team been identified and formed?
Shared Services	Have the Shared Services (DevOps, UX, Architecture, etc.) been identified?
Other attendees	Do we know what other key stakeholders (IT, infrastructure, etc.) should attend?
Agile project management tooling	Do we know how and where iterations, PIs, features, stories, status, etc., will be maintained?
Development infrastructure	Do we understand the impact on and/or plans for environments (for example, continuous integration and build environments)?
Quality practices	Is there a strategy for unit testing and test automation?

Figure 17-4. ART readiness checklist: Optional items

Prepare the Program Backlog

The forcing function of the upcoming date focuses the collective minds on making sure everyone knows exactly what they are supposed to be building. After all, no one wants to show up at PI planning without a solid sense of the mission and definition of the system. While it's easy to assume that should be the case prior to the event, experience shows that this is not always the reality. Often, requirements and design options and diverse stakeholder viewpoints have not come together into a single view of "this thing we are building."

"What gets built" is controlled fairy exclusively by the program backlog, which contains the set of upcoming features, NFRs, and architectural work that define the future behavior of the evolving system. (Team backlogs also provide some more specific definition.) To that end, SPCs and LACE stakeholders often facilitate a process of bringing the ART stakeholders together to prepare a common backlog. Typically, more than one such session is required, and other activities also occur during this planning period, as illustrated in Figure 17-5.

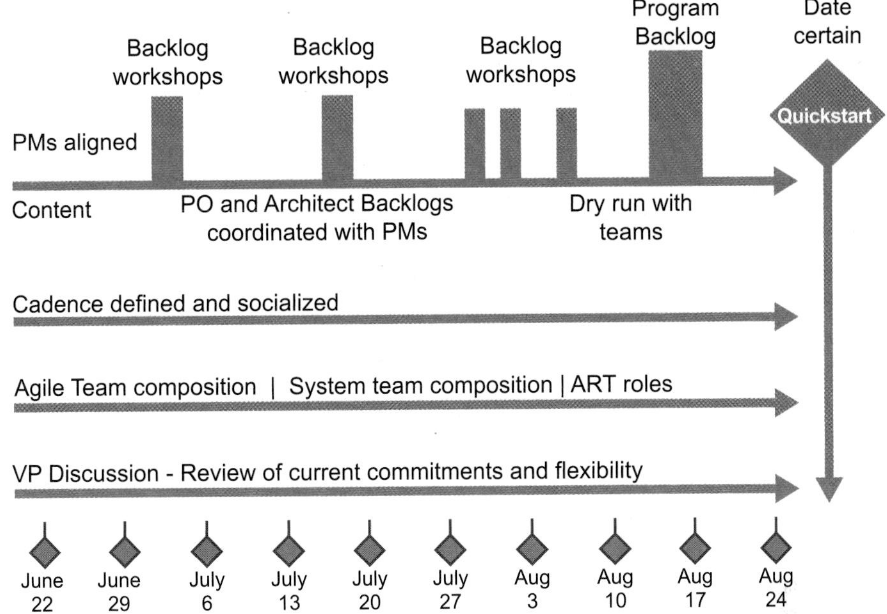

Figure 17-5. Preparing the program backlog and related activities

Train Teams and Launch the ART

At this point, key ART stakeholders are trained and on board, and launch plans are in place. The LACE and various SPCs are ready and prepared to help.

Training the Agile Teams

But it is the practitioners, now tentatively formed into Agile teams, who do the actual implementation. Before launching the ART, it's likely that many have never participated in Agile development. Therefore, the next significant task is to train all the teams in the SAFe Lean-Agile way of working.

SAI's two-day SAFe for Teams (S4T) course is designed specifically for this purpose. This training includes an introduction to Agile development, including the Agile Manifesto and its values and principles. It also includes core Scrum elements: the roles of the Scrum Master, Product Owner, and Development Team; the purpose and mechanics of the basic events, including iteration planning, team demo ("review in Scrum"), retrospective, and DSU; and building a kanban board for tracking stories. In addition, teams need to prepare their team backlog of the user stories and other work items necessary to evolve the system incrementally.

It's equally likely that a significant number of practitioners on the Agile teams already know Agile development. (After all, the manifesto was written in 2001.) In that case, there may be some potential resistance to "more basic Agile training," as many individuals and their management may think that they have already accomplished that. However, this team training is critically important for SAFe success, as it provides coaching substantially beyond the core Scrum practices. In particular, there are a number of elements of Agile at scale that are unique to SAFe. These include the following:

- The role of the team in PI planning, I&A, and the IP iteration
- Focus and participation on the system demo
- Applying features, user stories, and acceptance criteria to define and validate system behavior
- Using story points as the measure of velocity and estimating
- Understanding the flow of work through the kanban systems, including the team's local kanban
- Collaboration with other teams and other roles, including Product Management and System Architecture
- Introduction/application of technical practices including continuous integration, test-first with test automation, and pair work

The Benefits of "Big Room Training"

In some rollouts, training is performed team by team over time, which can be effective. However, we recommend a more accelerated approach, which includes training all the team members *at the same time*. This strong recommendation and practice has raised some eyebrows in the industry. Many picture 100+ people in a room being trained at the same time, compare it to the more intimate setting of a small team with a single instructor, and can't imagine that it delivers equivalent benefits. In fact, it delivers far more. The tangible benefits include following:

- *Accelerated learning.* This training happens in two days, rather than over a period of months. That speeds up the timing and learning by all the members of the train and accelerates the launch.
- *A common scaled Agile paradigm.* All team members receive the same training, at the same time, from the same instructor, eliminating the variability from different training sessions over time, by different instructors, using different courseware.
- *Cost efficiency.* One of the challenges with Agile implementation at scale has been the availability and expense of training. Talented and proven instructors are hard to find, they are not always available, and their value and cost are commensurately high. The Big Room Training approach typically provides three to five times the cost efficiency of individual team training.

Simply, there is no substitute for the power and dynamic of Big Room Training. But this is something you almost have to experience to believe. Or perhaps you can benefit from Australia's SAFe SPCT Mark Richards, as he reflects:[3]

> How on earth do you get a high impact training experience with 100 people in the room? I was initially unconvinced, so I worked with my clients to schedule four or five SAFe team-level courses over the period leading up to the first PI planning. I'd request that they send entire teams to the same course so they could sit and learn together, and they would promise to do their best. Then the pain would start. Firstly, the teams would often be in flux up until the last moment. Then they would be too busy on current commitments to all come together so they would dribble through two or three at a time. And distributed team members would go to different courses.
>
> Finally, I came to understand the motivation and some of the benefits of the big room—and eventually got convinced enough to try it. After the first "big room training," I was blown away and spent some time sorting through how on earth it could be so powerful. Following are some of the key insights it yielded:
>
> - The teams will be fully formed. The whole team can sit at the same table. Not only do they get to learn together and share their insights as they learn, but it's actually a very powerful team formation event. Teams choose their names on Day 1, and we watch team identity grow before our eyes.
> - The team engages in collective learning, with the chance to dissect their different interpretations in discussions and exercises. They are not reliant on "one brain—the Scrum Master" to ensure they get value from the agile approach, they have many brains that each captured different nuances.
> - The features for the PI will be ready. The team training exercises involving the identification, splitting, estimation and evolution of stories were done on real features the teams will be dealing with in PI planning.
> - Not only do the teams form their own identities, but they begin to form the shared identity of the train. As the discussions and debriefs progress, they start to learn about each other's worlds.

As different as it is, "all-in" Big Room Training remains one of our strongest recommendations and one of SAFe's most cost-effective and valuable implementation strategies.

3. www.agilenotanarchy.com/2016/01/the-case-for-safe-quickstart.html

The Quick-Start Approach to ART Launch

There are many ways to successfully start an ART, and there is no specific timeline for the readiness activities we've described. However, experience has shown that an accelerated—and frankly the easiest—way to launch an ART is via the "ART quick-start" approach, as illustrated in Figure 17-6.

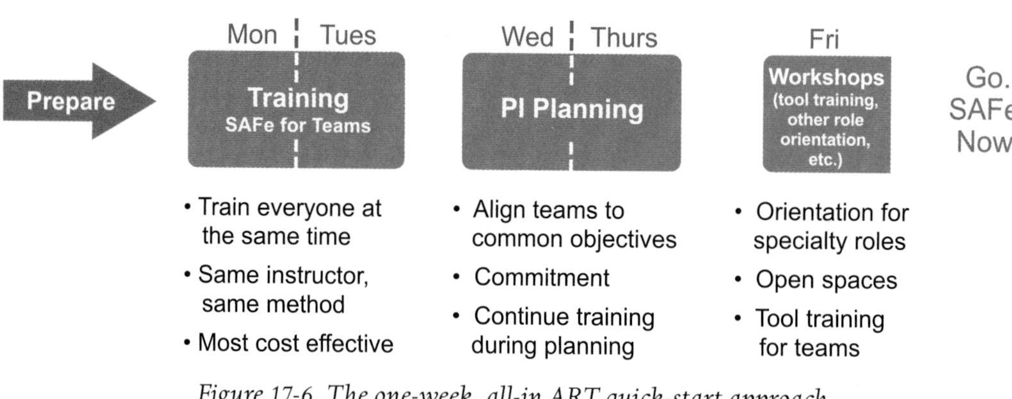

Figure 17-6. The one-week, all-in ART quick-start approach

In this approach, the training of Agile teams and the first PI planning session are all scheduled in a *single week*. While this may seem daunting, experience has shown that this is the easiest and most pragmatic way to help 100+ people move to a new way of working. There are three elements of this approach:

- *Day 1–2.* Agile team Big Room Training takes place, as described earlier.
- *Day 3–4.* Team training is followed immediately by PI planning. In this way, the teams are still present and in-context, and their first PI planning experience builds on the training of the prior day.
- *Day 5.* This is reserved for specialty role orientation, tool training, discussion of needed Agile technical practices, open space, or any other activities that the teams need to get ready for the first iteration.

PI planning serves to help build the teams' backlogs based on current priorities. The very next week, teams plan their iteration in the normal fashion and thereby start the execution of the PI.

Coach ART Execution

A successful launch and PI planning event sets the stage for a more empowered, engaged, and aligned team-of-Agile-teams to go about the business of building the solutions that deliver value. However, it's important to understand that training and planning do not make the newly formed teams ARTs or Agile. They simply provide the opportunity to *begin*. In support of this, leadership—and SPCs in particular—must be mindful that achieving even effective team-level Agile practices takes significant time. While the PIs serve as the envelope for facilitating effective Agile behaviors at both the iteration and PI levels, significant coaching is required.

To foster ART progress, coaching opportunities include the following:

- Helping to build and maintain the vision and roadmap
- Defining and managing the program kanban and program backlog
- Coaching Product Managers, System Architects, and RTEs in their new or adjusted roles
- Supporting frequent system-level integration
- Participating in Scrum of Scrums and system demo
- Helping to facilitate I&A and follow-up on improvement items
- Supporting the System Team and others in building development and deployment infrastructure and automation
- Keeping a focus on the architectural runway
- Supporting Release Management in the new way of working
- Supporting or delivering additional training

But the teams, especially those who are new to Agile, will need significant help, too. Here, coaching opportunities include the following:

- Helping teams plan, execute, and retrospect the first iterations
- Coaching new Scrum Masters and Product Owners in their roles
- Initiating and supporting Agile technical practices
- Helping teams establish the infrastructure, practices, and culture needed for continuous integration

I&A

And finally, there is no coaching opportunity more critical than the first I&A workshop. There, everyone will learn how the PI went, how the teams performed against their commitments, and how the solution *really* works at that point in time. In addition, SPCs and coaches can teach the first real corrective action and problem-solving workshop. This gives teams the tools they need to independently improve their performance, as well as how to work together—along with their management stakeholders—to collaboratively address the larger impediments that they face.

Launch More ARTs in the Value Stream

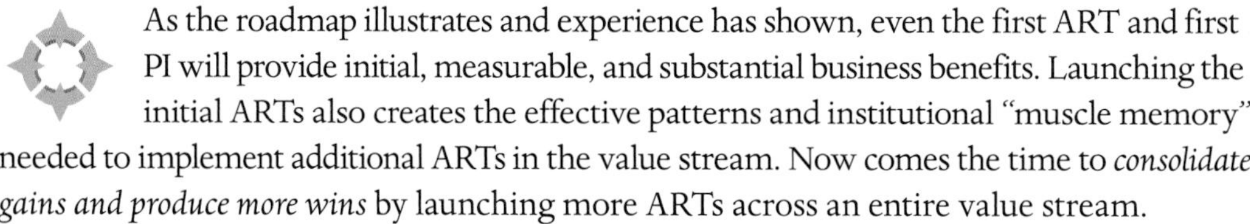

As the roadmap illustrates and experience has shown, even the first ART and first PI will provide initial, measurable, and substantial business benefits. Launching the initial ARTs also creates the effective patterns and institutional "muscle memory" needed to implement additional ARTs in the value stream. Now comes the time to *consolidate gains and produce more wins* by launching more ARTs across an entire value stream.

Launch More ARTs

The combination of good news and experience supports a rapid expansion via the launch of additional ARTs. While the ART pattern is now somewhat proven, and perhaps many ARTs can effectively launch themselves, more typically SPCs and LACE team members play an ongoing role, including the following:

- Coaching the current ARTs to generate effective results
- Training more teams and stakeholders
- Facilitating the first PI planning and I&A workshops
- Coaching the ARTs
- Communicating the positive results
- Modernizing governance documents
- Addressing implementation and process impediments

Implement Value Stream Roles, Artifacts, and Events

In smaller value streams, one or two ARTs can generally manage their own affairs, coordinate dependencies, and even release without much more structure or formality. That is the purpose of three-level SAFe.

However, for larger value streams—and for high-assurance systems, where more rigor of system definition and quality assurance is required—some or all of the additional value stream roles, events, and artifacts of four-level SAFe are required. In this case, the next stage of the rollout is typically concerned with establishing these additional practices. Activities include the following:

- *Establishing roles.* Identify responsibility for the three value stream roles—Value Stream Engineer (VSE), Solution Management, and Solution Architect/Engineering.
- *Establishing solution intent and solution context.* Determine the persistent responsibilities, process, and tooling to define and document solution intent and solution context. For high-assurance systems, establish and/or evolve Lean verification and validation practices.[4]
- *Establishing value stream vision, roadmap, and metrics.* Many elements of the floating tool palette may be required for large value streams. These include vision, roadmap, metrics, shared services, System Team and DevOps strategies, User Experience (UX) design, milestones, and releases.
- *Introducing capabilities and the value stream backlog.* Large value streams benefit from the use of the capabilities backlog item, in which case the value stream kanban must also be established.
- *Implementing pre- and post-planning, solution demo, value stream I&A.* These events are required to prepare for individual PI planning, to follow up and coordinate value stream objectives after planning, and to demonstrate the full solution to value stream stakeholders to assure that solution intent evolves in accordance with the value stream mission.
- *Integrating suppliers.* Large value streams typically have internal and/or external suppliers. Whether they are already working down a Lean/Agile/SAFe path or not, they must be integrated into the new way of working. Lean enterprises often take an active role in helping their suppliers adopt SAFe, as it improves the economics of the larger value stream. In any case, the suppliers must at least be integrated into SAFe value stream–level events.

4. "Building High Assurance Systems with SAFe 4.0" (www.scaledagileframework.com/safe-in-high-assurance-environments)

Launch More Value Streams in the Portfolio

It's quite an accomplishment to have implemented SAFe across a full value stream. Most importantly, measurable benefits in time-to-market, quality, productivity, and employee engagement begin accruing to the enterprise. As a result, the overall competitiveness of the enterprise starts to improve. But now, the larger goal is coming into view: a Lean-Agile enterprise with a fully implemented and Agile portfolio of SAFe value streams. Now comes time to expand the new way of working across the entire portfolio and *anchor the new approach in the culture.*

Launch More Value Streams

In the large enterprise, value streams are not necessarily homogenous. Rather, they can be entirely different businesses, operating units, or subsidiaries. They may be located in different countries, offer markedly different solutions and services, and have different chains of command that may meet again only at the highest, corporate level. When this is the case, even the spread of good news to other value streams may not cause an automatic embrace of SAFe across the enterprise. Many may well think that "what worked there will not work here."

In this case, the LACE may need to expand itself via a local satellite team in the other value streams and perhaps even start over at step 1 of the implementation roadmap. That's okay. It took many years to develop the current, largely successful way of working. It makes sense that it might take a few more to evolve to the more effective new way.

Whether the launch of additional value streams happens via pull, push, crises, or something in between, now is the time to expand the implementation to the full portfolio. In so doing, the following aspects must be accomplished:

- *Establish Agile Program Portfolio Management.* This includes implementing Lean-Agile budgeting, forecasting, Lean capital expenses and operating expenses, new Program Management Office (PMO) mindsets, and more. (See chapters 13, 14, and 18.)
- *Implement the Epic Owner role and portfolio kanban.* The role of the Epic Owners, the adoption of epics and the lightweight business case, and the portfolio kanban system and portfolio backlog must all be established. The Enterprise Architect

role is directly involved in this process as well, in part by establishing enabler epics that provide common technological underpinnings and support the broader use cases across the full solution portfolio.

- *Align the value streams with strategic themes.* Value streams exist for one reason: to meet the strategic goals of the portfolio. This can be assured by implementing a process of establishing and communicating the strategic themes that organize the portfolio into an integrated and unified solution offering.

Summary

In this chapter, we described how to prepare for the ART launch, how to train teams and launch the ART, how to launch more ARTs in the value stream, and how to launch more ARTs in the portfolio.

The key takeaways from this chapter are as follows:

- It takes time and effort to prepare to launch the first ART. Setting the launch date and cadence calendar is a great forcing function.
- Agile teams must be established to focus on new features and system components.
- If not already trained, key stakeholders of the ART will want to attend a Leading SAFe class held specifically in support of the launch. An extra workshop day can help facilitate ART launch planning and readiness.
- The teams, specialty roles and stakeholders, must all be trained. Big Room Training is the recommended model for the most effective and cost-efficient team training.
- There are other activities and roles as well, as described in the ART launch readiness checklist and associated templates. But no launch is ever perfect, and the important thing is to just do it. Experience and I&A will take care of the rest.
- After a period of preparation, the one-week "quick-start" approach is a proven way to rapidly implement the new SAFe way of working.
- Any ART launch is just that, the initial launch; each will generally require extensive coaching from experience leaders, Agile team and enterprise coaches, and SPCs.

- Launching one ART begets success, which begets more ARTs. The best assumption is that new ARTs will require about the same level of preparation as does the initial ART, although experience and knowledge facilitates take-up and success.
- For larger value streams with multiple ARTs, expansion requires that many of the value stream roles, artifacts, and activities will need to be instantiated.
- The ultimate goal is a Lean-Agile SAFe portfolio. Achieving that requires implementation of an Agile PPM function, adoption of epics for larger crosscutting initiatives, the Epic Owner role, and alignment via strategic themes.

18

Sustain and Improve

Excellent firms don't believe in excellence—only in constant improvement and constant change.

—Tom Peters

Introduction 287
Advance Organizational Maturity 288
Implement Agile HR Practices 292
Measure and Take Action 293
Improve Agile Architecture and Technical Practices 295
Focus on DevOps and Continuous Delivery 297
Reduce Time to Market with Value Stream Mapping 298
Summary 299

Introduction

In the past three chapters, we described a pattern for the successful implementation of the Scaled Agile Framework (SAFe). One Agile Release Train (ART) at a time and one value stream at a time, the business will move to this new way of working. Most importantly, substantial business benefits will occur.

But even after the initial business benefits are in place, this initial state of Lean-Agile adoption is not the end of the journey. It's just the next stage in the process of "relentless improvement." Of course, that means continuous change, which can be a hard thing for an enterprise to grapple with. By now, however, the emerging Lean-Agile enterprise will have started to build a new operating model and culture, one for whom continuous improvement is the norm.

In this chapter, we'll describe the next and ongoing steps, things the enterprise can do to continuously *sustain and improve* its business performance.

Advance Organizational Maturity

We'll start with the mindset and culture of the organization by focusing on the following practices:

- Persisting the Lean-Agile mindset
- Lean-Agile Program Portfolio Management (PPM)
- Communities of Practice (CoPs)
- Advancing facilitation skills

Persisting the Lean-Agile Mindset

It continues right where it began, with leadership and the Lean-Agile mindset. Figure 18-1 illustrates the direct connection between leadership and relentless improvement. You can't have one without the other.

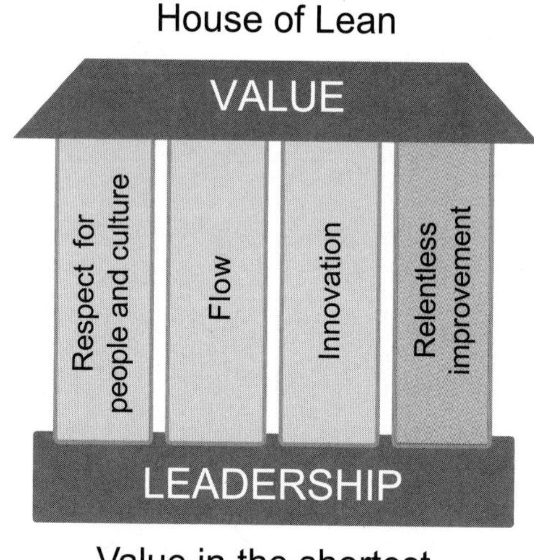

Figure 18-1. Lean leadership is the foundation for relentless improvement

Leaders provide a continuous sense of urgency for change and improvement and exhibit the same by their behavior. They also foster and support the other elements of sustain and improve, as described in the following sections.

Lean-Agile Program Portfolio Management

Nowhere is this Lean-Agile leadership more important than when addressing some of the legacy challenges of traditional Program Portfolio Management (PPM). In chapter 13, "Portfolio Level Overview," we illustrated how these mindsets evolve (Figure 18-2) as part of implementing SAFe.

	From Traditional Approach		To Lean-Agile Approach
#1	Centralized control	➡	Decentralized decision-making
#2	Project overload	➡	Demand management; continuous value flow
#3	Detailed project plans	➡	Lightweight, epic-only business cases
#4	Centralized annual planning	➡	Decentralized, rolling-wave planning
#5	Work breakdown structure	➡	Agile estimating and planning
#6	Project-based funding and control	➡	Lean-Agile budgeting and self-managing Agile Release Trains
#7	Waterfall milestones	➡	Objective, fact-based measures and milestones

Figure 18-2. Evolving traditional PPM mindsets to Lean-Agile thinking

And under the mantra of "it is better to lead than follow," the new, Lean-Agile Program Management Office (PMO) can take a lead role and thereby do the following:

- Lead the Lean-Agile transformation.
- Foster the Lean-Agile Center of Excellence (LACE) and other related CoPs.
- Apply objective milestones.
- Evolve leaner and more objective governance practices.
- Lead the move to Lean-Agile budgeting, forecasting, and capital expenses.
- Coach the ARTs in effective SAFe program delivery practices.
- Foster Agile contracts.

Lean-Agile Center of Excellence

We've described the LACE to this point as a focus on the transitional role of this change team, an engine of the "sufficiently powerful coalition for change." As such, it is primarily involved in implementing the new way of working within the organization. However, this change is not a one-time event; rather, the focus on Lean is to continually lower costs, reduce time to market, and increase the velocity of value delivery. There is no end. Therefore, the LACE often becomes a semipermanent body, a true center for excellence. This group understands the new way of working and continually advances its individual skills and uses its expertise to facilitate and foster the leaner, more Agile ways of working. But the LACE is only one such element of the coalition. To really sustain and improve, we need additional help.

Communities of Practice

As we have described throughout this book, SAFe organizes people with different skills around a value stream. However, organizing this way has an unintended consequence: It can limit the opportunities to share knowledge and learn new skills with other people in the same role. That's one of the advantages of the functional organization that SAFe leaves behind. After all, we have to decide what to optimize for, and we can't have it both ways.

CoPs help overcome this limitation by organizing people around a subject domain, work roles, or other areas of interest. Community members regularly interact with other like-minded practitioners to share knowledge, experiences, and practices. This gives practitioners with common interests the opportunity to collaborate and share knowledge outside of their team or program. For example, Scrum Masters from different Agile teams or trains may form a CoP to exchange best facilitation practices and experiences in building high-performing Agile teams. Product Owners may form a CoP to improve how they write user stories and prioritize their backlog.

Figure 18-3 illustrates an example of how members of different Agile teams may form a role-based CoP.

CoPs form and disband based on current need and context. For example, an automated testing CoP could be comprised of test engineers and developers interested in advancing their skills. An architecture and design CoP might foster the adoption of practices such as emergent design, intentional architecture, and user experience. It could also support building and maintaining the architecture of a solution, foster designing for testability and deployment readiness, retire old platforms, and more. Still others may be formed around Agile coaching, DevOps, and continuous delivery.

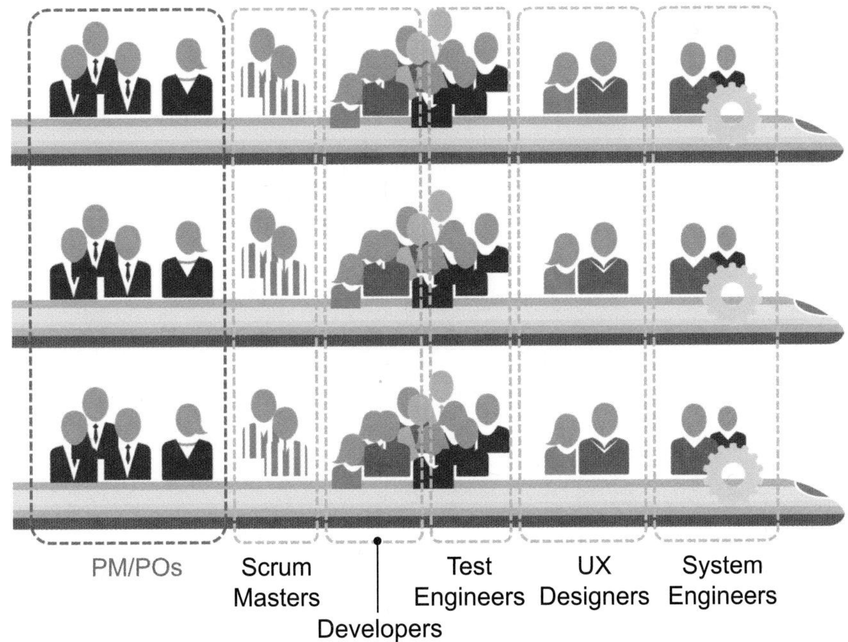

Figure 18-3. Example CoP

Advancing Facilitation Skills

Effective SAFe is built on effective Agile teams. We've already highlighted the critical role that the Scrum Master plays in helping develop effective Agile teams. Once Scrum Masters become adept in handling their basic responsibilities, many will be ready to take the next step to enhance and cultivate their skills.

This can provide the spark that can help drive higher team performance and simultaneously provide personal and career growth opportunities for this critical role.

Many benefit by taking a two-day SAFe Advanced Scrum Master course. It prepares current Scrum Masters for their leadership role in facilitating Agile team, program, and enterprise success in the larger and more mature SAFe implementation. The course covers facilitation of cross-team interactions in support of the program execution and relentless improvement. It enhances the Scrum paradigm with the following:

- An introduction to scalable engineering and DevOps pipeline practices
- The application of kanban to facilitate the flow of value
- Support of interactions with architects, product management, and other critical stakeholders

The course offers actionable tools for building high-performing teams and explores practical ways of addressing Agile and Scrum anti-patterns in the enterprise.

In a similar fashion, with equivalent trainings and CoPs, Release Train Engineers can improve their skills as Agile program managers, team coaches, and program-level facilitators.

Implement Agile HR Practices

"Respect for people" is a pillar of the House of Lean. It is *people* who build these critical systems we all depend on. These knowledge workers come to work intrinsically motivated to build high-quality, innovative systems. Given the importance of their work, management's challenge is to provide an *environment* in which they can prosper and do their best work.

While SAFe provides many of the values and practices of that environment, it also puts extreme pressure on traditional Human Resources (HR) practices. This compels enterprises to embrace a new, Lean-Agile HR perspective to accommodate the modern knowledge worker. There are six major themes of this new dynamic.

1. Embrace a new talent contract, one that explicitly acknowledges the need for value, autonomy, and empowerment.
2. Foster *continuous* engagement, to both the business and technical mission.
3. Hire people for Agile attitude, team orientation, and cultural fit.
4. Eliminate annual performance reviews; replace with continuous, iterative performance feedback and evaluation.
5. Establish compensation policies that effectively compensate for their efforts. Eliminate destructive individual financial incentives. "Take the issue of money off the table."
6. Support meaningful, impactful, and continuous learning and growth.

> For more on this topic, read the SAFe guidance white paper "Agile HR with SAFe: Bringing People Operations into the 21st Century with Lean Agile Values and Principles."[1]

---

1. http://www.scaledagileframework.com/agile-hr-with-safe

Measure and Take Action

We haven't focused much on measures in this book, other than the continued presence, evolution, and evaluation of working systems. But you can't knowingly improve what you can't measure, so in this section we'll take a quick look at a few of the many opportunities to measure and improve.

Inspect and Adapt

ARTs are created for a single reason: to gather the right people together and cultivate an environment in which they can build the best possible systems in the shortest possible time. To that end, it's hard to overemphasize the importance of ART (and value stream) Inspect and Adapt (I&A). That's why it is the entire subject of chapter 9, "Inspect and Adapt."

These are the cornerstone events of program execution and improvement. And unlike simpler forms of retrospectives, these bring the key stakeholders—the people who can change the systems in which they and others work—into an objective demonstration, measurement, and structured root-cause analysis and corrective action workshop. Here, they create and execute the changes to systems and processes needed to continually increase delivery velocity.

Leaders must actively encourage and participate in I&A problem-solving. This "closes the loop" on the Program Increment (PI) learning cycles and is the basis for continuously improving enterprise performance.

Lean Metrics

With its timeboxes, work physics (stories and features), fast feedback, and transparency, Lean-Agile development is inherently more measurable than prior methods. (For more, see scaledagileframework.com/metrics.) But metrics are a double-edged sword; people tend to focus on the measures, which are, at best, a proxy for the desired outcomes. However, without measurement, progress cannot really be certain. And since there is an investment required to fund any change, some measures must be put in place to assure a commensurate return.

In the spirit of the "simplest thing that can possibly work," we provide Figure 18-4, a set of seven measures that have been used to effectively measure SAFe transformations of significant size.

Benefit	Expected Result	Metric Used
Employee Engagement	Improved employee satisfaction; lower turnover	Employee survey; HR statistics
Customer Satisfaction	Improved Net Promoter Score	Net Promoter Score survey
Productivity	Reduced average feature cycle time	Feature cycle time
Agility	Continuous improvement in team and program measures	Team, Program, and Portfolio self-assessments; Release Predictability Measure
Time to Market	More frequent releases	Number of releases per year
Quality	Reduced defect counts and support call volume	Defect data and support call volume
Partner Health	Improving ecosystem relationships	Partner and vendor surveys

Figure 18-4. Lean portfolio metrics example

Enhance Performance with SAFe Self-Assessments

But when it comes to people, people don't generally like to be measured. After all, a person can be evaluated only by being compared to some other person. And only the person at the top can feel good about that outcome.

Further, many measures traditionally applied to the development process, and its people, are now obsolete. What's more, being measured by others is anathema to empowered, self-managing Agile thinking.

Instead, we suggest that teams self-assess against agreed-to Agile values. This is not new. The Scrum community has promoted various team-level self-assessments for years. To our larger purpose, SAFe provides a set of self-assessment worksheets for each of the team, program, value stream, and portfolio levels. Figure 18-5 shows an example of a typical radar chart for an ART self-assessment.

These can be used periodically to help teams advance their team, program, value stream, and, ultimately, portfolio performance.

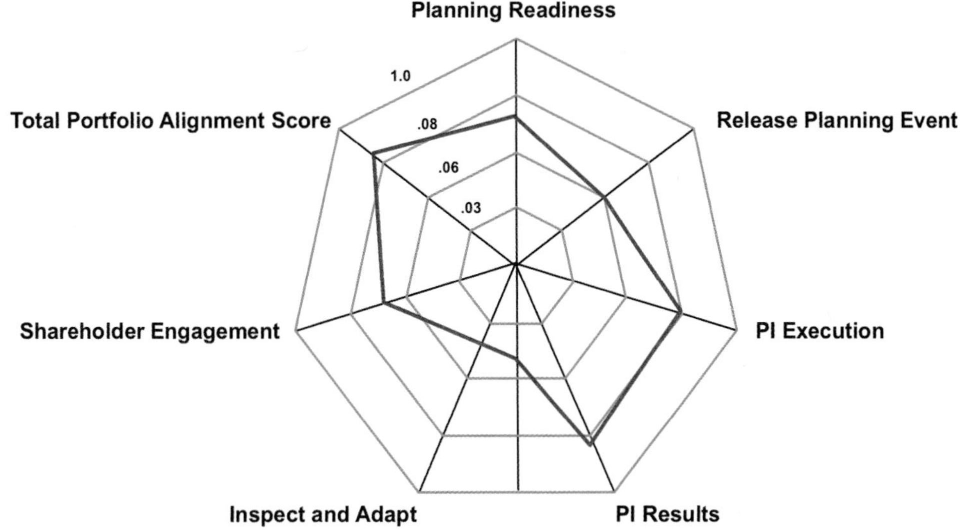

Figure 18-5. Example of an ART self-assessment radar chart

Improve Agile Architecture and Technical Practices

Agile Architecture

Agile or not, it's impossible to build significant world-class systems without some degree of intentional architecture. However, the Big Design Up Front (BDUF) practices of waterfall development are no longer relevant.

That means solution architecture must be built in concert with building the solution. This includes the creation of new architectural underpinnings (architectural runway) and practices for incrementally evolving legacy systems into the new platforms of choice. (In other words, yes, we do have to change the engine while we are driving to the destination.)

For this purpose, it's effective to create an Agile architecture CoP and/or a series of workshops. This allows System and Enterprise Architects to come together to define and learn the leaner and more incremental approaches to establishing and evolving solution architecture and to continuously advance their Agile architectural skills and craft. Topics addressed in this forum can include the following:

- Review and adopt SAFe's eight principles of Agile architecture.[2]
- Identify enabler epics and capabilities necessary to evolve the solution architecture.
- Establish the flow of enabler epics and features in the relevant kanban systems.
- Identify methods of splitting architectural epics into enabler capabilities and features for incremental implementation.
- Establish the decision-making framework and policies for architectural governance and capacity allocation.
- Identify relevant Nonfunctional Requirements (NFRs).

In many enterprises, such workshops are run on the PI cadence, often aligned with the Innovation and Planning iteration. This conveniently supports the availability of development teams for fast feedback spikes to help establish the technical viability of various design alternatives. Such timing also supports the pressing need to prepare architectural concepts and models for review in the upcoming PI planning session.

Agile Technical Practices

We've observed that within the first year or so of adoption, teams can quickly reach an apparent velocity limit by implementing only the basic role and team project management practices. After that, further improvements in velocity and quality can occur through effective implementation of Agile technical practices[3] (for example, built-in quality software practices, including continuous integration, test-first, and test automation). Mastering these takes an additional investment of focus and time, typically augmented by outside experts who have applied these practices in other contexts. Time must be allocated for this new learning. Again, the Innovation and Planning (IP) iteration can often provide the dedicated time needed for continuing education and practice in support of these new approaches.

In addition, companies building really large and/or high assurance systems need to focus on evolving fixed and variable solution intent and maintenance of architectural

2. http://www.scaledagileframework.com/agile-architecture
3. See http://scaledagileframework.com/built-in-quality for a complete list of built-in quality practices.

and other models that show how the system works. Implementing and advancing model-based systems engineering can provide a level of automation to develop and maintain these important artifacts.

Focus on DevOps and Continuous Delivery

Once Agile Release Trains are launched and value streams begin to better operate, that will increase visibility into the next set of bottlenecks and impediments to improved economics via more incremental delivery. Often, "leaning out" the development cycle just moves the bottleneck further down the value stream toward deployment. Since DevOps is integral to the value stream, SAFe ARTs include deployment personnel.

In order to establish an effective deployment pipeline—a continuous flow of new value from development to and through deployment—six specific practices are recommended as follows:

1. Build and maintain a production-equivalent staging environment
2. Maintain development and test environments to better match production
3. Deploy to staging every iteration; deploy to production frequently
4. Put everything under version control
5. Start creating the ability to automatically build environments
6. Start automating the actual deployment process

Another important aspect of assuring a continuous and reliable operating environment is the ability to automatically report system health and status. Development teams build application telemetry into the system to reduce the overhead and friction of manual monitoring and collection of data.

In addition, DevOps and continuous delivery provide faster feedback for ideation, design, implementation, and release. In other words, DevOps helps not just to deliver fast but also makes sure teams are delivering the *right thing*.

And finally, the impact on application architecture should not be underestimated. Long term, the continuous delivery pipeline requires systems that were designed—at least in part—with continuous delivery in mind. However, these practices involve a mindset shift and environment enablement, which includes things such as tooling and infrastructure for automation, and application telemetry. The shift in thinking requires strong leadership from managers and subject-matter experts who have the authority to create the environment for continuous value delivery. CoPs can also play a leading role.

Reduce Time to Market with Value Stream Mapping

The value stream is the most important organizational construct in SAFe. "Taking a systems view of value delivery" means understanding all the steps from ideation and feature approval to development, through deployment, all the way to release. The total average time for all these steps, including the delay times, is the average time to market for any new feature. This gives us one more, important tool in our toolbox. That is the process of *value stream mapping*, an analytical process teams can use to first understand, and then improve, time to market.

Figure 18-6 illustrates an example value stream map for a software company.[4]

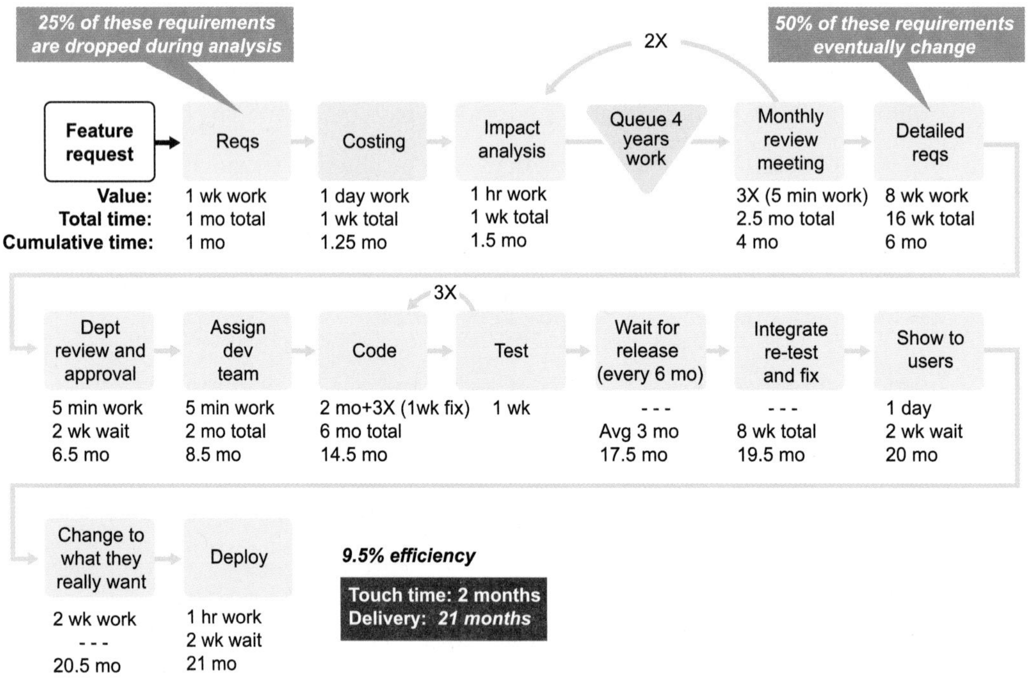

Figure 18-6. Example value stream map

4. Mary Poppendieck and Tom Poppendieck, *Implementing Lean Software Development: From Concept to Cash* (Addison-Wesley, 2006).

It is clear that this company's current process is complex and slow. Total time efficiency is such that a feature that takes two months to develop takes twenty-one months to get to market! Most all the time is spent waiting for the next step. (When a process runs at 100 percent utilization, every new thing has to wait for service.) Clearly there is substantial room for improvement.

As the SAFe enterprise matures its value stream thinking, an important improvement step is to map the value stream and make improvements. The steps are as follows:

- Map the current state by identifying all the steps, value-added times, handoffs, and delays, from receipt of customer request to release.
- Identify the largest sources of delays and handoffs as the feature moves through the system.
- Pick the biggest delay. Perform root-cause analysis. Create improvement backlog items to reduce the delay. Reduce batch sizes wherever possible.
- Implement the new improvement backlog items.
- Measure again, and repeat the process.

With this process, the maturing Lean enterprise has a systematic way to directly, aggressively, and continuously improve time to market, to its own business benefit.

Summary

In this chapter, we discussed the next and ongoing steps, things the enterprise can do to continuously *sustain and improve* its business performance.

The key takeaways from this chapter are as follows:

- Relentless improvement is a pillar of the SAFe House of Lean. Leaders provide a continuous sense of urgency for change and improvement and exhibit the same by their behavior.
- Nowhere is Lean-Agile leadership more important than when addressing some of the legacy challenges of traditional PPM.
- The LACE often becomes a semipermanent body, a true center for excellence. This group uses its advancing expertise to foster continuously leaner and more Agile ways of working.

- CoPs help overcome the limitation of organizing people around value streams. Community members regularly interact with other like-minded practitioners to share knowledge, experiences, and practices.
- Scrum Masters and Release Train Engineers play a particularly critical role in the culture of moving from centralized command and control to a distributed, facilitative, servant leadership culture. Advanced training is available for these and other roles.
- For some enterprises, Agile HR differs radically from the traditional approach. Agile HR establishes a new talent contract, one that fosters continuous engagement, empowerment, and autonomy, and eliminates demotivating policies and procedures.
- I&A is the cornerstone of relentless improvement. In addition, SAFe provides a variety of possible operating metrics, as well as self-assessment worksheets for each of the team, program, value stream, and portfolio levels.
- To accelerate delivery, teams adopt Agile architecture as well as various software and system technical and quality practices. These provide the foundation for fast iterations and efficient regression testing.
- Implementing DevOps and continuous delivery helps identify and eliminate bottlenecks and facilitates the goal of optimum economics via a continuum of fast, efficient, and high-quality releases.
- Value stream mapping provides a systematic way for a maturing lean enterprise to continuously improve its time to market.

19

Essential SAFe

Simplicity—the art of maximizing the amount of work not done—is essential.

—Agile Manifesto

Overview....301
Lean-Agile Principles....303
Agile Teams and Release Trains....306
Cadence and Synchronization....308
Essential Team and Program Roles....310
PI Planning....312
System Demo....313
Inspect and Adapt....314
IP Iteration....315
DevOps Pipeline....316
Lean-Agile Leadership....317
Summary....319

Overview

Throughout this book, we've described the Scaled Agile Framework (SAFe) in some detail. While it is indeed "distilled" from the larger body of knowledge,[1] the fact remains that it's a significant framework. Not surprisingly, we've observed that not every implementation realizes the full business benefits others achieve. When diagnosing these cases, we typically discover the root causes, which illustrates what happens when some essential SAFe practice is missing.

1. www.scaledagileframework.com

It's easy to see how that can happen. After all, it's a big framework, designed for people building big systems. And since it's a framework—not a method or recipe—some interpretation and context-specific implementation are typically required. So, the question arises, how would an enterprise know what's essential?

With that in mind, this final chapter introduces the "Essential SAFe" configuration, which provides the minimum—and essential—elements necessary to receive the majority of the business benefits.

Figure 19-1 illustrates the most essential elements of SAFe. This configuration of SAFe serves two purposes: one, it provides an excellent starting point for those implementing SAFe, and two, it can serve as a diagnostic assessment for those who are further down the road. And to make things as simple as possible for the reader, this chapter briefly summarizes the most critical elements of SAFe so that it can also serve as an introductory, stand-alone guide for either of these two purposes.

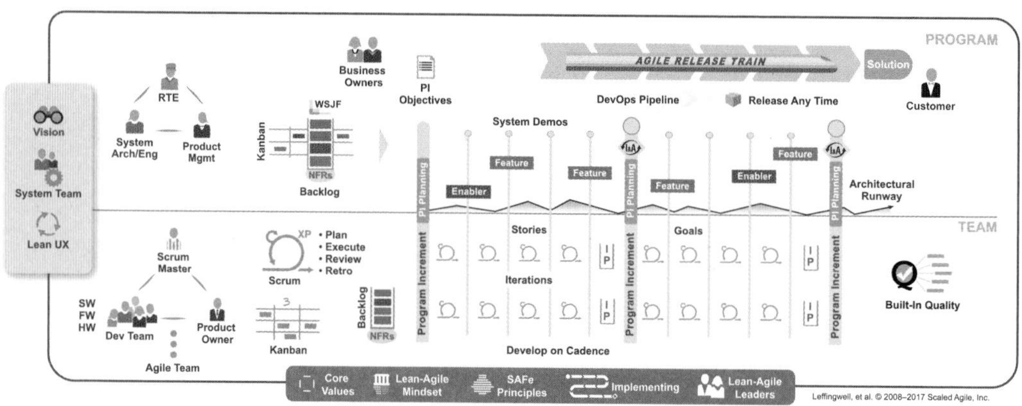

Figure 19-1. Essential SAFe is a subset of SAFe

The ten essential elements are as follows:

1. Lean-Agile principles
2. Agile teams and Agile Release Trains (ARTs)
3. Cadence and synchronization
4. Essential team and program roles
5. Program Increment (PI) planning
6. System demo
7. Inspect and Adapt (I&A)

8. Innovation and Planning (IP) iteration
9. DevOps pipeline
10. Lean-Agile leadership

Each is described in the sections that follow, along with a set of symptoms that typically occur when that element is missing from an implementation.

Lean-Agile Principles

An understanding of the nine fundamental Lean-Agile principles is critical to appreciate what SAFe is and how it helps the enterprise accomplish what it does. The following sections are abbreviated versions of the principles to help you focus on the most important aspects of the principles.

Principle #1: Take an Economic View

The over-arching goal is simple: to deliver the best value and quality to people and society in the shortest sustainable lead time. Doing so requires a fundamental understanding of the economics of the mission and makes sure that everyday decisions are made in a proper economic context. The primary aspects include developing and communicating the strategy for incremental value delivery and the creation of the economic framework. This helps define the trade-offs between risk, Cost of Delay (CoD), and operational and development costs, while supporting decentralized decision-making.

Principle #2: Apply Systems Thinking

W. Edwards Deming, one of the world's foremost systems thinkers, constantly focused on the larger view of problems and challenges faced by people building and deploying all types of systems: manufacturing, social, management, and even government. One central conclusion was the understanding that the problems faced in the workplace were a result of a series of complex interactions that occurred within the systems the workers used to accomplish their tasks. In SAFe, systems thinking addresses this and is applied to the organization that builds the system, as well as the system under development.

Principle #3: Assume Variability; Preserve Options

Traditional design and life-cycle practices drive picking a single requirement and design option early in the development process when there is high uncertainty. However, if the starting point is wrong, then future adjustments take too long and can lead to a suboptimal long-term design. Alternatively, a better approach is to maintain multiple requirements and design options for a longer period in the development cycle. Empirical data is then used to narrow focus, resulting in a design that creates better economic outcomes.

Principle #4: Build Incrementally with Fast, Integrated Learning Cycles

Lean-Agile teams develop solutions incrementally in a series of short iterations. Each results in an integrated increment of a working system. Subsequent iterations build upon the previous ones. Increments of the solution provide the opportunity for fast customer feedback and risk mitigation and also serve as minimum viable products or prototypes for market testing and validation. In addition, these early, fast feedback points allow teams to "pivot" when necessary to an alternate course of action.

Principle #5: Base Milestones on Objective Evaluation of Working Systems

Lean-Agile teams and customers have a shared responsibility to assure that investment in new solutions will deliver economic benefit. The sequential, phase-gate development model was designed to meet this challenge. But experience has shown that it does not mitigate risk as intended. In Lean-Agile development, each integration point provides an objective milestone in which to evaluate the solution frequently and throughout the development life cycle. This objective evaluation provides the financial, technical, and fitness-for-purpose governance needed to assure that continued investment will produce commensurate return.

Principle #6: Visualize and Limit Work in Process, Reduce Batch Sizes, and Manage Queue Lengths

Lean-Agile teams strive to achieve a state of continuous flow, allowing new capabilities to move quickly and visibly from concept to cash. The following are three keys to ensure flow:

- Visualize and limit the amount of Work in Process (WIP) to restrict demand to actual capacity.
- Reduce the batch sizes of work items to facilitate reliable flow through the system.
- Manage queue lengths to reduce the wait times for new capabilities.

Principle #7: Apply Cadence; Synchronize with Cross-Domain Planning

Cadence transforms unpredictable events into predictable ones and provides a rhythm for development. Synchronization causes multiple perspectives to be understood, resolved, and integrated at the same time. Applying development cadence and synchronization, coupled with periodic cross-domain planning, offers the Lean-Agile tools needed to operate effectively in the presence of product development uncertainty.

Principle #8: Unlock the Intrinsic Motivation of Knowledge Workers

Lean-Agile leaders understand that knowledge workers generally aren't motivated by incentive compensation approaches. Such individual Management by Objectives (MBOs) causes internal competition and destruction of the cooperation necessary to achieve the larger system aim. Providing autonomy, mission, and purpose while minimizing constraints leads to higher levels of employee engagement and results in better outcomes for customers and the enterprise.

Principle #9: Decentralize Decision-Making

Achieving fast value delivery requires fast, decentralized decision-making, as any decision escalated introduces delay. In addition, escalation can lead to lower-quality decisions because of the lack of local context and changes to facts that may occur during the wait time. Decentralized decision-making reduces delays, improves product development flow, and enables faster feedback and more innovative solutions. Some decisions, however, are strategic global choices that have economies of scale warranting centralized decision-making. Since both types of decisions occur, creating an established decision-making framework is a critical step in ensuring the fast flow of value.

What Happens If Your Implementation Is Not Based on SAFe Principles?

- Change agents, management, and other practitioners are unable to effectively adapt practices.
- Improvement of business outcomes over time is impaired; practices and measures that used to be beneficial become constraints.
- Lean-Agile mindset is unachievable; Agile practices deployed on a wrong-minded "mental platform" produce serious problems.
- Misalignment, conflict, and disagreement on processes and practices are impossible to resolve.

Agile Teams and Release Trains

ARTs are virtual organizations that have all the people they need to define and deliver value. Each ART is a long-lived, self-organizing team of Agile teams, a virtual organization (50–125 people) that plans, commits, and executes together. ARTs are organized around the enterprise's significant value streams and exist solely to realize the promise of that value by building solutions that deliver benefit to the end user. The ART aligns teams to a common mission via a single vision and program backlog.

In functional organizations, developers work with developers, testers work with other testers, and architects and systems engineers work with each other. While there are reasons why organizations have evolved that way, value doesn't flow easily, as it must cross *all* the silos. Daily involvement of managers and project managers is necessary to move the work across the silos. As a result, progress is slow, and handoffs and delays rule the day.

Instead, the ART takes a systems view and builds a cross-functional organization that includes all people needed to continuously define, build, test, and deploy valuable features. This means each train must include cross-functional Agile teams, as well as people from various other disciplines, as shown in Figure 19-2.

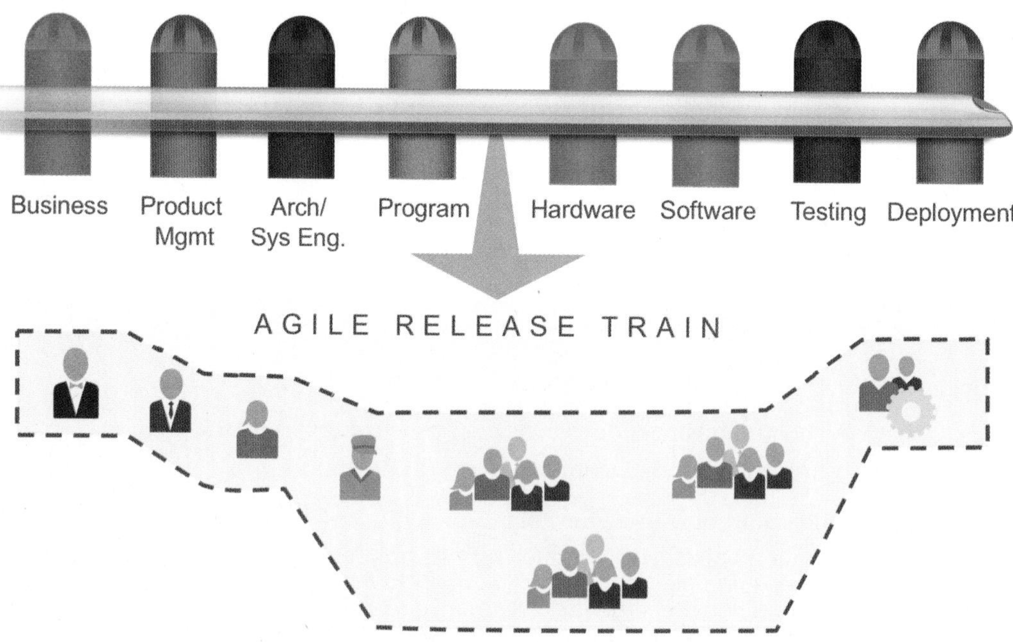

Figure 19-2. ARTs are cross-functional

In support of this, Agile teams are cross-functional too, as shown in Figure 19-3.

Figure 19-3. Agile teams are cross-functional

Each Agile team has the skills and people needed (for example, designers, developers, and testers) to effectively deliver a feature or component with a minimum number of dependencies on others.

Together, this fully cross-functional organization—whether physical (direct organizational reporting) or virtual (line of reporting is unchanged)—has everyone and everything necessary to define and deliver value. It is self-organizing and self-managing at the team and program levels. This creates a far leaner organization, one where traditional daily task management is no longer required. Value flows more quickly, with a minimum of overhead. That's the purpose of the ART.

What Happens When Agile Teams and ARTs Aren't Implemented Correctly?

- Teams are isolated and struggle to deliver value.
- There is a lack of collaboration among teams.
- Components become over-specialized, and bottlenecks are created.
- Teams are not aligned to a common mission.
- Release of value is late and problematic.
- There is no architectural and user experience integrity.
- There is too much WIP and multitasking, which leads to lower productivity and quality.

Cadence and Synchronization

Cadence provides a rhythmic pattern, the dependable heartbeat of the development process. It makes routine that which can be routine. This enables teams to focus on leveraging the variability inherent in solution development.

Synchronization causes multiple perspectives to be understood and resolved at the same time. For example, synchronization is used to pull the disparate assets of a system together to assess solution-level viability. It's also used to align development teams and the business to a common mission at PI planning.

Together, cadence and synchronization are the primary tools used to manage the inherent variability of Research and Development (R&D).

The first cadence of SAFe is the iteration cycle; each is a Plan-Do-Check-Adjust (PDCA) learning cycle. During this short period, the team plans, builds, integrates, and demonstrates the result, followed by a short retrospective. As illustrated in Figure 19-4, iterations provide the basic cadence, or tempo, for development.

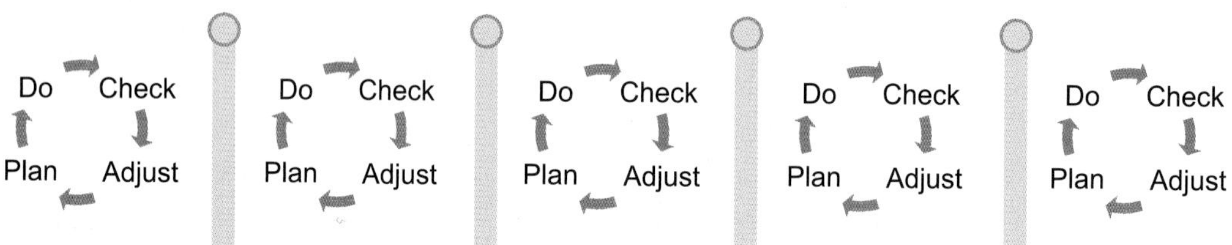

Figure 19-4. The basic iteration cadence, each a Plan-Do-Check-Adjust cycle

However, because significant solutions require integration across multiple teams, it is critical for the teams to work on a common cadence, using the same iteration duration. Otherwise, the teams may be iterating, but integration is difficult, and the slowest cycle delays problem discovery. The net result is that the teams may be iterating, but the system isn't, as shown in Figure 19-5.

To address this, SAFe provides two synchronized PDCA feedback loops. The inner team's PDCA loops are synchronized; all teams start and end the iterations at the same time. The inner loop iterations occur inside an ART PDCA cycle, or PI, as Figure 19-6 illustrates.

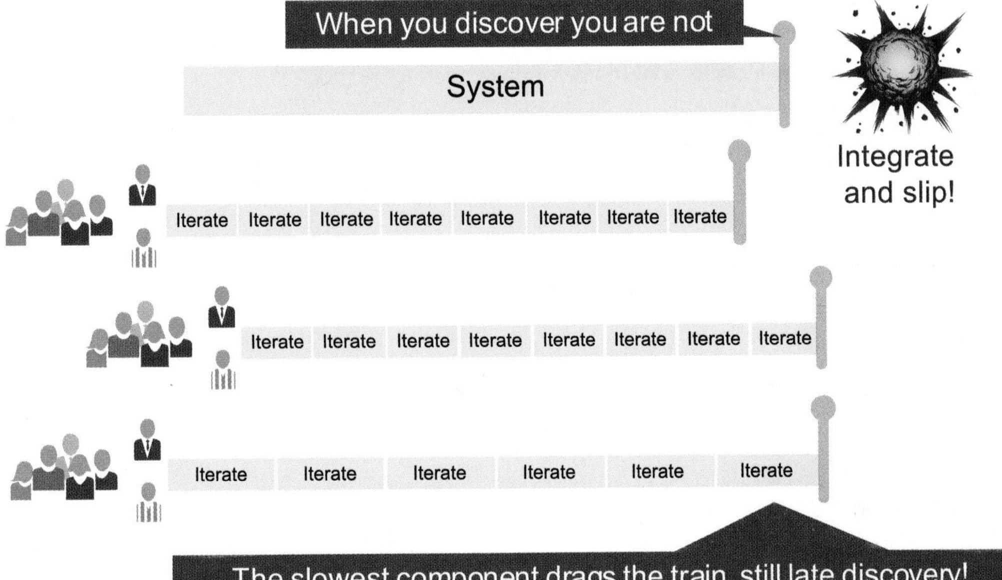

Figure 19-5. Cadence without synchronization is not enough

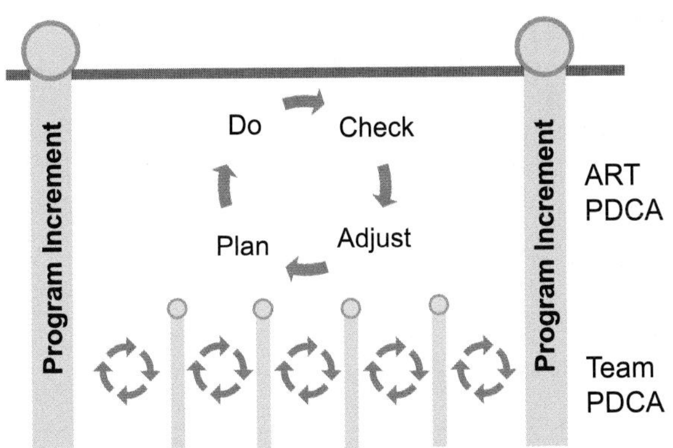

Figure 19-6. Iterations and PIs provide nested learning cycles

The PI provides a larger and more strategic PDCA timebox in which to accumulate and assess system-level performance. It also provides the cadence for the entire train to perform cross-domain planning, integration, demo, and I&A.

Develop on Cadence; Release Any Time

We've described how cadence and synchronization are the primary tools in managing the inherent variability of R&D. But it's important to note that the development cycle is distinct from the release cycle. These are two separate concerns. While in some situations the train may release solutions at the end of a PI, other programs may need to release less or more frequently than the PI cadence. Still others will have multiple, independent release cycles for the various subsystems of the solution.

What Happens without Cadence and Synchronization?

- There is gradual decline into disorder and lack of predictability.
- Getting the right people to meetings is impossible.
- Integration comes late, resulting in slips of value delivery.
- There are no forced integration and evaluation points.
- Individual teams may be Agile, but the system is not iterating.
- Enterprise agility is not achievable.

Essential Team and Program Roles

Effective implementations require the right people in the right roles, fulfilling the right set of responsibilities.

Essential Team Roles

- *Scrum Master.* Scrum Masters coach a high-performing and self-managing team. They do that by facilitating team meetings, driving Agile behavior, removing impediments, helping maintain the team's focus by protecting the team, and attending ART sync meetings.
- *Product Owner.* The Product Owner maintains the team backlog, acts as the customer for team questions, prioritizes the work, and collaborates with Product Management to plan PIs.
- *Development Team.* Developers, testers, and various specialists create and refine user stories and acceptance criteria. They define, build, test, and deliver software, hardware, and other system components or features.

Essential Program Roles

- *The Release Train Engineer (RTE).* The RTE acts as the chief Scrum Master for the train. RTEs facilitate ART-level events and meetings and help drive Agile behavior with the teams, the ART, and other stakeholders. They help manage risk, coordinate dependencies, and coach the ART to relentless improvement.
- *Product Management.* Product Management is responsible for identifying customer needs. They own the vision and product backlog, and they sequence features for optimal Return on Investment (ROI). They drive PI objectives and release content via prioritized features and acceptance criteria.
- *System Architect-Engineering.* System Architect-Engineering aligns ARTs with a common technological and architectural vision. They participate in defining the system and subsystems and their interfaces, validating technological assumptions, and evaluating alternatives. They support robust system development by providing, communicating, and evolving the larger technological and architectural view of the solution.
- *Business Owners.* Business Owners are a small group of stakeholders who have the ultimate fiduciary, governance, and ROI responsibility for the value delivered by a specific ART. Business Owners typically have management responsibility in one or more areas, such as customer relationships, development, solution quality, deployment, operations, Product Management, and architecture. They work with the ART to continuously define the business value of plans and working systems.
- *Customer.* The customer is whoever consumes the work of an ART. Whether internal or external to the development organization, they are an integral part of the value stream and thereby participate in ART events.

What Happens without the Essential Team and Program Roles?

- Responsibilities for requirements, design, architecture, implementation, and deployment are unclear.
- Meetings are less productive and end without clear outcomes.
- Teams find it hard to integrate because of incompatible components.
- Vision and requirements are not clear, and there is a lack of prioritization.
- Deliverables do not meet stakeholder expectations.
- It is difficult to improve processes.

PI Planning

There is no other, more powerful event than PI planning. It is the cornerstone of the PI—which provides the rhythm for the ART.

It's amazing how much alignment and energy are created when there are 100 or so people all working together toward a common mission, vision, and shared purpose. Gaining that alignment in just two days can save weeks, if not months, of delays waiting on decisions and coming to agreement via a flurry of emails.

More importantly, this event represents a critical and cultural milestone for the implementation of SAFe.

- The teams come together periodically to better define and design the system that fulfills the vision and commit to near-term PI objectives.
- The ART uses this event to create, foster, and sustain a sense of shared mission, responsibility, and cooperation and collaboration.
- The responsibility for planning moves from central authority to the teams who do the work; this sends a signal of true change from management that the teams are now empowered.
- It builds the social network that the ART depends on; after all, building large-scale, complex solutions is a social endeavor.

Whenever possible, attendees include all members of the ART. After all, they are the ones doing the work, so they are the only ones who can design the system, plan, and then commit to the plan.

What Happens without Effective PI Planning?

- Stakeholders and teams don't have a clear understanding of the vision.
- Teams don't know the business context and the most important objectives.
- There is a lack of alignment between business and technology.
- Dependencies are discovered too late.
- Planning is centralized and ineffective.
- Teams are not committed to the business objectives.

System Demo

The primary measure of ART progress is the objective evidence provided by a working solution in the system demo. Every two weeks, the full system—the integrated work of all teams on the train for that iteration—is demoed to the train's stakeholders. (This is in addition to each team's iteration demo.) Stakeholders provide the feedback the train needs to stay on course and take corrective action, as shown in Figure 19-7.

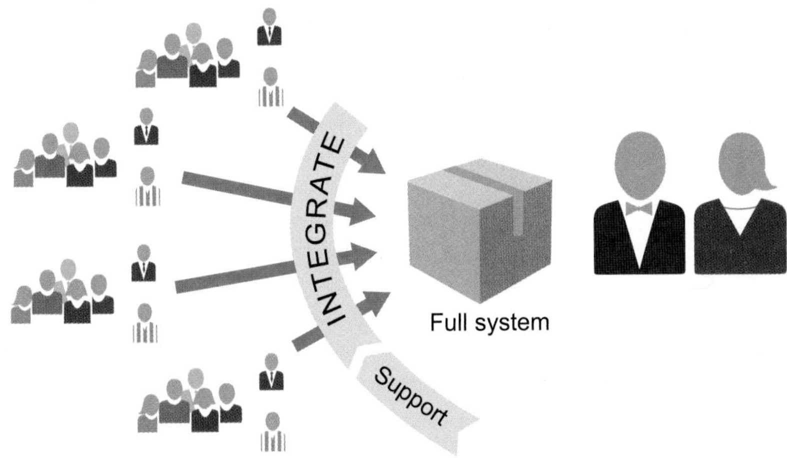

Figure 19-7. Teams integrate every iteration to demo the full system

At the end of each PI, a final system demo is held. That demo is a significant and somewhat more structured affair, as it demonstrates the accumulation of all the features (from all teams on the train) that have been developed over the course of the PI.

What Happens without the System Demo?

- There is late discovery of integration problems.
- Business Owners are unclear about solution progress, which reduces trust between the business and development organizations.
- Management relies on traditional proxy metrics.
- Quality and velocity are uncertain.
- There is little to no meaningful feedback.
- There is no forcing function for continuous integration and test automation.
- Teams might be iterating, but the system as a whole is not.

Inspect and Adapt

The I&A workshop is a significant event held at the end of each PI and that serves as its capstone.

A regular time to reflect, collect data, and solve problems, the workshop is where teams and stakeholders assess the solution in process and define and take action on the improvements needed to increase the velocity, quality, and reliability of the next PI.

All program stakeholders participate, resulting in a full understanding of the current context, along with a set of improvement stories that can be added to the backlog for the upcoming PI planning. As a result, every ART improves every PI. Continuous improvement is assured with implementation of the identified backlog improvement items.

The I&A has three parts.

- *PI system demo.* This is a demo of all features completed by the ART during the previous PI.
- *Quantitative measurement.* A review of any quantitative metrics that teams have agreed to collect and discuss.
- *Problem-solving workshop.* A short retrospective for the PI, along with a structured problem-solving workshop (as shown in Figure 19-8), which focuses on identifying the root causes of the problems faced by the ART and, most importantly, pinpoints a small number of improvement items that can be added to the backlog for the upcoming PI.

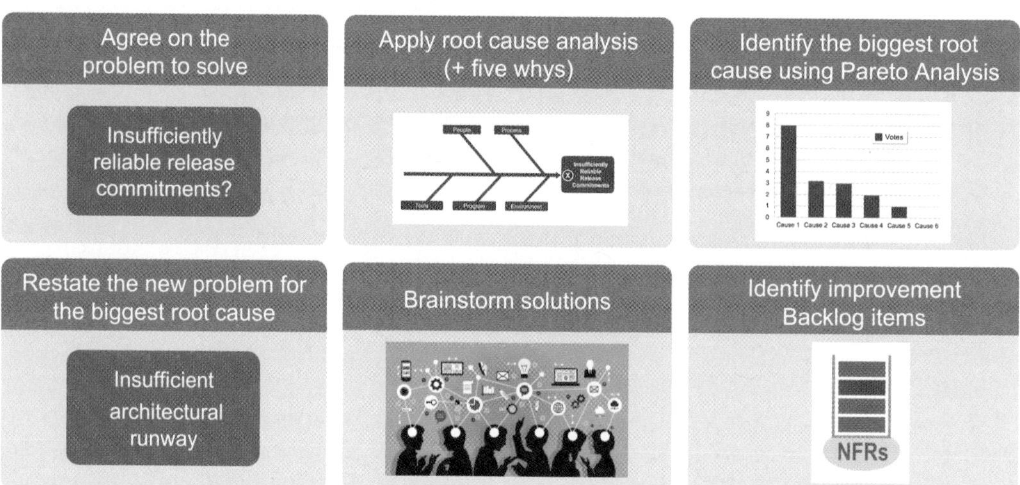

Figure 19-8. Problem-solving workshop format

What Happens without the Inspect & Adapt?

- Programs do not predictably deliver committed objectives.
- There is no way to improve systemically.
- Improvement efforts address symptoms, not root causes.
- Centralized improvement mandates don't reflect actual development problems.
- Management stakeholders are not involved in changing the system.

IP Iteration

Every PI delivers value. During the PI, teams are busy working on the PI objectives that they committed to in PI planning. Every iteration counts, and the teams are mostly "heads down," focused on near-term delivery. There is a sense of urgency about every iteration and every PI. Given this urgency, there's a risk that if time is not put aside for innovation, improvement, and planning, the "tyranny of the urgent" will outweigh all other activities.

To address this, the IP iteration provides a regular, cadence-based opportunity for teams to work on activities that are difficult to fit into a continuous delivery model. These can include time for innovation and exploration, a dedicated time for the scheduled PI system demo, the I&A workshop, PI planning events, backlog refinement for the next PI, and even time for continuing education.

The IP iterations fulfill another critical role: They provide an estimating buffer for meeting PI objectives and enhancing release predictability. Lean teaches us that operating at near 100 percent utilization drives unpredictable results. Put simply, if everyone is planned to full capacity, there is no one available to flex when problems inevitably occur. The result is unpredictability and delays in value delivery.

To address this, the IP iteration is also treated as a "guard band" or estimating buffer. During PI planning, no features or stories are planned for development in this iteration. This buffer gives the teams extra time to respond to unforeseen events, delays in dependencies, and other issues, which increases their ability to meet PI objectives. This substantially improves the predictability of the program's outcomes, an attribute that's extremely important to Business Owners.

Routinely using that time for completing the work, however, is a failure pattern. Teams must also take care that the IP iteration does not simply become a crutch for poor planning or, worse, a time for the quality activities that must occur during the iterations themselves. It defeats the primary purpose of the IP iteration; innovation will surely suffer.

What Happens without IP Iterations?

- There is no capacity buffer, and the ARTs are not predictable.
- There is no time for innovation because of delivery urgency.
- Technical debt just grows and grows.
- People burn out.
- Cadence and schedule become a challenge as there is no time allocated for teams to plan together, demo together, and improve together.
- There is no time for continuing education.
- The real velocity slows down.

DevOps Pipeline

The goal of software and systems engineering is to deliver usable and reliable solutions to the end users. Lean and Agile both emphasize the ability to do so more frequently and reliably.

Once Agile Release Trains are launched and value streams begin to better operate, that will increase visibility into the next set of bottlenecks and impediments to improved economics through more incremental delivery. Often, "leaning out" the development cycle just moves the bottleneck further down the value stream toward deployment. The countermeasure is the implementation of the DevOps pipeline, which was covered in chapter 8, "Executing a Program Increment." Because DevOps is integral to the value stream, SAFe ARTs include deployment personnel.

What Happens without the DevOps Pipeline?

- Value delivery is greatly delayed.
- Reduced quality of deployments and a higher rate of production defects.
- More frequent releases of the solution are not possible, increasing time to market and loss of first-mover advantage.

- Large batches of code are pushed to production, resulting in production emergencies.
- There is increased friction between development and operations, limiting collaboration, learning, and cultural change.

Lean-Agile Leadership

SAFe is based on a number of modern systems and software engineering disciplines, including systems thinking, Lean product development, and Agile development. Agile provides the tools needed to empower and engage teams to achieve unprecedented levels of productivity, quality, and engagement. But a broader and deeper mindset is needed to support Lean and Agile development at scale across the entire enterprise.

For SAFe to be effective, the enterprise's leaders and managers must take responsibility for Lean-Agile adoption and success. Executives must become leaders who are trained—and become trainers—in these leaner ways of thinking and operating. Without such a change and without leadership taking responsibility for the implementation, the transformation will fail to achieve the intended benefits. That's why SAFe focuses first on a Lean-Agile leadership mindset, which includes the following:

- *Thinking Lean.* Lean thinking is represented in the SAFe "House of Lean" icon, organized around six key constructs. The "roof" represents the goal of delivering Value. The "pillars" support that goal through Respect for People and Culture, Flow, Innovation, and Relentless Improvement. Lean leadership provides the foundation on which everything else stands.
- *Embracing agility.* In addition, SAFe is built entirely on the skills, aptitude, and capabilities of Agile teams and their leaders. And while there is no one definition of what an Agile method is, the Agile Manifesto provides a unified value system that has helped inaugurate Agile methods into mainstream development.

However, thinking Lean and embracing Agile aren't enough. Leading is what's required. To this end, Lean-Agile leaders do the actions covered in the following sections.

#1: Lead the Change

Steering an organization toward Lean and Agile behaviors, habits, and results cannot be delegated. Leaders must exhibit and communicate the urgency for change, collaboratively build a plan, understand and manage the change process, and quickly solve problems. They must have knowledge of organizational change management and take a systems view for implementing the transformation.

#2: Know the Way; Emphasize Lifelong Learning

Create an environment that promotes continuous learning and fosters formal and informal groups for learning and improvement. Strive to learn and understand new developments in Lean, Agile, and contemporary management practices.

#3: Develop People

Focus on developing people's knowledge and skills rather than on being the go-to expert or coordinator of tasks. Create a team that is jointly responsible for success.

#4: Inspire and Align with Mission

Minimize constraints. Provide an inspirational mission and vision, and eliminate demotivating rules, policies, and procedures. Build Agile teams and trains organized around value.

Understand the power of self-organizing, self-managing teams. Create a safe, failure-tolerant environment for learning, growth, and mutual influence.

#5: Decentralize Decision-Making

Establish a decision-making framework. Empower others by setting the mission, developing people, and teaching them to problem-solve.

#6: Unlock the Intrinsic Motivation of Knowledge Workers

Understand the role that compensation plays in motivating knowledge work. Change from individual to shared rewards. Create an environment of mutual influence. Eliminate any and all management processes and objectives that cause internal competition.

What Happens without Lean-Agile Leadership?

- The team has no one to learn from.
- The development processes cannot continuously improve.
- We have "Agile" development with non-Agile governance, leading back to the "iron triangle" of scope, time, and budget as well as to centralized planning and commitments.

- Lead time is long as decisions must be escalated.
- Without sufficiently powerful coalition for change, Lean-Agile transformation wanes.
- People cannot experiment, fail, and learn.
- People are over-controlled, underutilized, and demotivated.

Summary

In this chapter, we provided an overview of "Essential SAFe," which represents the indispensable elements of the Scaled Agile Framework.

The key takeaways of this chapter are as follows:

- SAFe is a framework, not a method or recipe. Therefore, some interpretation and context-specific implementation are typically required.
- Not every implementation of SAFe realizes the full business benefits that others achieve. The root causes of this problem are typically because of what happens when some essential SAFe practice is missing.
- Essential SAFe provides an excellent starting point to begin implementation of the framework. It can also serve as a diagnostic assessment for those who have already implemented SAFe.
- There are ten essential elements of SAFe:
    1. Lean-Agile principles
    2. Agile teams and ARTs
    3. Cadence and synchronization
    4. Essential team and program roles
    5. PI planning
    6. System demo
    7. I&A
    8. IP iteration
    9. DevOps pipeline
    10. Lean-Agile leadership

Abbreviations

ART	Agile Release Train
BVIR	Big Visible Information Radiator
CapEx	Capital Expenses
CoD	Cost of Delay
CoPs	Communities of Practice
DSU	Daily Stand-Up
FW	Firmware
HW	Hardware
I&A	Inspect and Adapt
IP	Innovation and Planning
LACE	Lean Agile Center of Excellence
MBSE	Model-Based Systems Engineering
NFRs	Nonfunctional Requirements
PI	Program Increment
PPM	Program Portfolio Management
RTE	Release Train Engineer
SAFe	Scaled Agile Framework
UX	User Experience
VSE	Value Stream Engineer
WIP	Work in Progress
WSJF	Weighted Shortest Job First
XP	Extreme Programming

Glossary

The Scaled Agile Framework (SAFe) glossary defines all of the terms on the Big Picture.

A 323
B 324
C 324
D 325
E 325
F 326
GHI 326
JKL 327
MNO 327
PQ 328
R 330
S 330
T 332
UVW 333

A

Agile Architecture

Agile architecture is a set of values and practices that advances the design and architecture of a system while implementing new business functions.

Agile Release Train

The Agile Release Train (ART) is a long-lived team-of-Agile-teams, which along with other stakeholders, develops and delivers solutions incrementally, using a series of fixed iterations within a program increment timebox. The ART aligns teams to a common business and technology mission.

Agile Teams

Agile teams are a group of three to nine dedicated individual contributors, covering all the roles necessary to define, build, and test a quality increment of value in an iteration.

Architectural Runway

Architectural runway consists of the existing code, components, and technical infrastructure necessary to support the implementation of high-priority, near-term features, without excessive delay and redesign.

B

Budgets

See *Lean-Agile budgeting*.

Built-in Quality

Built-in quality practices ensure that each solution element, at every increment, meets appropriate quality standards throughout development.

Business Epic

See *epic*.

Business Owners

Business Owners are a small group of stakeholders who have the primary technical, fitness for use, governance, and Return on Investment responsibility for a solution developed by an Agile Release Train. They are key stakeholders on the train and actively participate in certain events.

C

Capability

A capability is a high-level solution behavior that typically spans multiple Agile Release Trains. They are sized and split as necessary to fit within a single program increment.

CapEx and OpEx

CapEx and OpEx describe Lean-Agile financial practices for tracking capital expenses (CapEx) and operating expenses (OpEx) in a value stream budget. In some cases, CapEx may include capitalized labor associated with development of intangible assets such as software, intellectual property, and patents.

Communities of Practice

Communities of Practice (CoPs) are groups of people who have a common interest in a specific technical or business domain. They collaborate regularly to share information, improve their skills and performance, and advance the general knowledge of the domain.

Continuous Integration

Continuous integration is a built-in quality practice, where team members constantly integrate and verify their work, using automated build-and-test environments that quickly identify problems and defects.

Coordination
See *value stream coordination*.

Core Values
Core values define the ideals and beliefs that are key to the effectiveness of the Scaled Agile Framework. They are alignment, built-in quality, transparency, and program execution.

Customer
The customer is anyone who consumes the work of a value stream. Customers are an integral part of the Agile development process and value stream.

D

Develop on Cadence
Develop on cadence is a strategy for managing the inherent variability in solution development by making sure important events and activities occur on a regular, predictable schedule.

DevOps
DevOps is a mindset, culture, and set of technical practices that foster communication, collaboration, and close cooperation among all the professionals needed to develop, test, deploy, and maintain a solution.

E

Economic Framework
The economic framework is a set of decision rules aligning everyone to the financial objectives of the mission, defining economic trade-off parameters, and assuring operation within the budget provided by the program portfolio.

Enablers
Enablers further the exploration, infrastructure, and architecture development activities needed to support future business functionality. Enablers arise from the backlog and occur at all levels of the framework where they are described as enabler portfolio epics, enabler capabilities, enabler features, or enabler stories.

Enterprise
The enterprise represents the business entity that has the ultimate strategic, fiduciary, and governance authority for all the development value streams that make up a portfolio.

Enterprise Architect
The Enterprise Architect fosters adaptive design and engineering practices and drives strategic architectural initiatives for a portfolio. Enterprise Architects facilitate the reuse of ideas, components, and proven patterns across solutions.

Epic

An epic is a significant initiative that typically affects multiple value streams and Agile Release Trains. Epics require analysis using a lightweight business case and financial approval before implementation. There are two types of epics, business epics and enabler epics, which may occur at the portfolio, value stream, and program levels.

Epic Owners

Epic Owners are responsible for coordinating portfolio epics through the portfolio kanban system. They develop the business case and, when approved, work directly with the key stakeholders on the selected trains to help realize the implementation.

F

Feature

A feature is a service provided by the system that fulfills stakeholder needs and can be delivered by a single Agile Release Train. Each feature includes a statement of benefits and acceptance criteria and is sized to fit within a program increment.

GHI

Implementing 1-2-3

Implementing 1-2-3 is a proven success pattern for launching the Scaled Agile Framework. It describes the three basic steps: 1) train Lean-Agile change agents; 2) train executives, managers, and leaders; and 3) train teams and launch Agile Release Trains.

Innovation and Planning Iteration

The Innovation and Planning iteration occurs every Program Increment (PI) and serves multiple purposes. It acts as an estimating buffer for meeting PI objectives, as well as providing dedicated time for innovation, continuing education, and PI planning and Inspect and Adapt events.

Inspect and Adapt

Inspect and Adapt (I&A) is a significant event, held at the end of each Program Increment, where the current state of the solution is demonstrated and evaluated. Teams then reflect and identify improvement backlog items via a structured, problem-solving workshop.

Iteration Execution

Iteration execution is how Agile teams manage their work throughout the iteration timebox, resulting in a high-quality, working, tested system increment. Each iteration follows a standard pattern: plan the iteration, commit to a goal, execute, demonstrate the work to the key stakeholders, and hold a retrospective.

Iteration Goals

Iteration goals are high-level summaries of the business and technical goals that the team and Product Owner agree to accomplish in an iteration. They serve as a communication mechanism within the team and to the team's stakeholders, and they help ensure alignment with the Program Increment objectives.

Iteration Planning

Iteration planning is an event at which all team members determine how much of the team backlog they can commit to delivering during an upcoming iteration. The team summarizes the work as a set of committed iteration goals.

Iteration Retrospective

The iteration retrospective is a meeting where the team members discuss the results of the iteration, review their practices and identify ways to improve.

Iterations

Iterations are a standard, fixed-length timebox during which teams deliver incremental value in the form of working, tested software and systems. Iteration length may be chosen from one to three weeks, with two weeks being the suggested, and most common, duration.

JKL

Lean-Agile Budgeting

Lean-Agile budgeting is a set of practices that fund and empower value streams, while maintaining financial and fitness-for-use governance through objective evaluation of working systems and dynamic budget adjustments.

Lean-Agile Leaders

Lean-Agile leaders are lifelong learners who are responsible for the successful adoption of the Scaled Agile Framework (SAFe) and the results it delivers. They help teams build better systems by learning, exhibiting, teaching, and coaching SAFe's Lean-Agile principles and practices.

Lean-Agile Mindset

A Lean-Agile mindset combines the concepts of the Agile Manifesto and Lean thinking, serving as the basis for Scaled Agile Framework principles and practices.

MNO

Metrics

Metrics are agreed-upon measures used to evaluate how well the enterprise is adopting the Scaled Agile Framework and progressing toward the portfolio, value stream, Agile Release Train, and team business and technical objectives.

Milestones
Milestones are used to track progress toward a specific goal or event. There are three types of Scaled Agile Framework milestones: fixed-date milestones, program increment milestones, and learning milestones.

Model-Based Systems Engineering
Model-Based Systems Engineering (MBSE) is a methodology that focuses on the development of various related system models that are used to define and design the system. Models provide an efficient way to explore, update, and communicate system aspects to stakeholders while significantly reducing or eliminating dependence on traditional documents.

Nonfunctional Requirements
Nonfunctional requirements (NFRs) define system attributes such as security, reliability, performance, maintainability, scalability, and usability. They serve as constraints or restrictions on the design of the system across the different backlogs.

PQ

Portfolio Backlog
The portfolio backlog is a prioritized list of epics that have been approved for implementation through the portfolio kanban system.

Portfolio Business Epic
Portfolio business epics are large business initiatives that often span value streams and require multiple program increments to deliver.

Portfolio Kanban
The portfolio kanban is a method used to visualize and manage the analysis, prioritization, and flow of portfolio epics from ideation to implementation and completion.

Portfolio Level
The portfolio level contains the roles, artifacts, and processes needed to meet the strategic intent of the portfolio. It defines the value streams and funding for the people and other resources that build the solutions.

Pre- and Post-PI Planning
Pre- and post–Program Increment (PI) planning meetings are used to prepare for, and follow-up, PI planning for multiple Agile Release Trains and suppliers in a large value stream.

Product Management
Product Management is the content authority for the program level and backlog. They are responsible for identifying customer needs, prioritizing features, and developing the program vision and roadmap.

Product Owner

The Product Owner is the content authority for the team level. The Product Owner is responsible for creating and maintaining the team backlog, prioritizing and accepting stories, and representing the customer to the Agile team.

Program Backlog

The program backlog is a prioritized list of features intended to address user needs and deliver business benefits. It also includes the enabler features necessary to build the architectural runway.

Program Epics

Program epics are initiatives significant enough to require analysis using a lightweight business case and financial approval before implementation. Their scope is limited to a single Agile Release Train and may take several Program Increments to develop.

Program Increment

A Program Increment (PI) is a timebox in which Agile Release Trains deliver incremental value in the form of working, tested software and systems. PIs are typically eight to twelve weeks long, and the most common pattern for a PI is four development iterations, followed by one Innovation and Planning iteration.

Program Increment Planning

Program Increment planning is a cadence-based, face-to-face planning event that serves as the heartbeat of the Agile Release Train (ART), aligning all the teams on the ART to a common goal.

Program Kanban

The program kanban is a method used to visualize and manage the analysis, prioritization and flow of program epics and features from ideation to completion for a single Agile Release Train.

Program Level

The program level contains the roles and activities needed to continuously deliver solutions via an Agile Release Train.

Program PI Objectives

Program PI (Program Increment) objectives are an integrated summary of all the teams' PI objectives for a train. They are used to communicate the plan to stakeholders and to measure accomplishments of the train for a program increment.

Program Portfolio Management

Program Portfolio Management is a function that contains the individuals who have the ultimate decision-making authority of a portfolio. It is responsible for strategy, investment funding, common program management elements, and portfolio governance.

R

Release

A release is the private or public delivery of valuable, working, and fully tested and validated solution increments.

Release Any Time

Release any time is a practice whereby the Agile Release Train separates the development cadence from the solution release cycle. Within appropriate technical and business governance, trains may release whatever is needed, at any time.

Release Management

Release Management is a function that communicates release status to stakeholders, validates that the solutions meet the relevant quality and governance criteria, and provides the final authorization for the release.

Release Train Engineer

The Release Train Engineer (RTE) is a servant leader and coach for the Agile Release Train, who facilitates the train's processes, events, and execution. He or she escalates impediments and helps manage risk, value delivery, and continuous improvement.

Roadmap

The roadmap is a schedule of events and milestones that communicate planned deliverables over a timeline. It includes commitments for the planned Program Increment (PI) and offers visibility into the forecasted deliverables of the next few PIs.

S

SAFe Principles

Scaled Agile Framework (SAFe) principles define the nine core beliefs, fundamental truths, and economic premises that drive effective roles and practices and successful SAFe implementation.

Scrum Master

Scrum Masters are servant leaders and coaches for an Agile team. They help educate the team in Scrum, Extreme Programming, kanban, and SAFe, and they ensure that the process is being followed. They also help remove impediments and foster an environment for high-performing team dynamics, continuous flow, and relentless improvement.

ScrumXP

ScrumXP is a lightweight process for cross-functional, self-organized teams to deliver value within the context of the Scaled Agile Framework. ScrumXP combines the power of Scrum project management practices with Extreme Programming–inspired technical practices.

Set-Based Design

Set-based design is a practice in which the requirements and design options are kept flexible for a longer period of time. Instead of choosing a single "point" solution up front, set-based design is used to identify design options and eliminate poorer choices over time, thereby enabling flexibility in the design process.

Shared Services

Shared Services represents the specialty roles, people, and services necessary for the success of an Agile Release Train or value stream but can't be dedicated to any specific train full-time (for example, security specialists, database administrators).

Solution

A solution is a final product, service, or system delivered to the customer or something that enables an operational value stream within the organization.

Solution Architect/Engineering

Solution Architect/Engineering represents the individuals and teams who have the technical responsibility for the overall architecture and engineering design of the solution. They help align the value stream and Agile Release Trains to a common technological and architectural vision.

Solution Context

Solution context identifies critical aspects of the target solution's environment. It identifies impact on the requirements, usage, installation, operation, and support of the solution itself.

Solution Demo

The solution demo is where the results of all the development efforts from multiple Agile Release Trains—along with the contributions from suppliers—are integrated, evaluated, and made visible to customers and other stakeholders.

Solution Intent

Solution intent represents the repository for storing, managing, and communicating knowledge of the current and intended solution, including traceability between the items where required.

Solution Management

Solution Management is the content authority for the value stream level. They work with customers to understand their needs, create the vision and roadmap, define requirements, and guide work through the value stream kanban.

Spanning Palette

The spanning palette contains various roles and artifacts that may be applicable at any level of the framework. It is used to apply various Scaled Agile Framework elements to a specific team, program, value stream, or portfolio context.

Stories

Stories are short, simple descriptions of a small piece of desired functionality, written in the user's language. Each story supports incremental development by implementing a small, vertical slice of system functionality.

Strategic Themes

Strategic themes are itemized, differentiated business objectives that connect a portfolio to the enterprise's business strategy. They provide business context for decision-making within the portfolio, and they serve as inputs to the budget, portfolio, solution, and program backlog.

Supplier

A supplier is an organization that develops and delivers components and subsystems that help value streams deliver value to its customers.

System Architect/Engineering

System Architect/Engineering represents an individual or small team that defines a common technical and architectural vision for the solution under development. They participate in defining the system, subsystems, and interfaces; validating technology assumptions, and evaluating alternatives.

System Demo

The system demo occurs at the end of every iteration and provides an integrated view of the new features, which have been delivered by all the teams in the Agile Release Train (ART) for the most recent iteration. It provides the ART with an objective measure of progress during a Program Increment (PI).

System Team

The System Team is a special Agile team that provides assistance in building and using the Agile development environment, including continuous integration and test automation. The System Team integrates assets from Agile teams, performs end-to-end solution testing where necessary, and assists with deployment. They often facilitate the system demo.

T

Team Backlog

The team backlog contains user and enabler stories that originate from the program backlog, as well as stories that arise locally from the team's specific context. It represents all the things a team needs to do to advance their portion of the system.

Team Demo

The team demo is used to measure progress and get feedback at the end of each iteration by demonstrating every story, spike, refactor, and new Nonfunctional Requirements developed in the recent iteration.

Team Kanban
Team kanban is a method that facilitates the flow of value by visualizing Work in Process (WIP) and establishing WIP limits, measuring throughput, and continuously improving the process.

Team Level
The team level contains the roles, activities, and process model for the teams who power the Agile Release Train.

Team PI Objectives
Team Program Increment (PI) objectives describe the business and technical goals that an Agile team intends to achieve in the upcoming PI. They summarize and validate business and technical intent, which enhances communication, alignment, and visibility.

Test-First
Test-first is a built-in quality practice to develop and test a system in small increments. Tests are developed in advance of the functionality and are used to better define the intended system behavior, before the system is implemented.

UVW

User Experience
User experience designers support a consistent user experience across the components and systems of the larger solution, while Agile teams have responsibility for implementing the solution, including the user-facing elements.

Value Stream Backlog
The value stream backlog is the repository for all upcoming capabilities and enablers, each of which can span multiple Agile Release Trains and is used to advance the solution and build the architectural runway.

Value Stream Coordination
Value stream coordination provides guidance for managing dependencies across value streams in a portfolio.

Value Stream Engineer
The Value Stream Engineer (VSE) is a servant leader and coach for a value stream. VSEs facilitate value stream processes, events, and execution, as well as driving continuous improvement.

Value Stream Epics
Value stream epics are significant initiatives that require analysis, using a lightweight business case, and require financial approval before implementation. Their scope is limited to a single value stream and may take several Program Increments to develop.

Value Stream Kanban

The value stream kanban is a method used to manage the analysis, prioritization, and flow of value stream epics and capabilities, from ideation to completion.

Value Stream Level

The value stream level provides the roles, responsibilities, and activities necessary to support those building large and complex solutions, which typically require multiple Agile Release Trains, as well as the contributions of suppliers. This optional level is used by enterprises that face the largest systems challenges, which require multidisciplinary software and system professionals.

Value Stream PI Objectives

Value stream Program Increment (PI) objectives are the business and technical goals identified by value stream stakeholders for a PI. They communicate to stakeholders what the value stream will deliver in the upcoming PI. They are used for large value streams that have multiple ARTs or suppliers.

Value Streams

Value streams represent the series of steps that an enterprise uses to build solutions that provide a continuous flow of value to a customer. Value streams are the primary means for understanding business objectives, organizing teams and trains, and delivering end value. They are realized by Agile Release Trains.

Vision

The vision is a description or future view of the solution to be developed, reflecting customer and stakeholder needs, as well as the proposed features and capabilities. It provides the larger, contextual overview and purpose of the solution under development.

Weighted Shortest Job First

Weighted Shortest Job First (WSJF) is a prioritization model used to sequence "jobs" (features and capabilities) so as to produce maximum economic benefit in a flow-based system. WSJF is calculated as the cost of delay divided by job duration (or job size as a proxy).

Index

A

Abbreviations, used in this book, 321

Accelerated learning, in Big Room Training, 278

Acceptance tests, user stories, 108

Accepted risk, ROAM, 131

Activity, user story voice, 108

Adaptability, team commitment and, 137

Agendas
  final plan review of, 129
  post-PI planning meeting, 201
  pre-PI planning meeting, 199
  standard PI planning meeting, 117

Agile architecture
  architectural runway implementing, 149
  define and build solutions via, 178
  documentation of solution intent, 189
  improve, 295–296
  software quality practice using, 142
  supports hardware/software quality, 18
  vision and development practices, 119

Agile capitalization strategies, 244–247

Agile development
  as body of knowledge, 6–7
  SAFe improves outcomes via, 9–10
  transform system development to, 5

Agile Lifecycle Management (ALM), 247

Agile Manifesto
  apply at scale, 37–40
  embrace Agility via, 33
  focus on quality, 141
  in Lean-Agile mindset, 30
  principles, 36–37
  values, 34–36

Agile Release Trains. *See* ARTs (Agile Release Trains)

Agile teams
  ART launch and, 272–273, 277–278, 280
  ARTs powered by, 105–106, 271–272
  Big Room Training benefits for, 278–279
  as cross-functional, 98
  as essential SAFe element, 306–307
  estimates using story points, 109
  improve flow with kanban, 143–146
  readiness for PI planning, 115
  roles, 19, 106–107
  user stories in team backlog, 109–110

Alignment
  as core value of SAFe, 23
  development manager provides, 56
  of SAFe instances to enterprise portfolio, 212–213
  SAFe practices for, 12–13

ALM (Agile Lifecycle Management), 247

Analysis
  kanban for program level, 148
  kanban for value stream flow, 180
  portfolio kanban for epics, 224

Annual performance reviews, eliminate, 31

Apply cadence/synchronize with cross-domain planning, Lean-Agile principle, 83–87, 305

Apply systems thinking, Lean-Agile principle, 70–74, 303

Architectural runway, 108, 149–150

Architecture. *See* Agile architecture

Artifacts
  develop solution intent, 188
  develop value stream level, 20
  implement continuous delivery pipeline, 152
  launch more ARTS in value stream, 282–283
  spanning palette containing, 24–25
  value stream planning outputs, 204

ARTs (Agile Release Trains)
  apply Agile Manifesto at scale, 39–40
  balance work with capacity allocation, 110–111
  capitalization strategies, 245–246
  deliver value via series of PIs, 135
  develop on cadence, release any time, 100–102
  as essential SAFe element, 306–307
  execute capabilities, 176

ARTs (Agile Release Trains) (*continued*)
features, 103–104
functional organization of, 97–98
I&A workshops for, 160–167
kanban teams participate in, 146
leaders consolidate gains/produce more wins, 46
leaders create vision for change via, 44
leaders generate short-term win for first, 45–46
Lean-Agile program management, 219
overview of, 95–97
PI planning in value stream context, 200–201
powered by Agile teams, 105–107
program backlog, 104
roadmap, 104–105
roles, 99
SAFe implementation. *See* Implementation, SAFe
SAFe program level, 18–20
SAFe value stream level, 20–21
summary review, 111–112
and suppliers in solution development, 185
user stories and team backlog, 107–110
value stream execution, 202–206
vision, 102–103

ARTs (Agile Release Trains), implementing
coach ART execution, 281–282
launch more ARTS in value stream, 282–283
launch more value streams in portfolio, 284–285
overview of, 269–270
prepare for launch, 270–277
quick-start approach to ART launch, 280
summary review, 285–286
train teams and launch ART, 277–279

ARTs (Agile Release Trains), managing value flow
architectural runway, 149–150
DevOps pipeline, 152–153
Lean UX, 150–151
overview of, 146
program backlog and kanban, 147–148
Release Management, 149
Sync meeting, 148

Assume variability/preserve options, Lean-Agile principle, 74–76, 303

Automation
build, 153
deployment process, 153
test, 25, 99, 152, 278, 296

Autonomy, workplace, 89

B

Backlog
classes of service execute items in, 145–146
create improvement items, 166
portfolio. *See* Portfolio backlog
program. *See* Program backlog
reduce length of queue in, 83
team. *See* Team backlog

Base milestones on objective evaluation of working systems, Lean-Agile principle, 79–80, 304

Batch size, Lean-Agile principle of reducing, 32, 81–83, 304

BDUF (Big Design Up Front)
caused by firm fixed-price contracts, 238
caused by software requirements, 35
software quality and, 142

Behaviors, of Lean-Agile leaders, 41–42

Benefits, Feature and Benefit (FAB) matrix, 103–104

Bids, firm fixed-price contracts based on, 237–238

Big Picture, SAFe, 15–17

Big Room Training, benefits, 278–279

Big Visible Information Radiator (BVIR), 46–47, 139

Bodies of knowledge, SAFe
Agile development, 6–7
applying, 5
books for lifelong learning, 47–48
Lean product development, 8–9
required to implement Lean-Agile development, 15
systems thinking, 7–8

Brainstorming, 119, 166

Budgeting. *See* Lean-Agile budgeting

Build
apply Lean UX at enterprise scale, 151
automated for deployment pipeline, 153
incrementally with fast/integrated learning cycles, 76–79, 151, 304

Built-in quality
as core value of SAFe, 23
development manager support for, 56
executing PIs, 140–143
SAFe practices for, 11
software and hardware, 18

Business
align each portfolio vision to strategy of, 213
apply Agile Manifesto at scale, 39
PI objectives expressed in terms of, 126
PI planning session, 118
readiness for PI planning, 115
SAFe portfolio level objectives, 21
sustain and improve. *See* Sustain and improve
value stream pre-PI planning, 199

Business need for SAFe
business benefits, 10–13
challenges of system development, 4–5
for competitive edge, 3–4
establish sense of urgency for change, 43
improve system development outcomes, 9–10
new bodies of knowledge, 5–9
summary review, 13–14

Business Owners
agreement with final plan summary review, 129–130
as essential program role, 99, 311
negotiate final team PI objectives, 126
set business value for team PI objectives, 127–128

Business value
calculate cost of delay, 66–67
final plan review of, 129
set for each objective in team PI, 127–128
user story voice format, 108

BVIR (Big Visible Information Radiator), 46–47, 139

C

Cadence
apply, synchronize with cross-domain planning, 83–87, 305
determine calendar for ART launch, 271
develop on; release any time, 100–102, 310
as essential SAFe element, 308–310
kanban team participation in, 146
PI providing for ART, 113
portfolio, 226–227

Capabilities
defined, 176
kanban for value stream level, 178–179
organize ARTs into, 189, 264–265
value stream backlog and, 176–177

Capacity allocation
balance types of work with, 110–111
forecasting with, 236
PI planning with, 121

Capacity-based PI planning, draft plans, 121–122

Capitalization, Agile strategies for, 243–247

CFD (Cumulative Flow Diagram), kanban, 145, 146

Change
Agile Manifesto at scale, 39
create coalition for, 255
embrace in innovation, 32
tipping point as imperative for, 253–255
train Lean-Agile agents in, 255–256
welcome vs. following a plan, 36

Change leaders
communicate vision, 254–255
overview of, 42–47
systems thinking/management in, 73–74
training, 256

Checklist, ART launch readiness, 275–276

Checkpoints, PI planning hourly, 122

CI (continuous integration)
for Agile at scale, 278
coaching teams in, 281
mastering, 296
measure progress using, 19
reduce batch size via, 82
role of System Team in, 25, 99
software quality via, 141

Classes of service, manage work with, 145–146

Coaching ART execution, 281–282

Coalition, lead change with powerful, 43, 255

CoD (Cost of Delay)
algorithm for job sequencing, 65
calculating, 66–67
create implementation plan, 266
economic framework decisions in, 174
Lean-Agile budgeting and, 175

Collaboration
Agile contracting and, 239–240
ART sync meetings for, 148
build larger solution with team, 267
define strategic themes for portfolio via, 213–214
develop solution intent via, 189
ensure solution correctness with continuous, 195
Epic Owner role in, 216–217
favor customer, 36

Collective ownership, software quality, 142

Commitment, 131–132, 137

Communication channels, facility readiness for PI planning, 116

Communities of Practice. *See* CoPs (Communities of Practice)

Compensation, 31, 88

Competitive bids, firm fixed-price contracts, 237–238

Components
frequent system integration of, 143
organize Agile teams for ART launch, 273
system thinking for optimizing, 7, 71–72

Conceptualization, of mission and vision, 58

Conductor, leader as, 49–50

Confidence vote, value stream post-PI planning, 203

Conformance to plan, respond to change vs., 36

Constraints, minimized by leaders, 52–53

Content readiness, in PI planning, 116

Continuous delivery pipeline
  DevOps in ART value flow, 152–153
  not optimal in some environments, 101
  sustain and improve with focus on, 297–298

Continuous flow
  built-in quality resulting in, 23
  focus on DevOps and, 297–298
  implement model for, 80–81
  keys to ensuring, 304
  Lean-Agile PPM, 219
  managing ART, 146–153
  as Second Pillar of Lean, 32
  sequence jobs for, 65

Continuous improvement, Kaizen, 8

Continuous integration. *See* CI (continuous integration)

Contracts. *See* Lean-Agile contracting

Coordination of value streams, portfolios, 225–228

Coordinator, leader as, 49–50

CoPs (Communities of Practice)
  improve Agile architecture with, 295–296
  lead change with guiding coalition, 43
  as spanning palette element, 25
  sustain and improve with role-based, 290–291

Cost of Delay. *See* CoD (Cost of Delay)

Costs
  benefits of Big Room Training, 278
  of change for software, firmware, and hardware, 142
  ignore sunk, 68
  reduce batch size to implement flow, 81
  in traditional stage-gated development, 76

Cross-domain planning, 85–87

Cross-functional organizations, 97–98, 306–307

Cross-value stream program management, 227

Culture, 31, 46–47

Cumulative Flow Diagram (CFD), kanban, 145, 146

Current states, solution intent, 187

Customer
  ART role of, 99
  ensure continuous collaboration with, 189, 195
  as essential program role, 311
  favor collaboration over contract negotiation, 36
  SAFe managed-investment contracts and, 240–241
  solution development and, 185
  validate innovation with, 32
  at value stream pre-PI planning, 198–200

Cyber attacks, 4

Cycle time, 68–69, 82

D

Daily Stand-Up (DSU), iteration cycle, 139

Date, set ART launch, 270

Decentralize decision-making
  economic frameworks and, 174
  as essential principle of SAFe, 89–91, 305
  Lean-Agile budgeting and, 175
  in Lean-Agile leadership, 53–54, 318

Decision-making
  centralize strategic, 90
  decentralizing, 89–91
  economic framework for fast/effective, 173–174
  framework for, 91
  influence of strategic themes on portfolio kanban, 214–215
  leaders decentralizing, 53–54

Decision rules, 70, 174

Definition of Done (DoD), 153

Delay
  cost of. *See* CoD (Cost of Delay)
  manage flow in Lean-Agile mindset, 32
  software requirements causing, 35

Delivery incrementally, early, and often, 63–65

Demand management, Lean-Agile PPM, 219

Deming, Edwards W., 4, 7–8, 29

Dependencies, 119, 186

Deployment, portfolio, 228

Design
  hardware/firmware practice of verifying, 143
  for implementation. *See* Implementation, SAFe
  solution intent, 187
  using IP iterations for, 155

Develop on cadence, release any time, 310

Develop people, Lean-Agile leadership, 48–52, 318

Development
  Agile capitalization strategies for, 243–247

build deployment pipeline with deployment/test environments, 153
economic trade-off parameters, 68–69
evolving role of managers, 55–58

Development Team
Agile team role of, 107
as essential team role, 310
iteration planning, 137
train Agile teams, 277–278

Development value streams, 5, 260

DevOps pipeline
ARTs build and maintain, 20
as essential SAFe element, 316–317
executing PIs with ART value flow, 152–153
sustain and improve, 297–298

Documentation
of epics, 221
favor working software over, 35
Lean-Agile development decreases, 102
of solution intent, 191–192

DoD (Definition of Done), 153

Done (kanban step)
for epics, 225
for program level, 148
for value stream flow, 180

Draft plans. *See* PI planning, draft plans

DSU (Daily Stand-Up), iteration cycle, 139

Duration, estimate job, 65–67

Dynamic budgeting, for fiscal governance, 234

E

Economic framework
Agile capitalization strategies, 243–247
Agile contract collaboration and, 239
managed-investment contract, 241
solution development governed by, 186
strategic themes influencing, 214–215
value stream level, 20, 173–174

Economic view
calculate cost of delay, 66
deliver incrementally, early, and often, 63–65
drive change in organization via, 254–255
estimate job duration, 66–67
as SAFe's first Lean-Agile principle, 62–63, 303
sequence jobs for maximum benefit, 65
support economic principles, 68–70

Economics
make choices continuously, 69
SAFe principle of. *See* Economic view
understand trade-off parameters, 68–69
use decision rules to decentralize control, 70

80/20 rule (Pareto Analysis), identify root cause, 165

Embrace Agility, Lean-Agile mindset, 30, 314

Emergent behavior, systems thinking, 7

Emergent design, 150, 188

Empathy, of servant leaders, 57

Employee engagement, 11, 45–47

Enabler epics, 221–222

Enabler stories, 108

Enablers, SAFe, 18, 20

Engineering managers, value stream pre-PI planning, 199–200

Enterprise Architects, 22, 217–218, 228

Environment, in systems thinking, 7

Epic Owners, 22, 216–217, 284

Epics
defined, 21
enterprise value flow through kanban systems, 223–224
Lean-Agile budgeting for, 234
Lean-Agile planning/forecasting for, 235–237
portfolio. *See* Portfolio epics
program, 147–148, 216
value stream. *See* Value stream epics

Essential SAFe. *See* SAFe, essential

Estimates
kanban team participation in, 146
Lean-Agile forecasting via, 235–237
Lean-Agile PPM and, 219

Estimating (planning) poker sizing, user stories, 109

Executive briefing, PI planning, 116

Expedite execution of backlog items, 146

Expert, leader as, 49

Exploration, of enabler stories, 108

Extreme Programming (XP), software quality, 141

F

FAB (Feature and Benefit) matrix, 103–104

Facilitation skills, sustain and improve via, 291–292

Facilitator role, PI planning event, 116–117

Facility readiness, prepare for PI planning, 116

FASB (Financial Accounting Standards Board) regulations, 244–245

Feature and Benefit (FAB) matrix, 103–104

Features
  build incrementally, 151
  development capital for, 246–247
  estimating, 236
  final plan review of, 129
  in kanban system, 147–148
  overview of, 103–104
  in PI planning, 107, 118
  in program backlog, 104
  splitting capabilities into, 176–177

Fibonacci numbers, 109

Final plan summary review, 129–130

Financial Accounting Standards Board (FASB) regulations, 244–245

Firm fixed-price contracts, 237–238

Firmware, quality practices, 142–143

Fishbone diagram, root-cause analysis, 164–165

Fitness for purpose, 234, 241

"Five whys," identify root cause, 165

Fixed date execution of backlog items, 145

Fixed intent, 188, 189–190

Flipchart paper, PI planning breakouts, 120

Flow. *See also* Continuous flow
  establish enterprise value, 8, 223–224
  improve with kanban, 143–146
  value stream, 179–180

Forecasting, Lean-Agile, 235–237

Foresight, of servant leaders, 58

Foundation, core values of SAFe, 22–24

Four-level SAFe, 17

Fowler, Martin, 6–7

Frequency, of release, 102

Frequent solution integration, value stream execution, 204–206

Funnel (kanban step)
  for epics, 224
  for program level, 147
  for value stream flow, 179

Future states, solution intent, 187

G

Gemba, innovation with, 32

Geographic location, Agile team roster template, 272

Goals
  iteration summary review, 140
  lead change by communicating, 43
  leaders inspire/align with mission, 52–53

Governance
  dynamic budgeting for fiscal, 234
  Lean-Agile PPM, 220
  Release Management, 149

Guiding coalition, implementing SAFe
  charter Lean-Agile Center of excellence, 257–258
  implementation roadmap, 252–253
  introduction, 251
  need for powerful coalition, 255
  reaching tipping point, 253–255
  summary review, 258
  train executives, managers, and leaders, 256
  train Lean-Agile change agents, 255–256

H

Hackathons, IP iterations for, 155

Hardware
  cost of change, 142
  quality practices, 18, 142–143

Healing, servant leaders as, 58

Holding cost, 81

Hourly planning checkpoints, PI planning, 122

House of Lean
  foundation, as leadership, 33
  as foundation of SAFe, 22
  four pillars of, 31–33
  goal, as value, 31
  Lean thinking represented in, 314
  summary review, 40

Human Resources (HR) practices, 292

I

I&A (Inspect and Adapt) workshop
  at end of each PI, 156, 159
  as essential SAFe element, 314–315
  final system demo as part of, 154
  foster execution of ARTs with, 282
  measure and improve via, 293
  overview of, 159–160
  PI system demo as first part of, 160

quantitative measurement as second part of, 160–162
responsibilities of LACE for, 257–258
retrospective and problem-solving workshop, 162–166
schedule in ART calendar of events, 271
summary review, 167–168
at value stream level, 166–167, 207
what happens without, 314

Implementation
Agile Release Train. *See* ARTs (Agile Release Trains), implementing
kanban program level, 148
kanban value stream flow, 180
portfolio kanban step for epics, 225

Implementation, SAFe
development value streams cross boundaries, 262
guiding coalition for. *See* Guiding coalition, implementing SAFe
identify value streams, 261–262
identify value streams and ARTs, 260
overview of, 259
realized value streams with ARTs, 263–264
review summary, 268–269
roadmap, 252–253
split large value streams into multiple ARTs, 264–265
types of value streams, 260–261

Improvement, Fourth Pillar of Lean as relentless, 33

Incremental builds, 76–79

Incremental releases, 63–65, 220

Infrastructure, enabler stories expressed by, 108

Innovation and Planning. *See* IP (Innovation and Planning) iteration

Innovation, as Third Pillar of Lean, 32

Inspect and Adapt. *See* I&A (Inspect and Adapt) workshop

Inspire and align with mission, Lean-Agile leaders, 52–53, 318

Integration
build incrementally with fast, 76–79
hardware/firmware development via frequent, 143
value stream execution with frequent solution, 204–206

Interconnections, in systems thinking, 7

Investment funding, Lean-Agile PPM, 216, 219

IP (Innovation and Planning) iteration
allocate time for Agile technical practices via, 296
each PI concludes with, 135–136
as essential SAFe element, 315–316
overview of, 154–155
PI planning event in, 115
what happens without, 314

Iron triangle, in firm fixed-price contracts, 238

Ishikawa diagram, 164–165

IT (Information Technology)
DevOps pipeline in ART value flow, 152–153
program execution in SAFe, 12
solution context for deployment, 194
value streams for complex systems, 20, 261

Iteration cycle, 136–140, 308

Iterations
applying fixed cadence to, 84
develop ARTs on cadence, release any time, 100–102
final plan summary of all, 129–130
start fast with capacity-based planning, 121

J

Job sequencing, 65–67, 174–175

K

Kaizen, 8

Kanban
analyze/prepare features with ARTs, 147–148
features developed/managed via, 104
improve team flow with, 143–146
manage capabilities through value stream, 178
portfolio. *See* Portfolio kanban
roles/size limits of teams, 18

Kanban board, 80, 143–144

Kettering, Charles, 163

Know the way/emphasize lifelong learning, Lean-Agile leaders, 47–48, 318

Knowledge
body of. *See* Bodies of knowledge, SAFe
convert uncertainty into new, 77–78
estimate work using story points, 108

Knowledge workers
leader as developer of people for, 51
unlock intrinsic motivation of, 54–55, 87–89, 305, 318

L

LACE (Lean-Agile Center of Excellence)
chartering, 257–258
create implementation plan, 266
focus change management activities, 255
lead change with guiding coalition, 43
sustain and improve by advancing role of, 290

Leadership. *See also* Change leaders; Lean-Agile leadership
causing organization to tip to SAFe, 254
as conductors, 49–50
empower in Lean product development, 9
as experts, 49
as foundation of Lean, 33
future of, 51–52
lead the change, 42–47, 317–318
select initial value stream for implementation, 267
training for ART, 271

"Leadership in Online Labs" article, *Harvard Business Review* summary, 51–52

Leading Change (Kotter), 42–43

Leading SAFe class, 47, 271

Lean-Agile budgeting
approach to, 231–234
approve epic initiatives, 234
economic framework decisions, 174
evidence of fitness for purpose in, 234
governance with dynamic budgeting, 234
at portfolio level, 22
process of, 175
value stream and, 175

Lean-Agile Center of Excellence. *See* LACE (Lean-Agile Center of Excellence)

Lean-Agile contracting
collaborative approach to Agile contracts, 239–240
customer collaboration vs., 36
firm fixed-price contracts, 237–238
range of traditional types, 237
SAFe managed-investment contracts, 240–243
time and materials contracts, 239

Lean-Agile leadership
decentralize decision-making, 53–54, 318
develop people, 48–52, 318
as essential SAFe element, 317–319
evolve development manager role, 55–58
exhibit Lean-Agile mindset, 42
inspire and align with mission, 52–53, 318
key behaviors of, 41–42
know the way and emphasize lifelong learning, 47–48
know the way/emphasize lifelong learning, 318
lead the change, 42–47, 317–318
summary review, 58–59
unlock intrinsic motivation of workers, 54–55, 318

Lean-Agile mindset
advance organizational maturity with, 288
Agile Manifesto applied at scale, 37–40
Agile Manifesto principles in, 36–37
Agile Manifesto values in, 34–36
core principle of built-in quality in, 140–141
enterprise leaders must exhibit, 42
House of Lean in, 31–33, 317
of Lean-Agile leaders, 42, 314
overview of, 29–30
summary review, 40

Lean-Agile planning and forecasting, 235–237

Lean-Agile principles
apply cadence/synchronize with cross-domain planning, 83–87, 305
apply systems thinking, 70–74, 303
assume variability/preserve options, 74–76, 303
base milestones on objective evaluation of working systems, 79–80, 304
build incrementally with fast, integrated learning cycles, 76–79, 304
decentralize decision-making, 89–91, 305
as essential SAFe element, 303–305
summary review, 91–92
take an economic view, 62–70, 303
understanding, 61–62
unlock intrinsic motivation of knowledge workers, 87–89, 305
visualize and limit WIP/reduce batch sizes/reduce batch sizes, 81–83, 304
when implementation is not based on, 305

Lean product development, 5, 8–10

Lean UX, 25, 150–151

Learning
leaders facilitate lifelong, 47–48
support meaningful and continuous, 31

Legacy systems, system development and, 4

Levels, SAFe
portfolio level, 21–22
program level, 18–20
team level, 17–18
value stream level, 20–21

Life-cycle governance, Lean-Agile PPM, 220

Listening, of servant leaders, 57

Little's law, queuing theory, 83

M

Managed-investment contracts, SAFe, 240–243

Management
- review/problem-solving meeting, 123–124
- systems thinking and, 70–74
- training in change, 256

Managing for Excellence (Bradford & Cohen), 48–49

Manifesto for Agile Software Development. See also Agile Manifesto, 6–7

Market. *See* Time to market

Measures
- improve team flow with kanban, 144
- innovation accounting, 32
- lead change with Lean-Agile, 43, 293
- quantitative, 313
- SAFe portfolio level using objective, 22
- self-assessment, 294–295
- as spanning palette element, 25
- sustain and improve via, 293–295

Milestones
- final plan review of, 129
- in Lean-Agile PPM, 220
- Lean UX at enterprise scale and, 151
- PI planning and, 114
- in relentless improvement, 33
- as spanning palette element, 25
- via objective evaluation of working systems, 78–80, 151, 304

Mindset. *See* Lean-Agile mindset

Minimum Viable Product (MVP), 8, 77

Mission
- for Agile Release Trains, 19
- Lean-Agile leaders align with, 52–53, 318
- SAFe practice of alignment to, 12–13

Mitigated risk category, ROAM, 131

Model-based systems engineering, 143, 178

Money, 68, 88

Motivation
- long queues of work lowering, 83
- unlock knowledge worker, 54–55, 87–89, 305, 318

Multisite PI planning, 114–115

MVP (Minimum Viable Product), 8, 77

N

NFRs (Nonfunctional Requirements)
- component teams for, 273
- deferring, 177
- identifying in Agile architecture, 119, 296
- in iteration planning, 137
- kanban steps for program level, 147
- in solution development, 185
- solution intent describing, 188
- System Architect/Engineer defining, 99

Nonmonetary incentives, 52

O

Objectives, PI
- in iteration cycle, 137–140
- overview of, 126–127
- set business value for, 127–128
- stretch, 127
- summarizing into set of program, 133
- team commitment to, 131–132
- Team PI Performance Reports, 161–162
- value stream, 202–204

Ohno, Taiichi, 8, 32

Online resources
- SAFe big picture graphic, 15–17
- sizing stories, 109

Operating expenses, Agile capitalization, 243–247

Operational value streams, 260

Opportunistic value streams, 266–267

Organizations
- advancing maturity of, 288–292
- readiness for PI planning event, 115–117
- traditional silo vs. ART, 97–98

Outcomes
- business benefits of SAFe, 10–13
- improve system development, 9–10

Outsourcing, risks and complexities of, 4

Owned risk, ROAM category, 131

P

Pair work, software practice, 141

Pareto Analysis (80/20 rule), identify root cause, 165

PDCA (Plan-Do-Check-Adjust) learning cycle, 78–79, 308–309

People
- develop, 48–52
- favor interaction with, 35
- First Pillar of Lean as respect for, 31
- implement Agile HR practices, 292
- lead change by anchoring new approaches in, 46–47
- leader as developer of, 50–51

People (*continued*)
respect in Lean product development, 8
servant leaders committed to growth of, 58
systems thinking and, 72

Performance
Agile HR practices for, 31
sustain and improve. *See* Sustain and improve

Persuasion, of servant leaders, 58

Phase-gated development
capitalization triggers, 245
economic costs, 76
problem with milestones, 79–80
software quality, 142

PI execution
build quality in, 140–143
improve team flow with kanban, 143–146
Innovation and Planning (IP) iteration, 154–155
Inspect and Adapt (I&A), 156
iteration cycle, 136–140
manage ART flow, 146–153
overview of, 135–136
SAFe managed-investment contracts, 242–243
summary review, 156–157
system demo, 154

PI planning
ART calendar of events setup, 271
ART roadmap for long-term view, 104–105
by ARTs in value stream context, 200–201
ARTs using face-to-face, 19
cadence for ART, 113
cadence in SAFe, 84–85
efficient communication during, 39
as essential SAFe element, 312
features broken into user stories in, 107
overview of, 113–115
preparation for event, 115–117
quick-start approach to ART launch, 280
reports, 202
SAFe managed-investment contract pre-commitment phase, 241
summary reports, 199
summary review, 133–134
user stories and team backlog during, 107–110
value stream post-PI planning, 201–204
value stream pre-PI planning, 198–200
what happens without, 312

PI planning, draft plans
architecture vision/development practices, 119
business context for, 118
hourly planning checkpoints, 122
management summary review/problem-solving meeting, 123–124
product/solution vision, 118
start fast with capacity-based planning, 121
summary review, 122–123
team planning breakouts, 119–121

PI planning, finalize plans/commit
commitment, 131–132
establish business value, 127–128
final plan review of, 129–130
move forward/final instructions to teams, 133
plan retrospective, 132–133
planning adjustments, 125–126
program board, 128–129
program risks/impediments, 130
ROAMing risks, 130–131
stretch objectives, 127
team breakouts continue, 126
team PI objectives, 126

PI (Program Increment)
as Agile milestone, 220, 243
consolidate gains/produce more wins, 46
I&A workshop at end of each. *See* I&A (Inspect and Adapt) workshop
portfolio cadence of, 226–227
program level organized around, 19
releasing at end of each, 102
SAFe managed-investment contracts execution, 242–243
size features delivered in single, 103–104
synchronize with cross-domain planning, 85–87
for value stream epics, 177
value stream level organized around, 21

Plan-Do-Check-Adjust (PDCA) learning cycle, 78–79, 308–309

Planning
implementation, 265–267
iterations, 136–137
Lean-Agile, 235–237
Lean-Agile program management, 219
Program Increment. *See* PI planning

Planning board, value stream, 204

PMO (Program Management Office), 218, 258–259

Point-based design, vs. set-based, 75

Portfolio backlog
approved epics in, 223
defined, 225
Epic Owner role in, 284
feature estimates in, 236
influence of strategic themes on, 215

Portfolio epics
advancing solution behavior with, 221–223
capitalization strategies, 246

continually re-prioritized in kanban, 69
enterprise value flow through kanban, 223–224
forecasting with, 236–237
new capabilities from splitting, 176
in portfolio kanban system, 224–225
solution intent driven by, 194
value stream epics from, 177

Portfolio kanban
Agile development capitalization strategies, 246
decision filters, 215
enterprise kanban system, 223–224
Epic Owners role with, 216
launch more value streams in portfolio, 284
overview of, 224–225
portfolio epics initially captured in, 222–223
program epic section, 147
strategic themes in, 214–215
value stream epic section, 179

Portfolio roadmap, 228

Portfolios
connecting to business, 213
coordinate value streams with, 225–228
establish enterprise value flow using, 223–225
launch more value streams in, 284
Lean-Agile budgeting and, 231–232
Lean-Agile PPM, 218–220
manage multiple solutions in, 186
overview, 211–213
roles, 215–218
in SAFe, 21–22
solution context and, 194–195
strategic themes and, 213–215
summary review, 228–229

PPM (Program Portfolio Management)
Agile PMO assisting, 218
defined, 21
establishing, 284
evolving traditional mindsets to Lean-Agile, 289
fiscal governance with dynamic budgeting, 234
funding for value stream, 186
Lean-Agile, 218–220
portfolio role of, 216

Pre-commitment phase, Lean-Agile contracts, 240–241

Predictability, 85–87, 161–162

Principles
Agile Manifesto, 36–40
Lean-Agile. *See* Lean-Agile principles

Principles of Product Development Flow (Reinertsen), 65

Proactive leadership, tipping organization to SAFe, 254

Problem-solving
I&A workshop for, 163–166, 313
management review of PI plan, 123–124

Product costs, economic trade-offs, 68–69

Product Management
ART role of, 19, 99
collaborating for solution intent, 189
as essential program role, 311
in PI planning, 118, 126, 129–130
preparing for ART launch, 274
responsibility for features, 104

Product Owners
Agile team role of, 106
as essential team role, 310
executing PIs with ART sync meetings, 148
iteration planning, 137
as owner of team backlog, 109–110
preparing for ART launch, 274

Product/solution vision, PI planning session, 118

Productivity, 11, 254–255

Program backlog
driving innovation from, 155
each ART aligns teams to mission/vision via single, 26
and kanban, 147–148
preparing for ART launch, 276–277
prioritize for PI planning, 241
Product Management role for features in, 99
refining in IP iterations, 154
solution behaviors influencing, 189
understanding, 104

Program epics, 147–148, 216, 223–224

Program execution
as core value of SAFe, 24
development manager assistance with, 57
SAFe practices for, 12

Program level, SAFe, 18–20

Program management, Lean-Agile, 219

Program Management Office (PMO), 218, 258–259

Program Portfolio Management. *See* PPM (Program Portfolio Management)

Program roles, essential, 311

Progress, measure against strategic themes, 215

Prototypes, integration points as, 77

Q

Q&A (Questions and Answers), draft plan, 123

Quality. *See* Built-in quality

Quantitative measurement, I&A workshop, 160–162, 313

Queue lengths, manage flow, 32, 81–82, 304

Quick-start approach to ART launch, 280

R

R&D (Research and Development), 12, 308–310

Readiness, assess and evolve ART launch, 275–276

Refactoring, as software quality practice, 141

Release
- any time; develop on cadence, 100–102
- portfolio, 228

Release Management, 149, 199–200

Release Train Engineer. *See* RTE (Release Train Engineer)

Relentless improvement, as Fourth Pillar of Lean, 33

Research and Development (R&D), 12, 308–310

Resolved risk, ROAM category, 131

Respect for people, 31, 292

Retrospectives
- I&A workshop, 162–163
- iteration, 140
- PI planning session, 132–133
- value stream post-PI planning, 204

Revision, value stream post-PI planning, 203

Risks
- addressing program, 130
- as business context for planning session, 118
- calculating cost of delay, 66–67
- economic trade-offs and, 68–69
- in final plan summary review, 129–130
- long queues of work increasing, 82
- move to ROAM category, 130–131
- set-based design managing, 76
- in value stream post-PI planning, 203

Roadmap
- longer-term view of solution with ART, 104–105
- portfolio, 228
- SAFe implementation, 252–253
- as spanning palette element, 25
- strategic themes influencing program, 214–215

ROAM categories, moving risks to, 130–131

Role(s)
- Agile team, 105–107
- determine individual ART, 273–274
- development manager, 55–58
- essential team and program, 310–311
- key ART, 19, 99
- launch ARTS with value stream, 282–283
- leadership, 48–52
- portfolio level, 215–218
- spanning palette containing, 24–25
- value stream, 172–173
- vision for change and, 44

Rolling-wave planning, Lean-Agile program management, 219

Rollout strategy
- implementation plan, 265–267
- vision for change, 44

Root-cause analysis, 164–165

RTE (Release Train Engineer)
- advance facilitation skills of, 292
- create program board for PI planning, 128–129
- creates set of program PI objectives, 133
- as essential program role, 311
- facilitate PI planning event, 117
- lead PI planning event, 114–115
- quantitative measurement for I&A, 160–162
- role in ART, 19, 99
- value stream post-PI planning, 202
- value stream pre-PI planning, 199–200

S

SAFe, essential
- Agile teams and ARTs, 306–307
- cadence and synchronization, 308–310
- DevOps pipeline, 316–317
- essential team and program roles, 310–311
- Inspect and Adapt (I&A) workshop, 314–315
- IP iterations, 315–316
- Lean-Agile leadership, 317–319
- Lean Agile principles, 303–305
- overview of, 301–303
- PI planning, 312
- summary review, 319
- system demo, 313

SAFe Program Consultants. *See* SPCs (SAFe Program Consultants)

SAFe (Scaled Agile Framework)
- big picture, 15–17
- business need for. *See* Business need for SAFe
- core values, 23–24
- foundation of, 22–24

graphical diagram of, 1
managed-investment contracts, 240–243
portfolio level, 21–22
program level, 18–20
spanning palette, 24–25
summary review, 25–26
team level, 17–18
value stream level, 20–21

Scale
apply Lean UX at enterprise, 150–151
applying Agile Manifesto at, 37–40
centralize decisions providing economies of, 90

Scaled Agile Framework. *See* SAFe (Scaled Agile Framework)

Scientific industrial principles of management (Taylor), 54–55

Scope, PI planning, 115

Scrum
iteration cycle as activity in, 136–140
roles and size limits of teams, 18

Scrum Master
advance facilitation skills of, 291–292
Agile team role of, 106
as essential team role, 310
iteration planning, 137
train for ART launch, 274

Scrum of Scrums (SoS), 122, 148

Self-assessments, enhance performance, 294–295

Self-awareness, of servant leaders, 58

Self-organizing teams, 39–40

Sequence jobs, for maximum benefit, 65–67

Sequential/cadence-based rollout, implementation plan, 265–267

Servant leadership, development managers, 57–58

Set-based design
define and build solution via, 178
as hardware/firmware practice, 143
variability in, 75–76

Shared Services, 25, 99

Software
capitalizing development costs, 244–247
cost of change, 142
measure progress via working, 35
quality practices, 18, 141–142

Solution Architect/Engineer
ART role, 21
PI planning, 115, 198–201
Release Management governance, 149
value stream role, 173

Solution context
defined, 185
for IT deployment environments, 194
overview of, 192–193
portfolio-level concerns, 194–195
SAFe value stream level, 20
for system of systems, 193

Solution demos, 185, 206, 234

Solution Engineering, 189, 206

Solution intent
aligning solution context with, 192–194
defined, 185
developing, 188–189
documenting, 191–192
fixed and variable, 187–188
in high assurance environments, 192
moving from variable to fixed, 189–190
overview of, 186–187
SAFe value stream level, 20
system of systems, 190–191

Solution Management, 173, 185, 189, 198–201

Solution/System Architects, 22, 189

Solutions
advancing behavior, 221–222
content readiness for PI planning, 116
define and build, 178
development, 184–186
portfolio management, 228
select initial value stream in implementation, 267
systems thinking and, 71
value stream execution with frequent integration, 204–206

Solutions, large/complex
developing solution intent, 188–191
documenting solution intent, 191–192
fixed and variable solution intent, 187–188
managing multiple solutions in portfolio, 186
overview of, 183
solution context, 192–195
solution development, 184–186
solution intent, 186–187
summary review, 196

SoS (Scrum of Scrums), 122, 148

Spanning palette elements, 23–24

SPCs (SAFe Program Consultants)
create implementation plan, 266
create powerful coalition for change, 255
lead change, 43

SPCs (SAFe Program Consultants) (*continued*)
  train ART leaders/stakeholders for launch, 271
  train Lean-Agile change agents, 256

Specifications, solution intent, 187

Staging environment, 153

Stakeholders
  ART PI planning in value stream, 200–201
  deliver value in series of PIs, 135
  iteration planning, 137
  launch training for ART, 271
  system demo sent bimonthly to, 154
  training in change, 256

Stand-alone unit, Lean-Agile Program Management Office (Agile PMO), 258

Standard execution of backlog items, 145

Stewardship, of servant leaders, 58

Stories. *See* User stories

Storyboard, iteration tracking via, 139

Strategic themes
  align value streams with, 284
  overview of, 213–215
  SAFe portfolio level, 21

Strategy, Lean-Agile PPM, 216, 219

Strengths, Weakness, Opportunities, Threats (SWOT) analysis, 118

Stretch objectives, 127, 161–162

Subsystems
  assume variability/preserve options, 74–76
  build incrementally with fast, integrated learning cycles, 151
  design verification between, 143
  frequent system integration of, 143
  organize ARTs into, 189, 264–265

Sunk cost, ignore, 68

Suppliers, 240–241

Sustain and improve
  advance organizational maturity, 288–292
  focus on DevOps/continuous delivery, 297–298
  implement Agile HR practices, 292
  improve Agile architecture/technical practices, 295–297
  introduction, 287
  measure and take action, 293–295
  reduce time to market, 298–299
  summary review, 299–300

Switch: How to Change Things When Change Is Hard (Heath & Heath), 44

SWOT (Strengths, Weakness, Opportunities, Threats) analysis, 118

Sync meetings, 148

Synchronization
  apply with cross-domain planning, 83–87, 305
  applying cadence-based, 85
  aspects of, 84
  as essential SAFe element, 308–310
  kanban teams participate in, 146
  portfolio cadence and, 226
  value stream, 206

System Architect/Engineering
  apply Agile Manifesto at scale, 39
  development manager works with, 56
  as key ART role, 19, 99
  in PI planning, 116, 119–120
  as program role, 311
  in value stream pre-PI planning, 199–200
  as value stream role, 173

System demos
  cadence in SAFe with, 84
  I&A workshop and, 160
  as measure of ART progress, 154, 313

System engineering disciplines, 20

System integration, at ART level, 204

System of systems solution intent, 190–191, 193

System Team, 25, 99

Systems
  applying cadence in SAFe, 84–85
  building large/complex. *See* Solutions, large/complex
  challenges of developing, 4–5

Systems thinking
  applying, 70–74, 303
  as body of knowledge, 7–8
  improved outcomes in SAFe via, 9–10
  Lean UX at enterprise scale with, 151
  SAFe principle of, 70–74
  unlock motivation of knowledge workers with, 87

T

Take an economic view, Lean-Agile principle, 62–70, 303

Talent
  Agile HR establishing new, 292
  development manager recruits/retains, 56
  unlock intrinsic motivation of knowledge workers, 54

Tasks, leader as expert defining, 49

Taylor, Frederick, 54

Team backlog
capacity allocation, 110–111
Product Owner maintains, 106, 310
refining in IP iterations, 154
training Agile teams, 277
user stories and, 109–110

Team level, SAFe, 17–18

Team PI Performance Reports, I&A, 161–162

Team planning breakouts
in all PI plans, 126
hourly checkpoints during, 122
PI planning session, 119–121
start fast with capacity-based planning, 121

Teams roles, essential, 310–311

Technology
Agile technical practices, 296–297
lead change by establishing sense of urgency, 43
leader as expert in, 49
need for rapid response to advances in, 3–4
SAFe practices for, 12

Templates
Agile team roster, 271–272
ART role assignments, 273

Test-first practices, software quality, 141

Tests
anatomy of solution intent, 187
build deployment pipeline for, 153

Thinking Lean
in Lean-Agile mindset, 30, 314
overview of, 30–31
SAFe House of Lean, 31–34

Three-level SAFe, 16

Time and materials contracts, 239

Time criticality
calculate cost of delay, 66–67
decentralize decisions on, 90

Time for innovation, Lean-Agile mindset, 32

Time to market
driving change for business benefits, 254–255
reduce with value stream mapping, 298–299
SAFe practices for, 12

Tipping point, causes organizations to change to SAFe, 253–255

Tools, individuals/interactions over, 35

Total cost, for batch of work, 81

Toyota Production System, 8

Tracking, iteration, 139

Traditional functional organizations, vs. ART, 97–98

Trailing indicators, strategic themes, 215

Training
Agile teams and launch ART, 277–278
ART leaders and stakeholders for launch, 271
benefits of Big Room, 278–279
executives, managers, and leaders, 256
Lean-Agile change agents, 255–256
Product Managers and Product Owners for ART launch, 274
quick-start approach to ART launch, 280
Scrum Masters for ART launch, 274

Transaction costs, batch of work, 81

Transparency, 12–13, 23, 56–57

Trust, time and materials contracts, 239

Tyranny of the urgent, avoid in Lean-Agile mindset, 32

U

Uncertainty
estimate work using story points, 108
integration points create knowledge from, 77–78
modified Fibonacci numbers reflecting, 109

Unlock intrinsic motivation of knowledge workers, Lean-Agile, 54–55, 87–89, 305, 318

Urgency, lead change by establishing sense of, 43

User Experience (UX), 20, 39–40

User role, user story voice, 108

User stories
capacity-based planning and, 121
capitalizing/expensing software for, 247
create improvement backlog items, 166
in iteration cycle, 137–140
team backlog and, 107–110
team PI planning breakouts using, 119
teams implement, 18

UX (User Experience), 20, 39–40

V

Value
economic trade-off parameters, 68–69
Lean-Agile Mindset of, 31
statement for portfolio epic, 221

Value stream backlog
capabilities and, 176–177, 178
kanban for value stream flow, 180
value stream pre-PI planning, 200

Value stream board, 202

Value Stream Engineer. *See* VSE (Value Stream Engineer)

Value stream epics
enterprise value flow through kanban, 223–224
Epic Owner role in, 216
overview of, 177
value stream kanban manages flow of, 179

Value stream execution
ART PI planning in value stream context, 200–201
frequent solution integration, 204–206
overview of, 197–198
solution demo, 206
summary review, 207–208
value stream I&A, 207
value stream post-PI planning, 201–204
value stream pre-PI planning, 198–200
value stream sync, 206

Value stream level
build large/complex solutions. *See* Solutions, large/complex
capabilities and value stream backlog, 176–177
define and build solution, 178
economic framework, 173–174
I&A workshop at, 166–167
Lean-Agile budgeting, 175
roles, 172–173
SAFe, 20–21
summary review, 180–181
understanding, 171–172
value stream epics, 177
value stream flow, 179–180

Value stream mapping, reduce time to market, 298–299

Value stream(s)
allocate budgets to, 233
ARTs organized around, 19
coordinate within portfolio, 225–228
create vision for change via, 44
development across boundaries, 262
each portfolio contains set of, 212
as focus of Lean product development, 8
identify, 260–265
influence of strategic themes on, 214–215
launch more ARTS in, 282–283
launch more in portfolio, 284–285
manage flow in Lean-Agile mindset, 32
portfolio contains multiple, 186
realize value streams with ARTs, 263–264
rollout patterns for, 265–267
in SAFe portfolio level, 21–22
split into multiple ARTs, 264–265
system thinking and optimizing full, 72–73
types of, 260–261

Variability, 74–76, 83, 151

Variable intent, 188–190

Velocity
capacity allocation alleviates degradation of, 110–111
defined, 109
kanban teams estimating, 146
PI planning session estimating team, 119
portfolio forecasting with program, 236–237

Verification, hardware/firmware design, 143

Version control, refining in IP iterations, 153

Visibility
Agile contracts, 239
sticky notes in PI planning, 120–121

Vision
content readiness for PI planning, 116
documentation replaced with program, 102–103
leaders must clearly communicate, 44
of product/solution for PI planning session, 118
solution intent begins with, 188–189
as spanning palette element, 25
strategic themes influencing program, 214–215
value stream, 199

Visualize and limit WIP/reduce batch sizes/manage queue length, Lean-Agile principle, 81–83, 304

Vollmer, Peter, 13

Volume, estimate work using story points, 108

VSE (Value Stream Engineer)
ART PI planning in value stream context, 201
facilitates value stream sync, 206
kanban step for value stream flow, 173
value stream post-PI planning, 202
value stream pre-PI planning, 198–200

W

Wait times, reduce queue length to reduce, 83

Waste elimination, 32, 150–151

Waterfall-based development
avoid in iteration execution, 138
capitalization triggers in, 245
challenges of companies using, 4

favor working software over comprehensive documentation, 35
firm fixed-price contracts creating, 238

White elephant sizing, user stories, 109

Win-lose scenario, firm fixed-price contracts, 238

Wins, lead change with, 45–46

WIP (Work-In-Process)
implement flow, 80–81
improve team flow with kanban, 143–146
manage flow in Lean-Agile mindset, 32
value stream backlog and, 178
visualize and limit, 81–83, 304

WSJF (Weighted Shortest Job First)
calculate for job sequencing, 66–67
economic framework decisions in, 174
job sequencing based on cost of delay, 175
manage features in program backlog, 104

X

XP (Extreme Programming), software quality, 141